PRIVACY AND FREEDOM OF EXPRESSION

PRIVACY AND FREEDOM OF EXPRESSION

by

RICHARD CLAYTON
Barrister, Devereux Chambers, London

HUGH TOMLINSON
Barrister, Matrix Chambers, London

OXFORD
UNIVERSITY PRESS

OXFORD

UNIVERSITY PRESS

Great Clarendon Street, Oxford OX2 6DP

Oxford University Press is a department of the University of Oxford.
It furthers the University's objective of excellence in research, scholarship,
and education by publishing worldwide in

Oxford New York

Athens Auckland Bangkok Bogotá Buenos Aires Cape Town
Chennai Dar es Salaam Delhi Florence Hong Kong Istanbul Karachi
Kolkata Kuala Lumpur Madrid Melbourne Mexico City Mumbai Nairobi
Paris São Paulo Shanghai Singapore Taipei Tokyo Toronto Warsaw

with associated companies in Berlin Ibadan

Oxford is a registered trade mark of Oxford University Press
in the UK and in certain other countries

Published in the United States
by Oxford University Press Inc., New York

British Library Cataloguing in Publication Data

Data available

Library of Congress Cataloging in Publication Data

Data available

ISBN 0–19–924638–6

1 3 5 7 9 10 8 6 4 2

Typeset in Garamond by
Cambrian Typesetters, Frimley, Surrey

Printed in Great Britain
on acid-free paper by
Antony Rowe Ltd.
Chippenham, Wilts.

PREFACE AND UPDATE

The rights

The rights to privacy and to freedom of expression are two of the most important Convention rights introduced into English law by the Human Rights Act 1998. The Article 8 right to respect for private life provides a much needed focus for the slow development of 'privacy' rights by the common law. The Article 10 right to freedom of expression reinforces the well-established domestic right so that this right, based on a 'constitutional or higher legal order foundation'[1] is now the starting point in all cases involving restrictions on expression.

This book is a reprint of the chapters on Privacy and Freedom of Expression from our book on *The Law of Human Rights.*[2] It sets out to provide a comprehensive and systematic treatment of human rights law and practice in England and Wales in relation to these areas, including detailed analysis of the impact of the incorporation of the European Convention on Human Rights into domestic law by the Human Rights Act 1998.

The book contains two parts: the chapters relating to privacy and freedom of expression respectively. Each part is, itself, divided into five substantive sections. After an introduction, there is a discussion of the right in English law before the coming into force of the Human Rights Act 1998. This is followed by an analysis of the case law under the European Convention on Human Rights. The likely impact of incorporation on English law is then examined. This impact is considered in relation to a number of subject areas, including business and commerce, criminal law and justice, education, employment, immigration, media, mental health, police and prisoners. Each section ends with an Appendix examining the case law under the Canadian Charter of Rights, the New Zealand Bill of Rights Act and the constitutional jurisprudence in other common law jurisdictions.

In the next three sections of this introduction we will consider the recent case law relating to privacy and freedom of expression including in particular, the English cases decided over the first 7 months of the operation of the Human Rights Act 1998.[3]

---

[1] *Per* Lord Steyn, *Reynolds v Times Newspapers Ltd* [1999] 3 WLR 1010, 1030; see also *McCartan Turkington Breen v Times Newspapers Ltd* [2000] 3 WLR 1670, 1686.

[2] Oxford University Press, 2000.

[3] The Act came into force on 2 October 2000, this Introduction covers cases decided up to 1 May 2001.

Article 8 case law

Article 8 of the Convention contains a right to respect for 'private and family life, home and correspondence'. These are 'qualified rights': restrictions on the rights are permitted provided that they are 'prescribed by law' and 'necessary in a democratic society'.[4] The right to family life is not considered in the present book.[5] The right to respect for private life has been considered in a relatively small number of cases.

The most important English case is the decision of the Court of Appeal in *Douglas v Hello! Ltd*.[6] The case concerned the publication of unauthorized photographs of the wedding of Michael Douglas and Catherine Zeta-Jones in *Hello!* magazine. The court decided that, despite the fact that they had sold the rights to photograph their wedding to *OK* magazine, they had arguable claims for breach of their rights of privacy.[7]

The Court of Appeal accepted that the Courts now have to take into account the right to respect for private and family life under Article 8 when interpreting the common law and that, as a result, the law of confidence should and did protect privacy. As Sedley LJ said:

> The law no longer needs to construct an artificial relationship of confidentiality between intruder and victim: it can recognise privacy itself as a legal principle drawn from the fundamental value of personal autonomy.[8]

The Court also gave some indications about the way in which Convention jurisprudence might be taken into account by the English courts in deciding 'privacy' disputes. The Court applied the Article 8 approach to 'privacy' as a 'qualified right'—a right which can only be interfered with for 'legitimate aims' and in ways which are 'proportionate'. In addition, the Court took into account the Convention jurisprudence which recognizes 'degrees of privacy': the more intimate the aspect of private life which is interfered with, the more serious must be the reasons for interference.[9]

The right to privacy was also recognized in the case of *Venables v News Group Newspapers*[10] in which injunctions were granted against the whole world to prevent the publication of confidential information which would or might lead to the identification of two notorious child murderers.

---

[4] For a full discussion of these concepts, see *The Law of Human Rights*, para 6.123ff.
[5] It forms the subject matter of Chapter 13 of *The Law of Human Rights*, recent case law will be considered in the Supplement (Oxford University Press, 2001—0199245800).
[6] *Douglas* [2001] 2 WLR 992.
[7] However, an injunction was refused on discretionary grounds.
[8] para 126, 1025E.
[9] *Per* Keene LJ, at para 168, 1036 G-H.
[10] [2001] 2 WLR 1038.

However, in a number of cases, the court has rejected Article 8 based challenges to the investigatory powers of public authorities. Thus, in *R (Morgan Grenfell) v Special Commissioners*[11] the court accepted that a Notice for the Production of privileged documents was an interference with Article 8 but that this was justified under Article 8(2). Similarly, in *A-G's Reference (No. 3 of 1999)*[12] the House of Lords held that the use of an unlawfully retained DNA sample in criminal proceedings was a justifiable interference with the defendant's Article 8 rights.

There have been a number of unsuccessful attempts to invoke the 'right to respect for home' in Article 8. Thus, in *Chapman v United Kingdom*[13] the Court of Human Rights held that Gypsies' Article 8 rights did not extend to a right to be provided with a home. Whether the state provided funds to enable everyone to have a home was a matter for political not judicial decision. In *Poplar Housing Association v Donoghue*[14] the Court of Appeal held that certain mandatory possession provisions of the Housing Act 1988 were compatible with Article 8. It observed that, in housing policy issues the courts had to treat the decisions of Parliament with particular deference.[15]

Article 10 case law

The Article 10 right to freedom of expression is also a 'qualified right'. However, its importance has been emphasized repeatedly in both the Convention and English case law. Thus, in *McCartan Turkington Breen v Times Newspapers*[16] Lord Steyn described 'freedom of expression' as the 'primary right in a democracy'. The exceptions in Article 10(2) must be strictly construed and the need for them must be 'convincingly established' on the basis of evidence rather than assertion.[17]

The potential impact of Article 10 on English defamation law is demonstrated by two recent decisions of the Court of Human Rights. In *Thoma v Luxembourg*[18] it was held that, when one journalist quoted a defamatory remark made by another, it was a breach of his Article 10 rights to require that he should formally distance himself from the quoted remark. This is, apparently, contrary to the very well-established rule of libel law that it is no defence for a defendant to prove that he is simply repeating what someone else has said.[19] In *Marônek v Slovakia*[20] the Court held that a judgment for defamation in respect of a letter which was made public

---

[11] [2000] STC 965.
[12] [2001] 2 WLR 56.
[13] Judgment, 18 Jan 2001.
[14] [2001] EWCA Civ 595.
[15] Ibid, paras 69–72.
[16] [2000] 3 WLR 1670, 1686.
[17] See the discussion in *Kelly v BBC* [2001] WLR 253, 264.
[18] Judgment, 29 Mar 2001.
[19] The so-called 'repetition rule': see *Stern v Piper* [1997] QB 123.
[20] Judgment, 19 Apr 2001.

and which contained accusations of dishonesty was a disproportionate interference with the Article 10 rights of the writer. The basis of the decision appears to be the fact that the Slovakian courts had awarded damages and costs of 25 times the average monthly salary at the relevant time. In English terms this would amount to a total payment of the order of £40,000 which, in the context of defamation proceedings, would not be a substantial sum to pay in damages and costs. These two cases have, potentially, extremely far reaching consequences for the English law of defamation.

The decision of the House of Lords in *Reynolds v Times Newspapers*[21] was intended to ensure the common law of England harmonized with the Convention.[22] In *Loutchansky v Times Newspapers*[23] the Court of Appeal accepted that the principles of qualified privilege, as explained in *Reynolds*, were compatible with Article 10. However the court stressed that the matter had to be approached on a 'case by case basis'.[24] In *O'Shea v MGN Ltd*[25] it was held that the principle of strict liability for 'unintentional reference' by a defamatory photograph was an unjustifiable interference with Article 10 rights.

The need for 'convincing evidence' to justify interference with the right of freedom of expression has been demonstrated in several cases. Thus, in *Re X (a child)*[26] it was held that an injunction to restrain the publication of a local authority's policy with regard to fostering could not be justified. In *A-G v Times Newspapers*[27] the Court of Appeal held that an injunction which allowed the publication of information 'to such an extent that the information is in the public domain' should not be qualified by a requirement that the defendants obtain the Attorney-General's approval for publication was not consistent with Article 10.

A number of Article 10 challenges to restrictions on the use of confidential information have been unsuccessful. In *Ashdown v Telegraph Group*[28] the Liberal Democrat leader brought an action for breach of confidence and copyright in relation to the publication of a confidential minute of a meeting he had had with the Prime Minister. It was held that, although the claim for breach of copyright was a restriction on freedom of expression, the provisions of the Copyright Act 1988 struck a proper balance between freedom of expression and the protection of property. In *Imutran v Uncaged Campaigns*[29] an Article 10 challenge

---

[21] [1999] 3 WLR 1010.
[22] Ibid, 1688, *per* Lord Cooke.
[23] [2001] EWCA Civ 536; see also the subsequent decision at the trial, 27 Apr 2001, Gray J.
[24] *Per* Brooke LJ, para 46.
[25] 4 May 2001, Morland J.
[26] [2001] 1 FCR 541.
[27] [2001] 1 WLR 885.
[28] [2001] 2 WLR 967 (the case is subject to an appeal).
[29] *The Times*, 30 Jan 2001.

to an injunction restraining the use of confidential material concerning animal experiments was unsuccessful. It was held that the Human Rights Act did not substantially alter the test for the grant of injunctions.

Privacy versus Freedom of Expression

The rights to privacy and to freedom of expression are both of fundamental importance. However, in many cases they are in potential conflict. The freedom of expression of the media often involves an infringement of the right to privacy of the person whose affairs are being discussed. Any extension of the protection of privacy poses problems for the protection of freedom of expression.

Section 12 of the Human Rights Act was intended to provide additional protection for the media when injunctions were sought to restrain the publication of private information. Section 12(4) provides that the Court must 'have particular regard to the importance of the Convention right to freedom of expression'.

This provision was considered in *Douglas v Hello Ltd*.[30] The Court of Appeal held that because the Convention right to freedom of expression is qualified in favour of the reputation and rights of others (which include the right to respect for private life under Article 8), when considering an injunction against the media, 'privacy' and 'reputation' rights are as relevant as freedom of expression. As section 12(4) directs attention to 'any relevant privacy code', it was likely that any newspaper which breached paragraph 3 of the Press Complaints Commission Code of Practice would have its claim to freedom of expression 'trumped' by privacy considerations.[31]

The strength of the 'privacy' interest required to justify a severe restriction on freedom of expression was emphasized in the *Venables* case. The most important consideration was the potential risk to the claimants' lives if the injunctions were refused and the judge was uncertain as to whether it would have been appropriate to grant injunctions to prevent the disclosure of the claimants' new identities if only Article 8 was likely to be breached:

> Serious though the breach of the claimant's right to respect for family life and privacy would be, once the journalists and photographers discovered either of them . . . it might not be sufficient to meet the importance of the preservation of the freedom of expression in article 10(1).[32]

Conclusion

The importance of the two fundamental rights covered by this book is illustrated by the rapid development of the case law over the short period since the Human

---

[30] [2001] 2 WLR 992, 1027F–1029D, paras 133–136 (Sedley LJ).
[31] 1018F, para 94 (Brooke LJ).
[32] [2001] 2 WLR 1038, 1066G–H, para 86.

Rights Act came into force. The development of a law of privacy, drawing on Article 8, has only just begun. The importance of the right of freedom of expression is likely to be demonstrated by continuing 'liberalization' of the tort of defamation and the rules governing the publication of confidential information.

Richard Clayton

Devereux Chambers
Devereux Court
London WC2R 3JJ

Hugh Tomlinson

Matrix Chambers
Gray's Inn
London WC1R 5LN

10 May 2001

CONTENTS

12

THE RIGHT TO RESPECT FOR PRIVACY AND THE HOME

A. The Nature of the Rights

12.01   The rights to privacy and respect for the home are less well established in human rights jurisprudence than traditional civil rights such as life, liberty or freedom from slavery. Although the right of persons to be secure in their homes from unreasonable searches has long been acknowledged,[1] a more general right to privacy and respect for the home was only clearly recognised in the twentieth century.[2] Most modern international human rights instruments now protect the right of the individual to 'privacy' or 'private life', but the limits of the right are still not clearly defined. Article 12 of the Universal Declaration provides that:

> No one shall be subjected to arbitrary interference with his privacy, family, home, or correspondence, nor to attacks upon his honour and reputation. Everyone has the right to protection of the law against such interference or attacks.

Article 17 of the International Covenant on Civil and Political Rights describes it in similar terms.[3] Article 8 of the Convention refers to 'respect for private and family life, home and correspondence'.

12.02   At the heart of the right to privacy lies the notion of personal liberty and autonomy.[4] There is an enormous literature on 'privacy rights'[5] in which a variety of different definitions of the scope of the rights have been suggested. In addition to the

---

   [1] See, eg Fourth Amendment, US Constitution which reflected the English common law, cf A Amar, *The Bill of Rights* (Yale University Press, 1998) 65ff and see para 12.10 below; for a recent discussion of the position under the Fourth Amendment, see *Minnesota v Carter* (1998) 5 BHRC 457.
   [2] It has been suggested that the need to recognise privacy did not arise earlier because, in small rural communities, there was less distinction between 'private' and 'public' life, see F Schoeman, *Privacy and Social Freedom* (Cambridge University Press, 1992) Chap 7.
   [3] See App J in Vol 2, Art 17 refers to 'arbitrary *or unlawful* interference . . .'. For the effect of the latter term, see Human Rights Committee, General Comment 16, Doc A 43/40, 181–3.
   [4] See generally, D Feldman, *Civil Liberties and Human Rights in England and Wales* (Clarendon Press, 1993) Chap 8; see also E Barendt, 'Privacy as a Constitutional Right and Value' in B Markesinis (ed), *Protecting Privacy* (Oxford University Press, 1999).
   [5] See eg A Westin, *Privacy and Freedom* (Bodley Head, 1967); JUSTICE Report, *Privacy and the Law* (Stevens, 1970); R Wacks, *The Protection of Privacy* (Sweet & Maxwell, 1980); R Wacks *Privacy and Press Freedom* (Blackstone, 1995). For a full discussion of privacy in the human rights context, see D Feldman, (n 4 above) Pt III.

'right to be let alone',[6] privacy rights have been said to cover matters as diverse as an individual's dignity or moral integrity,[7] the unauthorised circulation of portraits,[8] the control of personal information,[9] the establishment and development of emotional relationships with others[10] and the freedom from media intrusion.[11] The wide range of areas in which the right has been invoked have led to scepticism as to whether it is helpful to speak of a general 'right to privacy' at all.[12] However, in analysing privacy rights it is important to distinguish between the 'human right' to privacy as against the state and the right to privacy as against private individuals or organisations.[13] Although the two are closely connected, the range of the former has been greater than that of the latter because of the greater power of the state over all aspects of private life as compared to private organisations.

The right to respect for private life in human rights instruments has its origin in traditional human rights concerns about state interference with the individual. Thus, the constitutional right to privacy in American law arises as an 'emanation'[14] derived from liberty rights enshrined in the Bill of Rights.[15] The protection of the home from unreasonable searches has expanded to protection from surveillance and interception of telephones.[16] More generally, the constitutional right to privacy has been invoked in cases concerning state interference with private decisions relating to birth control[17] and abortion,[18] clothing and appearance[19] and sexual conduct.[20] **12.03**

In the private law sphere, the right to privacy has been more limited. It was first suggested at the end of the nineteenth century in the United States,[21] where it has **12.04**

---

[6] S Warren and L Brandeis, 'The Right to Privacy' (1890) 4 Harv LR 193.

[7] See eg J C Inness; *Privacy, Intimacy and Isolation* (Oxford University Press, 1992); S Stoljar, 'A Re-examination of Privacy' (1984) 4 LS 67; D Feldman, 'Secrecy, Dignity or Autonomy? Views of Privacy as a Social Value' (1994) 47 CLP 41.

[8] See Warren and Brandeis (n 6 above) 195.

[9] See eg Westin, (n 5 above); R Wacks, *The Protection of Privacy* (Sweet & Maxwell, 1980).

[10] *X v Iceland* (1976) 5 DR 86, EComm HR.

[11] See eg *Kaye v Robertson* [1991] FSR 62.

[12] See eg R Wacks, 'The Poverty of "Privacy" ' (1980) 96 LQR 73.

[13] For a discussion about the debate between proponents of the vertical as against the horizontal approach towards human rights, see para 5.39ff above.

[14] Or a 'penumbra' or 'shadow'; see *Whalen v Roe* (1977) 429 US 589.

[15] The right has evolved, for example, from due process clauses of the Fifth and Fourteenth Amendments (see *Roe v Wade* (1973) 410 US 113, 153), the Ninth Amendment (see *Griswold v Connecticut* (1965) 381 US 479, 486–499) (Goldberg J concurring); see generally, L Tribe, *American Constitutional Law* (2nd edn, Foundation Press, 1988) 15–03.

[16] See eg the Convention cases, para 12.138ff below.

[17] *Griswold v Connecticut* (1965) 381 US 479.

[18] *Roe v Wade* (1973) 410 US 113, see para 12.259 below.

[19] See eg *Kelley v Johnson* (1976) 425 US 238 (police department regulations on officers' hair styles).

[20] See eg *Dudgeon v United Kingdom* (1981) 4 EHRR 149.

[21] See S Warren and L Brandeis, 'The Right to Privacy', (1890) 4 Harv L Rev 193.

been extensively analysed and developed in the case law.[22] It has, however, usually been restricted to the four areas summarised in the *Restatement of the Law of Torts*[23] which states that:

> The right to privacy is invaded by
> (a) the unreasonable intrusion upon the seclusion of another;
> (b) the appropriation of the other's name or likeness;
> (c) unreasonable publicity given to the other's private life;
> (d) publicity that unreasonably places the other in a false light before the public.

Private law privacy issues most commonly arise in the context of media intrusion into a person's private life. This can take a wide variety of forms including intrusive photography, the publication of personal information and 'harassment' by journalists and photographers. Such activities may give rise to causes of action in private law. However, they also indirectly bring the 'human right' to privacy into play as a result of the state's positive obligations to ensure that the private lives of its citizens are protected. The extent to which these obligations require the courts, as emanations of state to provide the individual with private law remedies for 'breach of privacy' is of fundamental importance in English law because of its failure to provide full protection for private law privacy rights.[24]

12.05   The issues arising in relation to the right to privacy in the context of human rights law can be conveniently considered under four heads:

> **Misuse of personal information**: A right to restrict the use of 'personal' or 'private' information about an individual is central to the right to privacy. A large volume of such information is held by public bodies and is, potentially, open to misuse. The extent to which the use of this information is controlled or restricted is one of the most important 'privacy' issues.

> **Intrusion into the home**: The right of the individual to respect for his home is fundamental to any notion of privacy. The issues which arise under this head include, in particular, protection of the citizen against unreasonable entries, searches and seizures by public officials.

> **Photography, surveillance and telephone tapping**: The 'private sphere' is not only invaded by physical intrusion into the home. The right of privacy is generally understood to extend to private 'correspondence'. Modern technology provides a wide range of means of surveillance including telephone tapping, 'bugging' and photography of various forms. When surveillance is carried out by public officials there is potentially a 'direct' infringement of privacy rights.

---

[22] See *Restatement of the Law of Torts*, 2nd edn, para 625A ff.
[23] Ibid 2nd edn, para 625A; save for the right in para 2(b), an action for invasion of privacy can be maintained only by a living individual whose privacy is invaded (ibid para 652I).
[24] See para 12.06ff below.

However, surveillance may also be carried out by private organisations, in particular, the media. This gives rise to difficult issues as to the applicability of human rights instruments in the private sphere.[25]

The extent of other privacy rights: Finally, there are a range of other 'privacy rights' to be considered. These cover all forms of interference in the 'private sphere' including appropriation of a person's image, interference with private sexual behaviour and questions of the sexual identity of transsexuals.

Difficulties arise in each of these areas as to the extent to which interference with the privacy rights of the individual can be justified by the interests of society as a whole in, for example, the investigation of suspected criminal offences or the exposing of wrongdoing. The English courts already have to strike a balance in such cases.[26] After the Human Rights Act comes into force, the policy issues will have to be confronted in a wide range of cases.

B.   The Rights in English Law Before the Human Rights Act

(1)   Introduction

It is well established that English law does not recognise a right to privacy as such.[27] The point was considered by the Court of Appeal in *Kaye v Robertson*.[28] In that case, a well known actor had undergone extensive surgery and was in hospital when he was photographed and allegedly interviewed by a tabloid newspaper. He sought an injunction to restrain publication of the interview. The case was argued on a number of bases, the most straightforward of which was infringement of privacy. In rejecting this head of claim, Glidewell LJ remarked that the case was

12.06

> a graphic example of the desirability of Parliament considering whether and in what circumstances statutory provision should be made to protect the privacy of individuals.[29]

The House of Lords considered the issue in *R v Khan*[30] in the course of deciding whether surveillance evidence obtained in breach of Article 8 of the Convention was admissible in a criminal trial; Lord Nolan[31] (with whom Lord Keith concurred)

---

[25] See generally, para 5.40ff above.

[26] See eg the cases concerning the disclosure of allegations of sex abuse, para 12.38 below.

[27] See the remarks of Lord Denning MR in *Re X (A Minor)* [1975] Fam 47, 58; *Malone v Metropolitan Police Commissioner* [1979] Ch 344, 372; for a useful collection of material on all aspects of this topic see S Bailey, D Harris and B Jones, *Civil Liberties: Cases and Materials* (4th edn. Butterworths, 1995) Chap 8.

[28] [1991] FSR 62.

[29] Ibid 66; an injunction was granted on the basis of a potential claim in malicious falsehood.

[30] [1997] AC 558, see also *Khan v United Kingdom*, Application 35394/97, 20 April 1999 (Commission admissibility decision).

[31] *R v Khan* (n 30 above) 577.

expressed the view that there was no right to privacy but Lord Browne-Wilkinson,[32] Lord Slynn[33] and Lord Nicholls[34] preferred to leave the question open.

12.07 Despite the absence of a developed 'right of privacy', the courts have taken 'privacy interests' into account in a number of cases. Thus, in *Derby v Weldon (No 2)*[35] Sir Nicholas Browne-Wilkinson recognised that:

> discovery[36] in the course of an action is an interference with the right of privacy which an individual would otherwise enjoy to his own documents. As a result of the public interest in ensuring that all relevant information is before the court in adjudicating on the claim in the action that right of privacy is invaded and the litigant is forced, under compulsion by the process of discovery, to disclose his private documents. But such invasion of privacy being only for the purpose enabling a proper trial of the action in which the discovery is given, the court is astute to prevent a document so obtained from being used for any other purpose.

However, such recognition has been sporadic. The consequences of the refusal of the courts to recognise a right of privacy was vividly illustrated by the case of *R v Brentwood Borough Council, ex p Peck*[37] in which it was held that a local authority had lawfully released to the media the closed-circuit television footage of the applicant's attempted suicide.[38]

12.08 The question of reform of the English law in this area has received considerable attention over the last thirty years.[39] The impetus for reform has come largely from the perceived need to curb the excesses of the tabloid press. In response to a 1969 private members bill on the subject, the Younger Committee on Privacy was established. In 1972, the Committee decided, by a majority, against creating a 'general right to privacy', primarily because it would confer upon the courts an exceedingly wide discretion to enforce the law.[40] An attempt to introduce a Protection of Privacy Bill in the 1988–89 session of Parliament failed to achieve a Third Reading. In 1990, the Calcutt Committee on Privacy concluded that no tort of infringement of privacy should be introduced.[41] The Committee recommended the establishment of a Press Complaints Commission. This Commission

---

[32] Ibid 571.
[33] Ibid 571.
[34] Ibid 582, 583.
[35] *The Times*, 20 Oct 1988; for a recent example, see *Haig v Aitken* [2000] 3 All ER 80 (sale of bankrupt's private correspondence would be an infringement of his right of privacy).
[36] Now 'disclosure' under CPR, Pt 31.
[37] *The Times*, 18 Dec 1997.
[38] See also *M v BBC* [1997] 1 FLR 51; but see *Marcel v Commissioner of Police of the Metropolis* [1992] Ch 225, 234C–D, taking into account the 'fundamental human right' of privacy in relation to disclosure of documents.
[39] For recent general discussions, see D Eady, 'A Statutory Right to Privacy' [1996] EHRLR 243; Lord Bingham, 'Should there be a Law to Protect Rights of Personal Privacy?' [1996] EHRLR 450.
[40] *Report of the Committee on Privacy*, Cmnd 5012 (1972) paras 33–44 and 661–666.
[41] See *Report of the Committee on Privacy and Related Matters*, Cmnd 1102 (1990).

was established but attracted considerable criticism, and in his 1993 Review of Press Self-Regulation Sir David Calcutt QC recommended that further consideration be given to the introduction of a tort of infringement of privacy.[42] The debate still continues.[43] Increasing numbers of senior judges have, however, expressed the view that it is open to the courts to develop a privacy law. As Lord Irvine LC said in the course of debates on the Human Rights Bill:

> I believe that the true view is that the courts will be able to adapt and develop the common law by relying on existing domestic principles in the laws of trespass, nuisance, copyright, confidence and the like to fashion a common law right to privacy.[44]

Despite the absence of a general 'right of privacy' in English law, such rights do receive a degree of *indirect* protection from a number of sources.[45] The torts of trespass to land and goods protect individuals against direct intrusions into their homes. The law of breach of confidence provides some protection against the disclosure of information and possibly against some forms of surveillance. There is limited statutory protection in relation to police surveillance and the use of information held on computer. These protections will be considered in the next four sections. **12.09**

(2) Intrusion into the home: entry, search and seizure

(a) Introduction

The common law has always treated the right to freedom from interference with personal property[46] as fundamental.[47] It has given rise to perhaps the most well-known of all maxims of the English law: **12.10**

> 'An Englishman's home is his castle' is one of the few principles of law known to every citizen . . . The rule is, of course, subject to exceptions, but they are few . . .[48]

In fact, the principle has always been subject to numerous limitations: by 1604 it

---

[42] (1993) Cm 2315, para 17; see also the House of Commons, National Heritage Committee, Fourth Report on Privacy and Media Intrusion, Mar 1993, (1992–93) HC Papers 294; and Lord Chancellor's Consultation Paper, *Infringement of Privacy* (Jul 1993).

[43] See eg the debate in House of Lords on the Human Rights Bill, *Hansard*, HL cols 771–787 (24 Nov 1997).

[44] Ibid col 785; see also Lord Bingham, 'Should there be a Law to Protect Rights of Personal Privacy?' [1996] EHRLR 450.

[45] See generally, B Neill, 'Privacy: A Challenge for the Next Century', in B Markesinis (ed), *Protecting Privacy* (Oxford University Press, 1999).

[46] For a fuller treatment, see eg D Feldman, *The Law relating to Entry, Seizure and Search* (Butterworths, 1986); R Clayton and H Tomlinson, *Civil Actions Against the Police* (3rd edn, Sweet & Maxwell, 2001) Chap 7.

[47] R Kerr (ed), *Blackstone's Commentaries on the Laws of England* (4th edn, John Murray, 1876) 100 ff.

[48] *McLorie v Oxford* [1982] 1 QB 1290 *per* Donaldson LJ.

provided protection only against the forcible entry of outer doors of dwelling houses, and gave way to legal process in the name of the King.[49] Nevertheless, it remains the case that the police or other public officials can enter premises only in the limited situations defined by statute or common law and that the burden is on them to justify the entry.

12.11 In the famous constitutional case of *Entick v Carrington*,[50] an entry and seizure by the King's messengers was said to be justified by a warrant issued by one of the four principal secretaries of state. Lord Camden CJ dismissed this defence in stirring words:

> The great end, for which men entered into society was to secure their property. That right is preserved sacred and incommunicable in all instances, where it has not been taken away or abridged by some public law for the good of the whole. . . . By the laws of England every invasion of private property, be it ever so minute, is a trespass.

This approach, which applies both to searches of property and seizures of goods has been applied, somewhat unevenly, ever since. Search, seizure and retention by public officials will be unlawful unless justified by some common law or statutory power.[51]

12.12 However, the idea of 'respect for the home' under Article 8(1)[52] has rather broader implications in the public law field; and has been successfully utilised in some recent judicial review cases. For example, in *R v North and East Devon District Health Authority, ex p Coughlan*[53] the Court of Appeal held that moving a disabled person out of a long stay residence after giving her an express assurance that she could remain there for life constituted an interference with the right to her home which required the public body to comply with its duty to act fairly.

(b) Interference with land and goods

12.13 Any unjustified direct physical intrusion onto land in possession of another is a trespass at common law. The slightest entry, such as putting a foot in the door or a microphone on a window, is sufficient. The person who enters must justify the entry. Honest belief in a right to enter is not a defence.[54] A public official who enters under an authority given by law becomes a trespasser *ab initio* if he abuses that

---

[49] See D Feldman, *Civil Liberties and Human Rights in England and Wales* (Clarendon Press, 1993) 403–4.

[50] (1765) 2 Wils 275; 19 State Trials 1029.

[51] For an illuminating general discussion see Feldman (n 46 above).

[52] See para 12.95ff below.

[53] [2000] 2 WLR 622.

[54] *Hewlitt v Bickerton* (1947) 150 EG 421; and see *Entick v Carrington* (n 50 above) 1066G: 'No man can set his foot upon my ground without my licence, but he is liable to an action, though the damage be nothing'.

authority.[55] This means that the occupier of the land can recover damages for the whole period that the wrongdoer is on the land and not just for the period after the abuse.[56]

Any interference with a person's goods is also, *prima facie*, tortious. An unjustified direct physical interference with goods in the possession of a person will be sufficient to constitute a trespass to goods.[57] If the person interfering with the goods acts in a manner inconsistent with the rights of the person in possession, he will be guilty of conversion. Conversion covers actions such as keeping and refusing to return, using, destroying, and returning the goods to a third party. Proceedings can be brought for trespass to goods when goods are removed, damaged or even touched. Conversion will be more appropriate if the plaintiff is prevented from gaining access to his goods, if lawfully seized goods are lost or damaged, or if there is a refusal to return goods which are no longer needed for the purpose for which they were seized.

12.14

(c) Powers of entry under warrant

A warrant is a legal authority to carry out acts which would, otherwise, be unlawful.[58] A large number of statutes empower justices of the peace to issue search warrants to police officers and other public officials.[59] Constables who act 'in obedience' to such a warrant are protected from claims in trespass if the warrant is issued without jurisdiction.[60] However, where police officers have acted maliciously in procuring the search warrant, they will be liable in damages.[61]

12.15

Applications for search warrants by police officers must be made in accordance with the procedure laid down in section 15 of the Police and Criminal Evidence Act 1984 ('PACE'). An application must be supported by an 'information' in writing.[62] The warrant must specify the name of the person who applies for it, the date on which it is issued, the enactment under which it is issued, the premises to be searched[63] and the articles or persons to be sought.[64] The execution of warrants

12.16

---

[55] *Six Carpenters Case* (1610) 8 Co Rep 146a; and see *Cinnamond v British Airports Authority* [1980] 1 WLR 582, 588; and generally, Clayton and Tomlinson (n 46 above) Chap 6.

[56] See *Shorland v Govett* (1826) 5 B & C 485.

[57] *Fouldes v Willoughby* (1841) 8 M & W 540, 549.

[58] For a comprehensive discussion, see D Feldman, *The Law Relating to Entry Search and Seizure* (Butterworths, 1986).

[59] For a comprehensive list of statutory police powers to enter and search premises, see H Levenson, F Fairweather and E Cape, *Police Powers: A Practitioner's Guide* (3rd ed, Legal Action Group, 1996), App 6.

[60] Constables Protection Act 1750, s 6; see generally, R Clayton and H Tomlinson, *Civil Actions Against the Police* (3rd edn Sweet & Maxwell, 2001) Chap 7.

[61] See, most recently, *Gibbs v Rea* [1998] AC 786 and see generally, Clayton and Tomlinson (n 60 above) Chap 8.

[62] s 15(3).

[63] *R v Southwestern Magistrates' Court, ex p Cofie* [1997] 1 WLR 885.

[64] s 15(6).

by police officers is governed by section 16 of PACE. The constable must, if the occupier is present, identify himself, produce the warrant and supply a copy.[65] If the occupier is not present, a copy of the warrant must be left at the premises.[66] A warrant does not permit a 'general search' of the premises:[67] a search under a warrant may only be a search 'to the extent required for the purpose for which the warrant was issued'.[68] The warrant must be endorsed, stating whether the articles which were sought were found and what other articles were seized.[69] The safeguards imposed by sections 15 and 16 of PACE are 'stringent in effect'.[70] Any search which is not carried out in accordance with these provisions will be unlawful.[71] Thus, searches have been held to be unlawful where copies of the schedules to the warrants were not supplied to the applicant at the time of the search[72] and where the enactment under which the warrant was issued was not specified.[73]

12.17   Special provisions apply to 'items subject to legal privilege',[74] 'excluded material'[75] and 'special procedure material'.[76] A provision of any enactment, passed prior to PACE, which permits searches for any of these three types of material, is of no effect.[77] A constable can, however, obtain access to excluded material or special procedure material by obtaining an appropriate order from a circuit judge if a number of special access conditions are fulfilled.[78] It has been emphasised that this procedure is 'a serious inroad upon the liberty of the subject' and that 'it is of cardinal importance that circuit judges should be scrupulous in discharging that responsibility'.[79] There is no power to search for or seize items subject to legal privilege. PACE provides, however, that this privilege is lost if the material is held 'with the intention of furthering a criminal purpose'.[80] The relevant provision[81] was given a very broad interpretation by the House of Lords in *R v Central Criminal Court, ex p*

---

[65]   s 16(5).

[66]   s 16(7).

[67]   See eg *R v Chief Constable of Warwick Constabulary, ex p Fitzpatrick* [1999] 1 WLR 564.

[68]   s 16(8).

[69]   s 16(9).

[70]   *R v Central Criminal Court, ex p A J D Holdings* [1992] Crim LR 669.

[71]   s 15(1) which covers the composite process of entering and searching; *R v Chief Constable of Lancashire, ex p Parker* [1993] QB 577.

[72]   Ibid.

[73]   *R v Reading Justices, ex p South West Meats* (1992) 4 Admin LR 401.

[74]   As defined in s 10(1).

[75]   That is personal records, human tissue or journalistic material held in confidence: see s 11(1).

[76]   That is, non-confidential journalistic material and confidential business material, s 14(1); for the impact of freedom of expression under Art 10 on these applications, see para 15.126 below.

[77]   s 9(2).

[78]   s 9 and Sch 1.

[79]   *R v Maidstone Crown Court, ex p Waitt* [1988] CLR 384; as a result, there is an implied obligation to give reasons for the decision: see *R v Southampton Crown Court, ex p J and P* [1993] Crim LR 962.

[80]   s 10(2).

[81]   Ibid.

Francis and Francis[82] in which it was found that, although the material was held innocently, the privilege was lost as a result of the 'criminal purpose' of a third party.[83]

In cases involving the use of warrants, the courts have emphasised the need to carry out a balancing exercise between, the public interest in the effective investigation and prosecution of crime and the public interest in protecting the personal and property rights of citizens against infringement and invasion:[84]

> [PACE] . . . seeks to effect a carefully judged balance between these interests and that it why it is a detailed and complex Act. If the scheme intended by Parliament is to be implemented it is important that the provisions laid down in the Act should be fully and fairly enforced.[85]

This approach has led to warrants being quashed in a number of cases.[86] However, there is no obligation on magistrates to give reasons for the grant of a warrant[87] and no record of the proceedings. As a result, it remains extremely difficult, in practice, to mount a successful challenge to a search warrant.[88]

(d) Powers of entry without warrant

A police officer has a common law power of entry into premises 'to deal with or prevent a breach of the peace'.[89] The power allows police officers to enter whether the breach is actually in progress or merely apprehended.[90] They may also enter in the fresh pursuit of someone suspected of a breach of the peace committed elsewhere. When the pursuit ends, however, and there is no likelihood of the breach recurring, the common law power to enter is terminated.[91]

PACE provides police officers with a number of statutory powers of entry. Officers may enter to:

12.18

12.19

12.20

---

[82] [1989] AC 346.

[83] The dispute arose when solicitors were ordered to produce material, comprising advice to a client, to assist in the tracing of proceeds of crime; the police argued that the material was held by the solicitors as a result of the plan of suspected drug traffickers for laundering their criminal gains. This decision has been subject to considerable criticism: see A Newbold, 'The Crime/Fraud Exception to Legal Professional Privilege' (1990) 53 MLR 472; and see generally, D Feldman, *Civil Liberties and Human Rights in England and Wales* (Clarendon Press, 1993), 448–450.

[84] *R v Crown Court at Lewes, ex p Hill* (1990) 93 Cr App R 60, 65.

[85] Ibid *per* Bingham LJ.

[86] See eg *R v Lewes Crown Court, ex p Nigel Weller & Co*, unreported, 12 May 1999.

[87] Although it is desirable, see *R v Marylebone Magistrates' Court, ex p Amdrell Ltd (trading as 'Get Stuffed')* (1998) 162 JP 719.

[88] See eg *ex p Amdrell* (n 87 above) in that case, the fact that the police did not disclose an intention to invite the media to attend the execution of a warrant did not invalidate its issue or execution.

[89] PACE, s 17(6); for a discussion of the meaning of breach of the peace, see para 16.13 below.

[90] See *Thomas v Sawkins* [1935] 2 KB 249; and see *McLeod v Commissioner of Police of the Metropolis* [1994] 4 All ER 553.

[91] *R v Marsden* (1868) LR 1 CCR 131.

- execute an arrest warrant;[92]
- arrest for an arrestable offence;[93]
- arrest for certain specified offences;[94]
- recapture a person unlawfully at large;[95]
- save life, limb or property;[96]
- search the premises of a person under arrest for evidence;[97] and
- search premises attended by a person immediately prior to or at the time of his arrest.[98]

The first four powers are only exercisable if the constable has reasonable grounds to believe that the person sought is on the premises.[99] The last requires reasonable grounds for believing that evidence which would justify the search is located on the premises.

(e) Powers of seizure and retention of goods

12.21 Police officers have a common law power to seize the 'fruits', 'evidence' or 'instruments' of serious crime from anyone 'implicated' in the crime or who unreasonably refuses to hand them over.[100] These powers have been superseded, but not replaced, by powers of seizure under PACE which are 'in addition to any power otherwise conferred'.[101]

12.22 Police officers have powers to enter premises and seize goods under a wide range of statutes. PACE provides for seven powers of seizure without warrant. The police may seize:

- items obtained through crime which may be disposed of;[102]
- evidence of crime which may be disposed of;[103]
- information on a computer which may be disposed of;[104]
- evidence found on the premises of a person under arrest;[105]

---

[92] PACE, s 17(1)(a).
[93] PACE, s 17(1)(b).
[94] PACE, s 17(1)(c).
[95] PACE, s 17(1)(d).
[96] PACE, s 17(1)(e).
[97] PACE, s 18(1).
[98] PACE, s 32(2)(b).
[99] PACE, s 17(2)(a).
[100] *Ghani v Jones* [1970] 1 QB 693, 708–709; the last category was added by Lord Denning MR when revising the judgment and is of dubious authority: see Jackson [1970] CLJ 1; and see generally, D Feldman, *The Law Relating to Entry Search and Seizure* (Butterworths, 1986), 409–416.
[101] PACE, s 19(5).
[102] PACE, s 19(2).
[103] PACE, s 19(3).
[104] PACE, s 19(4).
[105] PACE, s 18(1).

- evidence obtained through a stop and search procedure;[106]
- evidence found after arrest;[107]
- property located on a person brought to a police station.[108]

When the police seize large quantities of goods they must consider each item separately and decide whether or not there are reasonable grounds for believing that it is seizable. If proper consideration is not given to each item, a trespass to goods will result.[109] Where the search or seizure is unlawful, the goods must be returned.[110] As the Divisional Court stressed in *R v Chesterfield Justices, ex p Bramley*,[111] it is not unlawful to seize documents which are legally privileged if the police officer who did so did not have reasonable grounds for believing they were. However, the police are not entitled to remove documents to carry out a preliminary sift to investigate the position and must return documents immediately as soon as they have reasonable grounds for believing the documents are privileged.

Even if goods have been lawfully seized, the police will be guilty of wrongful interference with goods if they cannot justify the continued retention of them. When the police seize an item under their common law powers they must not keep it for longer than is reasonably necessary for their investigations.[112] The property must be returned when charges are dropped or the proceedings have been disposed of. **12.23**

The common law position is confirmed by section 22 of PACE, under which any material seized may be retained for 'so long as is necessary in all the circumstances'. Goods may be retained if there are reasonable grounds for believing they are the fruits of crime.[113] If goods are seized from a person in custody, on grounds that they might be used to cause injury, damage to property, interfere with evidence or assist in escape, they must be returned when the person is released from custody.[114] No goods can be retained for use as evidence at a trial or for investigation if a photograph or a copy would be sufficient.[115] Section 21 of PACE provides that the owner of documents has rights of access and copying. There is also a right of access to anything retained for the purpose of investigation of an offence, unless the police have reasonable grounds for believing that to give access would prejudice the investigation.[116] Owners of documents nevertheless often experience considerable practical difficulty in obtaining access or copies. **12.24**

---

[106] PACE, s 1(6).
[107] PACE, s 32(2)(a).
[108] PACE, s 54(1) and (3).
[109] *Reynolds v Commissioner of Police of the Metropolis* [1985] QB 881.
[110] See *R v Chief Constable of Lancashire, ex p Parker* [1993] QB 577.
[111] [2000] 1 All ER 411.
[112] *Ghani v Jones* [1970] 1 QB 693.
[113] PACE, s 22(2)(b).
[114] PACE, s 22(3).
[115] PACE, s 22(4).
[116] PACE, s 21(8).

12.25   The powers to seize and retain documents are conferred for the performance of public functions and cannot be used to make information available to private individuals for private purposes. This is because

> Search and seizure under statutory powers constitute fundamental infringements of the individual's immunity from interference by the state with his property and privacy—fundamental human rights.[117]

The police must nevertheless respond to a subpoena to produce documents to the court for the purposes of a civil action.[118]

(3) The misuse of personal information

(a) Introduction

12.26   The English law in relation to the protection of rights in personal information can be considered under two headings. First, there are the common law rights to protect the dissemination of information which is 'confidential'.[119] Although much of the earlier case law relates to trade secrets, these rights now also extend to many categories of 'personal' information. Secondly, there are a number of statutory rights of access to inaccurate information held in confidential files by public authorities and to correct inaccurate information which they may contain.

(b) Breach of confidence

12.27   **Introduction.**   The nineteenth century case law on 'breach of confidence' was the inspiration for the development of the right of privacy in the United States. The doctrine derives from a case in which Prince Albert obtained an injunction on the basis of breach of confidence to prevent an exhibition of etchings by himself and Queen Victoria: the injunction was granted against a defendant who had acquired copies without their consent.[120] The doctrine has proved to be extremely flexible and protects not merely trade secrets, but also confidential information about an individual's private life such as marital secrets,[121] sexual relationships,[122] a medical condition (such as having AIDS)[123] as well as artistic confidences.[124] The approach

---

[117] See *Marcel v Commissioner of Police of the Metropolis* [1992] Ch 225, 235D–E *per* Browne-Wilkinson J; approved by the Court of Appeal, 256D; and see also *Taylor v Director of the Serious Fraud Office* [1998] 3 WLR 1040.
[118] See *Marcel v Commissioner of Police* (n 117 above) 257D, 265D–G (the Court of Appeal overruling Browne-Wilkinson J on this point).
[119] For a fuller treatment, see eg R Toulson and C Phipps, *Confidentiality* (Sweet & Maxwell, 1996).
[120] *Prince Albert v Strange* (1848) 2 De G & Sm 652; the decision was heavily relied on by Warren and Brandeis (n 6 above).
[121] *Argyll (Duchess) v Argyll (Duke)* [1967] 1 Ch 302.
[122] *Stephens v Avery* [1988] Ch 449; *Barrymore v News Group* [1997] FSR 600.
[123] *X v Y* [1990] 1 QB 220.
[124] See eg *Gilbert v Star Newspapers* (1894) 11 TLR 4.

of the courts has been pragmatic and breach of confidence has developed into an adaptable remedy for the protection of privacy in an important class of cases.[125]

In order to establish a breach of confidence a claimant must show:

12.28

- that the information was confidential;
- that it was imparted in circumstances of confidence and
- that there has been or will be a misuse of that information.[126]

All three elements have been the subject of detailed consideration by the courts.

The nature of the information. First it must be shown that the information in question has the 'necessary quality of confidentiality'. This will not attach to 'trivial or useless information'[127] or to 'tittle tattle or gossip'.[128] More importantly, it will not attach to information which is already in the public domain. As Megarry J said in *Coco v A N Clarke (Engineerings) Ltd*:[129]

12.29

> something which is public property and public knowledge cannot *per se* provide any foundation for proceedings for breach of confidence. However confidential the circumstances of the communication, there can be no breach of confidence in revealing to others something which is already common knowledge.

Whether the publication of information has been so extensive as to destroy confidentiality is 'a question of degree depending on the facts of the particular case'.[130] Where marital secrets had been discussed by both parties in a number of newspaper articles, they were no longer 'confidential information'.[131] Furthermore, the confidentiality of information may be lost by the passage of time or change of circumstances.[132]

The fact that a matter has once been in the public domain cannot, however, prevent its resurrection, possibly many years later, from being an infringement of privacy; the determination is matter of fact and degree.[133] It has been held that

12.30

---

[125] See generally, F Gurry, *Breach of Confidence* (Oxford University Press, 1984), and Toulson and Phipps (n 119 above).

[126] See generally, *Saltman Engineering Co Ltd v Campbell Engineering Co Ltd* [1963] 3 All ER 413; and Toulson and Phipps (n 119 above) Chap III.

[127] See *McNicol v Sportsman's Books* (1930) McG CC 116.

[128] Cf *Stephens v Avery* [1988] Ch 449.

[129] [1969] RPC 41, 47.

[130] *Franchi v Franchi* [1967] RPC 149, 153; for a discussion as to the effect of foreign publication see *A-G v Guardian Newspapers Ltd (No 2)* [1990] 1 AC 109; and see Toulson and Phipps (n 119 above) Chap IV.

[131] *Lennon v News Group Newspapers* [1978] FSR 573, CA.

[132] See eg *A-G v Jonathan Cape Ltd* [1976] 1 QB 752 regarding the confidentiality of Cabinet discussions lost after 10 years; publication of 'Crossman Diaries' not restrained.

[133] *R v Broadcasting Complaints Commission, ex p Granada TV* [1995] EMLR 163, 168; see also *R v Chief Constable of North Wales Police, ex p Thorpe* [1999] QB 396, 429A.

previous convictions and sentences cannot be confidential information,[134] but this may be an overstatement of the position.[135]

12.31 **'Circumstances of confidence'.**   In order to be 'confidential', the information must have been imparted in circumstances importing an obligation of confidence. In many cases, the obligation will arise from the nature of the relationship between the persons giving and receiving the information. Thus, a relationship of confidence exists between doctor and patient,[136] journalist and source,[137] husband and wife[138] and between the parties to any sexual relationship.[139] Questions of confidentiality will, of course, only arise if the information being imparted is confidential in nature.

12.32 The general test is whether or not a reasonable man in the position of the recipient 'would have realised, upon reasonable grounds, that the information was being given to him in confidence'.[140] However, in the *Spycatcher* case,[141] Lord Goff suggested that the notion of a 'confidential relationship' could have a wider meaning. He accepted:

> the broad general principle . . . that a duty of confidence arises when confidential information comes to the knowledge of a person (the confidant) in circumstances where he has notice, or is held to have agreed, that the information is confidential, with the effect that it would be just in all the circumstances that he should be precluded form disclosing the information to others.[142]

He went on to state that the majority of cases in which a duty of confidence arises are those in which there is a pre-existing relationship between confider and confidant. Nevertheless, he said:

> It is well settled that a duty of confidence may arise in equity independently of such cases; and I have expressed the circumstances in which the duty arises in broad terms, not merely to embrace those cases where a third party receives information from a person who is under a duty of confidence in respect of it, knowing that it has been disclosed by that person to him in breach of his duty of confidence, but also to include certain situations, beloved of law teachers—where an obviously confidential document is wafted by an electric fan out of a window into a crowded street, or

---

[134] *Elliott v Chief Constable of Wiltshire The Times*, 5 Dec 1996.

[135] Cf *Melvin v Reid* (1931) 112 Cal App 285 (a film identifying the plaintiff as a prostitute who, seven years earlier, had been acquitted of murder was a breach of privacy after she had 'abandoned her life of shame, had rehabilitated herself'); and see W Prosser, 'Privacy', (1960) 48 Calif Rev 383, 396.

[136] *W v Edgell* [1990] 1 Ch 359.

[137] *A-G v Mulholland* [1963] 2 QB 477, and see *In re an Inquiry under the Company Securities (Insider Dealing) Act 1985* [1988] AC 660.

[138] *Argyll (Duchess) v Argyll (Duke)* [1967] 1 Ch 302.

[139] *Barrymore v News Group Newspapers* [1997] FSR 600.

[140] *Coco v A N Clarke (Engineerings) Ltd* [1969] RPC 41, 48.

[141] *A-G v Guardian Newspapers Ltd (No 2)* [1990] 1 AC 109.

[142] Ibid 281.

where an obviously confidential document, such as a private diary, is dropped in a public place, and is then picked up by a passer by.

Interesting and difficult questions have arisen as to the extent to which a court can 'impute' an obligation of confidence in circumstances in which no actual 'passing of information' takes place. These are considered below in relation to surveillance.[143]

Misuse of the information.   In order to maintain an action for breach of confidence, the information must have been disclosed to, or come into the hands of, a third party without the authorisation of the 'confider', or been used for a purpose other than that for which it was imparted to the confidant.[144] Thus, information obtained by the police from an interview under caution[145] or documents seized by the police when performing public functions (such as investigating and prosecuting crime) cannot be disclosed to private individuals for their private purposes;[146] and documents disclosed during the course of civil[147] or criminal[148] proceedings are likewise subject to an implied undertaking that they cannot be used for a collateral purpose. It is not clear whether it is necessary for the claimant to show 'detriment'. The better view, at least in relation to 'personal information', appears to be that this is not necessary.[149] It has been suggested that the test for determining whether there has been a misuse is whether a reasonable confidant's conscience would be affected by the disclosure.[149a] Applying this test, it has been held that the disclosure by doctors and pharmacists of anonymised information about prescribing habits was not a breach of confidence.[149b]

12.33

The defence of 'public interest'.   The English courts have recognised that the duty of confidence can be a restriction on the freedom of expression and that there may be occasions on which the public interest in the preserving of confidence is outweighed by other public interests. This is sometimes known as the defence of 'public interest'.[150] One aspect of this defence is the refusal of the courts to intervene to protect disclosure of information regarding 'wrongdoing'. This is because 'there is no confidence as to the disclosure of iniquity'.[151] This defence

12.34

---

[143] See para 12.52ff below.

[144] See generally, *Coco v A N Clark (Engineers) Ltd* [1969] RPC 41.

[145] *Bunn v British Broadcasting Corporation* [1998] 3 All ER 552.

[146] *Marcel v Commissioner of Police of the Metropolis* [1992] Ch 225, 255, 256 *per* Dillon LJ.

[147] *Home Office v Harman* [1983] AC 280; and see *Crest Homes plc v Marks* [1987] AC 829; and *Sybron Corporation v Barclays Bank plc* [1985] Ch 299.

[148] *Taylor v Director of the Serious Fraud Office* [1998] 1 WLR 1040.

[149] Cf Lord Keith's example of the 'anonymous donor' in *A-G v Guardian Newspapers Ltd (No 2)* [1990] 1 AC 109, 255–6.

[149a] See *R v The Department of Health ex p Source Informatics Ltd* [2000] 1 All ER 786.

[149b] Ibid.

[150] See *Beloff v Pressdram Ltd* [1973] 1 All ER 241, 260; but see *Price Waterhouse v BCCI* [1992] BCLC 583; and R Toulson and C Phipps *Confidentiality* (Sweet & Maxwell, 1996) 81–83.

[151] *Gartside v Outram* (1857) 26 LJ Ch 113.

extends to any misconduct of such a nature that it ought to be in the public interest to disclose it to others . . . The exception should extend to crimes, frauds, misdeeds, both those actually committed as well as those in contemplation provided always— and this is essential—that the disclosure is justified in the public interest. The reason is because 'no private obligation can dispense with that universal one which lies on every member of society to discover every design which be formed contrary to the laws of society, to destroy the public welfare'.[152]

12.35 This principle has been held to justify disclosure of suspected criminal conduct,[153] disclosure by the police of a photograph of a suspect where they make reasonable use of it for the purpose of the prevention and detection of crime and the apprehension of suspects or persons unlawfully at large,[154] disclosure of fraudulent business practices,[155] alleged miscarriages of justice and corrupt and disgraceful police practices,[156] alleged corruption by a local authority,[156a] dangerous medical practices which endanger the public,[157] dangerous medical hazards[158] and information about 'cults'.[159] It has also been held to justify the voluntary disclosure of confidential information to an inquiry set up under the Banking Act[160] and to regulators[161] (including disclosure of information acquired from police interview).[162] In matters of sexual conduct, however, the court will not refuse to enforce a duty of confidence simply because some people might regard the conduct as immoral.[163]

12.36 It is important to note that the defence of public interest does not depend upon proof of the iniquity of the person claiming breach of confidence; it involves balancing the public interest in favour of publication against the public interest in maintaining the right of confidentiality.[164] It has been extended to situations in which entertainers have sought to restrain revelations by their former

---

[152] *Initial Services v Putterill* [1968] 1 QB 398, 405.
[153] *Malone v Metropolitan Police Commissioner* [1979] Ch 344.
[154] *Hellewell v Chief Constable of Derbyshire* [1995] 1 WLR 804.
[155] *Gartside v Outram* (1857) 26 LJ Ch 113.
[156] *Cork v McVicar The Times*, 31 Oct 1984.
[156a] *Preston Borough Council v McGrath The Times*, 19 May 2000.
[157] *Schering Chemicals Ltd v Falkman Ltd* [1982] 1 QB 1.
[158] *W v Egdell* [1990] 1 Ch 359.
[159] *Hubbard v Vosper* [1972] 2 QB 84 (in relation to a book about Scientology).
[160] See *Price Waterhouse v BCCI* [1992] BCLC 583; cf the criticism of this decision in Toulson and Phipps (n 150 above) 81–83.
[161] See *Re A Company's Application* [1989] Ch 477.
[162] *Woolgar v Chief Constable of Sussex The Times*, 28 May 1999.
[163] *Stephens v Avery* [1988] Ch 449 (a married woman's lesbian relationship).
[164] *Lion Laboratories Ltd v Evans* [1985] QB 526: injunction refused in relation to information suggesting doubts about the accuracy of a breathalyser device; see also *X v Y* [1988] 2 All ER 648: injunction granted to restrain publication of information from medical records that two doctors were suffering from AIDS.

press agents.[165] The broad ambit of the 'public interest' defence has been criticised[166] and the defence has not been recognised in Australia.[167]

(c) Disclosure of information by public bodies

It appears that the obligations of public bodies in relation to the disclosure of confidential information may be different from those imposed in private law. In *R v Chief Constable of North Wales Police, ex p Thorpe*[168] the applicants were convicted sex offenders who sought judicial review of a decision to inform the owner of a caravan site where they were living of their convictions. Lord Bingham CJ held that where a public body acquires information relating to a member of the public which is not generally available and is potentially damaging: **12.37**

> the body ought not to disclose such information save for the purpose of and to the extent necessary for performance of its public duty or enabling some other public body to perform its public duty.[169]

He went on to hold that this principle did not rest on a duty of confidence but on a 'fundamental rule of good administration'.[170] Buxton J was of the view that, because of the overriding obligation of police officers to enforce the law and prevent crime, they did 'not have power or *vires* to acquire information on terms that preclude their using that information in a case where their public duty demands such use'.[171] This approach was approved by the Court of Appeal who said that:

> The issue here is not the same as it would be in private law. The fact that the convictions of the applicants had been in the public domain did not mean that the police as a public authority were free to publish information about their previous offending absent any public interest in this being done.[172]

The Court went on to say that both under Article 8 of the European Convention on Human Rights and under English administrative law, the police were entitled to use information when they reasonably conclude that this is what is required in order to protect the public.

---

[165] *Woodward v Hutchins* [1977] 1 WLR 760; see also *Khasshogi v Smith* (1980) 130 NLJ 168.
[166] See Toulson and Phipps (n 150 above) 81.
[167] See *Castrol Australia v Emtech Associates* (1980) 33 ALR 31, 54; and *Corrs Pavey Whiting and Byrne v Collector of Customs* (1987) 74 ALR 428, 445–50.
[168] [1999] QB 396.
[169] Ibid 409H.
[170] Ibid 410.
[171] Ibid 415B; this analysis gives rise to a number of difficulties which have not been explored in the case law which have proceeded on the basis that public bodies have the same obligations in relation to confidential information as private ones, see Toulson and Phipps (n 150 above) Chap V 'Public Sector Confidentiality'.
[172] [1999] QB 396, 429A–B, *per* Lord Woolf MR.

12.38 The general principle appears to be that a public body should not disclose information which is confidential or of a confidential character[173] unless there is a 'pressing need'[174] for disclosure in the interests of public health or safety,[175]
corruption[175a] or similar purposes.[175b] Such disclosure could be made without a
request from the third party but should be on the basis that the confidentiality of
the information should be maintained save insofar as the third party needs to use
the material for the purpose for which it was disclosed.[176] The balance has to be
struck between the competing public interests and, in a case involving disclosure
of information by the police concerning a past investigation it was said that:

> In order to safeguard the interests of the individual, it is . . . desirable that where the
> police are minded to disclose, they should . . . inform the person affected of what
> they propose to do in such time as to enable that person, if so advised, to seek assis-
> tance from the court.[177]

(d) Confidential files

12.39 Public bodies hold on file very large quantities of personal information about individuals. This is often, but not always, stored on computer. Until the enactment
of the Data Protection Act, the only potential remedy for misuse of this information would be a finding of breach of confidence: the claimant had to show that the
information concerned was originally acquired 'in confidence' and that the recipient had notice of its confidential nature.

12.40 The Younger Committee on Privacy[178] recommended legislation to keep under
review the techniques of collecting and processing personal information on computer. In 1975, a white paper was published proposing a permanent statutory
agency to protect data subjects and the Lindop Committee on Data Protection
was appointed the following year. In 1978, this Committee recommended the establishment of a Data Protection Authority.[179] The proposal was not accepted. In
1984, however, the Data Protection Act 1984 was passed in order to comply with

[173] For example, information which has been in the public domain at some earlier date and which
may not, therefore, attract the protection of the private law: see R Toulson and C Phipps,
Confidentiality (Sweet & Maxwell, 1996) para 3–08ff.
[174] *Re L (Sexual Abuse: Disclosure)* [1999] 1 WLR 307, 306A (in that case, the Court of Appeal
quashed the decision to disclose findings made in care proceedings because there were no pending
investigations); *R v A Police Authority, ex p LM*, 6 Sep 1999 (decision to disclose past unproven allegations of sex abuse quashed).
[175] See *Woolgar v Chief Constable of Sussex Police* [1999] 3 All ER 604.
[175a] *Preston Borough Council v McGrath The Times*, 19 May 2000.
[175b] See also *R v Secretary of the State for the Home Department, ex p Amnesty International*, 15 Feb
2000, unreported where the Divisional Court held that fairness required that medical reports concerning General Pinochet be disclosed to the states who had requested his extradition.
[176] Ibid, 615.
[177] Ibid.
[178] *Report of the Committee on Privacy*, Cmnd 5012 (1972) para 621.
[179] *Report of the Committee on Data Protection* (1978) Cmnd 7341.

the provisions of the European Convention for the Protection of the Individual With Regard to the Automatic Processing of Personal Data.[180] The Act has now been replaced by the Data Protection Act 1998, which gave effect to the European directive[181] on the processing and free movement of personal data.

The purpose of the Data Protection Act is to protect personal data. 'Personal' does not, however, mean 'private'. Whereas the 1984 Act only applied to automatically processed data, the definition of data under the 1998 Act includes information which is recorded as part of a relevant filing system (or with the intention of forming a relevant filing system) or part of an accessible record.[182] The Act applies to data which relates to a living individual who can be identified from the data or from the data and other information which is in the possession (or is likely to come into the possession) of the data controller[183] and includes expressions of personal opinion.[184]   **12.41**

An individual who is the subject of personal data is entitled[185] if he makes a request in writing to a data controller[186] to be promptly informed of whether there is any personal data which is being processed.[187] The data controller may charge a fee for the service. Where the processing of personal data is causing (or is likely to cause) unwarranted and substantial damage to the data subject[188] or another, the data subject is entitled to require the data controller, after the expiry of a reasonable period, to cease processing[189] (or not to begin processing) unless one of several specified exceptions apply.[190] He may also apply to the court[191] to rectify, block, erase or destroy personal data if the court is satisfied[192] that the data processed by the data controller is incorrect or misleading as to any matter of fact.[193] Any individual who suffers damage as a result of a data controller contravening the Act is entitled to compensation.[194]   **12.42**

The Act provides that data must be used in accordance with the data protection principles. Part I of Schedule I of the Act lists these principles; guidance concerning their interpretation is contained in Part II of the Schedule. The data protection principles are as follows: **12.43**

---

[180] See R Austin, 'The Data Protection Act 1984: The Public Law Implications' [1984] PL 618.
[181] EC Directive (EC) 95/46.
[182] s 1(1) of the 1998 Act.
[183] As defined by s 1(1) of the 1998 Act.
[184] Ibid s 1(3).
[185] Under s 7 of the 1998 Act.
[186] As defined by s 1(1) of the 1998 Act.
[187] As defined by s 1(1) of the 1998 Act.
[188] As defined by s 1(1) of the 1998 Act.
[189] As defined by s 1(1) of the 1998 Act.
[190] s 10 of the 1998 Act.
[191] See s 15 of the 1998 Act.
[192] Under s 14 of the 1998 Act.
[193] s 70(2) of the 1998 Act.
[194] Ibid s 13.

- personal data shall be processed fairly and lawfully and, in particular, shall not be processed unless at least one of the conditions in Schedule 2 is met and, in the case of sensitive personal data,[195] at least one of the conditions in Schedule 3 is met;[196]
- personal data shall be obtained only for one or more specified and lawful purposes, and shall not be processed in any manner incompatible with that purpose or those purposes;
- personal data held shall be adequate, relevant and not excessive in relation to the purpose or purposes for which they are processed;
- personal data shall be accurate and, where necessary, kept up to date;
- personal data processed for any purpose or purposes shall not be kept longer than is necessary for that purpose or those purposes;
- personal data shall be processed in accordance with the rights of data subjects under the Act;
- appropriate technical and organisational measures shall be taken against unauthorised or unlawful processing of personal data and against accidental loss or destruction of, or damage to, personal data; and
- personal data shall not be transferred to a country or territory outside the European Economic Area unless that country or territory ensures an adequate level of protection for the rights and freedoms of data subjects in relation to the processing of personal data.

12.44   However, the Data Protection Act contains exemptions in the following areas:

- national security;[197]
- crime and taxation;[198]
- health education and social work;[199]
- regulatory activity;[200]
- journalism, literature and art;[201]
- research, history and statistics;[202]

---

[195] As defined by s 2 of the 1998 Act.

[196] The data subject must give his consent (para 1); the processing must be necessary for the purposes of exercising rights or obligations conferred by law on the date controller in connection with his employment (para 2); the processing must be necessary to protect the vital interests of the data subject (para 3); the processing is carried out by a non profit making body (para 4); the information is public as a result of steps deliberately taken by the data subject (para 5); the processing is necessary in connection with legal proceedings or advice (para 6), the administration of justice, statutory functions or governmental functions (para 7) or medical purposes (para 8); the processing consists of information relating to racial or ethnic origin (para 9) or is processed in circumstances specified by the Secretary of State (para 10).

[197] See s 28.

[198] See s 29.

[199] See s 30.

[200] See s 31.

[201] See s 32.

[202] See s 33.

- information available to the public by or under any enactment;[203]
- disclosures required by law or made in connection with legal proceedings;[204]
- domestic purposes;[205] and
- miscellaneous exemptions.[206]

The Secretary of State also has power to make further orders for exemptions.[207]

The Data Protection Commissioner has power to ensure that data controllers **12.45**
comply with the Act by using the enforcement procedures in Part V of the Act.
The Act also creates a number of criminal offences,[208] prosecutions for which
cannot be instituted except by the Commissioner or Director of Public
Prosecutions.

(e) Access to personal information

There are a number of statutory provisions which give individuals a right of access **12.46**
to personal information. These rights should be distinguished from obligations
on public bodies to provide freedom of information which are discussed in
Chapter 15.[209] The Labour Government elected in 1997 is committed to a
Freedom of Information Act and a draft Bill was published in 1999. A Freedom of
Information Act is likely to become law in the course of 2000.

Files which are held manually are subject to the provisions of the Access to **12.47**
Personal Files Act 1987. There is no equivalent of the Data Protection
Commissioner and the Act is not of general application. The authority holding
such records has such obligations with regard to access and accuracy 'as are imposed by the regulations'.[210] The only files which are covered are those held by social services[211] and housing departments.[212] There are a wide range of exemptions
and the Act has proved of limited value.[213]

There is a right of access to personal information in the following areas: **12.48**

---

[203] See s 34.
[204] See s 35.
[205] See s 36.
[206] See s 37 and Sch 7.
[207] See s 38.
[208] Such as unlawfully obtaining or disclosing personal data and selling or offering to sell personal data: see s 55.
[209] See para 15.133ff below.
[210] s 1(1).
[211] Access to Personal Files (Social Services) Regulations 1989, SI 1989/206, as amended by SI 1991/1587.
[212] Access to Personal Files (Housing) Regulations 1989, SI 1989/503.
[213] See generally, P Birkinshaw, *Freedom of Information: The Law, the Practice and the Ideal*, (2nd edn, Butterworths, 1996), 259ff.

- social services files;[214]
- housing files;[215]
- health records after 1 November 1989 under the Access to Health Records Act 1990;
- information concerning physical or mental health collected by or on behalf of health professionals under the Access to Medical Reports Act 1988;[216]
- special educational needs in England[217] and Wales;[218] and
- environmental information.[219]

(4) Photography, surveillance and telephone tapping

(a) Introduction

12.49 One important way in which privacy may be invaded is by the taking of unauthorised photographs or film of a person or his home.[220] A person may be photographed or filmed in a 'private setting', such as while sunbathing at home, or in a public place. The photographs or films may be taken by public officials such as police officers or by third parties such as journalists or private investigators.

12.50 Closely related is the invasion of privacy by means of 'listening devices'. Devices can be placed in the home or fixed to a telephone line; they can also take the form of 'long range' listening devices which record conversation in a building without any form of physical intrusion. Such surveillance may, again, be carried out by public officials or third parties.

(b) Photography

12.51 The traditional view is that the English law gives a person no 'right to his own image'[221] or to an image of his home.[222] The law has, however, undergone considerable development in recent years, and privacy rights in relation to photographs may now find some protection in the law of confidentiality.

12.52 Prior to *Spycatcher*, it had been assumed that the requirement of a pre-existing relationship between the 'confider' and 'confidant' prevented the law of breach of confidence from providing protection against unauthorised photography. On the

---

[214] Access to Personal Files (Social Services) Regulations 1989, SI 1989/206, as amended by SI 1991/1587.

[215] Access to Personal Files (Housing) Regulations 1989, SI 1989/503.

[216] See also, Access to Health Records (Control of Access) Regulations 1993, SI 1993/746.

[217] Education (Special Educational Needs)(Information) Regulations 1994, SI 1994/1048.

[218] Education (Special Educational Needs)(Information) Regulations 1999, SI 1999/1442.

[219] Environment Information Regulations 1992, SI 1992/1711, as amended by SI 1998/1447.

[220] This was one of the areas of mischief mentioned by S Warren and L Brandeis in 'The Right to Privacy' (1890) 4 Harv Law Rev 193.

[221] See *Sports Press Agency v Our Dogs* [1916] 2 KB 880.

[222] *Baron Bernstein of Leigh v Skyways View and General Ltd* [1978] 1 QB 479.

basis of an 'imputed confidential relationship' suggested by *Spycatcher*,[223] however, it has been held that a breach of an express or implied obligation not to take photographs may give rise to action for breach of confidence. Thus, in *Shelley Films v Rex Features*,[224] the defendant was restrained from using photographs of a mask and a film-set which had been taken in spite of clear signs which banned entry by non-authorised persons and prohibited photography. In finding a relationship of confidentiality, the judge relied on both *Spycatcher* and the Australian case of *Franklin v Gliddins*,[225] in which a thief was held to be under a duty of confidentiality.[226]

The position was put more generally in *Hellewell v The Chief Constable of Derbyshire*,[227] which dealt with the use which police officers could make of photographs taken of persons in custody. Laws J held that there was undoubtedly an obligation of confidence between the plaintiff and police, as the photograph was not a 'public fact' and could be described as a 'piece of confidential information'. Nevertheless, the public interest in the prevention of crime outweighed the public interest in maintaining confidentiality. Laws J said, *obiter*, that:

> If someone with a telephoto lens were to take from a distance, and with no authority, a picture of another engaged in some private act, his subsequent disclosure of the photograph would in my judgment as surely amount to a breach of confidence as if he had found or stolen a letter or diary in which the act was recounted, and proceeded to publish it. In such a case the law would protect what might reasonably be called a right of privacy, though the name accorded to the cause of action would be breach of confidence.[228]

It may be that a relationship of confidentiality would be found if unauthorised listening devices were used to monitor a person's conversations;[229] these points have not yet been given direct consideration in the cases. The potential availability of a claim for breach of confidence in relation to photographs taken with telephoto lenses has led the European Commission on Human Rights to reject a claim under Article 8 on the ground that the applicant had failed to exhaust domestic remedies.[230]

(c) Surveillance

The common law provides very limited protection to the victims of visual or aural **12.54** surveillance. If an individual is kept under constant observation he might have a

12.53

---

[223] See *A-G v Guardian Newspapers Ltd (No 2)* [1990] 1 AC 109; see para 12.32 above.
[224] [1994] EMLR 134.
[225] [1977] QR 72.
[226] See also *Creation Records v News Group Newspapers The Times*, 29 Apr 1997.
[227] [1995] 1 WLR 804.
[228] Ibid 807.
[229] See *Francome v Mirror Group Newspapers Ltd* [1984] 1 WLR 892.
[230] See *Earl and Countess Spencer v United Kingdom* [1998] EHRLR 348, EComm HR.

claim for harassment.[231] If his conversation is recorded by surveillance devices, he may have an action for breach of confidence on the basis of an 'imputed relationship of confidentiality'.[232] The most obvious remedies are found in nuisance and trespass to land but these suffer from important limitations.

12.55 If any person enters onto another's land to observe him or to plant a listening device, he will be guilty of trespass. Damages have accordingly been awarded for trespass where a defendant secretly installed a microphone in the flat of the plaintiff[233] and under a marital bed.[234] The significance of an action in trespass has, however, been undermined by the highly sophisticated nature of surveillance devices. Such technology has made it a simple matter to eavesdrop on a home without entering the premises to install the device.

12.56 A nuisance will be committed if an act or omission of one person unreasonably interferes with the enjoyment of land of another. In *Victoria Park Racing v Taylor*,[235] however, the High Court of Australia held that spying is not an actionable nuisance. It refused to prevent racing broadcasts from a high platform built to gain an unimpeded view over the race track of the plaintiff, since the activities of the defendant neither interfered with nor were intended to interfere with the land of the plaintiff, but merely rendered his business less profitable. Another action in nuisance failed in a case in which a dentist in Balham sought an injunction against neighbours who installed large mirrors to observe his study and surgery.[236]

12.57 In *Bernstein v Skyways*[237] it was held that aerial photography over the plaintiff's land did not constitute a trespass because the rights of the landowner in the airspace above his property are limited to such a height as is necessary for the ordinary use and enjoyment of the land. However, Griffiths J went on to say that:

> if the circumstances were such that the plaintiff was subjected to the harassment of constant surveillance of his house, accompanied by the photographing of his every activity, I am far from saying that the court would not regard such a monstrous invasion of his privacy as an actionable nuisance for which they would give relief.

In *Khorasandjian v Bush*,[238] it was held that persistent and protracted harassment by telephone constituted a nuisance. This attempt to extend the tort of nuisance to cover interference with privacy rights was, however, criticised by the House of Lords in *Hunter v Canary Wharf*[239] on the basis that the essence of the tort is injury

---

[231] See now Protection from Harassment Act 1997.
[232] See para 12.31ff above.
[233] *Greig v Greig* [1966] VR 376.
[234] *Sheen v Clegg The Daily Telegraph*, 22 Jun 1961.
[235] (1937) 58 CLR 479.
[236] C Kenny, *Cases on Tort* (4th edn, 1926) 367.
[237] [1978] 1 QB 479.
[238] [1993] QB 727.
[239] [1997] AC 655, 691G–692B, *per* Lord Goff; 706B–7–7E, *per* Lord Hoffmann.

to land. Harassment is now a statutory offence,[240] but a tort of harassment might have developed independently on the basis of an extension of the tort in *Wilkinson v Downton*[241] to cover cases in which the claimant only suffers distress or discomfort.[242]

The surveillance of citizens by the security services or the police was, until recently, entirely unregulated by statute. Police surveillance was regulated by Home Office Guidelines[243] which did not provide a lawful authority for the placing of listening devices on private premises. This constituted an actionable trespass. On a number of occasions, the courts have described the position as unsatisfactory. In *R v Khan*[244] the defendant sought to exclude evidence obtained by the use of a listening device on the basis that the device had been illegally installed. Even though it was accepted that the surveillance had been illegal, the evidence was admitted as the result of an exercise of judicial discretion in accordance with section 78 of PACE. **12.58**

A number of the judges in *R v Khan* expressed the view that it was highly desirable that police surveillance be given a statutory foundation. Counsel for the prosecution indicated that the Government intended to introduce such legislation.[245] The position is now governed by Part III of the Police Act 1997, entitled 'Authorisation of Action in Respect of Property'. This legislation deals only with those forms of police surveillance which involve 'interference with property'. It does not provide a general scheme to regulate the use of listening devices by the police. **12.59**

Section 92 of the Police Act 1997 provides that: **12.60**

> No entry on or interference with property or with wireless telegraphy shall be unlawful if it is authorised by an authorisation having effect under this Act.

Authorisation may be given in cases where the authorising officer believes:

> (a) that it is necessary for the action specified to be taken on the ground that it is likely to be of substantial value in the prevention or detection of serious crime, and
>
> (b) that what the action seeks to achieve cannot reasonably be achieved by other means.[246]

---

[240] See Protection from Harassment Act 1997.

[241] [1897] 2 QB 57.

[242] At present, the tort requires the claimant to have suffered nervous shock, see *Hunter v Canary Wharf* (n 239 above) 707E–G, *per* Lord Hoffmann; and see the discussion of the tort in R Wacks, *Privacy and Press Freedom* (Blackstone, 1995), 80–89.

[243] The Guidelines on the Use of Equipment in Police Surveillance Operations, 19 Dec 1984, Dep NS 1579.

[244] [1997] AC 558; see para 11.132 above.

[245] See *R v Khan* (n 244 above) 582, *per* Lord Nolan.

[246] s 93(2).

Conduct shall be regarded as 'serious crime' if:

(a) it involves the use of violence, results in substantial financial gain or is conduct by a large number of people in pursuance of a common purpose; or
(b) the offence . . . is an offence for which a person who has attained the age of twenty-one and has no previous convictions could reasonably be expected to be sentenced to imprisonment for a term of three years or more.[247]

The authorisation may be given by a chief officer of police or equivalent senior officer[248] or, if that is not reasonably practicable, by a designated deputy.[249] The authorisation should, save in an urgent case, be provided in writing.[250]

12.61　In some cases an authorisation is not permitted to take effect until it has been approved by a Commissioner[251] appointed under the provisions of the Act.[252] Such approval is required where the property to which the authorisation relates is a dwelling house, hotel bedroom or office or in which:

it is likely to result in any person acquiring knowledge of
(i) matters subject to legal privilege;[253]
(ii) confidential personal information;[254] or
(iii) confidential journalistic material.[255]

These provisions do not, however, apply to an authorisation 'where the person who gives it believes that the case is one of urgency'.[256] The Act provides for the Secretary of State to issue a Code of Practice in relation to the issuing of authorisations. It also provides for a 'complaints procedure'. Such complaints are to be investigated by a Commissioner.[257] A Commissioner who is satisfied that there are no reasonable grounds for believing the specified matters may quash the authorisation or renewal.[258] Wide-ranging changes to the statutory regime governing surveillance are proposed by the Regulation of Investigatory Powers Bill which, for the first time, provides a legal framework for non-intrusive surveillance and the use of 'covert human intelligence sources' such as informants and undercover police officers.[258a]

---

[247] s 93(4).
[248] s 93(5).
[249] s 94.
[250] s 95.
[251] s 97(1).
[252] See s 91.
[253] Defined in s 98.
[254] Defined in s 99.
[255] Defined in s 100; s 97(2).
[256] s 97(3).
[257] s 107 and Sch 7.
[258] s 103.
[258a] See para 12.215 below.

Surveillance by the security and intelligence services is also governed by statute. In **12.62**
Hewitt and Harman v United Kingdom[259] the Commission on Human Rights declared admissible a complaint by two former officials of Liberty who had allegedly
been under surveillance by MI5. This resulted in the enactment of the Security
Services Act 1989. which establishes MI5 as a statutory body and defines its func-
tions.[260] By section 5, the Home Secretary is authorised to issue warrants for entry
onto or interference with property or for interference with wireless telegraphy.
Similar provisions relating to MI6 and GCHQ are to be found in the Intelligence
Services Act 1994. Both regimes will be supplemented by the provisions of the
Regulation of Investigatory Powers Bill.

The Security Service Act 1996 extended the function of the Security Service to **12.63**
allow it to

> act in support of the activities of police forces and other law enforcement agencies
> in the prevention and detection of serious crime.[261]

The Act also extends the power of the Home Secretary to issue warrants authorising entry onto or interference with property or interference with wireless telegraphy for the purposes of this function. These warrants may relate to property in the
British Islands if either:

(a) the conduct concerned involves the use of violence, results in substantial financial gain or is conduct by a large number of persons in pursuit of a common purpose, or
(b) the offence or one of the offences is an offence for which a person who has attained the age of 21 and has no previous convictions could reasonably be expected to be sentenced to imprisonment of three years or more.[262]

These provisions involve an executive power to issue warrants which is not controlled by the courts.[263]

(d) Intercepting letters and telephone tapping

The interception of a letter does not constitute a trespass unless the letter is actually **12.64**
touched in an unauthorised manner: 'the eye cannot by the laws of England be
guilty of a trespass'.[264] Nevertheless, the interception of letters by warrant of the
Home Secretary is a practice of long standing, in spite of the absence of clear authority for it.[265] The lawfulness of telephone tapping was unsuccessfully challenged

---

[259] (1989) 67 DR 88, EComm HR.
[260] s 1(1).
[261] s 1(1), amending s 1 of the Security Service Act 1989.
[262] s 2, adding s 5(3B) to the Intelligence Services Act 1994.
[263] See P Duffy and M Hunt, 'Goodbye Entick v Carrington: the Security Service Act 1996',
[1997] EHRLR 11.
[264] *Entick v Carrington* (1765); 19 St Tr 1029, 1066.
[265] See *Report of Committee of Privy Councillors* (1957) Cmnd 283, 'the Birkett Committee'.

in *Malone v Commissioner of Police for the Metropolis*.[266] Sir Robert Megarry V-C rejected a number of arguments based on a 'right to privacy'[267] and the 'direct effect of the Convention'.[268] The European Court of Human Rights subsequently found a violation of Article 8 in this case.[269]

12.65 The lawfulness of the power of the Home Secretary to authorise telephone tapping was the subject of review in slightly different circumstances in *R v Secretary of State for Home Affairs, ex p Ruddock*.[270] An official of the Campaign for Nuclear Disarmament unsuccessfully alleged that the Home Secretary had acted unlawfully by authorising MI5 to tap her telephone for party political purposes. Taylor J accepted that the court had jurisdiction to hear the case. He held that, as the Home Secretary was under a duty to act fairly, the official must act in accordance with the published criteria governing the issuance of warrants. He was not prepared, however, to infer from the evidence that the Home Secretary had issued a warrant in breach of his criteria.

12.66 In response to the decision of the European Court of Human Rights in the *Malone* case the Government published a White Paper[271] and the Interception of Communications Act 1985 was the result. The Act regulates the interception of post as well as telephone tapping and covers any communication sent by a public telecommunications system.[272] The Secretary of State cannot issue a warrant unless

> he considers the warrant is necessary:
>
> (a) in the interests of national security;
> (b) for the purpose of preventing or detecting serious crime;
> (c) for the purpose of safeguarding the economic well-being of the United Kingdom.[273]

Serious crime has the same broad definition as that used subsequently in the Police Act 1997.[274] When considering whether to issue a warrant, the Secretary of State must specifically address whether the information could be reasonably obtained by other means.[275]

12.67 A warrant permits the interception of communications sent to or from one or more specific addresses. The addresses specified are those to or from which

---

[266] [1979] Ch 344.
[267] See para 12.06 above.
[268] See para 2.09ff above.
[269] *Malone v United Kingdom* (1984) 7 EHRR 14.
[270] [1987] 1 WLR 1482.
[271] *The Interception of Communications in the United Kingdom* (1985) Cmnd 9438.
[272] s 1.
[273] s 2(2).
[274] See s 93(4) and see para 12.59 above.
[275] s 2(3).

communications are likely to be made by the persons identified in the warrant. The interception of other communications is, however, permissible as necessary to intercept the communications described in the warrant.[276] A warrant issued by the Home Secretary is normally valid for a period of two months.[277] Warrants issued on the grounds of national security or economic well-being may be renewed for up to six months if they are endorsed to this effect; other warrants only benefit from a one-month renewal period.[278] The warrant may be modified by the Home Secretary at any time.[279]

There are a number of types of telephone tapping which are not covered by the **12.68** 1985 Act.[280] It does not extend to non-public networks.[281] Furthermore, the public network ends at the socket in the wall and, as a result, interceptions of cordless phones are not covered by the Act.[282] It is also unclear whether the interception of mobile telephones falls within the Act.[283] In addition, no authorisation is required if one of the participants in a telephone conversation consents to the interception.[284] Telephone metering, that is the recording of information about the use of a telephone but not the actual conversation does not require any warrant but is permitted under section 45 of the Telecommunications Act 1985 for 'the prevention and detection of crime or the purposes of criminal proceedings'.[285]

The Interception of Communications Act is designed to prohibit allegations of **12.69** telephone tapping or interception of post being made in any court proceedings. Thus, section 9(1) provides that:

> In any proceedings before any court or tribunal no evidence shall be adduced and no questions shall be asked which, in either case, tends to suggest

that an offence under section 1 was committed or a warrant issued. The Act provides that a tribunal will hear the application of any person who believes that his communications have been intercepted.[286] The issues which such a tribunal may consider are, however, extremely limited. Unless the complaint is frivolous or vexatious, the investigation of the tribunal is restricted to an assessment as to whether a warrant (or certificate) was issued in accordance with the authorisation requirements. The role of the tribunal is limited to the investigation of whether there is a

---

[276] s 3(1).
[277] s 4.
[278] s 4(6)(c).
[279] s 5.
[280] See generally, JUSTICE, *Under Surveillance: Covert Policing and Human Rights Standards* (Justice 1998), 16–18.
[281] Cf *Halford v United Kingdom* (1997) 24 EHRR 523.
[282] See *R v Effik* [1995] 1 AC 309.
[283] See JUSTICE (n 280 above).
[284] See eg *R v Rasool* [1987] Crim LR 448.
[285] Cf JUSTICE (n 280 above) 17.
[286] s 7 and Sch 1.

formally valid warrant, rather than the question of whether there were proper grounds for the issue of the warrant in the first place.

12.70   Even if the warrant is found to have been properly authorised, the tribunal is not at liberty to concern itself with the way in which the material intercepted is subsequently handled. There is therefore no remedy under the Act for improper disclosure of material following its interception. Furthermore, by section 7(8):

> The decision of the Tribunal (including any decision as to its jurisdiction) shall not be subject to appeal or liable to be reviewed in any court.

If the tribunal finds that there has been a contravention of the Act, it may quash the relevant warrant (or certificate), direct that copies of the intercepted material be destroyed and direct that the Secretary of State pay compensation in a specified sum.[287]

12.70A   The statutory regime governing the interception of communications is to be reformed to ensure that investigatory powers are used in accordance with human rights. The Regulation of Investigatory Powers Bill 2000 envisages the repeal of the above provisions of the Interception of Communications Act 1985. Part I deals with the interception of communications and extends to all types of telecommunications systems. Part IV of the Bill provides for increased scrutiny of Secretary of States powers to authorise interception of communications by an Interception of Communications Commissioner and the establishment of a Tribunal to consider complaints. The Tribunal will also be the appropriate tribunal for actions under section 7 of the Human Rights Act 1998 in relation to the interception of communications. It will apply the same principles for making a determination as would be applied by a court on an application for judicial review.

(5) Privacy and the media

(a) Introduction

12.71   A large proportion of all complaints of invasion of privacy relate to the activities of the media.[288] As noted above,[289] many advocates of a tort of invasion of privacy have been motivated by the perceived need to curb the excesses of the tabloid press. Some protection against invasion of privacy by the press is contained in the Code of Practice adopted by the Press Complaints Commissions. Invasion of privacy by radio or television broadcasters is regulated by the Broadcasting Act 1996.

---

[287] s 7(5).

[288] For a fuller treatment, see eg G Robertson and A Nicol, *Media Law* (3rd edn, Penguin Books, 1992).

[289] See para 12.07 above.

(b) Press regulation

The Press Complaints Commission ('PCC') was established in 1991 on the recommendation of the Calcutt Committee.[290] It is a non-statutory body established by the press. The Commission has 16 members, the majority of whom are from outside the industry. One of the most important functions of the Commission is the enforcing of a Code of Practice for newspapers and periodicals. This was adopted in April 1994 and has been amended on two occasions since.[291]   **12.72**

The Code of Conduct contains a number of provisions dealing with privacy issues. Paragraph 3 is headed 'Privacy' and provides: **12.73**

> (i) Everyone is entitled to respect for his or her private and family life, home, health and correspondence. A publication will be expected to justify intrusions into any individual's private life without consent.
> (ii) The use of long lens photography to take pictures of people in private places without their consent is unacceptable.

> Note—Private places are public or private property where there is a reasonable expectation of privacy.

Paragraph 4 is headed 'Harassment' and provides:

> (i) Journalists and photographers must neither obtain nor seek to obtain information or pictures through intimidation, harassment or persistent pursuit.
> (ii) They must not photograph individuals in private places (as defined by the note to clause 3) without their consent, must not persist in telephoning, questioning, pursuing or photographing individuals after having been asked to desist, must not remain on their property after having been asked to leave and must not follow them.

Paragraph 5 states that, enquiries in cases involving grief or shock should be made with sympathy and discretion. Paragraph 8 deals with listening devices and states:

> Journalists must not obtain or publish material obtained by using clandestine listening devices or by intercepting private telephone conversations.

The Code provides that exceptions may be made to all of these clauses 'where they can be demonstrated to be in the public interest'. The public interest is not exhaustively defined but is said to include:

> (i)   Detecting or exposing crime or a serious misdemeanour;
> (ii) Protecting public health and safety;
> (iii) Preventing the public from being misled by some statement or action of an individual or organisation.

If a complaint of breach of the Code is brought to the PCC, the Commission will make an adjudication. Any publication which is criticised by the PCC is required   **12.74**

---

[290] *Report of the Committee on Privacy and Related Matters* (1990) Cm 1102.
[291] The latest version is dated 26 Nov 1997.

to print the adjudication in full and with due prominence. The PCC has no power to award compensation. There is no procedure for appeal from a decision of the PCC. However, the PCC is arguably a 'public authority' and as such susceptible to judicial review.[292] The PCC has attracted considerable public criticism. In his second report on self-regulation, Sir David Calcutt concluded that the press freedom had been emphasised by the PCC to the detriment of fairness to the individual.[293]

(c) Regulation of broadcasting

12.75   Radio and television broadcasting has long been subject to statutory control in relation to standards and complaints. Part V of the Broadcasting Act 1996 establishes a Broadcasting Standards Commission ('BSC').[294] The BSC is an amalgam of the Broadcasting Complaints Commission[295] and the Broadcasting Standards Council.[296] The functions of the BSC are applicable to all television and radio services provided by the BBC and other television and radio companies in the United Kingdom. The BSC has a duty to

> draw up and from time to time review, a code giving guidance as to the principles to be observed and the practices to be followed in connection with the avoidance of—
>
> (a) unjust or unfair treatment in programmes . . .
> (b) unwarranted infringement of privacy in or in connection with the obtaining of material contained in such programmes.[297]

In addition, it has a duty to draw up a code giving guidance as to the practices to be followed in connection with the portrayal of violence and sexual conduct.[298]

12.76   The Act establishes a complaints procedure.[299] When the BSC has adjudicated upon a complaint involving allegations of infringement of privacy concerning a programme that has been broadcast,[300] it is under a duty to send a statement of findings to the complainant.[301] It may also give directions for the publication of

---

[292] The point was accepted as being 'at least arguable' in *R v Press Complaints Authority, ex p Stewart-Brady* (1997) 9 Admin LR 274; see the debate in House of Lords on the Human Rights Bill, *Hansard,* HL cols 771–787 (24 Nov 1997) in which Lord Irvine LC expressed the view that the PCC might well be a 'public authority' under the Human Rights Act.
[293] See *Review of Press Self-Regulation* (1993) Cm 2315.
[294] s 106.
[295] Established by the Broadcasting Act 1980, s 17 and continued by the Broadcasting Act 1981, s 53 and the Broadcasting Act 1990, s 142.
[296] See the Broadcasting Act 1990, s 151.
[297] 1996 Act, s 107.
[298] s 108.
[299] ss 110–20.
[300] *R v Broadcasting Complaints Commission, ex p Barclay* (1997) 9 Admin LR 265.
[301] s 115(8) and see, *R v Broadcasting Complaints Commission, ex p British Broadcasting Corporation The Times,* 24 Feb 1995; and *R v Broadcasting Complaints, ex p Channel Four Television* [1995] EMLR 170.

its findings.[302] The BSC has no power to award compensation to a person whose privacy has been infringed. The Act extends to unwarranted interference with the privacy of companies which do have activities of a private nature which need protection from unwarranted intrusion.[303]

There is no right of appeal against findings of the BSC, but it is a 'functional public authority'[304] and its decisions are susceptible to judicial review. It is unlikely however, that a court will be quick to interfere with findings of the BSC in relation to privacy: the BSC is a specialist body, has members with experience of broadcasting and is authorised to determine difficult questions of fact, degree and value judgment.[305] **12.77**

(6) Other privacy rights

(a) Introduction

English law gives little clear recognition to privacy rights outside the fields of misuse of information, surveillance and intrusion. Two particular areas give rise to concern: 'false light' claims in which the name or likeness of an individual is misappropriated by a third party, and restrictions relating to sexual preferences. **12.78**

(b) 'False light' and related claims

English law provides a limited range of remedies in relation to publications which cast a person in a 'false light'.[306] A defamatory publication will give rise to an action for damages.[307] A publication is defamatory if the image of a person is used in such a way that the estimation of him by others is lowered. Thus, in *Tolley v Fry*,[308] the use of a caricature of a well known amateur golfer in an advertisement for chocolate was held to be defamatory, on grounds that it suggested that he had prostituted his amateur status. The *Tolley* case may be contrasted with that of *Correlli v Wall*,[309] in which the plaintiff author failed to restrain the publication of postcards depicting imaginary scenes from her private life, as the cards were not libellous. Even if photographs which present a person in a 'false light' are defamatory, no action will **12.79**

---

[302] s 119.

[303] *R v Broadcasting Standards Commission, ex p BBC The Times,* 12 Apr 2000.

[304] See para 5.16ff above; for the purposes of judicial review, it is well established that the Broadcasting Complaints Commission is a public authority (see eg *R v Broadcasting Complaints Commission, ex p Owen* [1985] QB 1153.

[305] See *R v Broadcasting Complaints Commission, ex p Granada Television Ltd* [1995] EMLR 163, 167, Div Ct.

[306] On the appropriation of personality: T Frazer, 'Appropriation of Personality—A New Tort?' (1983) 99 LQR 281.

[307] See para 15.24ff below.

[308] [1931] AC 33.

[309] (1906) 22 TLR 532; see also *Monson v Tussauds* [1894] 1 QB 671: no injunction to restrain exhibition of waxwork model of a person accused of murder but acquitted.

lie in English law if the publication, read as a whole, makes the true position clear. Thus, no action lay against a newspaper which published 'doctored' photographs showing the plaintiffs' faces on bodies in pornographic poses because the article made it clear that the photographs had been produced without the knowledge of the plaintiffs.[310] There is no action open to a non-trader by which he might restrain the unauthorised use of his name in an advertisement.[311] The position is different if the defendant makes a false attribution of authorship, even in the context of a piece which many readers will read as a caricature.[312]

(c) Privacy and sexual identity

12.80 It has been suggested that a person has a right to his or her own sexual preferences and to determine his or her sexual identity and that this is an aspect of privacy rights. No such right is recognised in the law of the United Kingdom. Thus, attempts by transsexuals to have their birth certificates changed to reflect their new sexual identities have been rejected by the English courts.[313]

C. The Law Under the European Convention

(1) The scope of the right

(a) Introduction

12.81 Article 8 of the Convention provides:

> (1) Everyone has the right to respect for his private and family life, his home and his correspondence.
> (2) There shall be no interference by a public authority with the exercise of this right except such as is in accordance with the law and is necessary in a democratic society in the interests of national security, public safety or the economic well-being of the country, for the prevention of disorder or crime, for the protection of health or morals, or for the protection of the rights and freedoms of others.

The issues raised by Article 8(1) concern the scope and content of 'private life', home and correspondence and the obligation of the state to 'respect' those interests. They also address the lengths to which the state must go to ensure that the private life, home and correspondence of individuals are respected.[314]

---

[310] See *Charleston v News Group Newspapers Ltd* [1995] 2 AC 65.
[311] See *Dockerell v Dougall* (1899) 80 LT 556, 557.
[312] *Clark v Associated Newspapers Ltd* [1998] 1 WLR 1558.
[313] See *Re P and G (Transsexuals)* [1996] 2 FLR 90; the applicants have also failed before the European Court of Human Rights, see *Rees v United Kingdom* (1986) 9 EHRR 56; *Cossey v United Kingdom* (1990) 13 EHRR 622; *Sheffield and Horsham v United Kingdom* (1998) 27 EHRR 163.
[314] See eg D Feldman, 'The Developing Scope of Article 8 of the European Convention on Human Rights' [1997] EHRLR 265.

Article 8(2) provides the grounds for justifying an interference with the right to **12.82** privacy and the home. In each case, it is necessary to consider two questions: first, has the state failed to provide 'respect' for the privacy of individuals, and, if so, secondly, is that failure justified as being in accordance with the law, for a legitimate aim; and necessary in a democratic society?

Although Article 8 states that everyone has the right to respect for his private and **12.83** family life, home and correspondence, it is arguable that a company has no rights to privacy under Convention case law.[315] The right to 'family life' in Article 8 will be dealt with in conjunction with Article 12: the right to marry and found a family in Chapter 13. The meaning of 'respect' and the elements of 'private life', 'home' and 'correspondence' are examined in this chapter.

(b) 'Private life'

Introduction. The Court has given some guidance about the meaning of 'private **12.84** life' and has indicated that it extends beyond the Anglo-American idea of privacy with its stress on secrecy of personal information and seclusion.[316] In *Niemetz v Germany*[317] it said that:

> The Court does not consider it possible or necessary to attempt an exhaustive definition of the notion of 'private life'. However, it would be too restrictive to limit the notion to an 'inner circle' in which an individual may choose to live his personal life as he chooses and to exclude entirely the outside world not encompassed within that circle. Respect for private life must also comprise to a certain degree the right to establish and develop relationships with other human beings.
>
> There appears, furthermore, to be no reason in principle why this understanding of the notion of 'private life' should be taken to exclude the activities of a professional or business nature since it is, after all, in the course of their working lives that the majority of people have a significant, if not the greatest opportunity of developing relationships with the outside world.

The right to respect for private life and home must not be looked at in isolation. Article 8 must be read in conjunction with freedom of religion under Article 9,[318] the right to receive and impart information and ideas under Article 10[319] and the right to education under Article 2 of the First Protocol.[320]

---

[315] See para 22.21 below and see also *R v Broadcasting Standards Commission, ex p BBC The Times*, 12 Apr 2000 in which it was held that, under the Broadcasting Act 1996, a company did have privacy rights.

[316] *X v Iceland*, (1976) 5 DR 86, EComm HR.

[317] (1992) 16 EHRR 97 para 29.

[318] See para 14.36ff below.

[319] *Kjeldsen, Busk Madsen and Pedersen v Denmark* (1976) 1 EHRR 711; and see para 15.137ff below.

[320] See *Belgian Linguistics case (No 2)* (1968) 1 EHRR 252 para 7 which states that 'measures taken in the field of education may affect the right to respect for private and family life or derogate from it'; and see para 19.34ff below.

12.85   The following areas have been considered by the Court to form part of 'private life' within the terms of Article 8:

- moral and physical integrity;
- personal identity;
- personal information;
- personal sexuality; and
- personal or private space.

12.86   **Physical and moral integrity.**   'Private life' covers the physical and moral integrity of the person. It therefore includes physical or sexual assault,[321] corporal punishment[322] and a compulsory blood[323] and urine[324] test. However, not all interferences with moral or physical integrity of an individual will violate private life. Thus, in *Costello-Roberts*,[325] the Court indicated that Article 8 could in some circumstances provide protection against school discipline; but found that the punishment 'did not entail adverse effects sufficient to bring it within the scope of the prohibition contained in Article 8'. It is difficult to reconcile these views with other cases of slight physical intervention: except, perhaps, because the incident took place at school. On the other hand, the Court stressed in *Raninen v Finland*[326] that the right to physical and moral integrity guaranteed by Article 8 comes into play even though it is not so severe as to amount to inhuman treatment under Article 3.[327]

12.87   **Personal identity.**   At the heart of private life is the capacity of the individual to formulate a perception of himself and to choose his personal identity. An individual therefore has the right to choose his own name,[328] how he should dress[329] and how to determine his own sexual identity. He may also be entitled to information about his identity, such as the records of his upbringing in public foster care[330] or his paternity[331] if it is significant to the development or determination of his personal identity. Identity also involves the manner in which an individual presents himself to the state and to others.[332]

---

[321]   *X and Y v Netherlands* (1985) 8 EHRR 235, involved a sexual assault by a man on a mentally handicapped young woman: at para 22, the Court found that the facts concerned a matter of 'private life'.

[322]   *Costello-Roberts v United Kingdom* (1993) 19 EHRR 112, Com Rep para 49.

[323]   *X v Austria* (1979) 18 DR 154, EComm HR.

[324]   *Peters v Netherlands* (1994) 77–A DR 75, EComm HR.

[325]   (n 322 above).

[326]   (1997) 26 EHHR 563.

[327]   See para 8.15ff above.

[328]   *Burghartz v Switzerland* (1994) 18 EHRR 101; *Stjerna v Finland* (1994) 24 EHRR 194; *Konstandinis v Stadt Altensteigstandsamt* [1993] ECR-I 1191, ECJ.

[329]   See *McFeeley v United Kingdom* (1980) 20 DR 44, 91, EComm HR (prison dress).

[330]   *Gaskin v United Kingdom* (1989) 12 EHRR 36 paras 36–37.

[331]   *Rasmussen v Denmark* (1984) 7 EHRR 371 para 33; *M B v United Kingdom* (1994) 77–A DR 108, 114–116, EComm HR.

[332]   Cf the discussion of the transsexual cases at para 12.93 below.

Personal information. The collection of personal information by state authorities without consent is a violation of private life. This is most obvious where the
collection is surreptitious, by activities such as telephone tapping or interception
of post. In *Z v Finland*[333] the Court emphasised that the protection of personal
data, not least medical data, is of fundamental importance to a person's enjoyment
of his right to respect for privacy and family life; and that there must be appropriate safeguards to prevent communication or disclosure of personal health data.

12.88

There is also a *prima facie* breach of the right to respect for private life where personal information is collated by an official census,[334] fingerprinting and photography by the police,[335] a compulsory medical examination[336] and the maintenance
of medical records;[337] in contrast, the Commission held that an obligation to carry
an identity card and to show it on request was not a breach of private life.[338] A security check on a potential employee is not of itself a violation of private life unless it involves the collection of information about his private affairs.[339] Proof that
the information is used to the detriment of the applicant is unnecessary, so long as
the compilation and retention of such a dossier is adequately shown.[340]

12.89

In some circumstances Article 8 can give rise to a right of access to personal information. In *Gaskin v United Kingdom*[341] the Court declined to express an opinion
on whether a general right of access to personal data and information could be derived from Article 8. However, it took the view that information concerning
highly personal aspects of the applicant's childhood, development and history related to his private and family life in such a way that the question of access to it
came within the scope of Article 8. In *Guerra v Italy*[341a] the Court held that the
state's positive obligations to ensure effective protection of the right to respect for
private and family life included the provision of information which would have
enabled the applicants to assess the environmental dangers of living near a factory
where an accident might occur. Similarly, in *McGinley and Egan v United
Kingdom*[342] it decided that withholding documents about the exposure of the applicants to radiation at Christmas Island was a breach of Article 8.

12.90

---

[333] (1997) 25 EHRR 371.
[334] *X v United Kingdom* (1982) 30 DR 239, EComm HR.
[335] *Murray v United Kingdom* (1994) 19 EHRR 193 para 85; *McVeigh v United Kingdom* (1981)
25 DR 15, 49.
[336] *X v Austria* (1979) 18 DR 154.
[337] *Chare nee Jullien v France* (1991) 71 DR 141, 155, EComm HR.
[338] *Filip Reyntjens v Belgium* (1992) 73 DR 136.
[339] *Hilton v United Kingdom* (1988) 57 DR 108, 117.
[340] Ibid 118.
[341] (1989) 12 EHRR 36.
[341a] (1998) 26 EHRR 357.
[342] (1998) 27 EHRR 1; but contrast *LCB v United Kingdom* (1998) 27 EHRR 212 where no positive obligation to provide information arose on the facts.

12.91   It is unclear whether the state has a positive obligation to control intrusive activities by private bodies (such as the press) when they acquire personal information.[343] However, the Commission has taken the view that the range of English remedies protecting privacy rights (and, in particular, a claim for breach of confidence)[344] provides sufficient protection for the purposes of Article 8.[345]

12.92   **Personal sexuality.**   Private life also encompasses choice about personal relationships with others: in particular, social and sexual activities.[346] Sexual activity is clearly part of 'private life'. In *Dudgeon v United Kingdom*[347] the Court described sexual activity as 'a most intimate aspect of private life'; and the Commission acknowledged, in an abortion case, the importance of 'untroubled sexual relations' as a part of private life.[348] Most of the cases in this area deal with homosexuality. It is clear that adult, consenting homosexual activity is now universally accepted in Member states.[349] In the recent cases of *Lustig-Prean v United Kingdom*[350] and *Smith v United Kingdom*,[351] the Court confirmed that only weighty and convincing evidence could justify interfering with private life by investigating and dismissing members of the armed forces on grounds of their homosexuality.

12.93   A number of cases have considered the position of transsexuals. The Court has rejected a number of cases brought because the United Kingdom has failed to amend a birth certificate to reflect the applicant's change of identity, most recently in *Sheffield and Horsham v United Kingdom*.[352] However, a similar complaint succeeded in *B v France*,[353] primarily because of its greater impact on the applicant's social and professional life. The Court also found there was no breach of Article 8 where the United Kingdom failed to recognise a transsexual as the father of a child born after artificial insemination from a donor.[354]

---

[343] The Court rejected the government's argument in *A v France* (1993) 17 EHRR 462 that telephone tapping was not undertaken on behalf of the state; see para 12.105 below.

[344] See para 12.27ff above.

[345] See, *Winer v United Kingdom* (1986) 48 DR 154, EComm HR; *Earl Spencer and Countess Spencer v United Kingdom* (1998) 25 EHRR CD 105.

[346] Some aspects of relations with others will be treated under other Convention heads, whether they are strictly private or not: see Art 11 (freedom of association) and Art 8 (in relation to family life).

[347] (1981) 4 EHRR 149 para 52.

[348] *Brüggemann and Scheuten v Germany* (1978) 10 DR 100, EComm HR.

[349] *Dudgeon v United Kingdom* (1981) 4 EHRR 149 para 52; consensual homosexual acts between adult men in private; also *Norris v Ireland* (1988) 13 EHRR 186; *Modinos v Cyprus* (1993) 16 EHRR 485.

[350] (1999) 7 BHRC 65.

[351] *The Times*, 11 Oct 1999.

[352] (1998) 27 EHRR 163; see, also *Rees v United Kingdom* (1986) 9 EHRR 56 and *Cossey v United Kingdom* (1990) 13 EHRR 622.

[353] (1993) 16 EHRR 1 paras 55–62.

[354] *X, Y and Z v United Kingdom* (1997) 24 EHRR 143.

Personal or private space.   The noise nuisance cases[355] can be explained on the   **12.94**
basis of the infringement of private space, which is to be enjoyed free from un-
welcome interference, whether apparent or covert.[356] The difficult question is
whether 'private space' includes anything beyond those places in which the applicant has exclusive rights of occupancy. In *Friedl v Austria*[357] the Commission took
the view that police photography of the applicant participating in a 'sit-in' as part
of a political demonstration did not violate Article 8. By comparison, in *Murray v
United Kingdom*[358] a photograph which was taken at an army centre was held to
be an interference with her right to privacy. Some assistance can be derived from
the Court's approach in *Halford v United Kingdom*,[359] it decided that a telephone
call made from a private telephone line in an office came within the scope of
Article 8(1) because the applicant had a *reasonable expectation* of privacy.[360]

(c) 'Home'

In addition to protecting 'private life', Article 8 requires respect for the home and   **12.95**
correspondence of individuals. These concepts clearly overlap; and some actions,
such as searches and seizures or interference with telephone conversations in the
home, may constitute an invasion of privacy on two or more senses. In *Miailhe v
France*,[361] for example, the Court found it unnecessary to examine whether the
searches involved the 'home', as it was sufficient to base the interference on the
'private life' and 'correspondence' provisions.

Article 8 creates a right of 'respect for the home'. It does not establish a right to the   **12.96**
home as such; and the Commission has held that the failure to provide a refugee
with a decent home did not breach Article 8.[362] It emphasised in *Burton v United
Kingdom*[362a] that:

> the Commission does not consider that Article 8 can be interpreted in such a way as
> to extend a positive obligation to provide alternative accommodation of an appli-
> cant's choosing.

The Court takes the view that respect for 'home' involves more than the integrity
of home life; what is at stake is the physical security of a person's living quarters

---

[355] In *Powell and Rayner v United Kingdom* (1990) 12 EHRR 355, the complaint was directed at
the noise generated by the operation of four major airports; see also *Arrondelle v United Kingdom*
(1982) 26 DR 5 (F Sett), EComm HR and *Baggs v United Kingdom* (1987) 52 DR 29, EComm HR.
[356] D Harris, M O'Boyle and C Warbrick, *Law of the European Convention on Human Rights*
(Butterworths, 1995) 308.
[357] (1995) 21 EHRR 83, Com Rep paras 48 and 51; and see, generally, S Naismith, 'Photographs,
Privacy and Freedom of Expression' [1996] EHRLR 150.
[358] (1994) 19 EHRR 193.
[359] (1997) 24 EHRR 523.
[360] Ibid para 45.
[361] (1993) 16 EHRR 332.
[362] *X v Germany* (1956) 1 YB 202.
[362a] (1996) 22 EHRR CD 135.

and possessions.[363] It includes the ability (facilitated by the state) to live freely in the home and to enjoy it, not merely as a property right.[364] In *Buckley v United Kingdom*[365] the Court rejected the argument that Article 8 only protected a home which was lawfully established; and went on to find that a gypsy who had continuously occupied land for five years without planning permission was nevertheless entitled to respect for the home. The negotiation of a lease by a Tenants' Union, on the other hand, did not fall within the scope of Article 8; thus, the Court in *Langborger*[366] rejected the argument that the rights and obligations derived from a lease are rooted in the concept of 'home' and are protected by Article 8.

12.97 'Home' has been given a broad interpretation.[367] In general, the term is taken to mean the place where a person lives on a settled basis.[368] However, it might also include a caravan site where a gypsy and her family lived for several years in breach of planning permission[369] a holiday home,[370] or a place of intended, rather than actual, residence.[371] It does not, on the other hand, extend to a home which is to be built in the future.[372] The 'home' of a professional person also includes his business premises; since these activities can be conducted from a private residence and those which are not so related can be carried on in a business or commercial premises, it may be difficult to draw a clear distinction between the two. This approach is consistent with the use of 'domicile' in the French text of the Convention.[373] Premises used wholly for work purposes, however, are not likely to be protected under the right to respect for one's home.[374] A person may have more than one 'home'.

12.98 An interference with the home arises where there is a direct infringement (such as a forcible search by executing a seizure order[375] or searching of a lawyer's

---

[363] Ibid, *Gillow v United Kingdom* (1986) 11 EHRR 335; see also *Selcuk and Asker v Turkey* (1998) 26 EHRR 477 in which the burning of the property of the applicant constituted grave and unjustified interference.

[364] *Howard v United Kingdom* (1987) 52 DR 198, EComm HR.

[365] (1996) 23 EHHR 101 paras 52–55.

[366] *Langborger v Sweden* (1989) 12 EHRR 416.

[367] *Niemetz v Germany* (1992) 16 EHRR 97.

[368] *Murray v United Kingdom* (1994) 19 EHRR 193 paras 84–96.

[369] *Buckley v United Kingdom* (1996) 23 EHRR 101.

[370] *Kanthak v Germany* (1988) 58 DR 94, EComm HR, for example, raises the question as to whether a camper van could be 'home'.

[371] *Gillow v United Kingdom* (1986) 11 EHRR 335; the applicants had lived in several places around the world and had houses in England and Guernsey; the Court accepted that although they had been long absent from it, they had always intended to return to Guernsey and held that they had a right to re-establish home life in that particular house.

[372] *Loizidou v Turkey* (1996) 23 EHRR 513 para 66.

[373] *Niemetz v Germany* (1992) 16 EHRR 97 para 30.

[374] D Harris, M O'Boyle and C Warbrick, *Law of the European Convention on Human Rights* (Butterworths, 1995) 318–319.

[375] *Chappell v United Kingdom* (1989) 12 EHRR 1.

office)[376] or where the home itself is threatened (by, for example, a compulsory purchase order).[377] The protection of 'respect for home' implies a right of access and occupation,[378] and a right not to be displaced or prevented from the physical possibility of returning to the home.[379] This may be difficult to distinguish from the right to enjoyment of property protected by Article 1 of Protocol 1, and certain government measures might interfere with both Article 8 and the Protocol. In *Cyprus and Turkey*,[380] the Commission found that the failure to allow Greek Cypriots to return to their homes in the north of Cyprus was a breach of Article 8, while the taking and occupation of their houses and land by Cypriot and mainland Turks, both civilian and military, was held to be a continuing violation of Article 1 of Protocol 1. Physical removal of persons from their homes and the taking, occupation or destruction of possessions[381] might each be considered a violation of the Article 8 right to respect for the home.

Interference with the home also includes blights on the environment such as the **12.99** noise generated by aircraft,[382] and serious pollution.[383] Severe environmental pollution may affect individuals' well-being and prevent them from enjoying their homes in such a way as would affect their private and family life adversely, without, however, seriously endangering their health.[384] In *Powell and Rayner v United Kingdom*[385] the Court rejected a complaint that the noise disturbance created by Heathrow Airport breached Article 8. It stressed that a fair balance had to be struck between the competing interests of the individual and the community as a whole; and held that the operation of a major international airport pursued a legitimate aim and that the steps taken by the Government to control, abate and compensate for airport noise did not exceed its margin of appreciation. In *Lopez Ostra v Spain*[386] the applicant complained about the failure of the local authority to use its powers to prevent a waste treatment plant releasing fumes and smells. The Court again stated that regard must be had to the fair balance to be struck between the competing interests of the individual and the community as a whole;

---

[376] *Niemetz v Germany* (n 373 above).
[377] *Howard v United Kingdom* (1987) 52 DR 198, EComm HR.
[378] *Wiggins v United Kingdom* (1978) 13 DR 40, EComm HR; *Gillow v United Kingdom* (1986) 11 EHRR 335.
[379] *Cyprus v Turkey* (1976) 4 EHRR 482, 519–20, EComm HR; *Cyprus v Turkey* (1983) 72 DR 5, 41–43, EComm HR.
[380] (1983) 72 DR 5, 41–43, EComm HR.
[381] See also *Mentes v Turkey* (1997) 26 EHRR 595 where the homes of the applicants were burnt down.
[382] *Powell and Rayner v United Kingdom* (1990) 12 EHRR 355.
[383] *Guerra v Italy* (1998) 26 EHRR 375.
[384] See *Lopez-Ostra v Spain* (1994) 20 EHRR 277; and *Guerra v Italy* (1998) 26 EHRR 375.
[385] (1990) 12 EHRR 355; see also *Arrondelle v United Kingdom* (1982) 26 DR 5 (F Sett), EComm HR and *Baggs v United Kingdom* (1987) 52 DR 29, EComm HR.
[386] (1994) 20 EHRR 277; and see generally, P Sands, 'Human Rights, Environment and the *Lopez-Ostra* Case' [1996] EHRLR 597.

and decided that Article 8 had been breached. More recently, in *Guerra v Italy,*[387] the Court also ruled that a failure of the authorities to reduce the risk of pollution from a chemical factory violated Article 8.

(d) 'Correspondence'

12.100 **Introduction.** The right to respect for correspondence in Article 8 has been considered in relation to interference with postal delivery, search and seizures of written documents and the interception of telephone conversations.

12.101 **Interference with postal correspondence.** The cases concerning interference with correspondence have primarily been brought by prisoners. Control over prisoners' correspondence is not of itself incompatible with the Convention.[388] It is not clear whether this implies a threshold of permissible control that does not violate Article 8 or that some supervision of correspondence, while an interference, is justifiable under the second paragraph. The nature and extent of the interference, including the existence of a rule or regime of control, will be taken into account.

12.102 Preventing a prisoner from initiating correspondence with his solicitor was held to be the most far-reaching form of interference with the exercise of the right to respect for correspondence.[389] However, in *Campbell v United Kingdom*[390] correspondence between the applicant and his solicitor was opened and read in accordance with the Prison rules. The Court held in favour of the applicant who alleged that he was restricted from communications with his solicitor 'because he knew his letters would be read'.[391] Similarly, in *Campbell and Fell v United Kingdom,*[392] in which only one letter from the adviser to the applicant was stopped, the 'prior ventilation rule' was found to amount to an interference of Article 8 because it, in effect, prevented all correspondence between the applicants and their advisers concerning proposed litigation until the internal inquiry in question had been completed. Thus, the practice of a psychiatric hospital forwarding the applicant's correspondence to a curator for screening prior to delivery was conceded by the Government to be an interference.[393] Even supervision of correspondence 'to a certain extent' during detention of the applicant has been found by the Court

---

[387] (1998) 26 EHHR 375.
[388] See *Silver v United Kingdom* (1983) 5 EHRR 347; also *Boyle and Rice v United Kingdom* (1988) 10 EHRR 425: although the prisoner had previously benefited from a more liberal regime, he was nevertheless required to serve his time at his then current place of detention on the same terms and conditions as the other prisoners there.
[389] *Golder v United Kingdom* (1975) 1 EHRR 524.
[390] (1992) 15 EHRR 137.
[391] The Court rejected the Government's argument that the applicant had not made out his claim because he had not proved that a specific letter related to the pending proceedings had been opened.
[392] (1984) 7 EHRR 165.
[393] *Herczegfalvy v Austria* (1992) 15 EHRR 437.

unquestionably to constitute an 'interference by a public authority with the exercise of the right enshrined in paragraph 1 of Article 8'.[394]

The Court has found interference with respect for correspondence in a number of situations: where 64 letters were stopped or delayed;[395] where the investigating judge deleted certain passages from the applicant's letter;[396] and where the authorities failed to forward the applicant's letter to the addressee.[397] In *McCallum v United Kingdom*[398] the Court held that stopping letters, withholding copies of letters and a 28-day restriction on correspondence imposed by a prison disciplinary award violated Article 8. In *Messina v Italy*[399] there was a factual dispute as whether there had been an interference. The applicant claimed that he had not received his correspondence while the Government contended that the letters, postcard and telegram in question had been delivered. The Commission held that the onus was on the authorities to show that they had discharged their obligations, and that provision by the state of a record of a prisoner's incoming mail was not sufficient proof that the items reached their destination.   **12.103**

Searches and seizures.   The Court has taken the view that house searches and seizures raise issues in connection with all the rights secured in Article 8(1), with the exception of the right to respect for family life.[400] Searches and seizures are not restricted to certain types of 'correspondence'.[401] Where a warrant issued by a court ordered a search and seizure of 'documents' resulting in the examination of four cabinets containing client data and six individual files, the operations were found to be covered by 'correspondence' and the material was regarded as such for Article 8 purposes.[402] Furthermore, correspondence does not have to be 'personal' in nature; no mention was made in *Niemetz*[403] of the possibility that Article 8 might be inapplicable on the ground that correspondence with a lawyer was of a professional nature.[404]   **12.104**

Telephone tapping.   Although telephone conversations are not expressly mentioned in Article 8(1), the Court has made it clear that they are covered by the   **12.105**

---

[394] *De Wilde, Ooms and Versyp v Belgium (No 1)* (1971) 1 EHRR 373.
[395] *Silver v United Kingdom* (1983) 5 EHRR 347.
[396] *Pfeifer and Plankl v Austria* (1992) 14 EHRR 692.
[397] *Schönenberger and Durmaz v Switzerland* (1988) 11 EHRR 202.
[398] (1990) 13 EHRR 596.
[399] Series A No 257–H (1993).
[400] *Funke v France* (1993) 16 EHRR 297; *Crémieux v France* (1993) 16 EHRR 357; *Miailhe v France* (1993) 16 EHRR 332.
[401] *Niemetz v Germany* (1992) 16 EHRR 97
[402] Ibid.
[403] (1992) 16 EHRR 97.
[404] Ibid.

notion of 'private life', 'family life' and 'correspondence'.[405] As a result, telephone surveillance of individuals constitutes an 'interference' with Article 8 rights by a public authority.[406] The mere existence of legislation permitting surveillance constitutes an interference that:

> strikes at the freedom of communication between users of the . . . telecommunication services and . . . with the exercise of the applicants' right to respect for private and family life and correspondence.[407]

In *Malone v United Kingdom*[408] interception of only one call could be proved.[409] Nevertheless, the Court found that, because the system established in England and Wales for the surveillance of communications itself amounted to an 'interference', it was unnecessary to inquire into the claims of the applicant that the interceptions had spanned a number of years.[410] The broad approach taken by the Court was confirmed in *Halford v United Kingdom*,[411] where it held that respect for correspondence extended to private telephone calls at work on a personal line.

(e) 'Respect'

12.106   Article 8 does not protect privacy or family or home or correspondence *as such*. It guarantees a '*respect*' for these rights. In view of the diversity of circumstances and practices in the contracting states, the notion of 'respect' (and its requirements) are not clear-cut; they vary considerably from case to case.[412]

12.107   The main issue concerning the scope of 'respect' is whether the obligation on the public authority under Article 8(1) is a purely *negative* one or whether it also has a positive component. On the one hand, the state might be required to simply

---

[405] Telephone conversations between family members are covered by both 'family life' and 'correspondence' under Art 8: *Andersson v Sweden* (1992) 14 EHRR 615; see also *Kopp v Switzerland* (1998) 27 EHRR 91, in which it was undisputed that telephone calls to and from business premises may be covered by notions of 'private life' and 'correspondence' within the meaning of Art 8(1). The interception of the telephone conversations of the applicant constituted an interference with private life and correspondence: *Lüdi v Switzerland* (1992) 15 EHRR 173.

[406] But see *A v France* (1993) 17 EHRR 462: where two parties conceived and carried out a plan to make a recording of telephone conversations, it was conceded that the actions constituted an interference with 'correspondence' of the applicant. The issue was whether the actions involved a public authority so as to invoke the responsibility of the state under the Convention.

[407] *Klass v Germany* (1978) 2 EHRR 214.

[408] (1984) 7 EHRR 14.

[409] The Government declined to disclose to what extent, if at all, the telephone calls of the applicant had been otherwise intercepted on behalf of the police.

[410] See also *Huvig v France* (1990) 12 EHRR 528; which followed *Klass* and *Malone* in holding that telephone-tapping amounted to an 'interference by a public authority' with the exercise of the right to respect for 'correspondence' and 'private life'; *Kruslin v France* (1990) 12 EHRR 547: where a police wire-tap of a telephone line of one party resulted in the recording of several conversations of the applicant, leading to proceedings taken against him, the Government did not deny that there had been an 'interference'; and see *Valenzuela Contreras v Spain* (1998) 28 EHRR 483.

[411] (1997) 24 EHRR 523 paras 53–58.

[412] *Abdulaziz, Cabales and Balkandali v United Kingdom* (1985) 7 EHRR 471 para 67.

refrain from doing anything that might unduly infringe the right to private life. On the other hand, the state might be obliged to take positive action to protect individuals from the adverse consequences of its inaction: which might imply a further obligation to prevent acts; or even to require positive action by third parties (such as newspaper journalists) where there is a potential interference with private life. This important distinction between negative and positive obligations which flow from Convention rights was examined in Chapter 6.[413]

The Court has repeatedly stressed that the object of Article 8 is essentially that of protecting the individual against arbitrary interference by the public authorities:[414] this is a 'primarily negative' undertaking. Nevertheless, it has stressed that there may, in addition, be positive obligations upon states[415] that are inherent in an effective 'respect' for Article 8 rights.　**12.108**

Two further points should be made. First, the Court has allowed a certain margin of appreciation[416] to states to determine whether 'respect' for Article 8 rights demands positive action in the circumstances.[417] Secondly, there is a distinction to be made between the assessment of the content of the right under Article 8(1) and the justification process under Article 8(2). Under Article 8(1), 'in determining whether a positive obligation exists, a fair balance must be struck between the general interest of the community and the interests of the individual'.[418] In justifying an interference under subsection 8(2), the interests of the state are balanced against a right which has already been established and which has therefore, at least formally, some degree of weight attached to it.　**12.109**

In practice, the Court has treated the distinction rather casually.[419] It has found the applicable principles to be broadly similar, regardless of whether the issue is formulated as a 'positive duty on the state to take reasonable measures to secure　**12.110**

---

[413] See para 6.95ff above.

[414] *Belgian Linguistic (No 2)* (1968) 1 EHRR 252 para 7; cited in *Marckx v Belgium* (1979) 2 EHRR 330; *X and Y v Netherlands* (1985) 8 EHRR 235; *Abdulaziz, Cabales and Balkandali v United Kingdom* (1985) 7 EHRR 471; *Rees v United Kingdom* (1986) 9 EHRR 56; *Keegan v Ireland* (1994) 18 EHRR 342; *Hokkanen v Finland* (1994) 19 EHRR 139; *Kroon v Netherlands* (1994) 19 EHRR 263.

[415] *Marckx v Belgium* (1979) 2 EHRR 330 para 31; *Airey v Ireland* (1979) 2 EHRR 305 para 32; *X and Y v Netherlands* (1985) 8 EHRR 235 para 23; see also *Johnston v Ireland* (1986) 9 EHRR 203 para 55); *Powell and Rayner v United Kingdom* (1986) 47 DR 5, 12, EComm HR. All of these cases affirm or reaffirm that 'Article 8 does not merely compel the state to abstain from interference: in addition to this, there may be positive obligations inherent in an effective respect for private and family life even in the sphere of the relations of individuals between themselves'

[416] See generally, para 6.31ff above.

[417] *Lopez-Ostra v Spain* (1994) 20 EHRR 277 para 51; see also *Cossey v United Kingdom* (1990) 13 EHRR 622.

[418] *Cossey v United Kingdom* (n 417 above) para 37: 'the search for which balance is inherent in the whole of the Convention'.

[419] See eg C Warbrick, 'The Structure of Article 8' [1998] EHRLR 32.

the rights of the applicant under Article 8(1)', or as an 'interference by a public authority to be justified in accordance with paragraph 2'. The Court has stated that in both contexts regard must be had to the fair balance between the competing interests of the individual and of the community as a whole.[420] In striking the required balance in relation to the positive obligations flowing from Article 8(1), the aims under Article 8(2) will have some relevance.[421]

12.111 **Positive action where the applicant suffers directly from inaction.** In some circumstances, the state will be required to provide positive protection where the applicant stands to suffer directly from its inaction.[422] The transsexual cases are an illustration of this approach. In none of these cases was the physical transformation of the individuals in issue; no state had prevented the treatment, and in the United Kingdom the public health system had provided it. The complaint was that the Government had failed to respect the private life of the applicants by refusing to alter their birth certificates to reflect the change in gender once the physical procedure had been undergone. In *Van Oosterwijk v Belgium*[423] the Commission said that the state 'had refused to recognise an essential element of his personality' and the effect was to 'restrict the applicant to a sex which can scarcely be considered his own'. In the four cases which have come before it, the Court has regarded the interest at stake to be the right to keep private the applicant's original sex by ensuring it would not be revealed whenever they were required to rely upon their birth certificates. In the United Kingdom cases, *Rees*,[423a] *Cossey*[423b] and *Sheffield and Horsham*,[423c] the Court weighed the fact that the certificate was intended to register the position at birth and the burden on the state if it altered the system, against the applicant's interest to have the certificate amended. In each case it held there was no failure of the state to respect the

---

[420] *Powell and Rayner v United Kingdom* (1990) 12 EHRR 355 paras 37–46; also *Lopez-Ostra v Spain* (n 417 above) paras 47–58: 'Whether the question is analysed in terms of a positive duty on the state—to take reasonable and appropriate measures to secure the applicant's rights under para 1 of Article 8— . . . or in terms of an "interference by a public authority" to be justified in accordance with para 2, the applicable principles are broadly similar. In both contexts regard must be had to the fair balance between the competing interests of the individual and of the community as a whole, and in any case the state enjoys a certain margin of appreciation'.

[421] *Powell and Rayner v United Kingdom* (n 420 above) paras 37–46 (there was 'no violation of the Convention, however the claim was framed'); *Rees v United Kingdom* (1986) 9 EHRR 56 para 37.

[422] This was contemplated in *Stjerna v Finland* (1994) 24 EHRR 194, even though the applicant was unable to show that state refusal to allow registration of change of name was either a failure to respect his private life or an 'interference' requiring justification under Art 8(2). In *Gaskin v United Kingdom* (1989) 12 EHRR 36 the Court required that authorities take steps to release records of the applicant's foster care which were held to be of special importance to his private life.

[423] (1979) B 36 Com Rep para 52, EComm HR.

[423a] (1986) 9 EHRR 56.

[423b] (1990) 13 EHRR 622.

[423c] (1998) 27 EHRR 163.

applicant's private life. In *B v France*,[424] on the other hand, the applicant succeeded because the French administrative system could be more easily changed than that of the British, and the need to rely frequently in practice on the certificate meant that a failure to rectify it would have more serious consequences for the applicants.

In *McGinley and Egan v United Kingdom*[425] a complaint was made about the with-   **12.112**
holding of documents concerning the exposure of the applicants to radiation at Christmas Island. The Court took the view that where the government engages in hazardous activities with hidden consequences for health, respect for private and family life requires an effective and accessible procedure to ensure that all relevant and appropriate information is made available.

Positive action to prevent interference by a private individual.   States might   **12.113**
also be obliged to take positive action to prevent or stop another *individual* from interfering with private life. The argument that Article 8(2) refers only to justification of interference by a 'public authority' has been rejected by the Court as irrelevant to the question as to what rights are protected by Article 8(1). It is clear that in appropriate cases

> there may be positive obligations inherent in effective respect for private or family life. These obligations may involve the adoption of measures designed to secure respect for private life even in the sphere of the relations of individuals between themselves . . . In order to determine whether such obligations exist, regard must be had to the fair balance that has to be struck between the general interest and the interests of the individual.[426]

Thus, a failure to provide essential information concerning severe environmental pollution was a breach of Article 8.[427] However, the limits of this approach were illustrated by *Botta v Italy*[478] where the Court held that respect for private life did not extend to giving a disabled person a right of access to the beach and sea which was distant from his normal holiday residence. Similarly, in *Barreto v Portugal*[429] the Court held that respect for private and family life did not require the existence in national law of legal protection enabling each family to have a home for themselves or giving the landlord a right to recover possession of a rented house in any circumstances.

In *Winer v United Kingdom*[430] the Commission found that the government had   **12.114**

---

[424] (1992) 16 EHRR 1.
[425] (1998) 27 EHRR 1.
[426] *Botta v Italy* (1998) 26 EHRR 241 para 33.
[427] See *Guerra v Italy* (1998) 26 EHRR 357, para 58; see also *Lopez-Ostra v Spain* (1994) 20 EHRR 277 para 51 where the court referred to a positive duty to take 'reasonable and appropriate measures' to secure Art 8 rights.
[428] n 426 above para 34ff.
[429] [1996] EHRLR 214.
[430] (1986) 48 DR 154, EComm HR.

not failed to respect the private life of the applicant where the only remedies for protection of reputation were those available in defamation in respect of untrue statements. The Commission's reluctance to require a direct remedy for invading privacy was because this would infringe another Convention right, the freedom of expression. A similar conclusion was reached in *Earl and Countess Spencer v United Kingdom*[431] where the Commission decided that the failure to take proceedings for breach of confidence meant that the applicant had failed to exhaust his domestic remedies. The position concerning the invasion of privacy by photographs is uncertain.[432] However, it seems there is no interference with respect for privacy where the photograph is obtained in a public place.[433]

12.115 Whether or in what circumstances the positive obligation will extend to the criminalisation of private acts remains unresolved. In one instance the state was held to have a duty to provide an effective criminal remedy to ensure deterrence in relation to sexual assault,[434] but given the special facts of that case, it is unlikely to create a precedent for a wide obligation on the state to criminalise private activities. There may be cases which attract this type of obligation but it is difficult to predict whether there will be a duty to criminalise such activities as private surveillance, data collection or publication of true statements about matters of private life.

12.116 An issue arises as to whether the margin of appreciation will be different according to whether the dispute is a conflict between individual and state or one in which the state is exercising a duty of positive action in an essentially private dispute. Clapham has argued[435] that there should be a wider margin in the latter case, reflecting the greater complexity of questions which arise when the state is found to have a positive duty to intervene between individuals for the protection of human rights.

12.117 **Positive obligation to require positive action by private persons.** The obligation to provide 'respect' may impose a duty on the state to require positive action by private persons. States might be obliged to require that private data collection firms grant access to individuals to records kept about them or that the parent with custody of children allow access to the other parent or other relatives like grandparents.[436]

---

[431] (1998) 25 EHRR CD 105.

[432] See eg S Naismith, 'Photographs, Privacy and Freedom of Expression' [1996] EHRLR 150.

[433] See *Friedl v Austria* (1995) 21 EHRR 83, Com Rep paras 48 and 51.

[434] *X and Y v Netherlands* (1985) 8 EHRR 235 (failure to prosecute a sexual assault on a mentally defective girl of 16).

[435] A Clapham, *Human Rights in the Private Sphere* (Clarendon Press, 1993) 211–22.

[436] See *Hokkanen v Finland* (1994) 19 EHRR 139, Com Rep paras 129–146 which relates to family life.

(2) Justification under Article 8(2)

(a) Introduction

Under Article 8(2) interference by a public authority must be justified as being in accordance with the law and necessary in a democratic society in support of one of the following legitimate aims: **12.118**

- national security;
- public safety;
- the economic well-being of the country;
- the prevention of disorder or crime;
- the protection of health or morals; and
- the protection of the rights and freedoms of others.

(b) 'Interference by a public authority'

In order to make out his claim, the applicant must establish the fact of interference.[437] The question of whether a governmental act constitutes an interference is not usually contested by the state. The Court has therefore placed little emphasis on defining interference, focusing instead on its justification once it is determined that there is a protected right. Government acts which have been found to constitute interference include 'supervision' of correspondence,[438] stopping, delaying or failing to forward letters to the applicant,[439] impeding a person from even initiating correspondence,[440] 'secret surveillance' measures[441] including interception of telephone conversations,[442] house searches and seizures,[443] the imposition of a fine on the applicant for failing to obtain a licence to live in his own home,[444] the generation of airport noise pollution[445] and the storage and release of personal information on the applicant.[446] **12.119**

---

[437] *Campbell v United Kingdom* (1992) 15 EHRR 137 para 32; and see generally, para 6.100 above.

[438] *De Wilde, Ooms and Versyp v Belgium (No 1)* (1971) 1 EHRR 373.

[439] *Silver v United Kingdom* (1983) 5 EHRR 347; *Campbell and Fell v United Kingdom* (1984) 7 EHRR 165; *Schönenberger and Durmaz v Switzerland* (1988) 11 EHRR 202; *McCallum v United Kingdom* (1990) 13 EHRR 596; *Herczegfalvy v Austria* (1992) 15 EHRR 437.

[440] *Golder v United Kingdom* (1975) 1 EHRR 524.

[441] *Klass v Germany* (1978) 2 EHRR 214.

[442] *Malone v United Kingdom* (1984) 7 EHRR 14; *Huvig v France* (1990) 12 EHRR 528; *Kruslin v France* (1990) 12 EHRR 547; *Lüdi v Switzerland* (1992) 15 EHRR 173; *A v France* (1993) 17 EHRR 462.

[443] *Funke v France* (1993) 16 EHRR 297; *Crémieux v France* (1993) 16 EHRR 297; *Miailhe v France* (1993) 16 EHRR 332; *Murray v United Kingdom* (1994) 19 EHRR 193; *Chappell v United Kingdom* (1989) 12 EHRR 1; *Niemetz v Germany* (1992) 16 EHRR 97.

[444] *Gillow v United Kingdom* (1986) 11 EHRR 335.

[445] In *Powell and Rayner v United Kingdom* (1990) 12 EHRR 355, the Court stated that the quality of the private life of the applicant and enjoyment of amenities of his home were 'adversely affected'; see also *Lopez Ostra v Spain* (1994) 20 EHRR 277.

[446] *Leander v Sweden* (1987) 9 EHRR 433, where the storage and release of information was coupled with a refusal to allow the complainant to refute the information.

12.120 In addition, two issues have been addressed by the Court. First, it has considered whether a failure to act can be called an 'interference' requiring justification under Article 8(2). This question has been answered in the negative.[447] Where the substance of the complaint is not that the state has acted, but has failed or refused to act, it cannot be said to have 'interfered'.[448]

12.121 Secondly, the Court has considered whether an interference might be established in the absence of measures directly affecting the complainant. In these circumstances a 'victim' test has been employed: in other words, even when the alleged government acts cannot be proved the Court might nevertheless make a finding of interference on grounds that the existence of a legislative or administrative system may be sufficient in itself to constitute an interference with the Article 8 rights of the applicant. In several different contexts, the Court has held that a complainant may be victimised by an established system or legal regime if it is one which facilitates infringement, and which *might* be applied to him, whether or not an intrusion can be proven on the facts.[449] The 'victim' test[450] means that the applicant need only establish a sufficient threat or risk to the effective enjoyment of his rights, whether the potential impact is a material one or has only a psychological effect.

12.122 Thus, legislation which criminalised homosexual activity was found to be a 'continuing interference' with private life, even though the risk of proceedings against consenting adult male homosexuals was not great.[451] The applicant had, however, been investigated and the threat of prosecution was found not to be 'illusory or theoretical'. In this context it was held that the legislation affected the private life of male homosexuals, including the applicant. Similar reasoning was used by the Court in *Norris v Ireland*,[452] although there had been no criminal investigation into the homosexual activities of the applicant and in spite of arguments that the existence of the legislation posed no threat to his lifestyle.

12.123 In other areas of 'private life' and 'correspondence', a system which facilitates surreptitious interception of telephone conversations has been found to create a 'menace of surveillance', even where applicants could not prove actual interception.[453] The existence in England and Wales of laws and practices which permitted and

---

[447] See the discussion at para 6.100 above.

[448] *Airey v Ireland* (1979) 2 EHRR 305; however, the Court's approach to failures to carry out positive obligations has, in practice, been very similar; see, generally, para 6.100 above.

[449] Ibid; *Campbell* was a prison case involving intervention with the prisoner's correspondence; prison rules allowed for letters to be opened and read even though the applicant could not show that any particular letter had been opened.

[450] For comment on this see P Duffy, 'The Protection of Privacy, Family Life and Other Rights Under Article 8 of the European Convention on Human Rights' (1982) 2 YEL 191.

[451] *Dudgeon v United Kingdom* (1981) 4 EHRR 149 para 40.

[452] A 142 (1988) para 37.

[453] *Klass v Germany* (1978) 2 EHRR 214.

established a system for effecting secret surveillance of communications amounted in itself to an 'interference', whether or not any measures were actually taken against the applicant.[454] It was enough in the *Malone* case that the complainant, who was suspected of receiving stolen goods, was a member of a class of persons against whom measures of postal and telephone interception were liable to be employed.

A similar approach has been taken where there was a general policy of supervision **12.124** of correspondence of prisoners,[455] whether or not correspondence is actually interfered with. Although in *Campbell and Fell v United Kingdom*[456] it was proved that one letter had been stopped, the Court noted that the effect of the established 'prior ventilation rule' was to prevent all correspondence between the applicants and their advisers concerning the proposed litigation until an internal inquiry had been completed.

(c) 'In accordance with the law'

Justification of an interference under Article 8(2) requires that the measures in **12.125** question be imposed 'in accordance with law'. The Court has identified a number of requirements as flowing from that phrase[457] and these are examined in detail in Chapter 6.[458]

First, the acts being challenged must have a basis in domestic law.[459] Clearly 'in **12.126** accordance with law' refers to national law,[460] which includes statute,[461] other non-statutory enactments[462] and common law,[463] as the Court has interpreted 'law' in its substantive rather than its formal sense.[464] It does not, however, merely

---

[454] *Malone v United Kingdom* (1984) 7 EHRR 14.
[455] Supervision has been held to be 'unquestionably' an interference by a public authority with the exercise of Art 8 rights: *De Wilde, Ooms and Versyp v Belgium (No 1)* (1971) 1 EHRR 373; *Silver v United Kingdom* (1983) 5 EHRR 347 in which 64 letters were stopped or delayed.
[456] (1984) 7 EHRR 165.
[457] See *Olsson v Sweden (No 1)* (1988) 11 EHRR 259 in which the Court itemises them.
[458] See para 6.126ff above.
[459] *Leander v Sweden* (1987) 9 EHRR 433 para 50; *Chappell v United Kingdom* (1989) 12 EHRR 1 para 52; *Margareta and Roger Andersson v Sweden* (1992) 14 EHRR 615; *A v France* (1993) 17 EHRR 462 para 38; *Murray v United Kingdom* (1994) 19 EHRR 193 para 88.
[460] *Campbell and Fell v United Kingdom* (1984) 7 EHRR 165 para 37.
[461] *Norris v Ireland* (1988) 13 EHRR 186 para 40: the interference was plainly 'in accordance with the law' since it arose from the very existence of the impugned legislation.
[462] *De Wilde, Ooms and Versyp v Belgium (No 1)* (1971) 1 EHRR 373 para 93; *Golder v United Kingdom* (1975) 1 EHRR 524 para 45 involving Prison Rules 1964.
[463] See *Dudgeon v United Kingdom* (1981) 4 EHRR 149 para 44; *Kruslin v France* (1990) 12 EHRR 547 para 29; *Huvig v France* (1990) 12 EHRR 528 para 28; *Herczegfalvy v Austria* (1992) 15 EHRR 437 para 91: the provisions in question did not offer the minimum degree of protection against arbitrariness required by the rule of law and there was no case law to remedy the situation; *Murray v United Kingdom* (1994) 19 EHRR 193: the taking and retention of a photograph of the applicant without her consent had no statutory basis but was lawful under the common law.
[464] *Kruslin v France* (1990) 12 EHRR 547 para 29; *Huvig v France* (1990) 12 EHRR 258 para 28.

refer to the existence of domestic law, but to the quality of the law, requiring it to be compatible with the rule of law, which is expressly mentioned in the preamble to the Convention.[465] 'In accordance with law' thus implies that the interfering measures must be accompanied by adequate and effective safeguards in the domestic law to protect against arbitrary interferences by authorities with the rights guaranteed by Article 8(1).[466] In light of the necessity of determining that measures are rooted in national law, the Court has reiterated on several occasions that its role is not to interpret and apply domestic law: this is primarily the task of the national courts.[467] The role of the Court in reviewing compliance with domestic law is relatively limited.[468]

12.127 Secondly, the law must be accessible and foreseeable. It must be accessible to the persons concerned, and formulated with sufficient precision to enable the citizen to foresee, to a reasonable degree, the consequences which a given action may entail.[469] In determining whether this criterion has been met, the Court must take into account that absolute precision is unattainable and that, in order to avoid excessive rigidity and to keep pace with changing circumstances, many laws will inevitably be couched in terms which are to some extent vague.[470] The degree of precision required of the 'law' will depend upon the particular subject matter.[471] Thus, a prisoner who was unable to read unpublished regulations succeeded in establishing that the procedure was not in accordance with the law.[472]

12.128 In the special context of secret surveillance,[473] the Convention requirement of

---

[465] *Malone v United Kingdom* (1984) 7 EHRR 14 para 67; *Silver v United Kingdom* (1983) 5 EHRR 347 para 90; *Golder v United Kingdom* (1975) 1 EHRR 524 para 34.

[466] *Malone v United Kingdom* (n 465 above) para 67; *Herczegfalvy v Austria* (1992) 15 EHRR 437 para 91; *Rieme v Sweden* (1992) 16 EHRR 155 para 60: although a basis in Swedish law was undisputed, the applicant argued (unsuccessfully) that the law in question did not afford him adequate protection against arbitrary interference; *Chappell v United Kingdom* (1989) 12 EHRR 1 para 56 discusses Anton Piller orders in United Kingdom law and their associated dangers which necessitate accompanying provisions safeguarding against arbitrary interference and abuse; see also *Eriksson v Sweden* (1989) 12 EHRR 183 para 60 and *Olsson v Sweden (No 1)* (1988) 11 EHRR 259 para 62 which discuss safeguards in relation to taking children into public care: 'preparatory work' providing guidance as to the exercise of the discretion conferred, and administrative review at several levels.

[467] *Olsson v Sweden (No 2)* (1992) 17 EHRR 134 para 79; *Andersson v Sweden* (1992) 14 EHRR 615 para 82; *Kruslin v France* (1990) 12 EHRR 547 para 29; *Eriksson v Sweden* (1989) 12 EHRR 183 para 62; *Chappell v United Kingdom* (1989) 12 EHRR 1 para 54; *Campbell v United Kingdom* (1992)15 EHRR 137 para 37: it is not for the Court to examine the validity of secondary legislation.

[468] *Eriksson v Sweden* (1989) 12 EHRR 183 para 62.

[469] *Olsson v Sweden (No 1)* (1988) 11 EHRR 259 para 61.

[470] *Silver v United Kingdom* (1983) 5 EHRR 347 para 88; *Olsson v Sweden (No 1)* (n 469 above); see also *Sunday Times v United Kingdom (No 1)* (1979) 2 EHRR 245 para 49.

[471] *Sunday Times v United Kingdom* (n 470 above) para 49; *Malone v United Kingdom* (1984) 7 EHRR 14 para 67.

[472] *Silver v United Kingdom* (n 470 above); *Petra v Roumania* RJD 1998–VII 2844.

[473] *Malone v United Kingdom* (n 471 above) para 79; *Hewitt and Harman v United Kingdom* (1989) 67 DR 88, 99, EComm HR; *N v United Kingdom* (1989) 67 DR 123, 132, EComm HR; *Kruslin v France* (1990) 12 EHRR 547 para 17.

foreseeability cannot be exactly the same as it is where the law seeks to restrict the conduct of individuals. It obviously does not require the authorities to give the applicant advance warning of the surveillance: it is enough that he knows whether he might be subject to surveillance. Nevertheless, Article 8 requires that the law must be sufficiently clear in its terms to:

> give citizens an adequate indication as to the circumstances in which and the conditions on which public authorities are empowered to resort to this secret and potentially dangerous interference with the right to respect for private life and correspondence.[474]

It is essential to have clear, detailed rules on the subject.[475] The Court has made it clear that the following minimum safeguards should be set out in the statute in order to avoid abuse of power:

> a definition of the categories of people liable to have their telephones tapped by judicial order, the nature of the offences which may give rise to such an order, a limit on the duration of the telephone tapping, the procedure for drawing up the summary reports containing intercepted conversations, the precautions to be taken in order to communicate the recordings intact and in their entirety for possible inspection by the judge and by the defence and the circumstances in which recordings may or must be erased or the tapes destroyed, in particular where an accused has been discharged by an investigating judge or acquitted by a court.[476]

Thirdly, a law which confers a discretion is not in itself inconsistent with the requirement of foreseeability, provided that the scope of the discretion and the manner of its exercise are indicated with sufficient clarity, having regard to the legitimate aim of the measure in question, to give the individual adequate protection against arbitrary interference.[477] A related issue is the extent to which the necessary detail must itself be contained in the substantive law, as opposed to accompanying administrative practice and associated directives.[478] This point was considered in the *Silver*[479] case in which the Court stated that although the scope of the discretion must be indicated in the law, it is not necessary that the detailed procedures be contained in rules of substantive law. In that case administrative directives nonetheless constituted an established practice that was to be followed save in exceptional circumstances, rather than one that varied with each individual case.

12.129

---

[474] *Malone v United Kingdom* (n 471 above) para 67.
[475] See *Valenzuela Contreras v Spain* (1998) 28 EHRR 483 para 46, Principle (iii).
[476] Ibid para 46, Principle (iv), relying on *Kruslin v France* (1990) 12 EHRR 547 para 35 and *Huvig v France* (1990) 12 EHRR 528 para 34.
[477] *Malone v United Kingdom* (1984) 7 EHRR 14 para 67; *Gillow v United Kingdom* (1986) 11 EHRR 335 para 51; *Olsson v Sweden (No 1)* (1988) 11 EHRR 259 para 61; *Kruslin v France* (1990) 12 EHRR 547; *Andersson v Sweden* (1992) 14 EHRR 615; *Eriksson v Sweden* (1989) 12 EHRR 183 para 60.
[478] *Malone v United Kingdom* (n 477 above) para 68; *Silver v United Kingdom* (1983) 5 EHRR 347 paras 88–90.
[479] (1983) 5 EHRR 347.

On the other hand, where the practice applied in a particular case conflicted with the administrative safeguards in place, the applicant succeeded in proving that the authorities had not acted in accordance with the law.[480]

12.130 Following the decision in *Malone v United Kingdom*[481] that there was no legal basis in the United Kingdom for the interception of telephone conversations,[482] Parliament enacted the Interception of Communications Act 1985 which now provides a statutory foundation for telephone-tapping which meets the substantive as well as formal requirements of 'law'.[483] Similarly, the Security Services Act of 1989 remedied the lack of foundation for secret surveillance indicated in *Hewitt and Harman v United Kingdom*.[484] In France, the law that 'the investigating judge shall, in accordance with the law, take all investigative measures which he deems useful for establishing the truth',[485] and case law to the effect that such measures included telephone-tapping did not provide sufficient safeguards against abuse of the power to render it in accordance with 'law' under Article 8. Furthermore, where a court rejected a complaint about illegal surveillance on the ground that the telephone line that was tapped belonged to a third party, the Court held there was a breach of Article 8.[486] The law of telephone-tapping in Luxembourg, on the other hand, exhibited the necessary detail and provision for control of the use of the discretion so as to be in accordance with 'law.'[487]

(d) 'Necessary in a democratic society' for a legitimate aim

12.131 Article 8(2) provides that:

> there shall be no interference by a public authority with the exercise of this right except such as is in accordance with the law and is necessary in a democratic society in the interests of
>
> (a) national security,
> (b) public safety, or
> (c) the economic well-being of the country;
> (d) for the prevention of disorder or crime,

---

[480] *Kopp v Switzerland* (1998) 27 EHRR 91.
[481] (1984) 7 EHRR 14.
[482] (1984) 7 EHRR 14.
[483] *Christie v United Kingdom* (1993) 78–A DR 119, 133, EComm HR: the Commission declared inadmissible an application claiming that the legislation was not sufficient protection against abuse of the power to issue warrants, see generally, para 12.66ff above.
[484] (1989) 67 DR 88: for comment see I Leigh and L Lustgarten (1989) 52 MLR 801. The enactment of the Intelligence Services Act 1994 provides further statutory foundation for secret surveillance procedures: for comment see J Wadham, 'The Intelligence Services Act 1994' (1994) 57 MLR 916.
[485] Code of Criminal Procedure, Art 81.
[486] *Lambert v France* RJD 1998-V 2230.
[487] *Mersch v Luxembourg* (1985) 43 DR 34, 94, 114, EComm HR (the Commission acknowledged the presence of the ultimate safeguard: the Convention was directly applicable in Luxembourg law).

(e) for the protection of health or morals, or

(f) for the protection of the rights and freedoms of others.

The state must identify at least one of these objectives as a basis for its claim that its interference with privacy is necessary in a democratic society. The legitimate aims are similar to those set out in Articles 9 to 11 of the Convention, with the distinction that Article 8(2) permits interference in the interests of 'the economic well-being of the country'.[488]

The Court has dealt with the meaning of the phrase 'necessary in a democratic society', the nature of the functions of the Court in the examination of issues turning on that phrase, and the manner in which it performs those functions on a number of occasions.[489] The relevant principles are discussed in Chapter 6.[490] The following general points can be made. First, the term 'necessary' is not synonymous with 'indispensable' but does not have the flexibility of such expressions as 'admissible', 'ordinary', 'useful', 'reasonable' or 'desirable'.[491] Secondly, 'necessary in a democratic society', in the context of Article 8, as in connection with other Convention interests, requires the state to demonstrate that the interference corresponds to a 'pressing social need' and that it is 'proportionate' to the legitimate aim.[492] Thirdly, it is for the authorities of Member States to make the initial assessment as to necessity: a certain margin of appreciation[493] is left to them, subject to review by the Court. Fourthly, in search and seizure cases it is necessary to show that there are procedures in place which provide adequate and effective safeguards against abuse.[493a] Thus, in *Camenzind v Switzerland*[493b] the Court emphasised that if individuals are to be protected from arbitrary interference by the authorities with Article 8 rights, there must be a legal framework and very strict limits on the powers it confers. **12.132**

It is well established that the exceptions under Article 8(2) are to be interpreted narrowly and the need for them in a given case must be convincingly **12.133**

---

[488] See generally, para 6.144 above.

[489] See *Dudgeon v United Kingdom* (1981) 4 EHRR 149 paras 50–54, 60; *Silver v United Kingdom* (1983) 5 EHRR 347 paras 97–98.

[490] See para 6.146ff above.

[491] *Handyside v United Kingdom* (1976) 1 EHRR 737 para 48; cited in *Silver v United Kingdom* (1983) 5 EHRR 347 para 97; and see generally, para 6.148 above.

[492] *Handyside v United Kingdom* (1976) 1 EHRR 737 para 48; *Dudgeon v United Kingdom* (1981) 4 EHRR 149, para 51; *Silver v United Kingdom* (1983) 5 EHRR 347 para 97; *Gillow v United Kingdom* (1986) 11 EHRR 335 para 55; *Leander v Sweden* (1987) 9 EHRR 433 para 58; *Olsson v Sweden (No 1)* (1988) 11 EHRR 259, para 67; *Schönenberger and Durmaz v Switzerland* (1988) 11 EHRR 202 para 27; *Berrehab v Netherlands* (1988) 11 EHRR 322 para 28; *Moustaquim v Belgium* (1991) 13 EHRR 802 para 43 (as to family life); *Campbell v United Kingdom* (1992) 15 EHRR 137 paras 44, 53; *Beldjoudi v France* (1992) 14 EHRR 801 para 74; and see generally, para 6.147 above.

[493] See generally, para 6.31ff above.

[493a] See eg *Funke v France* (1993) 16 EHRR 297 para 56; *Miailhe v France* (1993) 16 EHRR 332 para 37; *Crémieux v France* (1993) A 256-B para 39.

[493b] RJD 1997–III 2880 para 45.

established.[494] There is no scope for implying limitations to Article 8.[495] Furthermore, as the Court emphasised in *Dudgeon v United Kingdom*,[496] where the restrictions concern a most intimate part of an individual's private life, there must be particularly serious reasons to satisfy the requirements of justifying Article 8(2). The detailed factual analysis which should be undertaken is illustrated in the recent cases of *Lustig-Prean v United Kingdom*[497] and *Smith and Grady v United Kingdom*;[498] the Government failed to show that the investigations into the applicant's sexual orientation (once they had confirmed their homosexuality) and subsequent dismissal were sufficiently convincing and weighty to comply with Article 8(2).

12.134 **National security and public safety.** Justification that has as its objective the protection of national security and public safety is readilyestablished. This is particularly true in the context of secret surveillance. While in most cases search and seizure procedures will be carried out under criminal law procedures and require at least judicial authorisation by warrant,[499] where the state can show that there are 'exceptional conditions', surreptitious measures of surveillance will be justified. For example, sophisticated techniques of foreign espionage in *Klass v Germany*[500] justified exceptional telephone tapping counteraction measures, and internal terrorist activity in *Leander* amounted to a serious threat to national security which justified the collection of information and maintenance of secret files on candidates for sensitive employment positions.[501]

12.135 **The economic well-being of the country.** The unusual ground of the economic well-being of the country has been found to justify a wide variety of government activities: a licensing scheme for the occupation of premises;[502] immigration control policy;[503] the operation of an international airport;[504] customs investigation

---

[494] See eg *Klass v Germany* (1978) 2 EHRR 214 para 42; *Silver v United Kingdom* (1983) 5 EHRR 347 para 97; *Funke v France* (1993) 16 EHRR 297 para 55.

[495] See *Golder v United Kingdom* (1975) 1 EHRR 524 para 44; and see para 6.116 above.

[496] (1981) 4 EHRR 149 para 52.

[497] (1999) 7 BHRC 65 paras 83–104.

[498] (2000) 29 EHRR 493 paras 90–111.

[499] See eg *Funke v France* (1993) 16 EHRR 297, in which the lack of prior judicial authorisation was determinative in regard to a search of the applicant's house resulting in seizure of documents and collection of information as to his foreign assets; even a warrant may not be sufficient: see *Niemetz v Germany* (1992) 16 EHRR 97 where a search for documents was found disproportionate to the aim of prevention of crime and protection of rights of others, even though a warrant had been procured.

[500] A 28 (1978) para 56: the aim of the G10 is to safeguard national security and/or prevent disorder or crime.

[501] *Leander v Sweden* (1987) 9 EHRR 433 para 60 in regard to the Swedish personnel control system.

[502] *Gillow v United Kingdom* (1986) 11 EHRR 335.

[503] *Berrehab v Netherlands* (1988) 11 EHRR 322.

[504] *Powell and Rayner v United Kingdom* (1990) 12 EHRR 355.

procedures;[505] and disclosure of medical records for the purpose of assessing a social security claim.[506]

In *Gillow v United Kingdom*,[507] as a consequence of a change in the law the applicants, who had lost their 'residence qualifications' and were refused the required licence to live in their house in Guernsey, were convicted and fined for unlawful occupation of the premises. The Court held that it was legitimate for the authorities to try to maintain the population within limits that would permit the balanced economic development of the island. It was also legitimate for them to discriminate in the granting of licences in favour of persons who had strong attachments to the island, or who were engaged in an employment essential to the community. However, there was a breach in the application of the legislation of the facts.

12.136

The existence of large international airports, even in densely populated urban areas, and the increasing use of jet aircraft have also become necessary in the interests of a country's economic well-being. The Court in *Powell and Rayner*[508] found that Heathrow Airport occupies a position of central importance in international trade and communications and in the economy of the United Kingdom. The applicants conceded that the Government had pursued a legitimate aim, and that the negative impact on the environment which resulted could not be entirely eliminated.

12.137

Customs investigations leading to seizure of information about assets abroad and documents concerning foreign bank accounts in connection with customs offences under French law, though 'perhaps also for the prevention of crime' as held by the Commission, were primarily in the interests of the economic well-being of the country.[509]

12.138

In *M S v Sweden*[510] the applicant had injured her back in an accident while at work. When, a number of years later, she made a claim for compensation under the Industrial Injury Insurance Act, it was discovered that copies of her confidential medical records had been submitted by the clinic to the Social Insurance Office, in breach of professional secrecy contrary to the Secrecy Act 1980. The Court decided that the interference was justified as all the information disclosed was necessary and relevant for the determination of the applicant's claim for compensation; and it was necessary for the economic well-being of the country to ensure that public funds were only allocated to deserving claimants.

12.139

---

[505] *Funke v France* (1993) 16 EHRR 297.
[506] *M S v Sweden* RJD 1997–IV 1437.
[507] (1986) 11 EHRR 335.
[508] *Powell and Rayner v United Kingdom* (1990) 12 EHRR 355.
[509] *Funke v France* (1993) 16 EHRR 297; also *Crémieux v France* (1993) 16 EHRR 357; and *Miailhe v France* (1993) 16 EHRR 332.
[510] RJD 1997–IV 1437.

12.140 **For the prevention of disorder or crime.**   Measures interfering with Article 8(1) rights which have been found to be for the legitimate aim of the prevention of disorder and crime include the supervision of prisoners' correspondence,[511] telephone interception and other forms of secret surveillance,[512] immigration control policy[513] and searches for and seizure of documents and other physical evidence in connection with alleged offences.

12.141 When considering whether searches and seizures for the prevention of disorder and crime are necessary, the Court will look at the seriousness of the interference, the nature of the crime involved and the presence or absence of judicial warrant. The search of the office of a lawyer who was accused of insulting and imposing pressure on a judge was found to be disproportionate to its aim[514] on grounds that the warrant was a broadly framed order for seizure of 'documents' without limitation, and unduly infringed professional secrecy. In *Funke v France*[515] the Court agreed that measures including house searches and seizures (which 'might' be for the prevention of crime but were undoubtedly in the interests of the economic well-being of the country) were necessary in order to obtain physical evidence of exchange-control offences and to prevent outflow of capital and tax evasion, but nevertheless held that the legislation did not provide adequate safeguards against abuse of the wide powers available to customs authorities. The Court also emphasised that in the absence of the requirement of a judicial warrant, conditions and restrictions on the law were too lax to ensure that interferences with the rights of the applicant were proportionate to the aim pursued.[516] In *McLeod v United Kingdom*[517] the entry of police officers into the applicant's home to prevent a breach of the peace was disproportionate to the legitimate aim of the prevention of disorder. On the other hand, in *Camenzind v Switzerland*[517a] the specific procedures in place and the limited scope of the search were a proportionate interference with the right of respect for the home. Similarly, in *Murray v United Kingdom*[518] entry and search of the Murray family home by military authorities in Northern Ireland was not disproportionate to the aim of arresting Mrs Murray,

---

[511] *De Wilde, Ooms and Versyp v Belgium (No 1)* (1971) 1 EHRR 373; *Schönenberger and Durmaz v Switzerland* (1988) 11 EHRR 202; *Pfeifer and Plankl v Austria* (1992) 14 EHRR 692; *Campbell v United Kingdom* (1992) 15 EHRR 137.

[512] *Lüdi v Switzerland* (1992) 15 EHRR 173; *Klass v Germany* (1978) 2 EHRR 214.

[513] *Beldjoudi v France* (1992) 14 EHRR 801.

[514] *Niemetz v Germany* (1992) 16 EHRR 97; (the interference pursued aims that were legitimate under Act 8(2), namely the prevention of crime and protection of the rights of others, that is the honour of the judge).

[515] (1993) 16 EHRR 297; *Miailhe v France* (1993) 16 EHRR 332; *Crémieux v France* (1993) A 256-B.

[516] See also *Crémieux v France* (n 515 above); and *Miailhe v France* (n 515 above).

[517] (1998) 27 EHRR 493; for the decision in English law see *McLeod v Commissioner of Police of the Metropolis* [1994] 4 All ER 553, see para 12.19 above.

[517a] RJD 1997–III 2880 paras 45–47.

[518] (1994) 19 EHRR 193.

who was reasonably suspected of terrorist-linked crime. The Court noted that special precautions were justified as a means to that end, given the 'conditions of extreme tension' under which such arrests in Northern Ireland had to be carried out.

The significance of the particular applicant's interest emerges clearly from the **12.142** cases involving interference with prisoners' correspondence. Although some measure of control of prisoners' correspondence is not incompatible with the Convention,[519] the Court has given high priority in this context to protecting the right of prisoners to communicate with their legal advisers. In *Golder v United Kingdom*[520] the Court rejected the Government's argument that a refusal of the authorities to transmit a letter from prisoner to solicitor regarding the prospect of action against a prison official, was necessary to prevent disorder. In *Campbell v United Kingdom*[521] the introduction of Standing Orders for English and Scottish prisons which allowed the opening and reading of letters regarding prospective legal proceedings, but not those already in progress, was held to infringe Article 8. Clearly no useful distinction could be made between instituted and contemplated proceedings and the privilege attached to all such letters was upheld, requiring that the government must at least show reasonable cause for suspecting that the correspondence contains illicit material before opening it.

Correspondence in general does not require the same degree of confidentiality as **12.143** lawyer-client communications, but powers of supervision,[522] interception and scrutiny must not be exercised under general terms which would expose the contents of unobjectionable letters, but must relate to some specific objection. However, in *Schönenberger and Durmaz v Switzerland*[523] the Court accepted that preventing disorder or crime may justify wider measures of interference for convicted prisoners than individuals who are at liberty. Nevertheless, measures such as stopping letters which hold the prison authorities up to contempt, or deleting passages of private letters may be disproportionate to the aim of ensuring the protection of the rights of others or the prevention of crime.[524] Telephone surveillance measures have been justified on grounds of prevention of disorder and crime as well as national security. In *Z v Finland*[525] the Court had to consider balancing the confidentiality of information about a person's HIV infection against the interests of the public in investigating and prosecuting crime and having public court proceedings; and stressed that interference with Article 8 could only be justified by an overriding requirement of the public interest.

---

[519] See eg *Pfeifer and Plankl v Austria* (1992) 14 EHRR 692 para 46.
[520] (1975) 1 EHRR 524 para 45.
[521] (1992) 15 EHRR 137 see also *Foxley v United Kingdom, The Times,* 4 Jul 2000.
[522] See *De Wilde, Ooms and Versyp v Belgium (No 1)* (1971) 1 EHRR 373.
[523] (1988) 11 EHRR 202.
[524] *Pfeifer and Plankl v Austria* (1992) 14 EHRR 692.
[525] (1997) 25 EHRR 371.

12.144 **For the protection of health or morals.** Interferences justified on grounds of the protection of health alone usually involve the taking of children into care by public authorities[526] and impact not on private life, home or correspondence but on family life.[527] The 'protection of morals and of the rights and freedoms of others'[528] or the 'protection of health and morals'[529] have been claimed as the basis for interference with prisoners' correspondence; and the 'protection of morals' alone has been asserted most often in conjunction with restrictions on sexual activity. This is an area in which the Court has required particularly substantial reasons to justify the interference. So, for example, the existence of legislation in Northern Ireland dating back to 1861 and 1885[530] nevertheless contravened the Article 8 rights of the applicant to his private life.[531] The decision of the Court was taken in the face of a contrary assessment by the United Kingdom and wide support for the existing position in Northern Ireland; it relied instead on the developing European consensus towards eliminating criminal sanctions and the absence of evidence to show that the failure of Northern Ireland authorities to implement the law had reduced moral standards. The Court affirmed the qualities of broad-mindedness and tolerance as features of a democratic society and held that the shock factor of homosexual practices was not sufficient justification for criminalising them.[532]

12.145 **For the protection of the rights and freedoms of others.** The protection of rights and freedoms of others is generally coupled with other bases for justification under Article 8(2) and has most often been cited in connection with cases involving 'family'[533] rather than 'private' life. In the *Vagrancy* case[534] the aim of restrictions in connection with the supervision of prisoners' correspondence was not discussed or questioned before the Court, but the Commission had considered whether each interference was necessary for one of the purposes pleaded by the

---

[526] See *W v United Kingdom* (1987) 10 EHRR 29; *B v United Kingdom* (1987) 10 EHRR 87; *R v United Kingdom* (1987) 10 EHRR 74.

[527] See para 13.119 below.

[528] *Silver v United Kingdom* (1983) 5 EHRR 347.

[529] *De Wilde, Ooms and Versyp v Belgium (No 1)* (1971) 1 EHRR 373.

[530] The scope of the legislation had been restricted in England, Scotland and Wales, but remained unchanged in Northern Ireland.

[531] *Dudgeon v United Kingdom* (1981) 4 EHRR 149.

[532] *Norris v Ireland* (1988) 13 EHRR 186.

[533] *W v United Kingdom* (1987) 10 EHRR 29; *B v United Kingdom* (1987) 10 EHRR 87; *R v United Kingdom* (1987) 10 EHRR 74; *Olsson v Sweden (No 1)* (1988) 11 EHRR 259: a decision to take children into care had legitimate aims of protecting health and morals and protecting the rights and freedoms of others; see also *Olsson v Sweden (No 2)* (1992) 17 EHRR 134; *Andersson v Sweden* (1992) 14 EHRR 615; *Keegan v Ireland* (1994) 18 EHRR 342; *Hokkanen v Finland* (1994) 19 EHRR 139; *Eriksson v Sweden* (1989) 12 EHRR 183: legislation was clearly designed to protect the rights of children on the lifting of a care order. Though restrictions had no basis in domestic law, the Court was convinced that they were imposed with the legitimate aim of protecting the health and rights of the child.

[534] *De Wilde, Ooms and Versyp v Belgium (No 1)* (1971) 1 EHRR 373.

Government: protection of morals or protection of the rights and freedoms of others.

In other contexts, the protection of the 'honour' of a judge, coupled with preven-   **12.146**
tion of crime, was not sufficient justification for a blanket warrant to search a
lawyer's office for 'documents'.[535] A search of the home of a video dealer being
sued in breach of copyright was, however, justified as a legitimate means of protecting the rights of others in that it served to defend the plaintiffs' copyright
against unauthorised infringement.[536] The proceedings were civil and a seizure
order (formerly an *Anton Piller* order) was employed in order to keep the evidence
from 'disappearing'; even though the invasion of privacy was 'disturbing, unfor-
tunate and regrettable' the order was not disproportionate to that end.[537]

Finally, the retention and use of personal information collected about an individ-   **12.147**
ual may require justification separate and apart from that of the collection itself. If
information is used for a purpose other than that for which it was legitimately collected, this may constitute an interference. For example, in *T V v Finland*[538] the
fact that a prisoner was HIV-positive was disclosed to prison staff directly involved
in his custody; they were themselves subject to rules of confidentiality and the disclosure of the information was found to be justified in 'the interests of others'.

D. The Impact of the Human Rights Act

(1) Introduction

The absence of a right to privacy in English law demonstrates the limited capacity   **12.148**
of the common law to evolve new ways of protecting human rights. As Sir Robert
Megarry V-C emphasised in *Malone v Metropolitan Police Commissioner*[539] when
rejecting a claim that telephone tapping breached the 'right to privacy':

> it is no function of the courts to legislate in a new field. The extension of the exist-
> ing laws and principles is one thing, the creation of an altogether new right is an-
> other. At times judges must, and do, legislate; but as Holmes J once said, they do so
> only interstitially, and with molecular rather than molar motion: see *Southern
> Pacific Co v Jensen* (1917) 244 US 205, 221, in a dissenting judgment. Anything be-
> yond that must be left for legislation. No new right in law, fully-fledged with all the
> appropriate safeguards, can spring from the head of a judge deciding a particular
> case; only Parliament can create such a right.

---

[535] *Niemetz v Germany* (1992) 16 EHRR 97.
[536] *Chappell v United Kingdom* (1989) 12 EHRR 1.
[537] Ibid para 65–66.
[538] (1994) 76A DR 140, EComm HR.
[539] [1979] Ch 344, 372; see also *Kaye v Robertson* [1991] FSR 62.

The bundle of rights which the English law provides[540] gives only patchy and incomplete protection for the citizen. However, the position will radically alter as a result of the Human Rights Act. Public authorities[541] will be required to respect privacy rights, reversing the decision in *Malone v Metropolitan Police Commissioner*. Furthermore, the fact that section 6(3) of the Act requires a court (or tribunal) in private litigation to act in a way which is not incompatible with privacy rights[542] may have a substantial impact on 'privacy' rights in the context of private litigation.

12.149   The obligation to 'respect for the home' will also have important ramifications for public authorities. Where an administrative decision interferes with the right,[543] the starting point will be that the decision–maker must not act incompatibly with Convention rights; although the public authority can justify the interference under Article 8(2), the exceptions are to be interpreted narrowly and the need for them in a given case must be convincingly established.[544]

12.150   The incorporation of Article 8 will therefore lead to some of the most important developments which result from the Human Rights Act. It will have an important impact on employment rights, on public bodies regulating the media and on police powers of search and surveillance. It will also have some effect on the areas of civil litigation, commercial and criminal law, freedom of information, local government, mental health and planning and environmental law.

12.151   The potential impact of the Human Rights Act on the media generated considerable concern during the passage of the Bill and led to the inclusion of section 12 which was designed to provide stricter tests for the granting of interlocutory injunctions to restrain interference with privacy.[545] These issues are considered in Chapter 15.[546] The impact of the Act on the 'privacy rights' of citizens against private bodies depends on the extent to which it has 'horizontal effect'. In accordance with the approach to 'horizontality' outlined above,[547] the Human Rights Act is likely to have a significant impact on the development of the common law in relation to privacy.

(2)   United Kingdom cases prior to the Human Rights Act

(a) Introduction

12.152   A large number of applications based on Article 8 have come before the Commission and the Court. The United Kingdom has been found to have vio-

---

[540] See para 12.09ff above.
[541] See para 5.03ff above.
[542] See generally, para 5.38ff above.
[543] See para 12.95ff above.
[544] *Funke v France* (1993) 16 EHRR 297 para 55.
[545] See *Hansard*, HC col 535 (2 Jul 1998) (Home Secretary introducing s 12).
[546] See para 15.237ff below.
[547] See Chap 4 above.

lated the right to respect for private life, home and correspondence on 17 occasions.[548] The majority of Article 8 cases under these had fallen into three general categories: prisoners' privacy rights, telephone tapping and surveillance and complaints concerning privacy and sexual relationships. However, several other important issues have also been considered.

(b) Prisoners' rights

Prisoners have successfully challenged the interference with their correspondence on several occasions. In *Golder v United Kingdom*[549] the letters of the applicant to his MP were stopped and he was refused permission to consult a solicitor. The Court held that these constituted the most far-reaching interference with the applicant's right to respect for correspondence. In *Silver v United Kingdom*[550] the applicants complained of letters being stopped because of a 'prior ventilation' rule and the Court found that the majority of them had not been legitimately stopped.[551] The case of *Campbell v United Kingdom*[552] concerned the regular opening and screening of a prisoner's letters to his solicitor. This was again held to be an unjustified interference with his Article 8 rights. However, it has been made clear that prisoners' rights to correspondence can be legitimately restricted in accordance with Article 8(2). Thus, the practices of reading prisoners' letters[553] and restricting the numbers of letters which prisoners may send[554] have been upheld. In *Galloway v United Kingdom*[554a] the Commission rejected a complaint that mandatory drug tests in prisons breached Article 8.

12.153

(c) Telephone tapping and surveillance

In *Malone v United Kingdom*[555] the applicant complained that his telephone had been tapped by the police. The Court held that the regulation of telephone tapping by administrative practice was not regulation 'in accordance with the law'. This case resulted in the enactment of the Interception of Communications Act

12.154

---

[548] *Golder v United Kingdom* (1975) 1 EHRR 524; *Dudgeon v United Kingdom* (1981) 4 EHRR 149; *Silver v United Kingdom* (1983) 5 EHRR 347; *Campbell and Fell v United Kingdom* (1984) 7 EHRR 165; *Malone v United Kingdom* (1984) 7 EHRR 14; *Gillow v United Kingdom* (1986) 11 EHRR 335; *Boyle and Rice v United Kingdom* (1988) 10 EHRR 425; *Gaskin v United Kingdom* (1989) 12 EHRR 36; *McCallum v United Kingdom* (1990) 13 EHRR 596; *Campbell v United Kingdom* (1992) 15 EHRR 137; *Halford v United Kingdom* (1997) 24 EHRR 523; *McLeod v United Kingdom* (1998) 27 EHRR 493; *Lustig-Prean v United Kingdom* (1999) 7 BHRC 65; *Smith and Grady v United Kingdom*, (2000) 29 EHRR 493; *Khan v United Kingdom*, *The Times*, 23 May 2000; *Foxley v United Kingdom*, *The Times*, 4 Jul 2000; *ADT v United Kingdom*, Judgment, 31 Jul 2000.
[549] (1975) 1 EHRR 524.
[550] (1983) 5 EHRR 347; and see also *McCallum v United Kingdom* (1990) 13 EHRR 596.
[551] See also *Campbell and Fell v United Kingdom* (1984) 7 EHRR 165.
[552] (1992) 15 EHRR 137.
[553] *Boyle and Rice v United Kingdom* (1988) 10 EHRR 425.
[554] See *Chester v United Kingdom* (1990) 60 DR 65.
[554a] (1998) 27 EHRR CD 241.
[555] (1984) 7 EHRR 14.

1985. The Act itself has been held to satisfy the requirements of Article 8.[556] However, the Act does not apply to tapping of calls on internal communications systems operated by public authorities. As a result, the interception of office telephone calls was held in *Halford v United Kingdom*[557] to constitute a breach of Article 8. Complaints have also been made about other forms of surveillance by the police. In *Govell v United Kingdom*[558] the Commission declared admissible an application relating to the lack of legal authority for intrusive police surveillance. In *Khan v United Kingdom*[558a] the Court held that, in the absence of a scheme of statutory regulation,[558b] the use of a secret listening device was not 'in accordance with the law'. As a result, the interference with the applicant's rights under Article 8 could not be justified.

12.155 Applications have also been brought in relation to surveillance by the security service. The Commission held that a security check was not, of itself, objectionable; but could be where it was based on information about a person's private life.[559] In *Hewitt and Harman (No 1) v United Kingdom*[560] the applicants were both employed by the National Council for Civil Liberties and complained that they had been placed under secret surveillance by the security service. The Commission ruled the complaint to be admissible on the basis that the interference with the private life of the applicant was not 'in accordance with the law'. A friendly settlement was reached with the applicants and the Security Service was placed on a statutory basis by the Security Services Act 1989.[561] In *Esbester v United Kingdom*[562] the Commission held that the Security Services Act meant that secret surveillance by the Security Service was 'in accordance with the law'. A similar challenge to the activities of the security services was rejected by the Commission in *Hewitt and Harman (No 2) v United Kingdom*[563] in which the Commission dismissed the application as 'manifestly ill-founded'.

(d) Privacy and sexual relationships

12.156 Complaints about interference with private life by legislation regulating sexual orientation have frequently been made. In *X v United Kingdom*[564] the applicant

---

[556] *Christie v United Kingdom* (1994) 78–A DR 119, EComm HR.
[557] (1997) 24 EHRR 523.
[558] (1996) 23 EHRR CD 101 (admissibility), [1999] EHRLR 191 (merits: the Commission found violations of Arts 8 and 13); see also *Khan v United Kingdom* Application 35394/97, 20 Apr 1999 (ECtHR: admissibility decision arising out of *R v Khan* [1997] AC 558).
[558a] *The Times*, 23 May 2000.
[558b] The use of such devices is now regarded by the Police Act 1997, see para 12.59ff above.
[559] *Hilton v United Kingdom* (1988) 57 DR 108, EComm HR; and *N v United Kingdom* (1989) 67 DR 123, EComm HR.
[560] (1991) 14 EHRR 657.
[561] See para 12.62ff above.
[562] (1994) 18 EHRR CD 72.
[563] (1991) 47 DR 88, EComm HR.
[564] (1978) 3 EHRR 63.

had been found guilty of buggery of two 18-year-old males. The Commission took the view that the age of consent of 21 for homosexuals was an interference with the applicant's private life under Article 8 but was 'justified as being necessary in a democratic society for the protection of the rights of others'.

The most important case in this area is the Northern Ireland case of *Dudgeon v United Kingdom*.[565] The applicant complained that the laws restricting homosexual conduct were an interference with his private life. The Court agreed, holding that, even though the applicant had not in fact been prosecuted, the very existence of the legislation continuously and directly affected his private life. It also rejected the Government's contention that the legislation was 'necessary in a democratic society', noting that it differed from the position in the large majority of Council of Europe states. This case led to the Homosexual Offences (NI) Order 1982 which brought the law in Northern Ireland into line with the rest of the United Kingdom. It was followed in cases relating to Ireland[566] and Cyprus[567] and it is now clear that legislation criminalising any type of homosexual activity is contrary to Article 8.[568]   **12.157**

Transsexuals have contended that the refusal of the United Kingdom authorities to change the sex indicated on the register of births constituted a breach of their rights under Article 8. Such a claim by a female to male transsexual was rejected by the Court in *Rees v United Kingdom*.[569] It was held that the mere refusal to alter the register of births could not constitute an 'interference' under Article 8 and that the positive obligations to protect privacy rights did not extend as far as making arrangements to assist transsexuals. A similar result was reached in the male to female transsexual case of *Cossey v United Kingdom*;[570] and again in the cases of *X, Y and Z v United Kingdom*[571] and *Sheffield and Horsham v United Kingdom*.[572]   **12.158**

In *Laskey, Jaggard and Brown v United Kingdom*[573] the applicants had engaged in sado-masochistic acts and were convicted of assault occasioning actual bodily harm. The applicants' argument that this constituted an unjustified interference with their right to private life was rejected by the Court. It was common ground that the interference pursued the legitimate aim of the 'protection of health or morals' and the Court held that the interference was 'necessary in a democratic   **12.159**

---

[565] (1981) 4 EHRR 149.
[566] *Norris v Ireland* (1988) 13 EHRR 186.
[567] *Modinos v Cyprus* (1993) 16 EHRR 485.
[568] See generally, R Wintemute, *Sexual Orientation and Human Rights* (Clarendon Press, 1995) Chap 4.
[569] (1986) 9 EHRR 56.
[570] (1990) 13 EHRR 622.
[571] (1997) 24 EHRR 143.
[572] (1998) 27 EHRR 163.
[573] (1997) 24 EHRR 39.

society'. The case of *Sutherland v United Kingdom*[574] on the age of consent is pending before the Court. In *ADT v United Kingdom*[575] the Court decided that the offence of gross indecency between men in private was a violation of Article 8.

(e) Other applications

12.160   **Personal information.**   The Court has considered two important cases involving the right to obtain personal information. In *Gaskin v United Kingdom*[576] it held that personal information about the applicant's childhood, development and history related to his private and personal life to such an extent that access to it came within the scope of Article 8. In *McGinley and Egan v United Kingdom*[577] it held that withholding documents concerning the exposure of the applicants to radiation at Christmas Island was a breach of Article 8.

12.161   However, the Commission has dismissed a number of recent applications where individuals have claimed access to personal information. In *Martin v United Kingdom*[578] the Commission decided that a fair balance had been struck between the applicant and the state where access to medical records was denied to a person suffering from catatonic schizophrenia on the ground that it protected his medical health. In *Wiltshire v United Kingdom*[579] the Commission held that there was no breach of Article 8 where the applicant's files were edited to protect third parties.

12.162   **Right to respect for home.**   In *Gillow v United Kingdom*,[580] the applicants complained about the refusal of the Guernsey authorities to allow them to occupy their house. It was held that the refusal of a licence to occupy was disproportionate to the legitimate aim of promoting the economic well being of the island; and constituted a violation of Article 8. In *Buckley v United Kingdom*,[581] however, the refusal to grant the applicant gypsy planning permission to keep caravans on her own land did not breach Article 8. The planning restrictions in question pursued the legitimate aims of public safety, economic well-being, the protection of health and the protection of the rights of others. In *McLeod*[582] the applicant complained that the police had entered her house at the request of her ex-husband. The Court held that the power to enter premises to prevent a breach of the peace was 'in

---

[574] [1997] EHRLR 117 (the Commission held by 14 votes to 4 that the fixing of a minimum age for lawful homosexual activities at 18 rather than 16 was in violation of Art 8 of the Convention).
[575] Judgment, 31 Jul 2000.
[576] (1989) 12 EHRR 36.
[577] (1998) 27 EHRR 1.
[578] (1996) 21 EHRR CD 112.
[579] (1997) 23 EHRR CD 188.
[580] (1986) 11 EHRR 335.
[581] (1996) 23 EHRR 101; see also two Commission decisions involving gypsies: *Turner v United Kingdom* (1997) 23 EHRR (CD) 181 and *Webb v United Kingdom* [1997] EHRLR 680.
[582] (1998) 27 EHRR 493.

accordance with the law'[583] and was for the legitimate aim of 'the prevention of crime or disorder'. However, on the facts, the entry of the police into the applicant's home was disproportionate as it did not strike a fair balance between her right to respect for home and the prevention of crime and disorder.[584]

Environmental cases.   The case of *Powell and Rayner v United Kingdom*[585] concerned a complaint by applicants living near Heathrow Airport that excessive aircraft noise was interfering with their private life and home. Such interference was established in one case but was held to be 'necessary in the interests of the economic well-being of the country'. In a number of other cases involving aircraft noise, friendly settlements have been reached following Commission admissibility decisions in favour of the applicants.[586]   **12.163**

Personal privacy.   In *Winer v United Kingdom*[587] the Commission found that there had been no failure to respect the private life of the applicant because the only remedies for protection of reputation were those available in defamation in respect of untrue statements. In *Earl and Countess Spencer v United Kingdom*[588] the Commission rejected a claim that the absence of a right to privacy in English law breached Article 8 on the basis that the applicant failed to bring a claim for breach of confidence. Similarly, in *Steward-Brady v United Kingdom*[588a] the Commission rejected the allegation that the state had breached its positive obligations under Article 8 because the Press Complaints Commission had dismissed the applicant's complaint that the publication of his photograph in the *Sun* newspaper breached his right to privacy under its Code of Practice.   **12.164**

(3) General impact issues

(a) Privacy and the common law

Although the Human Rights Act creates privacy rights against public authorities, we argued earlier that the Human Rights Act does not, in general, entitle the court to create new causes of action between *private* parties in litigation.[589] As a result, it   **12.165**

---

[583] Ibid paras 38–45.
[584] Ibid paras 49–58.
[585] (1990) 12 EHRR 355.
[586] *Arrondelle v United Kingdom* (1980) 19 DR 186; (1982) 26 DR 5, EComm HR: payment of £7,500 made re noise at Gatwick; *Baggs v United Kingdom* (1985) 44 DR 13; (1987) 52 DR 29, EComm HR: noise at Heathrow; see also *Vearncombe v United Kingdom and Germany* (1989) 59 DR 186, EComm HR: noise from a military shooting range not intolerable; application inadmissible.
[587] (1986) 48 DR 154, 170–1, EComm HR.
[588] (1998) 25 EHRR CD 105.
[588a] (1998) 27 EHRR CD 284.
[589] See para 5.95ff above.

will not result in the immediate establishment of a general 'private law' right to privacy. Furthermore, the rationale for a right to privacy is very different where the individual seeks protection from intrusion by the state rather than from a private person. For example, the constitutional rights to privacy in American law arise as 'emanations', 'penumbras' or 'shadows'[590] derived from liberty rights enshrined in the Bill of Rights.[591] The reasons for requiring protection from unjustified coercion by the state to a person's 'inner life' on issues such as abortion or personal sexuality are therefore not the same as those which warrant a court placing restrictions on the excesses of the tabloid press.

12.166 Nevertheless, the Human Rights Act may encourage development of the common law based on existing causes of action,[592] particularly breach of confidence.[593] Furthermore, the Act may justify the formulation of a new cause of action where the court is under a positive duty to ensure respect for privacy.[594] It seems likely, however, that, whatever view the English courts take of 'horizontality issues', the incorporation of Article 8 will lead to a decisive impetus towards the establishment of a common law tort of infringement of privacy.[595] The Convention case law may provide the English courts with considerable assistance in defining the limits of the tort and the defences available.[596]

12.167 Two general issues will arise in relation to such a tort: what constitutes an 'infringement of privacy'? and what defences should be available to a person who has infringed another's privacy? In relation to the first, the English Courts will doubtless draw some inspiration from the highly developed United States case law. A useful starting point is the US *Restatement on Torts* which suggests that the tort of infringement of privacy is committed, *inter alia*, by:

> One who gives publicity to a matter concerning the private life of another . . . if the matter publicized is of a kind that:
>
> (a) would be highly offensive to a reasonable person.[597]

---

[590] *Whalen v Roe* (1977) 429 US 589.

[591] The right has evolved, for example, from due process clauses of the Fifth and Fourteenth Amendments (see *Roe v Wade* (1973) 410 US 113, 153, the Ninth Amendment (see *Griswold v Connecticut* (1965) 381 US 479, 486 to 499 (Goldberg J concurring); see generally, L Tribe, *American Constitutional Law* (2nd edn, Foundation Press, 1988) 15–03.

[592] See para 5.91ff above.

[593] See para 12.27ff above.

[594] See para 12.111ff above.

[595] Cf Lord Bingham, 'Should There be a Law to Protect Rights of Personal Privacy?' [1996] EHRLR 450; and 'The Way we Live Now: Human Rights in the New Millennium' [1998] 1 Web J of Current Legal Issues; and contrast for example D Eady, 'A Statutory Right to Privacy' [1996] EHRLR 243.

[596] Cf R Mullender, 'Privacy, Paedophilia and the European Convention on Human Rights' [1998] PL 384.

[597] *Restatement of Torts*, 2d, §625D.

The Convention case law may provide some assistance in defining the limits of 'infringement'. This approach may mean that, unlike the present position in relation to breach of confidence,[598] the fact that information has, at one time, been in the public domain will not, of itself, prevent it from being private. Nevertheless, it is arguable that under Convention case law there will be no infringement of privacy by filming activities which take place in public in the absence of special circumstances.[599] This is, however, a controversial issue, as it has been held in a number of jurisdictions that the 'right to one's image' is included in the right to respect for private life.[600] It may also depend on whether the applicant has in the particular circumstances in question a reasonable expectation of privacy.[601]

12.168 By far the most important defence is likely to be 'public interest'.[602] The limits of that defence have been the subject of considerable debate; and the specific issues that arise concerning the conflict between the right to privacy and freedom of expression are considered in Chapter 15.[603] The Article 8 jurisprudence may again provide some assistance in two respects. First, the 'legitimate purposes' listed in Article 8(2) provide potential guidance as to the limits of a 'public interest' defence. Thus, it might be argued that the defence should not be available unless it can be shown that the infringement of privacy rights is necessary in the interests of national security, public safety or the economic well-being of the country, the prevention of disorder or crime, the protection of health or morals or the protection of the rights and freedoms of others.[604]

12.169 Secondly, the analysis of the 'public interest' defence may be assisted by the concept of 'proportionality'. Thus, even if an infringement of privacy is 'legitimate', its effects may be disproportionate to the legitimate aim to be achieved. This would give a 'sliding scale' for the application of the defence: the more substantial the interference with privacy, the more important the justification must be.

---

[598] See para 12.29ff above.

[599] See *Friedl v Austria* (1995) 21 EHRR 83, Com Rep paras 48, 51, but contrast *R v Broadcasting Standards Commission, ex p BBC*, *The Times*, 12 Apr 2000; see generally, para 12.114 above.

[600] For a general discussion, see *Aubry v Les Editions Vice-Versa* [1998] 1 SCR 591; and for the position in Germany see H Stoll, 'General Rights to Personality in German Law' in B Markesinis (ed), *Protecting Privacy* (Oxford University Press, 1999).

[601] See eg *Halford v United Kingdom* (1997) 24 EHRR 523 at para 12.94 above; and the Canadian cases at para 12.223ff below.

[602] In addition, to 'public interest', defences of 'innocent infringement', consent, privilege, legal authority and protection of property and legitimate business interests have also been suggested: see JUSTICE, *Privacy and the Law*, (Justice, 1970) 36–8. It may be that the last three of these would be subsumed under a broad 'public interest' defence.

[603] See para 15.245ff below.

[604] For a discussion of the effect of such limitations in the context of s 10 of the Contempt of Court Act 1981, see *X Ltd v Morgan-Grampian (Publishers) Ltd* [1991] 1 AC 1; discussed at para 15.76ff below.

12.170   A 'public interest' defence which is developed on these lines may be narrower than that which is presently available in breach of confidence cases. In particular, the broad 'iniquity' defence[605] might well be cut down by considerations of 'legitimate purpose' and 'proportionality'. The Convention can, in this area, provide a helpful guide to the development of the common law.

(b) The impact on civil procedure

12.171   For the purposes of litigation one of the parties may use surveillance or tape telephone discussions in order to assist its case; this is not uncommon where a defendant in personal injury cases wishes to challenge a claim that the claimant is unable to return to work or where an employer seeks to discover if an employee is breaching restrictive covenants. If the litigant in question is a standard public authority[606] or a functional authority which fails to show the nature of the act is private,[607] the surveillance will breach Article 8(1). However, the public authority is likely to succeed in justifying the interference under Article 8(2) on the basis that it is necessary for the protection of the rights of others.

12.172   Under section 6(3) of the Act, the court must not act in a way which is incompatible with Convention rights.[608] The admission of evidence which is obtained in breach of Article 8(1) can be justified under Article 8(2). In *Chappell v United Kingdom*[609] the Court held that an *Anton Piller* order (now a seizure order) was a proportionate interference which had a legitimate aim; and this decision provides useful general guidance under the Human Rights Act. The court will have to consider, in each case, whether the measure which inteferes with Article 8 rights is 'accompanied by safeguards calculated to keep its impact within reasonable bounds'.[610]

12.173   A number of issues arise concerning the impact of Article 8 on powers under the Civil Procedure Rules to order disclosure of legally privileged material. The power to order disclosure of privileged documents in applications for wasted costs under CPR 48.7.3 has been held to be *ultra vires* by Toulson J in *General Mediterranean Holdings v Patel*.[611] A similar argument may be advanced concerning the power to

---

[605] See paras 12.036–12.038 above.
[606] See para 5.14ff above.
[607] Under s 6(5): see para 5.28ff above.
[608] See para 5.120 above.
[609] (1989) 12 EHRR 1.
[610] Ibid para 60.
[611] [1999] 3 All ER 673 where Toulson J also took account of Art 6; see also the prisoner cases concerning the *vires* of prison rules which permitted inspection of legally privileged documents. In *R v Secretary of State for the Home Department, ex p Leech (No 2)* [1994] QB 198 the Court of Appeal declared the inspection of legally privileged correspondence unlawful. However, in *R v Secretary of State for the Home Department, ex p Simms* [1999] QB 349 the Court of Appeal accepted that the inspection of documents on security grounds in closed prisons was lawful; the decision was not subject to the appeal made to the House of Lords.

order experts to disclose the substance of their instructions under CPR, rule 35.10(3)(4).[612] It is unlikely that the Human Rights Act will add any additional arguments on these questions.

(c) The right of access to personal information

Article 8 may create a right of access to personal information held by public au- **12.174**
thorities. The right of access to personal information can be distinguished from the right to freedom of information which may arise under Article 10 because of the obligation on a public authority to impart information. Article 10 basically prohibits a government from restricting a person from receiving information that others wish or may be willing to impart to him.[613] Although the Court declined to express a view in *Gaskin v United Kingdom*[614] on whether a general right of access to personal data and information could be derived from Article 8, it held that information concerning highly personal aspects of the applicant's childhood, development and history created a right of access to that information. In *McGinley and Egan v United Kingdom*[615] the Court said that where the government engages in hazardous activities with hidden consequences for health, respect for private and family life requires an effective and accessible procedure to ensure that all relevant and appropriate information is made available. Nevertheless, Article 8 may also supplement the current statutory provisions which enable access to information[616] by, for example, reversing the effect of *R v Mid-Glamorgan Family Health Services Authority, ex p Martin*[617] in relation to older records which are not subject to these provisons.

(4) Specific areas of impact

(a) Commercial law

The 'horizontal impact' of Article 8 on the law relating to business may be very **12.175**
substantial. If the courts develop a tort of infringement of privacy, this will have a significant impact on employment practices.[618] It will also impact on the storage and use of information by business. The 'vertical' effect is likely to be most important in the 'media' and 'planning' areas.[619]

---

[612] Although Toulson J expressed the view in *General Mediterranean v Patel* (n 611 above) 693 that these rules did not infringe the substantive right to legal confidentiality.

[613] See *Leander v Sweden* (1987) 9 EHRR 433 para 74; *Guerra v Italy* (1998) 26 EHRR 357 para 53; and see, generally, para 15.253 below.

[614] (1989) 12 EHRR 36.

[615] (1998) 27 EHRR 1.

[616] See para 12.46ff above.

[617] [1995] 1 WLR 110.

[618] See para 12.181 below.

[619] See paras 12.190 and 12.193 below.

12.176 The privacy rights in Article 8 may, however, provide business with limited protection against the activities of regulatory bodies. The right to 'private life and home' in Article 8(1) covers office premises[620] of professionals and searches and removal of documents are subject to the 'justification' provisions of Article 8(2).[621] On the other hand, under the Convention jurisprudence it is arguable that a company is not entitled to privacy rights.[622]

(b) Criminal law

12.177 The impact of Article 8 on criminal proceedings seems likely to be limited. However, there are many instances where surveillance techniques breach Article 8.[623] Furthermore, the use of non-statutory guidelines to regulate the activities of informers or undercover police officers where they intrude into a suspect's home or private life may breach the requirement that interferences with Article 8 rights must be 'in accordance with the law'.[624]

12.178 One important question that arises is whether evidence obtained in breach of Article 8 would be inadmissible in criminal proceedings. This issue was considered by the House of Lords in the *Khan* case where it was said that:

> if evidence has been obtained in circumstances which involve an apparent breach of article 8 . . . that is a matter which may be relevant to the exercise of the section 78 power.[625]

In that case, the evidence was held to be admissible and it is unlikely that a breach of Article 8 would, of *itself*, be sufficient to exclude evidence.[626] The *Schenk*[627] case shows that challenges to admissibility must be considered in the broader context of Article 6 rights; and that was the approach taken by the Court in *Khan v United Kingdom*.[627a] On the other hand, it might be argued that the Human Rights Act creates constitutional rights so that a stricter test must be overcome to justify admitting evidence obtained in breach of Article 8.[628]

---

[620] See *Niemetz v Germany* (1992) 16 EHRR 97.

[621] Cf M Smyth, 'The United Kingdom's Incorporation of the European Convention and its Implications for Business' [1998] EHRLR 273, 276.

[622] See para 22.21 below but see *R v Broadcasting Standards Commission, ex p BBC The Times*, Apr 2000.

[623] See para 12.105 above.

[624] M Colvin, 'Surveillance and the Human Rights Act' in Centre for Public Law at the University of Cambridge, *The Human Rights Act and the Criminal Justice and Regulatory Process* (Hart Publishing, 1999).

[625] See *R v Khan* [1997] AC 558, 581.

[626] See generally, Chap 21.

[627] *Schenk v Switzerland* (1988) 13 EHRR 242.

[627a] *The Times*, 23 May 2000.

[628] See generally, para 21.142ff above.

In deciding issues such as the publicity to be given to private information about **12.179** defendants or witnesses, a court must take Article 8 into account. Thus, criminal courts may be required to make orders prohibiting the publication of information about HIV positive witnesses if such publication would infringe their right to privacy.[629] In spite of the decriminalisation of sexual activity between men in 1967, the criminal law currently maintains a discrepancy between heterosexuals and homosexuals in regard to the lawful age of consent which appears to be contrary to Article 8.[630] It may also be arguable that the offence of *possessing* indecent photographs of children under section 160 of the Criminal Justice Act 1988[631] is in breach of the right to privacy, impinging, as it does, on the 'private sphere'.[632]

It is possible that Article 8 will have an impact on sentencing practice in the crim- **12.180** inal courts. In *Laskey, Jaggard and Brown*[633] the European Court of Human Rights took the length of the sentences imposed into account in determining whether the measures taken were 'proportionate'. It has been suggested that a longer sentence might have led the Court to take a different view on whether there had been a breach of Article 8.[634] While any sentence of community service or imprisonment involves interference with the private and family life of a convicted person, it is submitted that Article 8 does not have the general consequence that the sentencing court must consider the proportionality of this impact in every case.

(c) Education

Children with special educational needs may become subject to a statement of ed- **12.181** ucational needs (which a local educational authority has accepted or which has been imposed by a special educational needs tribunal).[635] It has been strongly argued that Article 8 (together with the right to education)[636] imposes obligations to take sufficient or appropriate steps to protect the physical or psychological integrity of a child and members of his family and that these will be breached where the authority fails to deliver the obligations contained in the statement of special education needs.[637]

---

[629] See *Z v Finland* (1997) 25 EHRR 371: an order to make public in 2002 the transcripts of evidence given by the medical advisers of the applicant was a violation of Art 8.

[630] See para 12.188 below in relation to discrimination on the grounds of sexual orientation.

[631] As opposed to the offence of distributing such photographs under the Protection of Children Act 1978, see para 15.90 below.

[632] See the South African decision of *Case v Minister of Safety and Security* (1997) 1 BHRC 541 at para 12.168 below.

[633] (1997) 24 EHRR 39, 60 para 49.

[634] D Cheney, L Dickson, J Fitzpatrick and S Uglow, *Criminal Justice and the Human Rights Act 1998* (Jordans, 1999) 138.

[635] See generally, para 19.26 below.

[636] See para 19.34ff below.

[637] M Supperstone, J Goudie and J Coppel, *Local Authorities and the Human Rights Act 1998* (Butterworths, 1999) 64; it is also argued that the authority has breached the right to education: see, generally para 19.92 below.

(d) Employment and discrimination

12.182 **Introduction.** The Human Rights Act means that employees of standard public authorities will, in effect, have a 'right of privacy' against their employer. They will also have a right to respect for family life under Article 8: this is discussed in Chapter 13.[638] There are several important areas in which violations of Article 8 might take place: the monitoring of the activities of employees at work, the regulation of 'private aspects' of employees' conduct, the collection of personal data on employees and sexual orientation discrimination.

12.183 **Monitoring employees.** In relation to this area the important question is whether an employee has a 'reasonable expectation of privacy'[639] in relation to a particular work activity. In *Halford v United Kingdom*[640] the applicant had a reasonable expectation of privacy in using a 'private telephone line' in her own office because her employers had given her permission to use it in connection with the sex discrimination claim she had brought against them. However, if employers expressly warn employees that they will monitor telephone calls, then surveillance is unlikely to breach Article 8. There is a strong argument that an expectation of privacy would also arise in relation to telephones in employee rest rooms or staff canteens, regardless of whether the employers give a warning. On the other hand, considerable difficulty may arise in establishing a reasonable expectation of privacy concerning the use of telephones in shared offices or in circumstances in which private use is forbidden. Violations of Article 8 may also occur if a public authority employer monitors private e-mail messages or monitors rest rooms or toilets by closed-circuit television.

12.184 Employers may be entitled to monitor the activities of employees if Article 8 rights are waived in the contract of employment. In principle, Convention rights can be waived[641] and employees can sign away Convention rights in their contract of employment.[642] However, it is well established under Convention case law that any waiver of a Convention right must be established in an unequivocal manner.[643] It seems that simply signing a contract may not be sufficient to amount to a waiver.[644] It is submitted that in order to rely on a waiver of Convention rights, an employer will be obliged to draw the provision specifically to the attention of the employees. It has been suggested that the Court should take a different

---

[638] See para 13.148ff below.
[639] See para. 12.94 above for a discussion of the Canadian case law considering this phrase, see para 12.226 below.
[640] (1997) 24 EHRR 523.
[641] *Deweer v Belgium* (1980) 2 EHRR 439 para 49; see generally, para 6.148ff above.
[642] See eg *Vereinigung Rechtswinkels Utrecht v Netherlands* (1986) 46 DR 200, EComm HR.
[643] See para 6.153 above.
[644] See eg *Rommelfanger v Germany* (1989) 62 DR 151, EComm HR.

approach towards prospective rather than existing employees.[645] In the Convention cases a distinction has been made between employees who have the choice of whether or not to accept a job[646] and employees in post who are put at risk of losing their jobs if they refuse to sign a waiver.[647]

Regulation of 'private aspects' of employees' conduct. The Human Rights Act **12.185** may also affect the ability of public authority employers to restrict private areas of conduct by means of provisions such as dress codes. The EAT has held that a dress code preventing male employees from wearing their hair in pony tails did not constitute sex discrimination.[648] However, it could be argued that such codes constitute interference with the 'private life' of the employees.[649] The right to privacy will also have an impact on the scope of the implied term of mutual trust and confidence[650] and may be relevant to issues such as random drug tests.[651] Furthermore it may be a breach of Article 8 for health checks to be carried out on an employee without 'informed consent' having been given.[652]

When deciding whether a dismissal is unfair, section 6(3) of the Human Rights Act **12.186** requires that employment tribunals must not act incompatibly with Convention rights.[653] Privacy rights[654] must be taken into account when a tribunal decides cases

---

[645] J Carter, 'Employment and Labour Relations Law' in C Baker (ed), *Human Rights Act 1998: A Practitioner's Guide* (Sweet & Maxwell, 1998) para 13–47.

[646] See eg *Glasenapp v Germany* (1986) 9 EHRR 25; *Kosiek v Germany* (1986) 9 EHRR 328.

[647] See eg *Knudsen v Norway* (1985) 42 DR 247, EComm HR.

[648] *Smith v Safeway plc* [1996] ICR 686; see also *Schmidt v Austicks Bookshops Ltd* [1978] ICR 85. It has been forcefully argued that *Safeway* is inconsistent with the reasoning in *Jones v Eastleigh Borough Council* [1990] 2 AC 751 (see R Wintemute, 'Recognising New Kinds of Direct Sex Discrimination: Transsexualism, Sexual Orientation and Dress Codes' (1997) 60 MLR 334, 353ff); and see G Clayton and G Pitt, 'Dress Codes and Freedom of Expression' [1997] EHRLR 54.

[649] Cf *McFeeley v United Kingdom* (1980) 20 DR 44, 91, EComm HR (a case concerning prison dress); *Kara v United Kingdom* (1998) 27 EHRR CD 272 (a bisexual male transvestite who wore female clothes to express his identity established that restrictions placed on his dress breached the right to private life; however, the Commission took the view that the interference was legitimate and proportionate); there has been considerable litigation in the United States on the question as to whether the control of dress or grooming is unconstitutional: see L Tribe, *American Constitutional Law*, (2nd edn, Foundation Press, 1988) para 15–15 (he points to over 200 cases in the two decades up to 1988).

[650] *Mahmud v Bank of Credit and Commerce International SA* [1998] AC 20.

[651] J Wadham and H Mountfield, *Blackstone's Guide to the Human Rights Act* (Blackstone, 1999) para 9.8.6.

[652] See *X v Commission* [1995] IRLR 320 and generally, B Watt, 'The Legal Protection of HIV and Health Care Workers and the Human Rights Jurisprudence of the European Court of Justice' [1998] EHRLR 301.

[653] Employment Tribunals are 'public authorities' under s 6 of the Human Rights Act, see generally, para 5.05ff above.

[654] For an instructive article on the approach of the American courts to privacy in the employment relationship, see eg M Finkin, 'Employee Privacy, American Values and the Law' (1996–97) 72 Chicago-Kent LR 222.

involving, for example, dress regulations,[655] no smoking rules, private conduct outside the workplace which is alleged to affect working relationships (such as homosexuality[656] and mental illness)[657] or medical (including HIV and psychological) testing. However, the positive duty on public authorities to take 'reasonable and appropriate measures' to secure Article 8 rights[657a] does not oblige the courts to create a general right to privacy.[657b] The tribunal is not obliged to apply strict Article 8(2) tests to the acts of private employers. It seems likely that it will be sufficient for the tribunal to continue to decide unfair dismissal cases by applying the well established 'reasonable responses test' for determining whether a dismissal is unfair.[657c]

12.187 **Collection and use of personal data on employees.** Employers hold and collect substantial amounts of personal data on employees which may be subject to misuse. The International Labour Organisation has expressed concern about the need to protect such data from misuse.[658] Security checks on employees which involve the collection of information about their private affairs would be a breach of Article 8.[659]

12.188 **Sexual orientation discrimination.** Discrimination by public employers in connection with sexual orientation is also likely to breach Article 8.[660] In *Lustig-Prean v United Kingdom*[661] and *Smith and Grady v United Kingdom*[662] the Court held that the investigation and dismissal of homosexuals from the armed forces was a breach of Article 8. Public authorities will violate the right to private life if they conduct intrusive investigations into the sexuality of employees; and, in practice, they will be acting unlawfully by dismissing employees on the grounds of their sexual orientation. It may also be arguable that the principle of statutory horizontality[663] will mean that the Sex Discrimination Act[664] must be read to

---

[655] See eg *Boychuk v Symons Holdings* [1977] IRLR 395; see Clayton and Pitt (n 648 above) which relies on *Stevens v United Kingdom* (1986) DR 245, EComm HR to argue that the right of dress and appeareance is a manifestation of the right of freedom of expression (see, generally, para 15.271 below); cf Carter (n 645 above) paras 13-22–13-24.

[656] See eg *Saunders v Scottish National Camps Association* [1980] IRLR 174.

[657] See eg *O'Brien v Prudential Assurance* [1979] IRLR 140.

[657a] See para 12.113ff above.

[657b] See para 12.165ff above.

[657c] See eg *British Leyland v Swift* [1981] IRLR 91 and *Iceland Frozen Foods v Jones* [1982] IRLR 439. But note that this test is now open to question as a result of the decisions in *Haddon v Van den Bergh Foods* [1999] IRLR 672 and *Midland Bank v Madden* [2000] IRLR 288; see now, CA decision, 31 Jul 2000 which confirms the reasonable responses test.

[658] For the concerns expressed by the ILO see: *Protection of Workers' Personal Data: An ILO Code of Practice* (ILO, 1997).

[659] See *Hilton v United Kingdom* (1998) 57 DR, EComm HR.

[660] See generally, R Wintemute, *Sexual Orientation and Human Rights* (Clarendon Press, 1995) Chap 4; and see R Wintemute, 'Lesbian and Gay Britons, the Two Europes and the Bill of Rights Debate' [1997] EHRLR 466.

[661] (1999) 7 BHRC 65.

[662] (2000) 29 EHRR 493.

[663] See para 5.84ff above.

[664] Cf *Smith v Gardner Merchant Ltd* [1998] IRLR 510.

include sexual orientation discrimination: so that private employers will also be prohibited from dismissing or subjecting employees to a detriment because they are homosexual. Although the Court in *Lustig-Prean v United Kingdom*[665] and *Smith v United Kingdom*[666] did not make any separate ruling on the complaint of discrimination under Article 14[667] in conjuction with Article 8, it could nevertheless be argued that the obligation to construe the Sex Discrimination Act in accordance with Article 14 means that discrimination will now cover sexual orientation discrimination.[668]

Although the dismissal of a public employee on the grounds of sexual orientation will constitute a breach of Article 8, the public authority can justify such dismissal under Article 8(2). This may be straightforward in the police or armed forces[669] but the justification may be more difficult in other areas of employment. **12.189**

(e) Family law

The Article 8 issues which arise concerning the right of respect for family life are discussed in Chapter 13.[670] However, the power of the court to require disclosure of privileged material in child care proceedings under Part IV of the Children Act 1989 may require further consideration;[671] there is a duty on legal representatives to make full and frank disclosure even where it harms their clients' case.[672] When making interim care or supervision orders, the court has the power to give directions for the medical or psychiatric examination or other assesment of a child.[673] When making such an order, the court must not act incompatibly with the child's right to privacy. **12.190**

(f) Health care

It is arguable that a right to personal automony which can be derived from Article 8;[674] is relevant to the validity of a patient's consent to medical treatment which **12.191**

---

[665] n 661 above, paras 108–109.
[666] *The Times*, 11 Oct 1999 (paras 115–116 in the full judgment).
[667] See generally, para 17.130ff below.
[668] Contrast *Smith v Gardner Merchant Ltd* (n 664 above) under the Act; and under European Community law, *Grant v South-West Trains Ltd* [1998] ECR I–621; *R v Secretary of State of Defence, ex p Perkins (No 2)* [1998] IRLR 508.
[669] See *Boitteloup v France* (1988) 58 DR 127; also *Bruce v United Kingdom* (1983) 34 DR 68: dismissal of a gay soldier for engaging in sexual activity with a 20-year-old soldier was justified. However, under the Human Rights Act there will be no blanket exclusion for acts done to ensure the combat effectiveness of the armed forces as there is under s 85(4) of the Sex Discrimination Act as amended.
[670] See para 13.150ff below.
[671] See *In re L (A Minor) (Police Investigation Privilege)* [1997] AC 16; see, in particular, the dissenting judgment of Lord Nicholls at 34.
[672] See eg *Oxfordshire County Council v P* [1995] Fam 161; *Essex County Council v R* [1994] Fam 167; *Re D H (A Minor) (Child Abuse)* [1994] 1 FLR 679.
[673] Children Act 1989, s 38(6); and see *Re C (A Minor) (Interim Care Order: Residential Assessment)* [1997] AC 489.
[674] See para 12.84ff above.

would otherwise amount to a battery.[675] At common law the patient must understand in broad terms the nature of the procedure he is agreeing to[676] and the doctor is obliged to disclose the risks inherent in and the alternatives to the procedure. It is arguable, however, Article 8 may impose a stricter duty on doctors to provide more detailed information to patients.

12.192   The right to personal automony may also affect the controversial question of whether a parent can overule the refusal of a '*Gillick* competent'[677] child or a 16- or 17-year-old child[678] to have medical treatment.[679] At common law the court is not bound to implement the wishes of a *Gillick* competent[680] child or of the 16- or 17-year-old child.[681] However, under the Human Rights Act it will be arguable that the child's wishes should prevail over its parents.

(g) Housing law

12.193   Article 8 does not create a right to a home as such:[681a] the right is to respect for a home. This may affect a number of areas in the field of housing law. The Human Rights Act will apply directly to local authorities. It is likely that registered social landlords under the Housing Act 1996 (formerly housing associations) are functional public authorities.[682] Article 8 will therefore have an important impact on housing management questions. The implications of a right of respect for the home and private life are discussed below. The impact of the right to respect for the family are examined in Chapter 13.[683]

12.194   Article 8 may affect the housing allocation policies of some local authorities. It would be a breach of the right of respect for private life, for example, to give

---

[675] See generally, I Kennedy and A Grubb, *Principles of Medical Law* (Oxford University Press, 1998) paras 3.86–3.100.

[676] *Chatterton v Gerson* [1981] QB 432, 443; *Sidaway v Board of Governors of the Bethlem Royal Hospital and the Maudsley Hospital* [1984] 1 All ER 1018, 1026, CA *per* Sir John Donaldson MR and 1029 *per* Dunn LJ.

[677] A child can validly consent to medical treatment where he has sufficient understanding and intelligence to understand fully what is proposed: see *Gillick v West Norfolk and Wisbech Area Health Authority* [1986] AC 112, 169m 186, 188–189, 195, 201.

[678] Family Law Reform Act 1969, s 8.

[679] See, generally, Kennedy and Grubb (n 675 above) para 4.62–68.

[680] *In re R (A Minor)(Wardship: Consent to Treatment)* [1992] Fam 11; *In re W (A Minor)(Medical Treatment: Court's Jurisdiction)* [1993] Fam 64.

[681] *In re R (A Minor)(Wardship: Consent to Treatment)* (n 680 above); *In re W (A minor)(Medical Treatment: Court's Jurisdiction)* (n 680 above).

[681a] See para 12.96 above.

[682] The decision in *Peabody Housing Association v Green* (1978) 38 P & CR 633 deciding that a housing association is not amenable to judicial review does not require a court to hold it is a public authority and is unlikely to be applied to the Human Rights Act; see *Hoyle v Castlemilk East Housing Co-operative, The Times*, 16 May 1997; and see, generally, para 5–16ff above; and C Hunter and A Dymond; 'Housing Law' in C Baker (ed), *The Human Rights Act 1998: A Practitioner's Guide* (Sweet & Maxwell, 1998) para 7–08 and see also, *R v Servite Homes, ex p Goldsmith*, 12 May 2000, Div Ct, unreported.

[683] See 13.161 below.

preference to housing married couples; and it may well breach Article 8 to require applicants for council housing to disclose their criminal convictions, particularly if those convictions are spent under the Rehabilitation of Offenders Act.[684] It will also require local authority landlords to justify standard conditions in tenancy agreements such as the prohibition on tenants having pets[684a] by demonstrating, for example, that the condition is favoured by tenants and tenants' associations.

It is increasingly common for local authorities and housing associations to install closed circuit television cameras to monitor the common parts of housing estates to discourage and prevent crime and anti-social behaviour. It seems likely that, in some circumstances at least, these cameras will record 'private events' and their use will, therefore, constitute a *prima facie* interference with the right to respect for private life. Nevertheless, it is submitted that provided the public authority can adduce proper evidence that the use of such cameras is necessary for one of these legitimate purposes, these measures are a justifiable interference with the right to private life.

12.194A

Local authority landlords may be obliged to take positive steps[685] to protect their own tenants from noise,[686] fumes,[687] pollution[688] (which might extend to matters such as vermin and cockroaches) and anti-social neighbours.[689] These positive obligations may mean that a local authority will be liable, for example, if it fails to take proper steps to protect its tenants from nuisance caused by other local authority tenants[690] or to sound-proof local authority flats.[691] Article 8 may also be breached by the failure of the local authority to take action under Parts VI and IX of the Housing Act 1985 in relation to unfit housing for private tenants as well as local authority tenants.[692] The question of whether a positive obligation arises in these cases will depend on the balance struck by the court between the general interest of the community and the rights of the individual.[692a]

12.195

---

[684] s 1(1), s 4(1)(2) and s 5 of the Act.

[684a] See J Luba, 'Acting on Rights—The Housing Implications of the Human Rights Act', Lecture, Sep 1999.

[685] See para 12.108 above.

[686] *Arrondelle v United Kingdom* (1982) 26 DR 5, EComm HR; *Powell and Rayner v United Kingdom* (1990) 12 EHRR 394; contrast the position in domestic law where a tenant cannot make a claim for breach of the covenant of quiet enjoyment or nuisance: see *Southwark London Borough Council v Mills* [1999] 3 WLR 939.

[687] *Lopez Ostra v Spain* (1994) 20 EHRR 277.

[688] *Guerra v Italy* (1998) 26 EHRR 357.

[689] There is no implied covenant on a landlord to enforce a covenant not to commit a nuisance against a neighbour (see *O'Leary v Islington London Borough Council* (1983) 9 HLR 81); nor can the landlord be liable for the acts of the neighbour in nuisance: see *Smith v Scott* [1973] Ch 314; *Hussein v Lancaster City Council* [1999] 4 All ER 125.

[690] Requiring reconsideration of *Hussain v Lancaster City Council* (n 689 above).

[691] Requiring reconsideration of *Southwark London Borough Council v Mills* (n 686 above).

[692] A local authority cannot use the enforcement provisions of the Housing Act against itself: see *R v Cardiff City Council ex p Cross* (1981) 6 HLR 6.

[692a] See para 6.99ff above.

12.196   Under section 6(3) of the Act, the court must not act in a way which is incompatible with Convention rights.[693] It will therefore be necessary to consider the impact of Article 8 when the court considers whether to make a discretionary possession order in relation to an assured tenancy,[694] when considering whether it is reasonable to make a possession order in relation to a secure tenancy[695] and when considering mortgagee possesssion orders. It may, for example, be argued that, in a case involving modest rent arrears, it would be disproportionate to make a possession order.

12.197   **Private nuisance.**   The definition of 'private nuisance' in English law may have to be revised in the light of Article 8. In *Hunter v Canary Wharf Ltd*[696] the plaintiffs' claims for nuisance based on interference with television reception by large buildings were dismissed by the House of Lords. It is arguable that the Article 8 'respect for home' would require the courts to take a broader view of what types of 'interference' should be regarded as constituting an actionable nuisance and to develop the common law accordingly.[697]

(h) Immigration law

12.198   It seems likely that the law relating to immigration and deportation will be significantly affected by Article 8 of the Convention. Deportations have been subject to challenge on a number of occasions on the ground of interference with Article 8 rights.[698] However, these challenges have almost always been based on interference with 'family life' rather than 'private life' and are dealt with in Chapter 13.[699]

(i) Local government law

12.199   The obligation to respect the home may have a significant effect on a wide range of administrative decisions; the implications of the right of respect for family life (in particular, in relation to public law child care cases)[700] are discussed in Chapter 13.[701] In community care cases a failure to respect the home when moving disabled adults and children in residential accomodation will provide an additional ground for challenge in judicial review proceedings.[702]

---

[693] See para 5.120ff above.
[694] Under Housing Act 1988, Pt II, Sch 2.
[695] Cases 1 to 8 and 12 to 16 in Sch 2 of the Housing Act 1985 are subject to s 84(2).
[695a] See Luba (n 684a above).
[696] [1997] AC 655.
[697] See the dissenting judgment of Lord Cooke in *Hunter v Canary Wharf Ltd* (n 696 above); and see para 5.93 above.
[698] See para 13.142 below; and see A Sherlock, 'Deportation of Aliens and Article 8 ECHR' (1998) 23 ELR Checklist No 1, HR 62.
[699] But see, *C v Belgium* RJD 1996–III 915.
[700] See para 13.30ff below.
[701] See para 13.175 below.
[702] See eg *R v North and East Devon District Health Authority, ex p Coughlan* [2000] 2 WLR 622; see para 12.12 above.

The power to inspect small residential homes under the Residential Homes (Amendment) Act 1991 must not be used in an instrusive way so as to comply with the right of respect for private life. Although a failure to register such homes is a criminal offence, it would be a *prima facie* breach of Article 8 if a prosecution was brought where the arrangement was made out of friendship or in return for companionship.[703]

12.200

Article 8 will affect the use local authorities may make of information gathered in the course of carrying out their functions. It may facilitate the general right to freedom of information[704] by providing a right of access to personal information.[705] It is also difficult to see how the release to the media by a local authority of video material from closed-circuit television could be lawful after the coming into force of the Human Rights Act.[706]

12.201

(j) Media law

Even in the absence of 'horizontal' application, it is likely that the Human Rights Act will have considerable impact on media law. It is clear that there are many situations in which the media infringes the private life and home of individuals. Although the press is not subject to direct state regulation, it is strongly arguable that the Press Complaints Commission is a functional public authority[707] and, as result, must act in conformity with Article 8. The Broadcasting Standards Commission is a body established by statute and is also a functional public authority.[708] As a result, if the Press Complaints Commission and Broadcasting Standards Commission fail to establish and effectively police a regulatory regime which provides proper protection for Article 8 rights then their actions may be unlawful under section 6 of the Human Rights Act. A 'victim' may be entitled to damages or injunctive relief. The effect of 'privacy rights' in the media law context, however, gives rise to complex issues of balancing of rights under the Convention.[709] These issues are considered in relation to freedom of expression in Chapter 15.[710]

12.202

(k) Mental health law

Article 8 of the Convention will be relevant to mental health law insofar as it protects the right of persons detained under the Mental Health Act to 'respect for

12.203

---

[703] L Clements, *Community Care and the Law* (Legal Action Group, 1996) 82, 83.
[704] See para 15.253 below.
[705] See para 12.46 above.
[706] Reversing *R v Brentwood Borough Council, ex p Peck The Times*, 18 Dec 1997.
[707] See para 5.16ff above and *R v Press Complaints Authority, ex p Stewart-Brady* (1997) 9 Admin LR 274; and see para 12.74 above, n 292.
[708] See para 5.16ff above.
[709] See eg R Singh, 'Privacy and the Media After the Human Rights Act' [1998] EHRLR 712.
[710] See para 15.245ff below.

home and correspondence'. It seems likely that the present position in relation to the interception of correspondence is compatible with Article 8(2).[711]

12.204 Another matter raised by Article 8 is that of state-imposed controls in connection with the care and housing of conditionally discharged patients in the community. Under Article 8 the state will be required to demonstrate a social need for restrictions on home or private life such as a mandatory period of residence in monitored accommodation. This could amount to a significant departure from existing practice, under which many post-discharge restrictions are established on a relatively automatic basis.

12.205 When a person is in involuntary detention in a psychiatric institution important functions are exercised by the person designated as their 'nearest relative' under section 26 of the Mental Health Act 1983. The 'nearest relative' is privy to private information concerning the patient. In limited circumstances an application may be made to the County Court to change the person exercising the functions of the 'nearest relative'.[712] However, such a change cannot be made on the ground that the patient has concerns about the identity of the nearest relative and does not wish this person to have access to private information. The Commission took the view that this gives rise to a breach of Article 8[713] and a friendly settlement was reached involving an agreement to amend the legislation.[713a]

(l) Planning and environment law

12.206 **Introduction.** The right to respect for 'home' in Article 8 has a potential impact on planning law. Thus the refusal of planning permission to allow a person to continue to live in a particular place is a *prima facie* breach of Article 8.[714] However, Article 8 will only apply if the 'home' is already established. The right does not extend to land on which a person plans to build a house.[715]

12.207 More importantly, after the Human Rights Act comes into force planning authorities will have to take into account the potential impact of their decisions on the Article 8 rights of individuals. It is well established that personal circumstances are only relevant to planning decisions in exceptional circumstances.[716] However, the general approach of the Convention is that personal circumstances

---

[711] See O Thorold, 'The Implications of the European Convention on Human Rights for United Kingdom Mental Health Legislation' [1996] EHRLR, 619, 633.

[712] Mental Health Act 1983 s 29.

[713] See *J T v United Kingdom* [1999] EHRLR 443 (merits).

[713a] *JT v United Kingdom*, Judgment, 30 Mar 2000.

[714] Cf *Buckley v United Kingdom* (1996) 23 EHRR 101; and see *Chesterfield Properties v Secretary of State for the Environment* [1998] JPL 568 where Laws J dealt with a *Wednesbury* challenge to a compulsory purchase order on the basis it involved a fundamental human right.

[715] See *Loizidou v Turkey* (1996) 23 EHRR 513.

[716] *Great Portland Estate v City of Westminster Council* [1985] AC 661.

are put first[717] and any interference with those rights must be justified as 'necessary in a democratic society'. It has been suggested that this might require a fundamental change of approach:

> . . . the approach under the Convention is that interference with individual rights is unjustified unless public interest reasons are adduced which are of sufficient importance. In current planning policy, decisions are made in accordance with the public interest, with affected private rights being subsidiary.[718]

If such a change is implemented, planning authorities will have to make clear, in the reasons for their decisions that they have not acted incompatibly with Article 8 rights.[719] If the reasons given do not demonstrate that there is a 'Convention justification' for the interference, then the decision will be unlawful and liable to be quashed.

Enforcement powers. An authority must not use its powers to enforce compliance with planning controls under Part VII of the Town and Country Planning Act 1990 by evicting trespassing gypsies in a way which is incompatible with the right to respect for the home. Even before the enactment of the Human Rights Act, the courts have taken account of the fundamental right to shelter when considering local authority decisions to evict gypsies;[720] and gypsies will be able to rely directly on Article 8 as a defence to possession proceedings.[721] In *Buckley v United Kingdom*[722] the Court held that the refusal to grant a gypsy planning permission and the institution of criminal proceedings for failing to comply with an enforcement notice was a proportionate interference with Article 8 which had a legitimate aim. However, there are a number of similar applications before the Commission by gypsies alleging violation of Article 8 which have been ruled admissible.[723] It may also

12.208

---

[717] See the approach taken in *Britton v Secretary of State for the Environment* [1997] JPL 617.

[718] See T Corner, 'Planning, Environment and the European Convention on Human Rights' [1998] JPL 301, 312.

[719] See *Britton v Secretary of State for the Environment* [1997] JPL 617; and contrast *R v Leicestershire County Council, ex p Blackfordby and Boothorope Action Group* (unreported) 15 Mar 2000.

[720] See eg *R v Lincolnshire County Council, ex p Atkinson* [1996] 160 JPLCL 580 and *R v Wolverhampton Metropolitan Borough Council, ex p Dunne* (1997) 29 HLR 754 in relation to the powers to deal with unauthorised encampments under the Criminal Justice and Public Order Act 1994; and *R v Kerrier District Council, ex p Uzell* [1996] 71 P & CR 566 in relation to a decision of a planning authority to take enforcement action against gypsies occupying a site in breach of planning control; and contrast the approach taken where a local authority commences summary proceedings for possession in *R v Brighton and Hove Council, ex p Marman* [1998] 2 PLR 48 and *R v Hillingdon Borough Council, ex p McDonagh, The Times,* 9 Nov 1998.

[721] Until the Human Rights Act comes into force, gypsies have been obliged to apply to adjourn the possession proceedings so that judicial review proceedings can be brought to challenge the decision to commence the possession proceedings: see *Avon County Council v Buscott* [1988] QB 656.

[722] (1996) 23 EHHR 101; see also *Turner v United Kingdom* (1997) 23 EHRR CD 181.

[723] *Coster v United Kingdom* (1998) 25 EHRR CD 24; *Beard v United Kingdom* (1998) 25 EHRR CD 28; *Smith v United Kingdom* (1998) 25 EHRR CD 42; *Lee v United Kingdom* (1998) 25 EHRR CD 46; *Varey v United Kingdom* (1998) 25 EHRR CD 49; *Chapman v United Kingdom* (1998) 25 EHRR CD 64.

be argued that an authority discriminates against gypsies when taking possession proceedings against them.[724]

12.209 **Statutory nuisance.** The Human Rights Act may also have an impact on the extent to which local authorities are obliged to exercise their powers to require the abatement of statutory nuisances.[725] A failure to exercise these powers in circumstances in which noise,[726] fumes,[727] pollution[728] affect individuals' enjoyment of their homes could constitute a breach of Article 8.[729] It is also arguable that compulsory purchase orders must comply with Article 8 and the right to the enjoyment of possessions under Article 1 of the First Protocol. The issues they raise are considered in Chapter 18.[730]

(m) Police law

12.210 **Introduction.** Police powers of surveillance constitute an 'interference' with the rights guaranteed by Article 8 and must, therefore, be 'in accordance with the law' and 'necessary in a democratic society' for one of the specified purposes.[731] This does not necessarily mean that the machinery of supervision should be in the hands of a judge[732] but there must be adequate and effective safeguards against abuse and sufficient independence.

12.211 **The Interception of Communications Act.** The Interception of Communications Act 1985 was enacted as a direct result of the decision of the Court in *Malone v United Kingdom*.[733] Since the Act came into force, the Commission have held[734] that the 'review machinery' which it establishes (and the similar machinery relating to the security and intelligence services)[735] are sufficient to satisfy Article 8. Nevertheless, these decisions are not binding on the English courts and there are powerful arguments to the contrary. The Tribunal does not consider the merits of the issue of a warrant, does not conduct oral hearings and

---

[724] See para 17.165 below.

[725] Environmental Protection Act 1990, ss 79, 80.

[726] *Arrondelle v United Kingdom* (1982) 26 DR 5, EComm HR; *Powell and Rayner v United Kingdom* (1990) 12 EHRR 394.

[727] *Lopez Ostra v Spain* (1994) 20 EHRR 277.

[728] *Guerra v Italy* (1998) 26 EHRR 357.

[729] See generally, Corner (n 718 above) 313 and P Sands, 'Human Rights, Environment and the *Lopez Ostra* Case' [1996] EHRLR 597.

[730] See para 18.103 below.

[731] See generally, the Rt Hon Lord Justice Auld, 'Investigations and Surveillance' and M Colvin, 'Surveillance and the Human Rights Act' in Centre for Public Law at the University of Cambridge, *The Human Rights Act and the Criminal Justice and Regulatory Process* (Hart Publishing, 1999).

[732] See para 12.125ff above.

[733] (1984) 7 EHRR 14.

[734] See para 12.154 above.

[735] See para 12.155 above.

does not give reasons. Although there are about 50 complaints a year, the Tribunal has not yet found a breach of the Act. As Klug, Starmer and Weir point out:

> it is imperative that the tribunals set up to investigate surveillance by the secret services have power to question whether the surveillance complained about was justified; and to report their findings either way. Otherwise, whether they provide an adequate safeguard is unknowable. Equally the fact that the tribunal cannot 'go behind' a decision of the secret services to target an individual because he or she belonged to a group or category of people regarded by them as requiring investigation presents the tribunal with a circular obstacle . . .[736]

Furthermore, there are limitations on the impact of the Interception of Communications Act which mean that certain types of police surveillance is likely to be a breach of Article 8.[737] The 1985 Act does not apply to private telecommunications networks and does not, for example, cover interceptions of radio signals from cordless telephones[738] or of e-mails whilst travelling on internet service providers on the private network. The 1985 Act also does not apply to any interception carried out with the consent of one of the parties to the communication.[739] However, the regime governing the interception of communications will be radically recast when the Regulation of Investigatory Powers Bill becomes law. This extends the statutory regime to all forms of telecommunication and makes provision for a new Tribunal to deal with complaints concerning interception. This Tribunal will conduct hearings and allow legal representation and will meet some of the criticisms of the Interception of Communications Act 1985.[740]

12.212

The Security Services Act. The Security Service Act 1996 extended the functions of the Security Service to acting in support of the activities of the police force and other law enforcement agencies in the prevention and detection of serious crime.[741] By section 2, the Act extends the power of the Secretary of State to issue warrants[742] to cover applications in relation to the new function. These warrants may relate to property in the British Islands if they are in relation to 'serious crime'. It has been forcefully argued that this new power to issue warrants may be in breach of Article 8 because the Secretary of State is given a broad discretion which does not satisfy the requirements of 'foreseeability' and 'precision'.[743] In addition, there is a

12.213

---

[736] F Klug, K Starmer, S Weir, *The Three Pillars of Liberty* (Routledge, 1996) 230; also, JUSTICE, *Under Surveillance: Covert Policing and Human Rights Standards* (Justice, 1998) 24–27.

[737] See generally, Colvin (n 731 above).

[738] *R v Effik* (1994) 99 Crim App R 312.

[739] Interception of Communications Act 1985, s 1(2).

[740] For the background to the Bill see the Consultation Paper *Interception of Communications in the United Kingdom* (HMSO, 1999), CM 4368.

[741] Security Service Act 1996, s 1(1), amending Security Service Act 1989, s 1.

[742] Intelligence Services Act 1994, s 5.

[743] See P Duffy and M Hunt, 'Goodbye Entick v Carrington: the Security Service Act 1996' [1997] EHRLR 11, 15–16.

lack of effective judicial supervision. The various bodies established under the Security Service and Intelligence Service Acts are immune from judicial review. Duffy and Hunt argue that, in cases in which the purpose of the surveillance is not the protection of national security, these bodies do not provide an adequate substitute for judicial supervision.[744]

12.214 **Regulation of other forms of surveillance.** Other surveillance by public authorities in the United Kingdom has, traditionally, been unregulated by statute. In *Govell v United Kingdom*[745] the Commission declared admissible an application relating to the lack of legal authority for intrusive police surveillance. The concerns raised by the House of Lords in *R v Khan*[746] led to the enactment of the Police Act 1997. This brought in a system of review in relation to intrusive surveillance. In *Khan v United Kingdom*[746a] the Court confirmed that the system which had existed prior to the Police Act 1997 was not 'in accordance with law' and, as a result, constituted a breach of Article 8.

12.215 There are a number of serious issues concerning the compatibility of police surveillance with Article 8.[747] First, although it seems likely that the regime under the Police Act 1997, in general, satisfies Convention standards, there remain areas of concern. In particular, although the police now have to obtain prior approval of a Commissioner where surveillance would involve intrusion which could infringe privacy, this does not apply to an authorisation 'where the person who gives it believes that the case is one of urgency'.[748] It is arguable that authorisation of this type lacks the safeguards which the Court of Human Rights has identified as being necessary to ensure that interferences were proportionate.[749] Secondly, the Police Act 1997 does not cover 'non-intrusive' surveillance such as the tape recording of conversations using long range microphones, video surveillance and so on. These are also 'interferences' with Article 8 rights and remain unregulated by law in the United Kingdom. This is a plain breach of the Convention[750] and the Government is seeking to rectify the position by the provisions of Part II of the Regulation of Investigatory Powers Bill. This Bill applies

---

[744] Ibid 18–19.

[745] (1996) 23 EHRR CD 101.

[746] [1997] AC 558; see generally, para 12.54ff above.

[746a] *The Times*, 23 May 2000.

[747] For a general discussion, see M Colvin, 'Surveillance and the Human Rights Act' in Centre for Public Law at the University of Cambridge, *The Human Rights Act and the Criminal Justice and Regulatory Process* (Hart Publishing, 1999).

[748] Police Act 1997, s 97(3).

[749] See eg *Funke v France* (1993) 16 EHRR 297 para 54ff; and contrast *Camenzind v Switzerland* RJD 1998–III 2880 paras 45–47.

[750] But see *Hutcheon v United Kingdom* [1997] EHRLR 195 (visual surveillance of applicant's home by 75 ft observation tower held to be within the normal duties of RUC and thus 'in accordance with the law', for a legitimate aim).

to any surveillance which is 'intrusive',[750a] or 'directed'.[750b] It will also apply to the 'conduct and use of covert human intelligence sources' that is informants and undercover police officers. The Bill proposes an 'authorisation regime' similar to that in the Police Act 1997 with additional safeguards in the form of a Covert Investigations Commissioner and a Tribunal. The Tribunal will also be the appropriate tribunal for actions under section 7 of the Human Rights Act 1998 in relation to surveillance.[750c] The Tribunal will apply the same principles for making a determination as would be applied by a court on an application for judicial review.

Search warrants.   Police powers of search and seizure are largely regulated by the provisions of the Police and Criminal Evidence Act 1984 and appear, in general, to be in conformity with the Convention. However, an issue may arise as to whether the procedure for the issue of search warrants by magistrates[751] conforms with Article 8. This is because the procedure appears, in practice, to be little more than a 'rubber stamping exercise', with refusals being exceedingly rare.[752] A warrant does not show the grounds on which it was issued and the 'information in writing' is usually formal in nature. Justices have no obligation to give reasons for the grant of a warrant and no record is kept of proceedings.[753] This makes legal challenges extremely difficult. If a warrant is issued without proper grounds, then the person whose property is searched has no remedy against the police. The issuing justices are only liable if malice can be shown. No such action has been successful in modern times.[754] These factors lead Feldman to conclude:

12.216

> one is left with an impression that justices of the peace do not provide the independent judicial scrutiny of proposed entries and searches under warrants which is needed to ensure that interferences with the right to respect for a person's private life and home are justified . . . The formal trappings of scrutiny are there, but the substance is sadly lacking in most cases.[755]

As a result, it is arguable that the procedure for the grant of search warrants is in breach of Article 8. It should be noted, however, that a challenge to the issue of a

---

[750a] That is surveillance involving the presence of an individual or device on residential premises or private vehicle or which is carried out in relation to anything taking place on such premises or in such vehicle, clause 25(3).

[750b] That is surveillance undertaken for a specific operation which is likely to result in the obtaining of personal information, clause 25(2).

[750c] See clause 56 and generally, Part IV.

[751] See para 12.08 above.

[752] See K Lidstone and C Palmer, *Bevan and Lidstone's: The Investigation of Crime* (2nd edn, Butterworths, 1996) para 4.10; D Dixon, C Coleman and K Bottomley 'PACE in Practice' (1991) 141 NLJ 1586.

[753] *R v Marylebone Magistrates Court, ex p Amdrell Ltd (trading as 'Get Stuffed')* (1998) 162 JP 719, although giving reasons is desireable.

[754] See generally, R Clayton and H Tomlinson, *Civil Actions Against the Police* (3rd edn, Sweet & Maxwell, 2000) Chap 7.

[755] D Feldman, *Civil Liberties and Human Rights in England and Wales* (Clarendon Press, 1993), 414.

warrant under Article 8 was unsuccessful in the Scots case of *Birse v HM Advocate*.[755a] The evidence of the Justice was that his 'invariable practice' was to question the requesting officer as to the reason for applying for the warrant and the source of any information relied on. The Court also rejected the argument that there was a breach of Article 8 because no record had been kept of the proceedings because the complainer was deprived of a proper basis for ensuring that the application had been considered properly. There was no consideration of the extent to which the Justice's 'invariable procedure' provided an effective scrutiny of the warrant[755b] and the impact of the Article 8 requirement for 'procedural safeguards'.[755c]

12.217   There is increasing concern about the execution of search warrants in the presence of the media. A search warrant involves a serious interference with a person's home and private life. Media involvement and the publication of material relating to the search, including films of police entry, means that there is a much greater degree of interference. Although the Divisional Court has stated that any general practice of inviting the media to attend on the execution of warrants is deplorable[756] it refused to quash a warrant on the ground that television cameras had been invited to attend. In the United States, in contrast, the practice of inviting the media to attend the execution of a warrant, known as 'ride-along', has been held to be unconstitutional.[757] The Supreme Court held that media 'ride-alongs' could not be justified by matters such as the need to publicise law enforcement activities, minimise police abuses and protect suspects and officers: the right to the privacy of the home prevailed. It is strongly arguable that a similar approach will be taken under Article 8.

12.218   Another area of potential impact concerns police powers to seize material which is subject to legal professional privilege. Although there is no statutory power to search for or seize such material, privilege is lost if the material is held 'with the intention of furthering a criminal purpose'.[758] Case law establishes that the privilege is lost when the material was held innocently for a third party's 'criminal purpose'.[759] This can be contrasted with the approach taken by the European Court of Human Rights in *Niemetz v Germany*[760] in which a search of a lawyer's office was held to be a breach of Article 8, as disproportionate to the aim of prevention of crime and protection of rights of others. There is a good argument that the

---

[755a] Unreported, 13 Apr 2000.
[755b] No consideration was given to the question as to how often the Justice refused applications for warrants.
[755c] See para 12.132 above.
[756] *R v Marylebone Magistrates Court, ex p Amdrell Ltd (trading as 'Get Stuffed')* (1998) 162 JP 719.
[757] See *Wilson v Layne* (1999) 7 BHRC 274, SC, there was violation of Fourth Amendment rights.
[758] PACE, s 10(2).
[759] See *R v Central Criminal Court, ex p Francis and Francis* [1989] AC 346; see para 12.17 above.
[760] (1992) 16 EHRR 97; cf D Harris, M O'Boyle and C Warbrick, *Law of the European Convention on Human Rights* (Butterworths, 1995) 345.

Niemetz approach is to be preferred. An interference with legal professional privilege will be disproportionate unless it can be shown that the solicitor, or perhaps his client, was intending to further a criminal purpose.[761]

(n) Prison law

The United Kingdom Government has been found to be in violation of Article 8 on three occasions in cases relating to prisoners' correspondence.[762] The relevant standing orders were modified to take account of these decisions.[763] However, the Human Rights Act may have an impact in a number of other areas.[764] Any impact of the privacy aspects of Article 8[765] would be on matters relating to access to the outside world.[766] It appears that the present regime dealing with correspondence and family visits is in conformity with Article 8 requirements. The restrictions on visits by journalists and communication with the media are considered under Article 10.[767]

12.219

Appendix 1: The Canadian Charter of Rights

(1) Introduction

The Canadian Charter of Rights and Freedoms makes no special provision for the constitutional protection of privacy. However, the Federal Privacy Act provides extensive protection for this right in ordinary domestic law and some provinces have also enacted legislation.[768]

12.220

Two important cases have considered the impact of the right to privacy under section 5 of the Quebec Charter of Human Rights and Freedoms. This provides that every person has the right to respect for his private life.

12.221

In *Godbout v Longueil*[769] the Supreme Court of Canada took a liberal view of the concept of privacy and said that its purpose was to protect a sphere of individual autonomy for all decisions relating to choices which are of fundamentally private or inherently personal nature. The city of Longueil had adopted a resolution which required all permanent employees to reside within its boundaries; and the plaintiff had signed a declaration agreeing that her employment would be terminated if she moved outside the city. She moved out of the city, was dismissed and brought an action for damages and reinstatement. The

12.222

---

[761] See Feldman (n 755, above) 447–51.

[762] See para 12.153 above.

[763] See S Livingstone and T Owen *Prison Law* (2nd edn, Oxford University Press, 1999) para 7.23.

[764] See the general discussion in Livingstone and Owen (n 763 above) para 16.42ff.

[765] For the 'family law' aspects, see para 13.78 below.

[766] For the present position, see Livingstone and Owen (n 763 above) Chap 7.

[767] See para 15.286 below.

[768] For a survey, see J Craig and N Nolte, 'Privacy and Free Speech in Germany and Canada: Lessons for an English Privacy Tort' [1998] EHRLR 162.

[769] [1997] 3 SCR 844.

Supreme Court decided that the residence requirement deprived the plaintiff of the right to privacy: it deprived the plaintiff of the ability to choose where to establish her home.

12.223   In *Aubry v Les Editions Vice-Versa*[770] the Supreme Court had to consider the extent to which 'privacy' rights would protect material gathered in a public place. A photograph was taken of a young woman sitting on a step in front of a building and was published without her consent by a magazine. She then brought proceedings against the magazine. The Supreme Court took the view that the right to individual autonomy included the ability to control the use made of one's image; and that this right was infringed when the image was published without consent, enabling an individual to be identified. However, the right to privacy had to be balanced against the right to freedom of expression. The Supreme Court held that the balance depends both on the nature of the information and the situation of those concerned and concluded that the plaintiff's right to protection of her image was more important than the artist's right to publish a photograph without first obtaining her consent.

12.224   The conflict between privacy and freedom of expression has been considered in a number of other cases.[771] In *Silber v BCTV*[772] a televison company decided to make a film about a long and bitter strike at the plaintiff's company. A television crew were attempting to film from the car park because the plaintiff had been uncooperative and a violent struggle ensued which was broadcast on television. When damages were sought under the provincial privacy legislation, the television company relied on a public interest defence; and succeeded on the ground that the filming of the struggle took place in a parking lot which was open to the public, that both the plaintiff and the strike were newsworthy and that the television company was motivated by a desire to inform the public about a serious issue in the community. By comparison, in *Valiquette v The Gazette*[773] a teacher recovered damages when a newspaper disclosed the fact he had AIDs. The public interest defence was rejected because the plaintiff was not himself a public figure, the newspaper was motivated primarily by commercial interests and the revelations seriously affected his health.

12.225   The right to privacy has also been embraced by the Supreme Court of Canada as the rationale for the guarantee against unreasonable search and seizure under section 8 of the Charter.[774] Under the common law, police and government authorities were precluded from entering private property without authorisation to search for evidence of crime, subject to two exceptions: they could search for and seize evidence without warrant if it was incidental to a lawful arrest, and they could obtain a judicial warrant on sworn evidence of a strong basis for belief that the goods are concealed in the place to be searched. The common law against unreasonable search and seizure was founded on the protection of property rights rather than privacy. Entry onto private premises was trespass and removal of goods or paper amounted to conversion. Outside of the law regarding invasion of property rights,

---

[770] [1998] 1 SCR 591.

[771] See eg in relation to Quebec, *Field v United Amusements* [1971] SC 283; *Rebeiro v Shawningan Chemicals* [1973] SC 389; and in relation to British Columbia, *Pierre v Pacific Press* [1994] 7 WWR 759, BCCA; *Hollinsworth v BCTV* (1996) 34 CCLT (2d) 95; and see generally, Craig and Nolte (n 768 above).

[772] (1986) 69 BCLR 34.

[773] (1992) 8 CCLT (2n) 302; the case was unsuccessfully appealed on 10 Dec 1996 unreported.

[774] Section 8 of the Charter guarantees the right to be secure against unreasonable search and seizure.

there was no prohibition against evidence derived from what state officials might see or hear. Moreover, some of the common law safeguards, such as warrants, have been overridden in Canadian jurisdictions by enactment of statutory powers of search and seizure which omit them. However, where the police took hair samples, buccal swabs, and teeth impressions from a 17-year-old arrested for a brutal murder but failed to seize them in accordance with the Criminal Code or under common law powers, the seizure was held to be highly intrusive and in breach of section 8.[775]

The value protected by the law of search and seizure has now shifted from property rights to privacy. The Supreme Court of Canada in its interpretation of section 8 in *Hunter v Southam*[776] held that the Charter guaranteed against unreasonable search and seizure protected a 'reasonable expectation of privacy'. In doing so, it followed the American decision in *Katz v United States*[777] which involved police placement of an electronic listening device on the outside of a public telephone booth to record the accused's end of a telephone conversation. In the absence of police trespass onto private property, the US Supreme Court found that the 'bug' was an infringement of the Fourth Amendment which prohibits 'unreasonable searches and seizures', on grounds that there had been an invasion of the 'reasonable expectation of privacy' relied upon by the accused in using the telephone booth. The Supreme Court of Canada in *Hunter v Southam* adopted the 'reasonable expectation of privacy' basis even though that case involved actual entry onto the premises of a corporation for the purposes of a combines investigation. It found that a corporation has the same constitutionally protected expectation of privacy as an individual, and, because the purpose of section 8 is to 'protect individuals from unjustified state intrusions upon their privacy', that an *ex post facto* determination as to reasonableness of the search would not suffice. It said that the purpose of the section 'requires a means of preventing unjustifiable searches before they happen, not simply of determining, after the fact, whether they ought to have occurred in the first place'. **12.226**

(2) Section 8 principles[778]

The basic principles which apply to the right to be secure against unreasonable search or seizure under section 8 were summarised in *R v Edwards*:[779] **12.227**

- A claim for relief under section 24(2) of the Charter can be made only by the person whose Charter rights have been infringed.[780]
- Like all Charter rights, section 8 is a personal right; it protects people, not places.[781]
- The right to challenge the legality of a search depends upon the accused establishing that his personal rights to privacy have been violated.[782]

---

[775] *R v Stillman* [1997] 1 SCR 607.
[776] *Hunter v Southam* [1984] 2 SCR 145.
[777] *Katz v United States* (1967) 389 US 347; cf *Minnesota v Carter* (1998) 5 BHRC 457 (in which the majority of the US Supreme Court took a restrictive approach to this case).
[778] See generally, J Fontana, *The Law of Search and Seizure in Canada* (3rd edn, Butterwoth-Heinemann 1992) and P Hogg, *Constitutional Law of Canada* (4th edn, Carswell, 1997) para 45.5.
[779] [1996] 1 SCR 128.
[780] *R v Rahey* [1987] 1 SCR 588, 619.
[781] *Hunter v Southam* [1984] 2 SCR 145; citing Stewart J in *Katz v United States* (1967) 389 US 347.
[782] *R v Pugliese* (1992) 71 CCC (3d) 295.

- As a general rule, two distinct inquiries must be made in relation to section 8. The first is whether the accused had a reasonable expectation of privacy; the second, if such an expectation is present, is whether the police search was conducted reasonably.
- A reasonable expectation of privacy is to be determined on the basis of the totality of the circumstances.[783]
- The factors to be considered in assessing the totality of the circumstances may include, but are not restricted to, the following:

  (a) presence at the time of the search;
  (b) possession or control of the property or place searched;
  (c) ownership of the property or place;
  (d) historical use of the property or item;
  (e) the ability to regulate access, including the right to admit or exclude others from the place;
  (f) the existence of a subjective expectation of privacy; and
  (g) the objective reasonableness of the expectation.

(3) A personal right

12.228 The essence of section 8 protection is the existence of a personal privacy right.[784] The right allegedly infringed will, therefore, be that of the person, most often the accused, who makes the challenge.

12.229 A personal right of privacy is not coterminous with a possessory or property interest in premises or articles,[785] although possession or ownership might properly be considered evidence of that personal right.[786] For example, as the applicant in *Pugliese*[787] was unable to advance any ground for privacy beyond ownership of the building in question, the Court concluded that he had no expectation of privacy in a leased apartment in the building or the portion of it from which drugs were seized. Neither did possession of a driver's licence in *Hufsky* give its owner any right to withhold it from the authorities. Instead, the courts have indicated that a key element in privacy is the right to be free from intrusion or interference,[788] an element which could not be established in *Edwards* in which the accused had been no more than a 'privileged guest' in the home of his girlfriend. Particularly relevant was the fact that it was not the accused but his girlfriend who had the authority to regulate access to, and exclude others from, the premises.

12.230 It is possible, in some circumstances, to establish an expectation of privacy in goods themselves.[789] Such was the case in relation to the records of a business proprietorship in *Thomson Newspapers*[790] which were subject to an order for production under the federal

---

[783] *R v Colarusso* (1984) 13 DLR (4th) 680.

[784] *R v Edwards* [1996] 45 CR (4th) 307, 318, SCC; *R v Pugliese* (1992) 71 CCC (3d) 295.

[785] Dickson J in *Hunter v Southam* [1984] 2 SCR 145 emphatically rejected any requirement of a connection between the section 8 right and a property interest in the premises searched.

[786] *R v Edwards* [1996] 45 CR (4th) 307, 318 quoting Finlayson JA in *R v Pugliese* (1992) 71 CCC (3d) 295.

[787] Ibid.

[788] *R v Edwards* (n 786 above) 321.

[789] *R v Edwards* (n 786 above) 319: the appellant sought unsuccessfully to assert a right in the drugs seized, after having maintained in the Court of Appeal that they did not belong to him. The SCC precluded him from changing his position so as to raise a fresh defence.

[790] *Thomson Newspapers Ltd v Canada* [1990] (*Director of Investigation and Research, Restrictive Trade Practices Commission*) 1 SCR 425.

Combines Investigation Act. The accused in *R v Plant*,[791] on the other hand, failed to establish a right of privacy in his electricity bills. The accused in *Edwards* was also unsuccessful in arguing that an interest in seized drugs[792] created a reasonable expectation of privacy.

The expectation of privacy by third parties is not relevant to the disposition of an application under section 8. In *R v Edwards*, the police conducted a drug search of the premises of the girlfriend of the accused, who was persuaded to allow them access without a warrant, in the absence of her boyfriend. The majority held the search to be constitutional as the accused had no reasonable expectation of privacy in the apartment. The rights of his girlfriend were not in issue before the Court, although it was acknowledged that the intrusion of the search on third parties might have been relevant to the reasonableness of the search in the second stage of the analysis, had it been necessary to go that far.[793] Contrary to the view of the majority, Judge La Forest felt that section 8 protects a public interest in security from intrusion by unwarranted police searches and that the expectation of privacy of the girlfriend ought to have been taken into account in the first stage.

12.231

(4) Section 8 analysis: a two-step process

(a) Introduction

The determination as to whether section 8 has been infringed is a two stage process.[794] The expectation of privacy is relevant to each stage. First, the presence (or absence) of a reasonable expectation of privacy is relevant to whether the activity in question constitutes a search or seizure. Secondly, once a search or seizure has been established, the court must assess its reasonableness; and presumes the search or seizure is reasonable unless the contrary is proved. Where a reasonable expectation exists, but in a diminished form, the threshold will be lowered and the presumption of unreasonableness more easily rebutted. Whether a reasonable expectation of privacy exists is to be ascertained without reference to the police conduct during the search[795] or to the seriousness of the alleged offences.[796] Whether the search constitutes an unreasonable intrusion on that right to privacy is a separate question.

12.232

(b) 'Reasonable expectation of privacy'

The existence of a 'search' or 'seizure'. The Supreme Court of Canada has followed the American decision in *Katz*[797] to hold that electronic surveillance is a search or seizure under section 8 of the Charter.[798] A reasonable expectation of privacy is violated when a telephone conversation is intercepted without the knowledge or consent of the participants.[799]

12.233

---

[791] *R v Plant* [1993] 3 SCR 281.
[792] *R v Edwards* (n 786 above) 319; see also *R v Sandhu* (1993) 82 CCC (3d) 236 in which the question of ownership of a suitcase for drug delivery arose.
[793] *R v Edwards* (n 786 above) 316 for the two stages see para 12.232 below.
[794] *R v Edwards* [1996] 45 CR (4th) 307, 316 *per* Cory J.
[795] Ibid.
[796] *R v Plant* [1993] 3 SCR 281.
[797] *Katz v United States* (1967) 389 US 347.
[798] *R v Duarte* [1990] 1 SCR 30.
[799] *R v Thompson* [1990] 2 SCR 1111.

12.234 The Supreme Court has, however, refused to distinquish between 'participant electronic surveillance', in which one party to a conversation or interaction consents to its surreptitious electronic recording, and 'third-party electronic surveillance', in which none of the parties consents. In *Duarte*[800] the police obtained the cooperation of an informer to enable them to instal audio-visual equipment on his premises and to record his drug transaction with the accused; in *R v Wiggins*[801] the informer consented to wear a microphone which transmitted his conversations with the accused about the drug dealings to the police. In each of these cases, the surreptitious recording was found to invade a reasonable expectation of privacy. The difficulty with this approach is that the breaching of confidence is not an invasion of privacy and disclosure of a private conversation by one of the parties is therefore admissible evidence. As a result, evidence from informers is admissible whereas electronic recordings of a conversation is not.[802] Another problem is that if the recording is an invasion of privacy, it is so whether or not it is tendered as evidence, and thus police are prohibited from using recording devices even as a means of protection of undercover officers or informers.

12.235 In spite of these difficulties, the Supreme Court of Canada has maintained the view that a participant does not accept the risk of disclosure by another participant. It has extended the finding of reasonable expectation of privacy from private telephone conversations to the video-taping of an illegal gambling operation in a crowded hotel room. In *R v Wong*[803] the hotel consented to the installation of a hidden camera, and although few of the guests knew one another, the Court found that the recording of events in the room invaded their reasonable expectation of privacy, in violation of the Charter.

12.236 As a result, the police in Canada can lawfully use electronic surveillance techniques only where there is no reasonable expectation of privacy, such as a conversation or transaction taking place on the street or in a public venue. The Charter would not apply to a recording initiated by a private individual, but if, for example a shop proprietor installed a video camera at the suggestion of the police, he might be deemed an agent of the police.[804]

12.237 The collection of evidence, even in the absence of a search, might also amount to a 'seizure' on the basis of reasonable expectation of privacy. In *R v Dyment*[805] a doctor collected blood from the wound of an unconscious traffic accident victim for medical purposes, but then delivered it to a police officer for analysis, resulting in charges of impaired driving against the victim. Although section 8 did not apply to the private act of collection of the sample by the doctor, the Court found that the receipt of the sample by the police officer, without warrant and without the consent, was an unreasonable 'seizure' violating the expectation of privacy of the accused. The Court also used the expectation of privacy to distinguish the 'gathering' of evidence from that of an unconstitutional taking, citing the example of police collection of blood from the seat of a car, rather than that flowing from

---

800 *R v Duarte* [1990] 1 SCR 30.
801 *R v Wiggins* [1990] 1 SCR 62.
802 Evidence obtained in breach of the Charter is not admissible, unless it can be shown that the police were unaware that they had violated the Charter and were acting in good faith.
803 *R v Wong* [1990] 3 SCR 36.
804 *R v Broyles* [1991] 3 SCR 595 where a friend of a suspect visiting the suspect in prison at the suggestion of the police, and recording their conversation, was a police agent.
805 [1988] 2 SCR 417.

a wound. The individual in the former case would be considered to have 'abandoned' the blood, retaining no reasonable expectation of privacy in regard to it.

Where there is a reasonable expectation of privacy in relation to documents, an order for **12.238** their production also constitutes a 'search' or 'seizure' under section 8. In *R v Hufsky*[806] a demand by a police officer that a driver produce a driver's licence and vehicle insurance certificate was found not to be a 'search' under the section because it did not intrude on a reasonable expectation of privacy. It was clear that there could be no such intrusion by way of a request for evidence of compliance with a requirement that is a lawful condition of the exercise of a right or privilege.[807] While there is no reasonable expectation of privacy in regard to a motor vehicle licence, such expectation does exist in regard to business records.

In order for constitutional protection to be extended to commercial documents, the in- **12.239** formation seized must be of a 'personal and confidential nature';[808] this would include information revealing intimate details of the lifestyle of its owner. The computerised records of electricity consumption were found in *Plant*[809] to reflect a purely commercial relationship between appellant and utility, because they revealed little personal information of the occupant of the residence, and were available to the public. By contrast, in *Thomson Newspapers v Canada*[810] the records of a business proprietor were characterised as confidential communications. There, the order under the federal Combines Investigation Act to produce the documents was found to be a 'seizure', even though there was no entry or search of premises[811] on grounds that there was 'little difference between taking a thing and forcing a person to give it up'.[812]

The reasonableness of the search or seizure.   The expectation of privacy will also, **12.240** to some extent, be relevant in the assessment of the reasonableness of the search or seizure. The test of reasonableness was established by unanimous decision of the Supreme Court of Canada in *Hunter v Southam*;[813] the power of search and seizure in the Combines Investigation Act was found to infringe section 8 of the Charter because it authorised 'unreasonable' searches and seizures. The Court decided that a search or seizure is presumed to be unreasonable; and acknowledged that it would not always be feasible to satisfy the prescribed criteria. Nevertheless, a search without a warrant might be justified if a presumption of unreasonableness could be rebutted.

In relation to electronic surveillance, provided the requirements of the Criminal Code for **12.241** 'wiretaps' have been met,[814] the search or seizure will be not only lawful, but will not be

---

[806] [1988] 1 SCR 621; followed by *R v Ladouceur* [1990] 1 SCR 1257.

[807] *R v Hufsky* [1988] 1 SCR 621, 638.

[808] *R v Plant* [1993] 3 SCR 281.

[809] Ibid.

[810] [1990] 1 SCR 425.

[811] *Thomson Newspapers v Canada* [1990] 1 SCR 425.

[812] Note, though, that ultimately the seizure was found to be a reasonable one, in spite of the fact that it had been authorised by the investigating agency, rather than a court, on grounds that a demand to produce is far less intrusive upon privacy than an actual search of premises.

[813] *Hunter v Southam* [1984] 2 SCR 145: the Court said that a search was reasonable only if it was authorised by statute which stipulated three conditions: a prior warrant or other authorisation; issued by a person 'capable of acting judicially'; and on oath that there are 'reasonable and probable grounds' for believing that an offence has been committed and that evidence is located in the place to be searched.

[814] The Criminal Code requires a judicial warrant obtained on reasonable and probable grounds to authorise the electronic interception of telephone conversations.

'unreasonable' under section 8 of the Charter.[815] In subsequent cases, the Court has held the presumption of unreasonableness to be rebutted where the search or seizure is not significantly intrusive, or where the expectation of privacy itself is diminished, or both.[816]

12.242   The order for production of documents in *Thomson Newspapers*, for example, was considered minimally intrusive, in comparison with the imposition of an actual search, upon the undiminished expectation of privacy in the documents. As a result, the order for production, though issued under non-judicial authorisation, resulted in a reasonable 'seizure' when held up to a reduced standard or threshold of reasonableness in the circumstances. In *Plant*, on the other hand, the lower court decision that a perimeter search of premises was not unreasonable, given its minimal level of intrusion, was overturned by the Supreme Court of Canada which found that it could not be justified without warrant.

12.243   A lower expectation of privacy will also reduce the standard of reasonableness so as not to require fulfilment of the warrant requirements of *Hunter v Southam*. This will occur, for example, where prison inmates, while having some expectation of privacy, might be subject to random or routine searches of their person or cells;[817] in a school context, where it has been held reasonable for a teacher to search a student without warrant for possession of drugs;[818] at an international border, where the absence of a warrant requirement in the Customs Act was reasonable;[819] or during travel in an automobile.[820] The expectation of privacy will also be less if the activity in question is regulated: administrative inspections of commercial premises, or even private homes in order to check for compliance with building standards, zoning rules, public health and safety requirements are not unreasonable searches[821] and confiscation of an illegal or dangerous or diseased thing without a warrant in such circumstances is not an unreasonable seizure.[822]

---

[815]   See also *R v Garafoli* [1990] 2 SCR 1421; *R v Lachance* [1990] 2 SCR 1490; *Dersch v Can* [1990] 2 SCR 1505; *R v Zito* [1990] 2 SCR 1520.

[816]   See *R v Wise* [1992] 11 CR (4th) 253 which held that the expectation of privacy in a motor vehicle is reduced in comparison to that in a home or office and that installation of an unsophisticated tracking device in the interior of the motor vehicle was only minimally intrusive.

[817]   *Weatherall v Canada* [1991] 1 FC 85.

[818]   *R v JMG* (1986) 56 OR (2d) 705.

[819]   *R v Simmons* [1988] 2 SCR 495.

[820]   *R v Wise* [1992] 11 CR (4th) 253: the expectation of privacy in automobile travel is markedly decreased relative to the expectation of privacy in one's home or office; in *R v Belnais* [1997] 3 SCR 341 the Supreme Court held that the reasonable expectation depends on the totality of the circumstances.

[821]   See *Re Belgoma Transportation* (1985) 51 OR (2d) 509: employment standards; *R v Quesnel* (1985) 53 OR (2d) 338: marketing board inspection; *R v Bichel* (1986) 33 DLR (4th) 254: building inspection of private home; *Ontario Chrysler (1997) Ltd v Ontario* (1990) 72 OR (2d) 106: business practices inspection.

[822]   *R v Bertram S Miller* [1986] 3 FC 291: (confiscation and destruction of diseased plants); *Re Ozubko* (1986) 33 DLR (4th) 714 Man CA: (confiscation of illegal syringe); *Re Milton* (1986) 37 DLR (4th) 694: (confiscation of illegal fishing nets).

Appendix 2: The New Zealand Bill of Rights Act

(1) Introduction

Like the Canadian Charter of Rights and Freedoms, the New Zealand Bill of Rights Act **12.244**
1990 makes no express provision for the guarantee of respect to privacy. Section 21 of the
New Zealand Bill of Rights Act provides that:

Unreasonable search and seizure

Everyone has the right to be secure against unreasonable search or seizure, whether of the person, property or correspondence or otherwise.

The final words reflect the Fourth Amendment in the American Bill of Rights and have
some similarity to the privacy provision of the European Convention. The New Zealand
courts have followed the Canadian example and have dealt with the concept of privacy
under the heading of the section 21 guarantee against unreasonable search and seizure.

(2) The interpretation of section 21

The New Zealand approach to reasonableness of search and seizure places less emphasis **12.245**
on the protection of privacy than does that of the Canadian courts. Whether a search or
seizure has been unreasonable and evidence unfairly or improperly obtained is determined
by balancing all of the relevant interests in the circumstances, including, but not focusing
exclusively on an 'expectation of privacy'.

The Court of Appeal first considered the relationship of privacy to search and seizure in **12.246**
R v Jeffries,[823] in which the police, believing the accused and his companions to be fleeing
an armed robbery, stopped and searched the vehicle they were driving for weapons and
stolen goods. The search, conducted without warrant, would have been lawful under the
Arms Act had they identified themselves properly and advised the suspects of the section
of the Act under which the search was to take place; they did not so comply with the
statute and the search of the boot of the car revealed not arms but $30,000 worth of
cannabis. The issue before the Court of Appeal was whether the search was reasonable
under the New Zealand Bill of Rights Act. Five of the seven judges agreed that a search
may be 'unlawful' and yet reasonable under the Bill of Rights Act; four found that although the search was unlawful it had not been rendered unreasonable. Two judges held
that the search was lawful and reasonable; one judge in dissent held the unlawful search
was *ipso facto* unreasonable. The cannabis was admitted as evidence in the trial of the accused.

After consideration of the Canadian position on the relationship of privacy to the reason- **12.247**
ableness of a search,[824] Richardson J stated that: an analysis of section 21 would emphasise four considerations:

(i)   rights of the citizen reflect an amalgam of values: property, personal freedom, privacy
      and dignity. A search of premises or the person is an invasion of property rights, a restraint on individual liberty, an intrusion on privacy and an affront to dignity.

---

[823] [1994] 1 NZLR 290.
[824] In particular *Hunter v Southam* (1984) 14 CCC 3d 97 and the US case of *Katz v United States*
389 US 347.

(ii) neither the Bill of Rights Act nor the International Covenant provides a general guarantee of privacy, and New Zealand did not have a general privacy law. There is no one privacy value that applies in all cases; rather, the nature and significance of a privacy value depends on the circumstances in which it arises.

(iii) a section 21 inquiry is an exercise in balancing competing values and interests; in particular, the legitimate state interests in detection and prosecution of offending against the immunity of citizens from arbitrary and unlawful searches of their property and persons. Whether the intrusion is 'unreasonable' involves weighing all relevant public interest considerations and their application in the particular case.

(iv) protection against unreasonable search or seizure must be distinguished from a 'reasonable expectation of privacy'. The two would be the same if one could ignore the interests of society as a whole or the interests of anyone other than the person whose privacy is affected, but rights are never absolute and individual freedoms are necessarily limited by membership of society.

A section 21 assessment must start with the presumption that any search is a significant invasion of individual freedom. How significant it is will depend on the particular circumstances and the other values and interests including law enforcement considerations which weigh in the particular case.

The intrusiveness of the search and the extent of the violation of individual rights vary according to the subject-matter of the search and the manner in which it is carried out. Thus, frisking an individual is less intrusive than a search of body cavities; the home is more a sanctuary than the office. Reasonable expectations of privacy are lower in public places than within private property. While in a mobile society the privacy of one's motor vehicle is highly valued and may be perceived as a projection of the privacy of the home, road safety and the legitimate protection of other users of the roads justify extensive rules governing the use of vehicles and allowing surveillance and supervision of vehicles, drivers and passengers. The expectation of privacy may be less where the property searched belongs to a third party, particularly where that person purports to consent to the search, and the complainant is a guest or family member or shares the use of the property. The manner in which a search is carried out will also affect the degree of any intrusion on private rights. It follows that in assessing the reasonableness of a search or seizure it is important to consider 'both the subject-matter and the time, place and circumstance'.

12.248   Since 1994, the New Zealand Court of Appeal has been inundated with section 21 cases.[825] The Court has preferred the 'amalgam of values' approach taken in *Jeffries* to the 'expectation of privacy' perspective of the American and Canadian jurisprudence. The test of unreasonableness of a search or seizure involves an assessment of all of the circumstances: the relevant values and public interest considerations and their application in the particular case.[826]

---

[825] See eg *R v A* [1994] 1 NZLR 429; *R v H* [1994] 2 NZLR 143; *R v Ririnui* [1994] 2 NZLR 439; *R v Pratt* [1994] 3 NZLR 21; *Simpson v A-G (Baigent's case)* [1994] 3 NZLR 667; *Auckland Unemployed Workers' Rights Centre Inc v A-G* [1994] 3 NZLR 720; *R v McNicol* [1995] 1 NZLR 576; *R v Kahu* [1995] 2 NZLR 3; *R v Stockdale* [1995] 2 NZLR 129; *Television New Zealand Ltd v A-G* [1995] 2 NZLR 641; *R v Reuben* [1995] 3 NZLR 165; *R v Wojcik* (1994) 11 CRNZ 463; *Campbell v Police* [1994] 3 NZLR 260; *R v Wong-Tung* (1995) 13 CRNZ 422; *R v Smith* (1996) 13 CRNZ 481; *R v Barlow* (1995) 14 CRNZ 9; *R v Faasipa* (1995) 2 HRNZ 50; *Queen Street Backpackers Ltd v Commerce Commission* (1994) 2 HRNZ 94; *R v Dodgson* (1995) 2 HRNZ 300.

[826] *R v A* [1994] 1 NZLR 429; *R v Pratt* [1994] 3 NZLR 21, 24: the test 'whether the circumstances giving rise to it make the search itself unreasonable or if a search that is otherwise reasonable is carried out in an unreasonable manner'.

While *Jeffries* established that lawfulness does not always determine reasonableness, or vice **12.249**
versa, the unlawfulness of a search and seizure is highly relevant to reasonableness.[827] If a
warrant is readily obtainable, that will tell strongly against the reasonableness of an unauthorised search.[828] Only in rare cases will an unlawful search and seizure be reasonable.[829]
So for example, in *R v H* where the police deliberately decided to refrain from obtaining a
search warrant readily available under the Summary Proceedings Act, the search of the
premises of an accountant and seizure of the company records was found to be unreasonable. The principles were restated by the Court of Appeal in *R v Grayson and Taylor*.[830] In
that case, the police observed suspicious activity, including the construction of an electric
fence and erection of shadecloth on the appellants' kiwi fruit orchard. Believing that they
did not have enough evidence to obtain a search warrant, the police entered the property
for the purposes of corroborating the information they had received. The entry involved
negotiating electric fences and thick underbrush, but was not forceful. During their five
minutes on the property, the officers observed rows of cannabis plants growing between
the kiwifruit vines. A search warrant was subsequently obtained and surveillance videos
taken, plants seized and appellants charged with cultivation of cannabis. The trial judge
found the initial search unlawful but not unreasonable. The Court of Appeal dismissed
the appeal and held that in all the circumstances, entry onto the property was reasonable
and the evidence admissible.

The Court of Appeal in *Grayson* has set out a number of statutory and common law prin- **12.250**
ciples relevant to a challenge to the admissibility of evidence on grounds of breach of section 21. It was pointed out that entry and search of private property by state officials,
without permission, is an actionable trespass,[831] but that evidence obtained by illegal
searches is admissible, subject only to a discretion to exclude it on the ground of unfairness
to the accused.[832] This basis for a challenge to admissibility is not affected by section 21.
The Court noted that section 21 is a restraint on governmental action that does not confer any positive power[833] on the state to conduct a 'reasonable search'.

The Court of Appeal went on to hold that: **12.251**

> A search is unreasonable if the circumstances giving rise to it make the search itself unrea-
> sonable or if a search which would otherwise be reasonable is carried out in an unreasonable
> manner. So too seizure. Whether a police search or seizure is unreasonable depends on both
> the subject-matter and the particular time, place and circumstance.[834]

A prime purpose of section 21 is to ensure that governmental power is not exercised unreasonably. A section 21 enquiry is an exercise in balancing legitimate state interests
against any intrusions on individual interests. It requires weighing relevant values and
public interests.[835] The guarantee under section 21 to be free from unreasonable search
and seizure reflects an amalgam of values. A search of premises is an invasion of property
rights and an intrusion on privacy. It may also involve a restraint on individual liberty and

---

[827] See *R v H* [1994] 2 NZLR 143, 148.
[828] Ibid 148.
[829] *R v Pratt* [1994] 3 NZLR 21, 24.
[830] [1997] 1 NZLR 399.
[831] Ibid Principle 1, 406.
[832] Ibid Principle 2, 407.
[833] Ibid Principle 3, 407.
[834] Ibid Principle 4.
[835] Ibid Principle 5.

an affront to dignity. Any search is a significant invasion of individual freedom. How significant it will be depends on the circumstances.[836]

12.252 The Court gave express consideration to the role of 'privacy' in connection with the reasonableness of searches under section 21:

> Contemporary society attaches a high value to privacy and to the security of personal privacy against arbitrary intrusions by those in authority. Privacy values underlying the section 21 guarantee are those held by the community at large. They are not merely the subjective expectations of privacy which a particular owner or occupier may have and may demonstrate by signs or barricades. Reasonable expectations of privacy are lower in public places than on private property. They are higher for the home than for the surrounding land and for land not used for residential purposes. And the nature of the activities carried on, particularly if involving public engagement or governmental oversight, may affect reasonable expectations of privacy. An assessment of the seriousness of the particular intrusion involves considerations of fact and degree, not taking absolutist stances. In that regard, and unlike the thrust of the American Fourth Amendment jurisprudence, the object of section 21 is vindication of individual rights rather than deterrence and disciplining of police misconduct.[837]

Taking these matters into account, illegality was not the touchstone of unreasonableness. In terms of section 21, what is unlawful is not necessarily unreasonable. The lawfulness or unlawfulness of a search will always be highly relevant but will not be determinative either way.[838]

12.253 After considering the specific provisions of New Zealand law in relation to search warrants, the Court summarised the position in relation to the Bill of Rights Act as follows:

> The Bill of Rights is not a technical document. It has to be applied in our society in a realistic way. The application and interpretation of the Bill must also be true to its purposes as set out in its title of affirming, protecting and promoting human rights and fundamental freedoms in New Zealand, and affirming New Zealand's commitment to the International Covenant on Civil and Political Rights. The crucial question is whether what was done constituted an unreasonable search or seizure in the particular circumstances. Anyone complaining of a breach must invest the complaint with an air of reality and must lay a foundation for the complaint before the trial Court by explicit challenge or cross-examination or evidence.[839]

12.254 There are a large number of the decisions dealing with admissibility of evidence obtained under unlawful searches. A minor non-compliance with statutory procedural requirements was not sufficient to render a search 'unreasonable'.[840] The 'close surveillance' of a prisoner, involving collection and examination of bowel motions, was not unreasonable where authorities believed that he had controlled drugs secreted within his body for an unlawful purpose. The heroin packets recovered were admissible and the procedures, although 'draconian' were reasonable in the interests of the health of the prisoner and for prison safety.[841] However, evidence has been excluded in a number of search cases. In *R v*

---

[836] Ibid Principle 6.
[837] Ibid Principle 6.
[838] Ibid Principle 7.
[839] Ibid Principle 10, 409.
[840] *R v Jeffries* [1994] 1 NZLR 290.
[841] *R v Stockdale* [1995] 2 NZLR 129.

Pratt[842] the defendant had been strip searched in the street. The police had found keys in his pocket which were used to gain access to a building in which a quantity of cocaine was discovered. The evidence of the finding of the keys and what the police did with them was excluded. In *Frost v Police*[842a] the use of dogs and other forceful measures by police after two noise complaints were not reasonable, given that the intent was to conduct a warrantless search for drugs under the auspices of noise control legislation at premises where drug dealing was suspected, police had had ample time to obtain a search warrant. The courts have also excluded evidence from the warrantless search of bags in the back of the accused's car[842b] and of a car boot.[842c] When property was thrown away by an accused in the course of an unlawful and unreasonable search this was sufficiently linked to breaches of section 21 to require its exclusion.[842d]

(3) Electronic surveillance

(a) Non-participant surveillance

In *R v Fraser*[843] the police video-taped an accused drug dealer apparently concealing items **12.255** in the garden of an address where he was not a resident. The surveillance took place from outside the private property without a warrant. Under the Summary Proceedings Act, the police could have obtained a warrant to 'enter' and search for 'things', but the Court found that no such warrant was necessary to conduct a video-recording in the open area outside a private residence. The search was lawful, as there was no statutory or common law prohibition against observing or video-taping the open area surrounding a residential property.

Nevertheless, the search was not necessarily reasonable under the Bill of Rights Act; this **12.256** depended on what the accused might reasonably be subjected to in the circumstances, having regard to standards of the community concerning respect for privacy. It was necessary to consider all the circumstances prevailing at the time the search was undertaken and to balance the legitimate interests of the individual to a reasonable expectation of privacy with those of the state in the detection and prosecution of criminal activities. The Court found no evidence that the accused could have expected not to be observed in the area covered by the video camera. A similar result was reached in *R v Peita*[843a] where cannabis was discovered growing on the appellant's farm by a police spotter plane. It was held that the conduct of the aerial surveillance was not unreasonable and that evidence discovered as a result of that activity was admissible.

(b) Participant recording

In relation to 'participant recording' or 'participant surveillance' the New Zealand Court **12.257** has followed the United States rather than the Canadian approach and held that such surveillance is not unreasonable under the Act. The Court in *R v A*[844] provided four reasons for this position:

---

[842] [1994] 3 NZLR 21; see also *R v McNicol* [1995] 1 NZLR 576; *R v Kahu* [1995] 2 NZLR 3; *Campbell v Police* [1994] 3 NZLR 260.

[842a] [1996] 2 NZLR 716.

[842b] *Longley v Police* [1995] 1 NZLR 87.

[842c] *R v Brainbridge* (1999) 5 HRNZ 317.

[842d] Ibid, distinguishing *R v Reuben* [1995] 3 NZLR 165.

[843] [1997] 2 NZLR 442.

[843a] (1999) 5 HRNZ 250.

[844] [1994] 1 NZLR 429.

- It is not unlawful for any participant in a conversation to record a discussion surreptitiously. There is no basis in parliamentary consideration of electronic surveillance for the courts to conclude that public policy requires treatment of participant recording as inherently destructive of basic values.
- Advances in information technology have advantages as well as risks. The social answer to the problem turns on an examination of all of the circumstances rather than on an impossible quest for universally agreed moral absolutes. It is a matter of time, place and circumstance.
- The expectation of privacy, while important, is not the only consideration in determining whether a search or seizure is unreasonable.
- Characterising participant recording as always constituting unreasonable search and seizure would have significant consequences contrary to the public interest. First, if such recording is a breach of section 21 it would, *prima facie*, be excluded from evidence, while the intrusion on privacy would have occurred in any event. Secondly, it would necessarily inhibit the police from wiring a police officer for safety reasons.

Appendix 3: Human Rights Cases in Other Jurisdictions

(1) Introduction

12.258 The right to privacy is protected under the civil and criminal law of most European states. In France, Article 9 of the Civil Code was introduced in 1970 and provides for the right to 'respect for privacy'. This has now been recognised as a 'constitutional right'.[845] The German courts have developed a general 'right to personality' which has enabled them to protect a range of privacy rights.[846] The protection of privacy rights in Italy has also been a matter for judge made law.[847]

12.259 In many common law jurisdictions the right to privacy is now the subject of statutory protection.[848] The right has, however, been the subject of sustained consideration in the constitutional context in the American courts where the right has been recognised as covering both the interest in avoiding the disclosure of personal information and the 'interest in independence in making certain kinds of important decisions'.[849] This right has been used to provide constitutional protection for the use of contraception,[850] the distribution of

---

[845] See generally, E Picard, 'The Right to Privacy in French Law', in B Markesinis (ed), *Protecting Privacy* (Oxford University Press, 1999).

[846] See generally, P Quint, 'Free Speech and Private Law in German Constitutional Theory' (1989) 48 Maryland L Rev 247–346; B Markesinis, 'Privacy, Freedom of Expression and the Horizontal Effect of the Human Rights Bill: Lessons from Germany' [1999] 115 LQR 47; H Stoll, 'General Rights to Personality in German Law' in Markesinis (n 845 above); and see, J Craig and N Nolte, 'Privacy and Free Speech in Germany and Canada: Lessons for an English Privacy Tort' [1998] EHRLR 162.

[847] See G Alpa, 'Protection of Privacy in Italian Law' in Markesinis (n 845 above).

[848] See for example the Privacy Act 1988 (Australia).

[849] *Whalen v Roe* (1977) 429 US 589, 599–600 *per* Stevens J; a full discussion is outside the scope of this book but see generally, L Tribe, *American Constitutional Law* (2nd edn, Foundation Press, 1988) Chap 15 and also D Anderson, 'The Failure of American Privacy Law' in Markesinis (n 846 above).

[850] *Griswold v Connecticut* (1965) 381 US 479 (criminal law prohibiting the use of contraceptive unconstitutional).

contraceptives to unmarried persons[851] and abortion.[852] The right has not, however, been extended to sexual privacy generally, the Supreme Court refusing to strike down statutes criminalising sodomy.[853] Furthermore, the right to privacy is subject to freedom of expression rights, and the publication of false private information will only be actionable if malicious.[854]

The Fourth Amendment to the US Constitution affirms the right of the people to be secure 'in their persons, houses, papers and effects, against unreasonable searches and seizures'. This provision embodies the principle of respect for privacy of the home,[854a] but not a general right of privacy.[854b] It also protects persons on office premises[854c] overnight guests in hostels[854d] or houses[854e] but does not extend to 'open fields'[854f] or to a visitor to a house.[854g] It also covers the use of hidden microphones and telephone tapping,[854h] but not aerial inspection of a garden.[854i] Government officials are not permitted to undertake searches or seizures without an 'individualised suspicion' unless it was based on 'special needs' beyond the normal requirements of law enforcement.[854j]

12.259A

(2) Human Rights Committee[855]

Article 17 of the International Covenant on Civil and Political Rights provides that:

12.260

(1) No one shall be subjected to arbitrary or unlawful interference with his privacy home or correspondence, nor to unlawful attacks on his honour and reputation.

(2) Everyone has the right to the protection of the law against such interferences or attacks.

---

[851] *Eisenstad v Baird* (1972) 405 US 438.

[852] *Roe v Wade* (1973) 410 US 113 (law prohibiting abortion unconstitutional); this was, of course, one of the most controversial decisions of modern times, see generally, Tribe (n 849 above) para 15 10 and also *Planned Parenthood v Casey* (1992) 505 US 833.

[853] *Bowers v Hardwick* (1986) 478 US 186; but see *Romer v Evans* (1996) 517 US 620 (Colorado constitutional amendment prohibiting action designed to protect homosexuals from discrimination unconstitutional under Fourteenth Amendment 'Equal Protection' provisions); see generally, Tribe (n 849 above) para 15–21 and R Wintemute, *Sexual Orientation and Human Rights* (Clarendon Press, 1995) Chaps 2 and 3.

[854] *Time Inc v Hill* (1967) 385 US 374.

[854a] *Wilson v Layne* (1999) 7 BHRC 274 ('media ride alongs' unconstitutional).

[854b] *Katz v United States* (1967) 389 US 347, 350.

[854c] *Gouled v United States* (1921) 255 US 298.

[854d] *Lustig v United States* (1949) 338 US 74.

[854e] *Minnesota v Olson* (1990) 495 US 91.

[854f] *Oliver v United States* (1984) 466 US 170.

[854g] *Minnesotav v Carter* (1998) 5 BHRC 457.

[854h] *Katz v United States* (n 854b above; *United States v United States District Court for Eastern District of Michegan* (1972) 407 US 297.

[854i] *California v Ciraolo* (1986) 476 US 207; *Florida v Riley* (1989) 488 US 445.

[854j] *Chandler v Miller* (1997) 3 BHRC 234 (drug testing programme for candidates for state office unconstitutional); contrast the drug testing programmes approved in *National Treasury Employees Union v Von Raab* (1989) 489 US 109 (customs officials) and *Vernonia School District 47J v Acton* (1995) 515 US 646 (high school students engaged in athletic competitions).

[855] See generally, J Michael, 'Privacy' in D Harris and S Joseph (eds), *The International Covenant on Civil and Political Rights and United Kingdom Law* (Clarendon Press, 1995) 333–354.

This provision does not, unlike other Articles, specify the grounds on which a state party may interfere with privacy.

12.261 An interference will be 'unlawful' unless it is authorised by a domestic law which itself complies with 'the provisions, aims and objectives of the Covenant'.[856] An interference can be arbitrary even if it is lawful. The concept of arbitrariness is intended to guarantee that an interference is 'reasonable' in the circumstances.[857] Article 17 is the subject matter of General Comment 16, in which it was stated that:

> the competent public authorities should only be able to call for such information relating to an individual's private life the knowledge of which is essential in the interests of society as understood under the Covenant.[858]

12.262 In *Toonen v Australia*[859] the Committee took the view that the requirement of 'reasonableness' implied that 'any interference with privacy must be proportional to the end sought and be necessary in the circumstances of any given case'. It was held that laws in Tasmania prohibiting sex between men were an arbitrary interference with privacy.[860]

(3) India

12.263 Article 21 of the Constitution of India provides that:

> No person shall be deprived of his life or personal liberty except according to procedure established by law.

The Supreme Court has held that a right to privacy is implicit in this provision.[861] In *Rajagopal v State of Tamil Nadu*[862] B P Jeevan Reddy J summarised the position in relation to this implicit right as follows:

> This is a 'right to be let alone'. A citizen has a right to safeguard the privacy of his own, his family, marriage, procreation, motherhood, child-bearing and education among other matters. None can publish anything concerning the above matters without his consent— whether truthful or otherwise or whether laudatory or critical. If he did so, he would be violating the right to privacy of the person concerned . . .[863]

There are, however, exceptions in relation to the publication of information based on public records and the right to privacy is not available if public officials are acting in the course of their official duties unless, in the latter case, the publication is made with reckless disregard for the truth.[864]

---

856 General Comment 16 para 3.
857 Ibid paras 4 and 8.3.
858 Ibid para 7.
859 488/1992, 31 Mar 1994, UNHRC.
860 Cf the discussion in R Wintemute, *Sexual Orientation and Human Rights* (Clarendon Press, 1995) 143–149.
861 *Kharak Singh v State of UP* [1964] 1 SCR 332; *Gobind v State of MP* (1975) 2 SCC 148; *Rajagopal v State of Tamil Nadu* [1995] 3 LRC 566.
862 Ibid 581e.
863 Ibid 581d–f.
864 Ibid 581f–582b.

In *People's Union for Civil Liberties v Union of India*[865] it was held that telephone tapping **12.264** infringed Article 21 which had to be interpreted in accordance with Article 17 of the International Covenant on Civil and Political Rights.[866] Although there were statutory restrictions on the power to intercept messages or conversations, these had to be backed by procedural safeguards to ensure that the power was exercised in a fair and reasonable manner.[867] It was held that, as the Government had laid down no procedural safeguards it was necessary for the Court to do so. The Court specified who should authorise telephone tapping, the duration and scope of authorisations, the records which should be maintained and the limits on the use of intercepted material.

(4) Ireland[868]

The Irish Constitution does not make express provision for any right to privacy. In the **12.265** 1980s the courts rejected a number of attempts to establish such a right.[869] However, the right was finally recognised in the 'telephone tapping' case of *Kennedy v Ireland*.[870] It was held that:

> although not specifically guaranteed by the Constitution, the right to privacy is one of the fundamental personal rights of the citizen which flow from the Christian and democratic nature of the State. It is not an unqualified right. Its exercise may be restricted by the constitutional rights of others, or by the requirements of the common good, and it is subject to the requirements of public order and morality.

As a result, it was held that the unjustifiable tapping of the plaintiffs' telephones by the state was a breach of their rights to privacy. In one case,[871] the Supreme Court was prepared to assume, for the purpose of argument, that there might be a right to privacy in a public street. However, police surveillance was justified in that case and in a case in which a person in police custody was kept under observation.[872] In *Redmond v Mr Justice Flood*[873] the applicant complained that public hearings of a statutory tribunal relating to certain planning matters were an interference with his right to privacy. The Supreme Court dismissed the application holding that the constitutional right to privacy was not an absolute one and could be outweighed by the exigencies of the common good. The inquiry in question had to be held in public for the purpose of allaying the public disquiet that led to its appointment.

(5) South Africa

The Constitution of South Africa provides: **12.266**

> (14) Everyone has the right to privacy, which includes the right not to have—

---

[865] [1999] 2 LRC 1.

[866] See App J in Vol 2. It was also held that telephone tapping infringed rights of freedom of expression under Art 19 of the Constitution, see para 15.362 below.

[867] Applying *Maneka Ghandi v Union of India* (1978) 1 SCC 248.

[868] See generally, J M Kelly, *The Irish Constitution* (3rd edn, Butterworths, 1994) 767–770.

[869] *Norris v A-G* [1984] IR 36 (in relation to criminal laws penalising homosexuality); *Madigan v A-G* [1986] IRLM 136 (in relation to laws requiring disclosure of income).

[870] [1987] IR 587.

[871] *Kane v Governor of Mountjoy Prison* [1988] IR 757.

[872] *DPP v Kenny* [1992] 2 IR 141.

[873] [1999] 1 IRLM 241.

(a) their person or home searched;
(b) their property searched;
(c) their possessions seized; or
(d) the privacy of their communications infringed.

This is subject to the 'limitations' set out in section 36 'to the extent that the limitation is reasonable and justifiable in an open and democratic society based on human dignity, equality and freedom'. The South African Constitutional Court has considered this provision on a number of occasions.

12.267 In *Bernstein v Bester*[874] the applicants challenged the constitutionality of provisions of the Companies Acts[875] providing for the summoning and examination of persons in relation to the affairs of a company being wound up. It was contended that the examination mechanism infringed, *inter alia*, rights to privacy. These argument were rejected by the Court. Ackermann J said that:

> The truism that no right is to be considered absolute, implies that from the outset of interpretation each right is always already limited by every other right accruing to another citizen. In the context of privacy this would mean that it is only the inner sanctum of a person, such as his/her family life, sexual preference and home environment, which is shielded from erosion by conflicting rights of the community. This implies that community rights and the rights of fellow members place a corresponding obligation on a citizen, thereby shaping the abstract notion of individualism towards identifying a concrete member of civil society. Privacy is acknowledged in the truly personal realm, but as a person moves into communal relations and activities such as business and social interaction, the scope of personal space shrinks accordingly.[876]

12.268 The right to privacy was considered in the 'obscene publications' context in *Case v Minister of Safety and Security*.[877] It was held that a statutory provision forbidding the possession of 'indecent or obscene photographic matter' was a violation of the 'right to privacy'. Didcott J stated that:

> what erotic material I may choose to keep within the privacy of my home, and only for my personal use there, is nobody's business but mine.[878]

However, the majority took a more restrictive view, holding that the possession of such material could be subjected to limitation even in the privacy of one's own home.[879]

12.269 In *National Council for Gay and Lesbian Equality v Ministry of Justice*[880] the Constitutional Court held that the common law offence of sodomy and number of related statutory offences were unconstitutional and invalid. The applicants' arguments were based on the right to equality[881] but the Court stressed that the right to privacy was also infringed:

---

[874] 1996 (4) BCLR 449, CC paras 65 and 67.
[875] ss 417 and 418; analogous to Insolvency Act 1986, s 236.
[876] Ibid para 67; cf the discussion of the South African common law of privacy at paras 68ff.
[877] (1997) 1 BHRC 541 (the Court was dealing with the Interim Constitution, s 13 of which is in materially identical terms).
[878] *Case v Minister of Safety* (n 877 above) para 91, 575e–f.
[879] See Langa J, para 99, 578b–d; Madala J paras 103–107, 579a–580f.
[880] 9 Oct 1998; upholding Heher J (1998) (6) BCLR 726 (W).
[881] s 9 of the Constitution.

Privacy recognises that we all have a right to a sphere of private intimacy and autonomy which allows us to establish and nurture human relationships without interference from the outside community. The way in which we give expression to our sexuality is at the core of this area of private intimacy. . . . The fact that a law prohibiting forms of sexual conduct is discriminatory, does not, however, prevent it at the same time being an improper invasion of the intimate sphere of human life to which protection is given by the Constitution in section 14. We should not deny the importance of a right to privacy in our new constitutional order, even while we acknowledge the importance of equality.[882]

There will, however, be no invasion of the constitutional right of privacy if information is communicated in a situation analogous to a 'privileged occasion' at common law.[883] Thus, in *Mistry v Interim National Medical and Dental Council of South Africa*[884] the Constitutional Court held that there was no breach of the right to privacy when one medicines control inspector communicated information to another for the purpose of planning a search of premises for a regulatory inspection. The Court took into account, *inter alia*, the fact that the information had not been obtained in an intrusive manner, it did not concern intimate aspects of the applicant's life and it was communicated only to a person who had statutory regulatory responsibilities.

12.270

---

[882] *Per* Ackermann J at para 32; see also Sachs J concurring at paras 108 to 119 for an important analysis of the relationship between equality and privacy rights.
[883] M Chaskalson, J Kentridge, J Klaaren, G Marcus, D Spitz and S Woolman (eds), *Constitutional Law of South Africa* (Juta, 1996) para 18–12.
[884] 1998 (7) BCLR 880.

15

FREEDOM OF EXPRESSION

A. The Nature of the Right

15.01 Freedom of expression is often said to be essential to the operation of democracy.[1] It is sometimes claimed that freedom of expression establishes a market place of ideas[2] which promotes the search for truth;[3] or that free speech ensures individual development and self fulfilment[4] and is, for example, to be derived from the right to human dignity and to equality of concern and respect.[5] However, the most persuasive vindication of freedom of expression is that it secures the right of the citizen to participate in the democratic process.[6] Both the House of Lords[7] and the Supreme Court of Canada[8] have said that expression enjoys special protection on all three grounds.

---

[1] The philosophical underpinnings of the right have been much discussed. See E Barendt, *Freedom of Speech* (Clarendon Press, 1985); D Harris, M O'Boyle, and C Warbrick, *Law of the European Convention on Human Rights* (Butterworths, 1995) 373; F Schauer, *Free Speech: A Philosophical Enquiry* (Cambridge University Press, 1982).

[2] See eg the famous dissenting judgment of Holmes J in *Abrams v United States* 250 US 616 (1919) at 630; see para 15.344 below.

[3] See eg J Milton, 'Areopagitica: A Speech for Licensed Printing' in *Prose Writings* (Everyman, 1958); J S Mill, *On Liberty* (Cambridge University Press, 1989) Chap 2.

[4] Schauer (n 1 above) Chaps 4 and 5; and see the justification for freedom of expression recently reaffirmed by the European Court of Human Rights in *Zana v Turkey* (1997) 27 EHRR 667 para 51: see para 15.139 below.

[5] R Dworkin, *Taking Rights Seriously* (Duckworth, 1977) Chap 12.

[6] See eg Brandeis J in *Whitney v California* (1927) 274 US 357, 375; see para 15.344 below.

[7] *R v Secretary of State for the Home Department, ex p Simms* [1999] 3 All ER 400, 408 *per* Lord Steyn: see para 15.07 below.

[8] *Irwin Toy v Quebec* [1989] 1 SCR 927, 976 *per* Dickson CJ, Lamer and Wilson J; *R v Keegstra* [1990] 3 SCR 697, 762, 763 *per* Dickson CJ.

One of the earliest and most well-known constitutional rights provisions is the **15.02**
First Amendment to the Constitution of the United States which provides that:

> Congress shall make no law . . . abridging the freedom of speech, or of the press . . .

This has given rise to one of the most highly developed areas of human rights jurisprudence in the world.[9] All of the major international human rights instruments protect the right to freedom of expression. Article 19 of the International
Covenant on Civil and Political Rights, for example, states:

> (1) Everyone has the right to freedom of opinion and
> (2) Everyone shall have the right to freedom of expression; this right shall in-
> clude freedom to seek, receive and impart information and ideas of all kinds, re-
> gardless of frontiers, either orally, in writing or in print, in the form of art, or
> through any other media of his choice.
> (3) The exercise of the right provided for in paragraph 2 of this Article carries
> with it special duties and responsibilities. It may, therefore, be subject to certain re-
> strictions, but these shall only be
>
> > (a) For respect of the rights or reputations of others;
> > (b) For the protection of national security or of public order, or public health
> > or morals.[10]

The major rights instruments and constitutions nevertheless treat the right of ex-   **15.03**
pression very differently. Some, like the First Amendment, express it in unquali-
fied terms.[11] Typically, however, human rights instruments expressly define the
limitations on freedom of expression.[12] Article 10 of the Convention defines the
right in language which is weaker than that of Article 19 of the Covenant and circumscribes the right by provision of a full list of exceptions.[13]

The freedom of expression must be weighed against other public and private in-   **15.04**
terests. Expressions of opinion and the publication of information in the mass
media can violate other rights and freedoms and have a clear and direct impact on
the political process. As a result, they are subject to close governmental scrutiny.
Regulation of the press and broadcasting raises questions as to the extent of control that national authorities ought to maintain over the production and distribution of information, and the justifiable bases for such interference.

---

[9] For an overview, see Barendt (n 1 above); see generally, eg, L Tribe, *American Constitutional
Law* (2nd edn, Foundation Press, 1988) Chap 12; and for a general discussion of the relationship
between US and European approaches see I Loveland (ed), *Importing the First Amendment* (Hart
Publishing, 1998); and see para 15.344ff below.

[10] See also Universal Declaration, Art 19; the text is reproduced at App H in Vol 2.

[11] For a fuller treatment, see eg Tribe (n 9 above) Chap 12.

[12] See eg the Inter-American Convention, Art 13(2), which excludes from protection prior censorship.

[13] See generally, A Lester, 'Freedom of Expression', in R St J Macdonald, F Matscher and H
Petzold (eds), *The European System for the Protection of Human Rights* (Kluwer, 1983) 465–68.

15.05 The relationship between freedom of expression and the various limitations to which it may be subject is the subject of serious debate in a number of areas. Five areas can be highlighted:

> **Prior restraint**: an issue of immediate importance concerns the circumstances in which injunctions will be granted by the courts to restrain publication of material which is allegedly defamatory, or otherwise in breach of private or public law. Such injunctions are severely restrictive of freedom of expression but their refusal may lead to irreparable damage to more important interests.

> **Reputation and privacy**: the restriction of expression in order to protect reputation and privacy involves complex questions of the 'balancing' of competing rights particularly where public figures are involved.

> **Comment on court proceedings**: the curtailment of expression in the interests of the administration of justice has been particularly controversial in England where there are strict rules concerning the reporting of pending proceedings.

> **Blasphemy, obscenity and hate speech**: the censorship and regulation of media content on grounds of public morality is an area in which the balance has to be struck between freedom of expression and other important rights and values such as respect for religion and the protection of children. The regulation of 'hate speech' involves a particularly direct conflict of values and has been intensely disputed over recent decades.

> **Regulation of the media**: government regulation of the mass media has also been a focus of 'freedom of expression' debates in a number of jurisdictions.[14] These issues have been given new impetus by the growth of new media such as the Internet which are outside the traditional regulatory regimes.[14a]

B. The Right in English Law Before the Human Rights Act

(1) Introduction

15.06 Freedom of speech, like other fundamental freedoms in the common law, has traditionally been considered to be merely residual in character.[15] Now, however, 'freedom of expression' is increasingly being recognised as a common law, or even

---

[14] For the position in the United States see E Barendt, 'The First Amendment and the Media' in I Loveland (ed), *Importing the First Amendment* (Hart Publishing 1998); and see generally, T Gibbons, *Regulating the Media* (2nd edn, Sweet 8 Maxwell, 1998).

[14a] Cf *Reno v ACLU* (1997) 2 BHRC 405 (provisions regulating publication of indecent material on the Internet struck down by Supreme Court).

[15] Dicey did not refer to freedom of expression in his discussion of personal liberties, describing it instead in the context of wrongs and libel: see A Dicey, *An Introduction to the Study of the Law of the Constitution* (8th edn, (Macmillan, 1915) Chap 6 'The Right to Freedom of Discussion'; and see also A Boyle, 'Freedom of Expression as a Public Interest in English Law' [1992] PL 574.

'quasi-constitutional' principle[16] to be invoked by the judiciary in the interpretation of statutes, to limit or balance other public interests[17] and as a basis for refusing some types of relief.[18] This shift in the common law has been influenced by judicial consideration of Article 10 of the European Convention, so that to some extent domestic law already conforms to the requirements of the Convention.[19]

The justifications for the importance of the right of freedom of expression have been summarised by Lord Steyn as follows: **15.07**

> Freedom of expression is, of course, intrinsically important: it is value for its own sake. But it is well recognised that it is also instrumentally important. It serves a number of broad objectives. First it promotes the self-fulfilment of individuals in society. Secondly, in the famous words of Holmes J (echoing John Stuart Mill), 'the best test of truth is the power of the thought to get itself accepted in the competition of the market'[20] Thirdly, freedom of speech is the lifeblood of democracy. The free flow of information and ideas informs political debate. It is a safety valve: people are more ready to accept decisions that go against them if they can in principle seek to influence them. It acts as a brake on the abuse of power by public officials. It facilitates the exposure of errors in the governance and administration of justice of the country.[21]

Some types of speech in English law enjoy protection in positive terms. Debate   **15.08**
and proceedings in Parliament are absolutely privileged against impeachment or question in any court or place out of Parliament.[22] Media and journalists reporting on parliamentary proceedings are subject to absolute privilege. Reports of court[23] proceedings are also privileged against actions in defamation, so long as their publication is fair, accurate and not actuated by malice. Parliamentary papers and their publishers also receive statutory protection.

---

[16] See E Barendt, 'Libel and Freedom of Expression in English Law' [1993] PL 449, 450; at 459-60, Barendt suggests that freedom of expression may be a positive right. Boyle (n 15, above), suggests that freedom of expression as a public interest exists in addition to the residual categorisation which remains an important sense in which 'rights' exist in English law; see also T Allan, *Law, Liberty and Justice* (Clarendon Press, 1993) Chap 6; and for a discussion of positive rights in English law, see para 1.33ff above.

[17] See in regard to defamation: *Derbyshire County Council v Times Newspapers Ltd* [1993] AC 534; in connection with contempt of court and the defence of public interest disclosure to actions for breach of confidence: *A-G v Guardian Newspapers Ltd (No 2)* [1990] 1 AC 109.

[18] The prior restraint approach is exemplified by the rule in *Bonnard v Perryman* [1891] 2 Ch 269 which precluded an interim injunction in a libel action, where the defendant raised a defence of justification or fair comment; see generally, P Milmo and W Rogers (eds), *Gatley on Libel and Slander* (9th edn, Sweet & Maxwell, 1998) Chap 25.

[19] See para 2.18ff above.

[20] *Abrams v United States* (1919) 250 US 616, 630 *per* Holmes J (dissenting); see para 15.334 below.

[21] *R v Secretary of State for the Home Department, ex p Simms* [1999] 3 WLR 328, 337.

[22] Bill of Rights 1689, Art 9.

[23] See the Defamation Act 1952, s 7, extending heads of qualified privilege; also the Contempt of Court Act 1981, ss 5 and 10.

15.09   English law also imposes statutory duties on certain public bodies to facilitate freedom of speech. For example, free postal communications and broadcast time must be made available prior to parliamentary or European Assembly elections,[24] educational institutions must ensure freedom of speech for members, students, employees and visiting speakers,[25] and individuals who make disclosures of information about their employers are given a limited degree of protection.[26] The Monopolies and Mergers Commission is also required to consider 'the need for accurate presentation of news and free expression of opinion' in reporting on the impact of a newspaper merger upon public interests.[27] Outside these clearly defined areas, the protection of freedom of expression has traditionally been limited to preventing prior restraint of damaging material.[28] In particular, reputation was given greater importance than the right to freedom of expression.[29]

15.10   However, in recent years freedom of expression has gradually assumed a more important positive role. In 1994 the position was summarised by Hoffmann LJ in the following terms:

> There are in the law reports many impressive and emphatic statements about the importance of freedom of speech and the press. But they are often followed by a paragraph which begins with the word 'nevertheless'. The judge then goes on to explain that there are other interests which have to be balanced against press freedom. And in deciding upon the importance of press freedom in the particular case, he is likely to distinguish between what he thinks deserves publication in the public interest and things in which the public are merely interested . . . But a freedom which is restricted to what judges think to be responsible or in the public interest is no freedom. Freedom means the right to publish things which government and judges, however well motivated, think should not be published. It means the right to say things which 'right-thinking people' regard as dangerous or irresponsible. This freedom is subject only to clearly defined exceptions as laid down by common law and statute . . . It cannot be too strongly emphasised that outside the established exceptions . . . there is no question of balancing freedom of speech against other interests. It is a trump card which always wins.[30]

---

[24] Representation of the People Act 1983, ss 95-97, as amended by the Representation of the People Act 1985.

[25] Education (No 2) Act 1986, s 43; E Barendt, 'Freedom of Speech in the Universities' [1987] PL 344 refers to these as 'bizarre' provisions.

[26] Public Interest Disclosure Act 1998 amending the Employment Rights Act 1996.

[27] Fair Trading Act, 1973, s 59(3).

[28] See para 15.24ff below.

[29] It is regarded by Blackstone as part of the 'right of personal security', the first of the 'absolute rights of man', *Blackstone's Commentaries* (17th edn, 1830) Book I, Chap 1.

[30] *R v Central Independent Television plc* [1994] Fam 192; it should, however, be noted that this comment was made in the context of proceedings to restrain the publication of information about children, an area in which the courts have often been ready to place severe restraints on freedom of speech, see para 15.68ff below.

The importance of protecting unpopular speech has been emphasised by Sedley LJ who observed:

> Free speech includes not only the inoffensive but the irritating, the contentious, the eccentric, the heretical, the unwelcome and the provocative provided it does not provoke violence. Freedom only to speak inoffensively is not worth having.[31]

The 'established exceptions' to the freedom of expression are, however, widely drawn and often not clearly defined. The following are the most important: **15.11**

- the law of *defamation* which restricts expression which damages individual reputations or provokes public disorder;
- the law of *contempt of court* which requires that certain expression be curtailed in the interests of the administration of justice;
- the law of *obscenity and indecency* which gives rise to censorship and the regulation of media content on grounds of public morality;
- the *criminal law* which also prohibits certain forms of expression as likely to provoke public disorder or racial hatred, be offensive to the Christian religion or incite persons to violence against the state;
- the law relating to the *regulation and censorship* of broadcast media, film and video;
- civil and criminal law restraints on speech which disclose Government secrets or confidential information, in the interests of *national security*.

In practice, the rules governing the lawfulness of a particular 'item of expression'   **15.12**
can be extremely complex. It may be made by one of a number of public or private parties, through a variety of media and may be challenged under more than one head, each subject to various defences. The position is further confused because 'freedom of the press' is not treated consistently: sometimes the press are in the same position as ordinary 'publishers' and sometimes they are given special protection. As a result, the role which any positive principle of 'freedom of expression' will play in a decision is difficult to predict.

(2) Prior restraint

(a) Introduction

The power of the courts to *prevent* publication is the most stringent form of re-   **15.13**
striction upon freedom of expression. Prior restraint has always been approached with particular caution; as Blackstone said:

> The liberty of the press is indeed essential to the nature of a free state; but this consists in laying no *previous* restraints upon publications and not in freedom from

---

[31] *Redmond-Bate v DPP* (1999) 7 BHRC 375, 382, 383; and see *Silkin v Beaverbrook Newspapers Ltd* [1958] 1 WLR 743 in which Diplock J described freedom of speech as 'the right of the crank to say what he likes'.

censure for criminal matter when published. Every freeman has an undoubted right to lay what sentiments he pleases before the public: to forbid this, is to destroy the freedom of the press; but if he publishes what is improper, mischievous or illegal, he must take the consequence of his own temerity.[32]

This statement of principle appears to have had a significant influence on the development of the law in the United States.[33] The basic principle and its affinity with the provisions of Article 10 of the Convention has been acknowledged in a number of cases. As Laws J put it:

> there is a general principle in our law that the expression of opinion and the conveyance of information will not be restrained by the courts save on pressing grounds. Freedom of expression is as much a sinew of the common law as it is of the European Convention . . .[34]

(b) Defamation cases

15.14 It has long been recognised that freedom of expression is an important consideration in determining whether an interim injunction ought to be granted to restrain the publication of material which is alleged to be defamatory. In such cases, an injunction will not be granted if the defendant asserts a defence of justification on grounds that the words complained of are *true*. The fundamental approach was described in *Bonnard v Perryman*:[35]

> The right of free speech is one which it is for the public interest that individuals should possess and, indeed, that they should exercise without impediment, so long as no wrongful act is done; and unless an alleged libel is untrue there is no wrong committed . . .

This principle has been affirmed in a large number of cases.[36] Provided that the defendant advances some evidence to support a proposed plea of justification, an injunction will be granted only in the extremely rare case in which the claimant can satisfy the court than the plea of justification is bound to fail.[37] Furthermore, the rule in *Bonnard v Perryman* applies, irrespective of motive or the manner in which publication is threatened. A court refused an injunction,

---

[32] *Blackstone's Commentaries*, (17th edn, 1830) Book IV, 151-2; quoted in *Holley v Smyth* [1998] 2 WLR 742, 751D-H.

[33] See *Schering Chemicals Ltd v Falkman Ltd* [1982] 1 QB 1, 17C-H; see generally, L Levy, *The Emergence of a Free Press* (Oxford University Press, 1985); and see also L Tribe, *American Constitutional Law* (2nd edn, Foundation Press, 1988), 785ff.

[34] *R v Advertising Standards Authority Ltd, ex p Vernons Organisation Ltd* [1992] 1 WLR 1289, 1293A.

[35] [1891] 2 Ch 269, 284.

[36] See eg *Fraser v Evans* [1969] 1 QB 349, 360; *Bestobell Paints v Bigg* [1975] FSR 421; *Crest Homes v Ascott* [1980] FSR 396; *Khasshoggi v IPC Magazines Ltd* [1986] 1 WLR 1412.

[37] See generally, P Milmo and W Rogers (eds), *Gatley on Libel and Slander* (9th edn, Sweet & Maxwell, 1998) para 25.6.

for example, even where a defendant sought to extract money from the plaintiffs on threat of publication of what he said were damaging but true allegations about them.[38]

(c) Breach of confidence and other claims

The rule in *Bonnard v Perryman* preventing prior restraint in defamation cases also **15.15** extends to trade libel, injurious falsehood and related claims.[39] It does not, however, provide a defence against the imposition of interim injunctions sought on the basis of *other* causes of action.

A claimant attempting to restrain the publication of material which he believes to **15.16** be damaging will therefore often seek to do so on other grounds: conspiracy to injure, breach of copyright, trade mark infringement[40] and, most importantly, breach of confidence. A claim for an interlocutory injunction on the basis of an alleged conspiracy to injure was, for example, successful in *Gulf Oil (Great Britain) Ltd v Page*,[41] where the plaintiff obtained an injunction to restrain the defendant from displaying a defamatory airborne sign.

Attempts to obtain an injunction on grounds which would avoid the *Bonnard v* **15.17** *Perryman* defence may nevertheless be refused. The application for injunction in *Femis-Bank (Anguilla) Ltd v Lazar*[42] was unsuccessful on the basis that, whatever the cause of action, freedom of speech was an important factor to be taken into account in the exercise of the discretion of the court. Even though the rule in *Bonnard v Perryman* does not apply to trademark infringement or breach of copyright, the courts will not allow such a claim to be used as a 'vehicle' for what is, in essence, a claim for defamation.[43] In a claim for breach of a contract 'not to publish', demonstration by the claimant of a good arguable case will not be sufficient grounds for a grant of interim injunction: the court should be able to assess the relative strengths of the parties' cases.[44]

The most important basis upon which a claimant may obtain 'prior restraint' of **15.18** publication is that of a claim of *breach of confidence*. The rule in *Bonnard v Perryman* does not apply to prevent interim injunctions from being granted. Proceedings for confidential information are in a special category, because

> if, pending the trial, the court allows publication, there is no point in having a trial since the cloak of confidentiality can never be restored. Confidential information is

---

[38] See *Holley v Smyth* [1998] QB 726.
[39] *Lord Brabourne v Hough* [1981] FSR 79, 85.
[40] *Gallup Organization v Gallup International*, 29 Nov 1995.
[41] [1987] Ch 327.
[42] [1991] Ch 391.
[43] Cf *Service Corporation v Channel Four Television*, unreported, 12 May 1998, Lightman J.
[44] See *Cambridge Nutrition Ltd v British Broadcasting Corporation* [1990] 3 All ER 523.

like an ice cube . . . Give it to the party who has no refrigerator or will not agree to keep it in one, and by the time of the trial you just have a pool of water.[45]

As a result, the claimant need show only an arguable claim and that the 'balance of convenience' is in favour of granting the order.[46]

15.19 The availability of interim injunctions to restrain breaches of confidence is a serious threat to freedom of expression.[47] The most important example of such restraint was in the *Spycatcher* litigation, in which the British Government sought to restrain the publication of a book by a former intelligence officer, Peter Wright. The book had been written in breach of the Official Secrets Act and of the duty of confidentiality of the author. In June 1986, a number of British newspapers published articles containing allegations made by Mr Wright concerning the Security Service which the British Government was seeking to restrain in court proceedings in Australia.[48] On 27 June 1986, the Attorney-General obtained *ex parte* injunctions to restrain further publication. On 11 July 1986 these injunctions were continued in modified form by Millett J. The injunctions were upheld by the Court of Appeal.

15.20 The application for an injunction before the Australian courts by the British Government was unsuccessful. On 11 July 1987, the book was published in the United States. As a result, after hearing a preliminary issue in July 1987, Sir Nicholas Browne-Wilkinson V-C discharged the interlocutory injunctions.[49] Although the Judge accepted that the 'ice cube' of the confidential information needed to be preserved, he took the view that:

> It has been put in the refrigerator, but the American publication is as though somebody had turned off the refrigerator . . .[50]

The Court of Appeal nevertheless allowed in part the Attorney-General's appeal and granted a modified interlocutory injunction. This injunction was upheld by the House of Lords on 30 July 1987 on the ground that there was an arguable case for the protection of an important public interest, namely the maintenance of the secrecy of the Security Service.[51] However, Lords Bridge and Oliver dissented; and Lord Bridge was particularly critical:[52]

---

[45] *Per* Sir John Donaldson MR in *A-G v Newspaper Publishing plc* [1988] Ch 333, quoted in *A-G v Guardian Newspapers Ltd (No 1)* [1987] 1 WLR 1248, 1259F-H.

[46] In accordance with the principles in *American Cyanamid Company v Ethicon Ltd* [1975] AC 396; however it must be possible to frame an interlocutory injunction in clear terms: cf *Times Newspapers Ltd v MGN Ltd* [1993] EMLR 442 in which an injunction was refused on this ground.

[47] Concerns in relation to this were one reason for the addition of s 12 of the Human Rights Act; see para 15.238ff below.

[48] Mr Wright was resident in Australia and was proposing to publish a book there.

[49] *A-G v Guardian Newspapers Ltd (No 1)* [1987] 1 WLR 1248.

[50] Ibid 1268B-C.

[51] Ibid.

[52] The majority comprised Lords Brandon, Templeman and Ackner.

I have had confidence in the capacity of the common law to safeguard the fundamental freedoms essential to a free society including the right to freedom of speech
which is specifically safeguarded by Article 10 of the Convention. My confidence is
seriously undermined by your Lordships' decision . . . The maintenance of the ban,
as more and more copies of the book *Spycatcher* enter this country and circulate
here, will seem more and more ridiculous. If the Government are determined to
fight to maintain the ban to the end, they will face inevitable condemnation and hu-
miliation by the European Court of Human Rights in Strasbourg. Long before that
they will have been condemned at the bar of public opinion in the free world.[53]

Lord Templeman took the view that the restraints imposed were necessary in accordance with Article 10 of the Convention.[54]

The newspapers applied to the European Court of Human Rights. In the *Observer*   **15.21**
and The Guardian v United Kingdom[55] the Court accepted the argument of the
Government that the injunctions had the legitimate aim of 'maintaining the authority of the judiciary' and safeguarding the operation of the security services.
Nevertheless, the majority took the view that, the confidentiality of the material
having been destroyed by its publication, there was no sufficient reason for the
continuation of the injunction after 30 July 1987.[56]

(d) Contempt proceedings

The position concerning prior restraint is different for contempt proceedings.   **15.22**
The court has jurisdiction to grant an injunction to restrain the publication of any
material which may constitute a 'criminal' contempt.[57] Although only the
Attorney-General may institute proceedings for criminal contempt[58] it appears
that anyone with a sufficiently proximate interest may also apply.[59]

Because the prior restraint of a publication is a very serious interference with press   **15.23**
freedom, an injunction on grounds of contempt will only be granted where the
publication would, manifestly, be a contempt of court.[60] As a result, applications
for injunction have been refused in a number of cases.[61] It is clear, however, that

---

[53] At 1286C-H; when the case was heard before the Court of Human Rights, it held the injunction breached freedom of expression under Art 10: see *The Observer and The Guardian v United
Kingdom* (1991) 14 EHRR 153.
[54] At 1296F-1299G.
[55] n 53 above.
[56] Ibid para 68.
[57] For the distinction between 'civil' and 'criminal' contempts see para 15.42 below.
[58] Contempt of Court Act 1981, s 7.
[59] See *Peacock v London Weekend Television* (1985) 150 JP 71 (Police Federation granted injunction to restrain TV programme on grounds that it would prejudice a pending inquest) and *Leary v
BBC*, unreported, 29 Sep1989, CA; but see *Pickering v Liverpool Daily Post and Echo Newspapers plc*
[1991] 2 AC 370, 425 where Lord Bridge expressed doubt on this point; see generally, *Arlidge, Eady
and Smith on Contempt* (2nd edn, Sweet & Maxwell, 1999) paras 6-9–6.16.
[60] *A-G v British Broadcasting Corporation* [1981] AC 303, 311, 362.
[61] See eg *Schering Chemicals Ltd v Falkman Ltd* [1982] 1 QB 1, but an injunction was granted to
restrain breach of confidence; *A-G v News Group Newspapers Ltd* (Botham libel case) [1987] QB 1.

an application to restrain a manifestly contemptuous publication will not be refused simply because the defendant seeks to justify. The position was summarised by Sir John Donaldson MR as follows:

> In practice, I think that the rule in *Bonnard v Perryman* will be decisive unless and until the strict liability rule is invoked. Once it is invoked it will prevail, because, in the form in which it survives in 1981, if strictly construed and applied, the balance must always come down on the side of protecting the right to justice.[62]

It was, however, emphasised that section 5 of the Contempt Act would protect general discussion of topics with which forthcoming trials were incidentally concerned.[63] The result of these matters is that a 'gagging writ' will only be effective after the action becomes 'active' and will not limit discussion on matters of general public interest.[64]

(3) Protection of reputation: defamation

(a) Introduction

15.24   The English law of defamation protects the reputation of every person from defamatory statements about him made to third parties without lawful justification. Although many defamation cases refer to the importance of freedom of expression, the common law has always placed great emphasis on the right to reputation. As the Court of Appeal said in *Kiam v Neill*:[65]

> The right to protection of the law against attacks on honour and reputation are as important in a democratic society as the right to freedom of the press. History discloses examples which show that undermining the reputation of a political opponent of an arbitrary domineering or oppressive regime can be one of the first weapons deployed by the despot.

The effect of this emphasis is that the common law provides no special protection or defence to the press: press publications are subject to the same rules of law as apply to publications by private individuals.[66]

(b) The nature of the claim

15.25   A statement is defamatory if it tends to lower the claimant in the estimation of right thinking members of society generally.[67] The statement does not have to

---

[62] *A-G v News Group Newspapers Ltd* (n 61 above) 14.

[63] Ibid 14–15.

[64] See generally, N Lowe and B Sufrin, *Borrie and Lowe: The Law of Contempt* (3rd edn, Butterworths, 1996) 191–6; *Arlidge, Eady and Smith on Contempt* (n 59 above) para 6-1– 6-27.

[65] *The Times*, 29 Jul 1996; see also *Reynolds v Times Newspapers Ltd* [1999] 3 WLR 1010, 1023E-H (*per* Lord Nicholls).

[66] See P Milmo and W Rogers (eds), *Gatley on Libel and Slander* (9th edn, Sweet & Maxwell, 1998) para 1.9.

[67] *Per* Lord Atkin, *Sim v Stretch* (1936) 52 TLR 669; generally, *Gatley on Libel and Slander* (n 66 above) Chap 2.

have any actual effect on reputation: the law looks at its 'tendency'.[68] The court considers the 'natural and ordinary meaning' of the words used rather than the literal meaning: it can include any implication or inference which a reasonable reader would draw from the words.[68a] In addition, a statement may be defamatory on the basis of extrinsic facts known to some readers: this is known as an innuendo.[68b] The meaning of a particular statement and whether or not it is defamatory are matters for a jury[69] but the question of whether the words are 'capable' of being defamatory is decided by the judge.[70] The prominent role of the jury introduces a considerable degree of uncertainty: it is often difficult to predict with any accuracy whether a jury is likely to find particular words defamatory.

The law of defamation presumes that defamatory imputations are false[71] and that   **15.26**
the person defamed is of good reputation. The claimant is not required to prove actual damage to reputation or any other loss. The burden of establishing the truth of the words used, or any other defences, is on the publisher of the words. This burden is, inevitably, a considerable restriction on freedom of expression. When a defamatory statement is published in permanent form, the tort of *libel* is committed, and:

> the law presumes that *some* damage will flow in the ordinary course of things from the mere invasion of his absolute right to reputation.[72]

Defamation that is expressed orally or in a less than permanent form constitutes   **15.27**
the tort of *slander*. Slander is, in general, only actionable at common law if actual damage can be proved. There are, however, a number of forms of slander which are actionable without proof of damage.[73] Once a cause of action in slander is established, damages are 'at large'.

(c) Who can bring a defamation action?

An action for defamation can be brought by a natural person or by a company.   **15.28**
A trading corporation can sue for damage to its trading reputation[74] and a

---

[68]   See *Hough v London Express Newspapers Ltd* [1940] 2 KB 507, 515.

[68a]   *Lewis v Daily Telegraph* [1964] AC 234, 258; *Jones v Skelton* [1963] 1 WLR 1362, 1370; *Gatley on Libel and Slander* (n 66 above) para 3.14ff. Note that an 'inferred' imputation is sometimes called a 'popular' or 'false' innuendo (*Lewis*, 280).

[68b]   This is a 'true innuendo', see generally, *Gatley on Libel and Slander* (n 66 above) para 31.8ff.

[69]   There remains a right to trial by jury in libel actions under the Supreme Court Act 1981, s 69(1). This right may be lost if the case involves prolonged examination of documents or accounts: see *Aitken v Guardian Newspapers, The Times*, 21 May 1997.

[70]   See eg *Gillick v BBC* [1996] EMLR 267; and *Gatley on Libel and Slander* (n 66 above) para 30.2ff.

[71]   *Gatley on Libel and Slander* (n 66 above) para 11.3.

[72]   *Ratcliffe v Evans* [1892] 2 QB 524, 528.

[73]   These are: an imputation of a criminal offence punishable by imprisonment, an imputation of a contagious disease, an imputation of unchastity against a woman under the Slander of Women Act 1891, and words calculated to disparage a person in any office, calling, trade or business.

[74]   *Gatley on Libel and Slander* (n 66 above) para 2.16.

non-trading corporation can bring an action in respect of imputations which are damaging to its property or finances.[75] A trade union cannot, however, sue for libel because it is not a body corporate.[76]

15.29 It is now clear that a local government corporation cannot sue for libel. The point arose in *Derbyshire County Council v Times Newspapers*,[77] in which the Court of Appeal, placing considerable reliance on Article 10 of the Convention,[78] denied a local authority the right to sue for libel. This decision was upheld by the House of Lords on the basis of the common law, without any reliance upon the Convention. Lord Keith was of the view that it was:

> of the highest public importance that a democratically elected governmental body, or indeed any governmental body, should be open to uninhibited public criticism.[79]

As a result, he concluded that:

> not only is there no public interest favouring the right of organs of government whether central or local, to sue for libel, but . . . it is contrary to the public interest that they should have it. It is contrary to the public interest because to admit such actions would place an undesirable fetter on freedom of speech.[80]

This principle has been applied to governmental bodies[81] and to political parties.[82] It does not, however, extend to individually elected officials, public employees or members of political parties.

(d) Defences to an action for defamation

15.30 **Introduction.** The most important defences[83] to actions for defamation are 'justification' on grounds of truth, fair comment on a matter of public interest, absolute privilege and qualified privilege. The 1996 Defamation Act has also introduced a defence of an offer to make amends[84] where a defendant is prepared to pay damages assessed by a judge.

15.31 **Justification.** 'Justification' or proof of the substantial truth of a defamatory imputation is a complete defence. The defendant carries the burden of proving the truth of the defamatory imputations which the words bear:

---

[75] Ibid para 2.19.

[76] *Electrical, Electronic, Telecommunications and Plumbing Union v Times Newspapers Ltd* [1980] QB 585.

[77] [1992] QB 770, CA; [1993] AC 534, HL.

[78] See para 2.19 above.

[79] Ibid 547F–G.

[80] Ibid 549.

[81] *British Coal Corporation v NUM*, unreported, 28 Jun 1996.

[82] *Goldsmith v Bhoyrul* [1998] QB 459.

[83] See generally, P Milmo and W Rogers (eds), *Gatley on Libel and Slander* (9th edn, Sweet & Maxwell, 1998) Pt 2.

[84] See s 3(5); the defence of 'offer to make amends' replaces the statutory defence of unintentional defamation contained in the 1952 Act, s 4.

> When a plea of justification is pleaded, it involves the justification of every injurious imputation which a jury may think is to be found in the alleged libel.[85]

The operation of the defence of justification in the modern law of libel is highly technical. The following points should be noted:

- the claimant must set out the 'sting' of the libel on which he relies;[86]
- the claimant can 'pick and choose' from a publication containing more than one defamatory imputation, basing his claim on only some of the imputations;[87]
- the defendant must justify either the 'sting' relied on by the claimant or a 'lesser' defamatory meaning which he says the words bear;[88]
- if the claimant picks one defamatory imputation, the defendant cannot justify another separate and distinct imputation in the same publication;[89]
- if the claimant complains that the publication contains several defamatory imputations, the defence of justification does not fail only because the truth of every charge is not proved, *if* the untrue words 'do not materially injure the claimant's reputation' having regard to the remaining charges.[90]

The burden on a defendant is a high one. Uncertainty results from the fact that the jury determines the meaning of the words used and is obliged to find a single meaning.[91] The result is that a defendant who can prove the truth of almost everything in a long publication could still be successfully sued if the jury finds that the publication contains one defamatory imputation the truth of which the defendant cannot prove.

Fair comment.   Another defence that may be established by the defendant to an **15.32** action in defamation is that the words used were fair comment[92] on a matter of public interest.[93] There are three stages in proving fair comment. First, the defendant must show that the words used were 'comment', rather than assertions of fact. The test is 'how the words would be understood by an ordinary reader'.[94] In practice, the line between comment and factual assertion is difficult to draw.[95]

---

[85] *Digby v Financial News* [1907] 1 KB 502.

[86] See *Lucas-Box v News Group Newspapers Ltd* [1986] 1 WLR 147, 151-152.

[87] *Cruise v Express Newspapers* [1999] 2 WLR 327.

[88] This must be specifically set out in the defence and is known as a 'Lucas-Box' meaning, see *Lucas-Box v News Group Newspapers Ltd* (n 86 above).

[89] *Cruise v Express Newspapers* (n 89 above); *Polly Peck (Holdings) plc v Trelford* [1986] QB 1000.

[90] Defamation Act 1952, s 5.

[91] See *Charleston v News Group Newspapers Ltd* [1995] 2 AC 65.

[92] The defence is, more accurately described as 'honest comment', *per* Lord Nicholls, *Reynolds v Times Newspapers Ltd* [1999] 3 WLR 1010, 1061A.

[93] 'Public interest' in this sense is not confined within narrow limits: see *London Artists Ltd v Littler* [1969] QB 375.

[94] *Slim v Daily Telegraph Ltd* [1968] 2 QB 157.

[95] See generally, *Gatley on Libel and Slander* (n 83 above) para 12.6ff.

Secondly, the facts on which the comment is based must be shown to be true.[96] The defence will not fail, however, solely for lack of proof of the truth of every allegation of fact, if the defendant can show that the expression of opinion is fair comment, having regard to the facts which are proved.[97] Thirdly, the defendant must show that the comment was 'fair'. This is the least onerous requirement because 'fair', in this context, simply means 'capable of being honestly held'. As Diplock J said to the jury in *Silkin v Beaverbrook Newspapers Ltd*:[98]

> do not apply the test of whether you agree with it. If juries did that, freedom of speech, the right of the crank to say what he likes, would go. Would a fair minded man holding strong views, obstinate views, prejudiced views, have been capable of making this comment? If the answer to that is yes then [the defence succeeds].

The defence of fair comment can be rebutted by proof that the defendant was actuated by malice.[99]

15.33 **Absolute privilege.**   The public interest requires that individuals be permitted in certain circumstances to express themselves with complete freedom. Certain speech is therefore privileged, which may be absolute or qualified. Absolute privilege is a complete defence, no matter how damaging or defamatory the statements may be, precluding a court from any jurisdiction to hear an action in defamation. The most important heads of 'absolute privilege' are:

• Statements made by witnesses, advocates or judges in the course of litigation.[100] This privilege extends to witness statements,[101] court documents and to any statement made as part of the process of investigating crime.[102] It does not, however, extend to fabricating evidence.[102a]
• Statements made in the debates or proceedings in Parliament, and evidence given by witnesses to select committees.[103] The fact that proceedings in Parliament cannot be 'questioned' means that a party cannot rely, in an action, on anything said in Parliament.[104] A member of Parliament may, however, waive the privilege for the purposes of defamation proceedings.[105]

---

[96] See *Broadway Approvals Ltd v Odhams Press Ltd* [1964] 2 QB 683.
[97] Defamation Act 1952, s 6.
[98] [1958] 1 WLR 743.
[99] For malice, see para 15.37 below.
[100] *Munster v Lamb* (1883) 11 QBD 588, 607; see *Gatley on Libel and Slander* (n 83 above) para 13.3–13.14.
[101] *Watson v M'Ewan* [1905] AC 480.
[102] *Taylor v Director of the Serious Fraud Office* [1998] 1 WLR 1040.
[102a] *Docker v Chief Constable of West Midlands Police, The Times,* 1 Aug 2000 (HL).
[103] Bill of Rights 1688, Art 9.
[104] *Prebble v Television New Zealand* [1995] 1 AC 321.
[105] Defamation Act 1996, s 13(1); *Gatley on Libel and Slander* (n 83 above) para 13.29–13.30; and see *Hamilton v Al-Fayed* [1999] 1 WLR 1569.

• Fair and accurate reports of court proceedings if they are published contemporaneously with the proceedings.[106]

The courts are cautious about extending the categories of absolute privilege,[107] but the categories are not closed.[108]

Qualified privilege. Words spoken in good faith on other occasions may also be subject to privilege, albeit of a qualified nature. There is now statutory provision for qualified privilege which protects the publication of reports or statements from across a wide range of subject matter,[109] so long as they are 'fair and accurate'.[110] These include fair and accurate reports of the proceedings of foreign legislatures, courts, public commission inquiries, public meetings and local authorities or local authority committees.[111]

15.34

Qualified privilege protects expression at common law on the premise that there exists a legal, moral, or social duty on the person to communicate a statement, and a corresponding interest or duty on the person who receives the publication. It covers matters such as 'reply to attack'[112] and ordinary business communications. The categories of qualified privilege are not closed: they are no more than applications, in particular circumstances, of an underlying principle of public policy to the effect that both the maker and the recipient of the statement must have a 'duty or interest' in making or receiving it.[113] However:

15.35

> The essence of this defence lies in the law's recognition of the need, in the public interest, for a particular recipient to receive frank and uninhibited communication of particular information from a particular source.[114]

In determining whether an occasion is subject to qualified privilege, the court has regard to all the circumstances.[115] The question in each case is whether the public was entitled to know the particular information: this 'duty interest' or 'right to know' test cannot be carried out in isolation from factors such as the nature,

---

[106] Defamation Act 1996, s 14: the privilege extends to reports of proceedings before the European Court of Justice, the European Court of Human Rights, and defined international criminal tribunals.

[107] *Royal Aquarium and Summer and Winter Garden Society Ltd v Parkinson* [1892] 1 QB 431, 451.

[108] See *Merricks v Nott-Bower* [1965] 1 QB 57, 73; and cf *Hasselblad (GB) Ltd v Orbinson* [1985] QB 475.

[109] See Defamation Act 1996, s 15 and Sch 1.

[110] For the case law on this phrase, see P Milmo and W Rogers (eds), *Gatley on Libel and Slander* (9th edn, Sweet & Maxwell, 1998) para 15.4.

[111] See Ibid Chap 15.

[112] *Adam v Ward* [1917] AC 309.

[113] Ibid 334.

[114] *Per* Lord Nicholls, *Reynolds v Times Newspapers Ltd* [1999] 3 WLR 1010, 1017F–G.

[115] *London Association for the Protection of Trade v Greenlands Ltd* [1916] 2 AC 15, 23.

status and source of the material and the circumstances of the publication[116] but there is no separate 'circumstantial test'.[117]

15.36   One important issue that arises is the extent to which qualified privilege protects media reports. Qualified privilege might apply because the media arguably have a duty to supply and the public have an interest in receiving information as to issues of contemporary importance. In *Reynolds v Times Newspapers Ltd*[118] the House of Lords rejected the argument that there should be a new category of qualified privilege for 'political information'[119] on the basis that such a privilege would not provide adequate protection for reputation and that it would be unsound in principle to distinguish 'political expression' from other matters of serious public concern. Lord Hobhouse commented that, to allow for such a privilege:

> would be handing to what are essentially commercial entities a power which would deprive the subjects of such publications of the protection against damaging misinformation. Such persons and the public are entitled to the disinterested and objective involvement of the law. It is for the publisher to establish to the satisfaction of the law that the publication was privileged.[120]

Nevertheless, it was recognised that the 'powerful arguments in favour of the constitutional right of free speech' meant that, 'where politicians are involved, the interest and duty tests are likely to be satisfied in most cases without too much difficulty'.[121] Subsequent case law suggests that, in practice, the 'right to know' test may be easy to satisfy[121a] and that, as a result, media reports on a wide range of matters of 'public interest' may be protected by qualified privilege. This is a rapidly developing area of the law which will be strongly influenced by the Human Rights Act.[121b]

15.37   Once the defendant has established qualified privilege, his good faith is presumed. The onus then shifts to the claimant to rebut the defence by showing that the publication was actuated by express malice. 'Express malice' entails either that the

---

[116] For a list of 'illustrative' circumstances, see *per* Lord Nicholls, *Reynolds v Times Newspapers Ltd* (n 114 above).

[117] See n 114 above, disapproving the approach of the Court of Appeal [1998] 3 WLR 862, 899E–H.

[118] [1999] 3 WLR 1010.

[119] The House of Lords were not persuaded to follow US and Commonwealth cases which recognised, in various degrees, a 'public figure' defence: see *Sullivan v New York Times* (1964) 376 US 254; *Rajagopal v State of Tamil Nadu JT* 1994 6 SC 524; *Lange v Australian Broadcasting Corporation* (1997) 189 CLR 520; *Lange v Atkinson and Australian Consolidated Press NZ Ltd* [1998] 3 NZLR 424.

[120] [1999] 3 WLR 1010, 1061A–B.

[121] Ibid 1056E, *per* Lord Hope.

[121a] See *GKR Karate v Yorkshire Post Newspapers*, unreported, 17 Jan 2000 (Sir Oliver Popplewell)—test satisfied in relation to an article relating to 'dodgy karate lessons' despite the fact that the local newspaper had not given the claimant a reasonable opportunity to respond and had inaccurately quoted the source.

[121b] See para 15.247ff below.

defendant had some improper motive for publication, such as injuring the claimant, or that he knew the words were false or was reckless as to whether they were true or false.[122] The burden imposed is a heavy one, and, if the evidence at trial is equally consistent with malice or its absence, there will be no case for the defendant to answer and the claim may be dismissed without hearing the defendant's evidence.[123]

(e) Remedies

The primary remedy for defamation is damages. The value of the award has traditionally been in the sole province of the jury; judges and counsel were not permitted to influence the decision of the jury by mentioning specific figures that might be appropriate.[124] The powers of intervention of the Court of Appeal were limited to ordering a re-trial if the award was 'divorced from reality'.[125] As a result, jury awards varied over an enormous range. Jury awards were first scrutinised in Convention terms by the Court of Appeal in *Rantzen v Mirror Group Newspapers*[126] which held that the power of the Court to order a new trial or to substitute a different damage award[127] should be applied consistently with Article 10.

15.38

More recently, in *John v MGN Ltd*,[128] it was held that the reasonableness of jury awards could be tempered by directing the jury to the level of damages in personal injury cases. In practice, both the judiciary and counsel are now permitted to mention figures to the jury. The effect of *Rantzen* and of *John* has been to depress the value of damages awards and settlements in libel cases although a 'tariff' of Court of Appeal approved awards has been slow to develop.[129] The value of settlements in cases against newspapers, in particular, has been substantially reduced.

15.39

The courts also have power to award permanent injunctions if a claim in defamation is established at trial. An injunction will be granted if there is any reason to believe that the defendant is likely to publish the same or similar defamatory words. Such injunction may also affect the position of third parties who publish the defamatory imputations. It is clear that, where an interim injunction has been granted, a third party will be in contempt of court if his publication is likely to

15.40

---

[122] See *Horrocks v Lowe* [1975] AC 135; and P Milmo and W Rogers (eds), *Gatley on Libel and Slander* (9th edn, Sweet & Maxwell, 1998) Chap 16.

[123] See *Telnikoff v Matusevitch* [1991] 1 QB 102, 121: overruled, but not on this point [1992] 2 AC 343; and *Gatley on Libel and Slander* (n 122 above) para 32.28ff.

[124] See *Ward v James* [1966] 1 QB 273; see also *Sutcliffe v Pressdram Ltd* [1991] QB 153.

[125] See *McCarey v Associated Newspapers (No 2)* [1965] 2 QB 86, 111; see generally, *Gatley on Libel and Slander* (n 122 above) para 36.26.

[126] [1994] QB 670.

[127] Under the Courts and Legal Services Act 1990, s 8.

[128] [1997] QB 586.

[129] For such awards, see the Appendix of Court of Appeal 'Approved Libel Awards' in *Gatley on Libel and Slander* (n 122 above) A3.1–A3.6.

interfere with the course of justice between the claimant and the defendant.[130] It is not clear whether the same is true in the case of permanent injunctions.[131] It seems unlikely that, in the absence of a specific intention to interfere with the course of justice, the publication of the libel by a third party would constitute a breach of either an interim or final injunction against a defendant.[132]

(4) Comment on court proceedings: contempt of court

(a) Introduction

15.41 'Contempt of court' means interference with the due administration of justice.[133] Its purpose is to ensure respect for the administration of justice as a whole and for the remedies ordered by the court.[134] Nevertheless, the law of contempt appears to be unduly restrictive of freedom of expression, which the courts have traditionally treated as having secondary importance. It is also open to criticism in its summary trial procedures,[135] absence of maximum sentences[136] and, in particular, its uncertain scope.[137]

15.42 The classification of contempt at common law is not straightforward. 'Civil' contempts such as non-compliance with court orders or undertakings[138] in civil proceedings are generally[139] distinguished from 'criminal'[140] contempts. Criminal contempts can be divided into at least three categories:

- 'contempt in the face of the court' (which refers to conduct of persons in the courtroom);

---

[130] *A-G v News Group Newspapers Ltd* [1987] QB 1.

[131] See *Gatley on Libel and Slander* (n 122 above) para 9.31.

[132] In contrast to the position in breach of confidence, where the purpose of the injunction is to restrain the publication of particular items of confidential information.

[133] See eg *A-G v Times Newspapers Ltd* [1974] AC 273, 322.

[134] See eg *Morris v Crown Office* [1970] 2 QB 114.

[135] The summary trial procedures used in contempt cases may lack the elements of procedural fairness that are normally required for criminal trials, see generally *Arlidge Eady and Smith on Contempt* (2nd edn, Sweet & Maxwell, 1999) paras 2-17–2-25.

[136] With limited exceptions where statutes have intervened, no maximum sentences are prescribed, leaving the court free to impose whatever form of punishment it feels is appropriate, including coercive sanctions for civil contempts.

[137] The substantive criteria for contempt are vague and uncertain in spite of the fact that liability attracts potentially heavy penal sanctions.

[138] These can include injunctions or orders restricting or postponing reporting of trials when the administration of justice may be affected. Such restrictions may be imposed when trials are held in private, when reporting might prejudice the fairness of proceedings, when children, rape or blackmail are involved, or in regard to material disclosed on discovery.

[139] Except in Scotland.

[140] For discussion of the technical distinction between civil and criminal contempt see N Lowe and B Sufrin, *Borrie and Lowe: The Law of Contempt* (3rd edn, Butterworths, 1996) Chap 2; *Arlidge, Eady and Smith on Contempt* (2nd edn, Sweet and Maxwell, 1999) Chap 3; see also the judgments of the Australian High Court in *Witham v Holloway* (1995) 183 CLR 525, 530-49.

- 'scandalising the court' (which involves publications which undermine public confidence in the judicial system or otherwise interfere with the course of justice as a continuing process); and
- 'prejudicing active legal proceedings' under the '*sub judice* rule' (which prohibits publication of material tending to prejudice or impede specific civil or criminal proceedings before the courts).

The law of contempt applies only to 'courts of justice properly so-called'.[141] These include Mental Health Tribunals[142] and Employment Tribunals.[143] The authorities were reviewed by the Court of Appeal in *General Medical Council v British Broadcasting Corporation*[144] which decided that the Professional Conduct Committee of the General Medical Council is not a 'court' for the purposes of the law of contempt. There may be jurisdiction to restrain grave and obvious interference with proceedings before non-curial tribunals but no such order has ever been 'made.[145]   **15.43**

The contempts most likely to be committed by the press or broadcasting media are the criminal contempts of publication of material which prejudices active proceedings or scandalises the court and breaches of civil undertakings or court orders which prohibit media publication.   **15.44**

(b) Prejudicing or impeding proceedings

At common law, this type of contempt restricted the media from discussing or reporting on issues being addressed in civil and criminal proceedings on the basis that those proceedings might be prejudiced. The time before and after the trial when a publication was *sub judice* started from the point at which proceedings were 'imminent'.[146] However, the test was criticised for being broad and vague. The *actus reus* involved creating a *real risk* of prejudice to proceedings even if no detriment was suffered. Although it was essential to prove *intent to publish*[147] it was not necessary to show that the contemnor intended that the publication should interfere with the course of justice and, as a result, liability was strict.   **15.45**

The House of Lords in the *Sunday Times* case[148] held that a risk of prejudice to proceedings might be brought about by a publication which 'prejudged' the matter at trial, on the basis of policy arguments against 'trial by newspaper' or 'trial by   **15.46**

---

[141] *Badry v DPP* [1983] 2 AC 297, 307; cf Contempt of Court Act 1981, s 19: 'court' includes 'any tribunal or body exercising the judicial power of the state'.

[142] *Pickering v Liverpool Daily Post and Echo Newspapers plc* [1991] 2 AC 270.

[143] *Peach Grey and Company v Sommers* [1995] 1 ICR 549.

[144] [1998] 1 WLR 1573.

[145] *A-G v British Broadcasting Corporation* [1981] AC 303, 344; see *General Medical Council v British Broadcasting Corporation* (n 144 above).

[146] *R v Savundranayagan* [1968] 1 WLR 1761; [1968] 3 All ER 439.

[147] *R v Thompson Newspapers Ltd, ex p A-G* [1968] 1 WLR 1.

[148] *A-G v Times Newspapers Ltd* [1974] AC 273.

television'. The case involved an attempt to prevent the publication of an article in the *Sunday Times* newspaper which was potentially prejudicial to civil proceedings against the manufacturer of the drug thalidomide. Distillers Limited had manufactured and marketed the drug in the United Kingdom from 1958 to 1961 which, when prescribed to treat nausea in pregnant women, resulted in appalling deformities in hundreds of babies. During Distillers' negotiations to establish a trust fund for the children, the *Sunday Times* ran an article[149] which criticised the company's proposals and announced that a further article, in relation to the history of the tragedy, would be forthcoming. Distillers' complaint to the Attorney-General resulted in an injunction, which was later quashed by the Court of Appeal, to prevent publication of the second article. The House of Lords reinstated it on the basis that the proposed article would 'prejudge' the negligence issue and thereby interfere with the administration of justice. In effect, the House of Lords held that any 'prejudgment' would amount to contempt, whether or not it had a direct effect on the litigant. Previously, only a 'real risk' of influence upon the tribunal, witnesses or parties would amount to contempt, and it had been assumed that this would not normally be found in the absence of a jury trial.[150] The decision imposed greater limitations on the media without any greater certainty as to what was publishable.

15.47   In 1974, in light of the *Sunday Times* case, the Phillimore Committee was established to address the need for reform. Although the Committee stressed the desirability of avoiding trial by media, it criticised the prejudgment test of the House of Lords.[151] It is difficult to distinguish between balanced comment (which would be permissible) and prejudgment (which would not): judicious comment and expressions of opinion may often be difficult to distinguish from prejudgment. Furthermore, the prejudgment test was little different from the requirement to cause a risk of prejudice to the due administration of justice; but its uncertainty made it an unsatisfactory basis for creating a strict liability offence which significantly restricted freedom of expression.

15.48   The Phillimore Committee recommended that this type of contempt remain governed by strict liability.[152] Its report, together with the decision of the European Court of Human Rights in the *Sunday Times* case,[153] prompted the UK Government to enact the Contempt of Court Act 1981.

---

[149] 24 Sep 1972.

[150] In the *Sunday Times* case the Divisional Court applied the principle that a deliberate attempt to influence the settlement of pending proceedings by bringing public pressure to bear on a party amounted to a contempt of court: see [1973] QB 710.

[151] See S Bailey, D Harris, and B Jones, *Civil Liberties: Cases and Materials* (4th edn, Butterworths, 1995) 409.

[152] This is now reflected in the Contempt of Court Act 1981, ss 1 and 2.

[153] *Sunday Times v United Kingdom* (1979) 2 EHRR 245. The ECHR disagreed with the prejudgment test, and found that the restriction on freedom of expression was not founded on a sufficiently pressing social need to justify it in a democratic society.

Contempt of Court Act 1981. The Act does not codify the common law of **15.49**
contempt: it addresses only publications which may prejudice active legal proceedings, with the aim of bringing the law into line with the European
Convention. The Act was intended to be a 'liberalising measure'.[154] It establishes
a rule of strict liability, as recommended by the Phillimore Committee, which
changes the common law on three important respects: it defines contempt more
narrowly, it requires active proceedings and it provides for a public interest defence. Any ambiguity in the Act is presumed to have been intended to avoid future conflict between the law of contempt of court and the obligations of the
United Kingdom under the Convention.[155] The statutory purpose of the Act

> was to effect a permanent shift in the balance of public interest away from the pro-
> tection of the administration of justice and in favour of freedom of speech.[156]

When considering whether or not a particular publication is in contempt, the
court will, in each case, look at the 'localised balance' between freedom of speech
and the right to a fair trial, looking at the significance of the interference in each
case.[157]

First, publications[158] which tend to interfere with the course of justice generally **15.50**
(and legal proceedings in particular), are subject to strict liability,[159] regardless of
intent. The principles were summarised in *A-G v MGN Ltd*.[160] The test is whether
the publication will create a 'substantial risk'[161] that the course of justice in the
'proceedings in question'[162] will be seriously impeded or prejudiced.[163] This test is
difficult to apply in practice. Concern has been expressed that the courts have
taken a robust attitude when considering applications for the stay of criminal proceedings or appeals based on prejudicial publicity but have been more sensitive
when dealing with contempt.[164] It has been suggested that this is because section
2(2) postulates a lesser degree of prejudice than is required to make good an

---

[154] See *Arlidge, Eady and Smith on Contempt*, (2nd edn, Sweet & Maxwell, 1999) para 1–114.

[155] *Re Lonrho plc* [1990] 2 AC 154, 208.

[156] *Per* Lloyd LJ, *A-G v Newspaper Publishing plc* [1988] Ch 333, 382.

[157] *Per* Sedley LJ, *A-G v Guardian Newspapers* [1999] EMLR 904.

[158] Defined to include speech or writing or whatever form addressed to the public at large or any
section of the public: see s 2(1).

[159] s 1.

[160] [1997] 1 All ER 456; see generally, *Arlidge, Eady and Smith on Contempt* (n 154 above) para
4–79ff and also A Nicol and H Rogers, 'Contempt of Court, Reporting Restrictions and Disclosure
of Sources' in *Yearbook of Media and Entertainment Law, 1999* (Oxford University Press, 1999).

[161] Contempt of Court Act 1981, s 2(2); *A-G v MGN Ltd* (n 160 above) 461, Principle 4; 'substantial' means that the risk of influence is 'more than remote', for any risk that is more than remote
must be 'substantial' (see *A-G v English* [1983] 1 AC 116, 141F–G).

[162] *A-G v MGN Ltd* (n 160 above) 461, Principle 5; it is noteworthy that the provision does not
protect the administration of justice generally.

[163] See also *A-G v Independent Television News Ltd* [1995] 2 All ER 370.

[164] *A-G v Birmingham Post and Mail* [1999] 1 WLR 361 DC; *A-G v Unger* [1998] 1 Cr App Rep
308.

appeal against conviction.[165] However, the better view appears to be that there is a single standard which operates differently in the two contexts.[166]

15.51 Secondly, this rule of strict liability applies only to proceedings which are 'active' at the time of publication, as defined by the Act. Criminal proceedings are considered to be active from the time of arrest without warrant or the issue of warrant or summons.[167] Civil proceedings, on the other hand, are active from the time that 'arrangements for trial are made'.[168] This was the date of 'setting down' but, under the CPR, is likely to be an earlier date.[169] The Act creates a defence of 'innocent publication and distribution'.[170] This is available to a publisher who, having taken all reasonable care, either:

- does not know and has no reason to suspect that relevant legal proceedings are active;[171] or
- does not know and has no reason to suspect that the publication contains matter to which the strict liability rule applies.[172]

The innocent publication defence is only available in respect of prosecutions under the 'strict liability' rule.[173] Furthermore, it does not alter the general common law principle that publishing offending material by mistake is no defence.[174]

15.52 Thirdly, section 5 of the Act states that:

> A publication made as or as part of a discussion in good faith of public affairs, or other matters of general public interest is not to be treated as a contempt of court under the strict liability rule if the risk of impediment or prejudice to particular legal proceedings is merely incidental to the discussion.

Strictly speaking, the provision of section 5 is not a 'defence' at all: the burden is on the prosecution to show that the publication does not fall within the section.[175] The House of Lords in *A-G v English*[176] held that the only question raised by

---

[165] As was suggested by Simon Brown LJ in *A-G v Birmingham Post and Mail* [1999] 1 WLR 361, 369H.

[166] See *A-G v Guardian Newspapers*, 23 Jul 1999, DC.

[167] Sch I para 4.

[168] Sch I para 13. Under the CPR, there is no procedure for 'setting down'.

[169] The date on which the trial date is fixed under CPR, r 29.2(2).

[170] Contrast the common law position: neither ignorance of the proceedings (*R v Odhams Press Ltd, ex p A-G* [1957] 1 QB 73) nor the content of imported publications (*R v Griffiths, ex p A-G* [1957] 2 QB 192) was a defence.

[171] s 3(1).

[172] s 3(2).

[173] N Lowe and B Sufrin, *Borrie and Lowe: The Law of Contempt* (3rd edn, Butterworths, 1996) 398–400.

[174] See *R v Evening Standard Company Ltd* [1954] 1 QB 578: editor had every reason to believe that the case report was accurate; *R v Thomson Newspapers Ltd, ex p A-G* [1968] 1 WLR 1: editor had established a proper system to avoid prejudicial publication.

[175] *A-G v English* [1983] 1 AC 116.

[176] Ibid.

section 5 is whether the risk of prejudice is 'merely incidental' to the main theme of the publication. The publication complained of in *English* did not refer to any actual proceedings, but it would seem that even if an accused is mentioned by name, section 5 may apply.[177]

Intentional contempt.   Since the enactment of the Contempt of Court Act, it   **15.53**
has been uncertain whether publications that intentionally threaten to prejudice pending proceedings[178] might be prosecuted at common law to circumvent the more stringent requirements of the Act. The 1981 Act itself, in section 6(c), preserves liability for intentional contempt at common law.[179]

Lord Donaldson suggested in the *Spycatcher* case[180] that 'intention' requires a 'spe-   **15.54**
cific intent to interfere with the administration of justice'; and that 'recklessness' is therefore not a sufficient basis for liability under section 6. The necessary intent might, however, be inferred from the foreseeability of the consequences of the conduct. In that case, foresight on the part of the editor of the *Independent* that publication would prejudice the action of the Attorney-General against the *Guardian* and the *Observer* could support an inference of intention to prejudice the administration of justice amounting to contempt under the common law. The decision was followed in *A-G v Observer Ltd*[181] which found that libraries which innocently made copies of *Spycatcher* available to the public pending the trial of the action must have had sufficient knowledge of the circumstances to infer intention for the purposes of contempt.

Intention to prejudice proceedings was also established where the defendants   **15.55**
sought to bring improper pressure to bear on the other party.[182] In *A-G v Hislop*[182a] the defendants published material in *Private Eye* which, it was held, was intended to persuade Sonia Sutcliffe, the wife of the 'Yorkshire Ripper,' to discontinue her defamation action[183] against the publication. There was a substantial risk that the articles might have prejudiced the course of justice because Mrs Sutcliffe might have been deterred from having her complaint tried before a court.

---

[177] See *A-G v Times Newspapers Ltd* (the *Fagan* case), *The Times*, 12 Feb 1983; also *A-G v Guardian Newspapers* [1992] 3 All ER 38; see also *A-G v Guardian Newspapers*, 23 Jul 1999, DC.

[178] Among other reforms, the Report of the Phillimore Committee, at Cmnd 5794, published Dec 1974, recommended that intentional contempt should be dealt with through proper criminal rather than summary procedures, and that contempt in the absence of intention ought to be more narrowly defined.

[179] s 6(3) states that nothing in the previous sections of the Act 'restricts liability for contempt of court in respect of conduct *intended* to impede or prejudice the administration of justice'.

[180] See *A-G v Guardian Newspapers Ltd (No 2)* [1988] Ch 333, 374-5.

[181] [1988] 1 All ER 385; see also *A-G v News Group Newspapers plc* [1989] QB 110.

[182] *A-G v Hislop* [1991] 1 QB 514.

[182a] Ibid.

[183] The magazine was also guilty of statutory contempt.

(c) Scandalising the court

15.56 'Scandalising the court' is a form of contempt that developed to protect the judicial system from media criticism. It has been defined as 'any act done or writing published calculated to bring a court or a judge into contempt or to lower his authority . . .'[184] Scandalising the court is not affected by the Contempt of Court Act 1981, as there are generally no active proceedings which might be prejudiced. Even if the publication occurred when proceedings were active, the effect of any abuse of a court or judge is likely to create a risk of prejudice to the administration of justice in general rather than a risk to particular proceedings. The *actus reus* of the offence may be fulfilled in two ways: by a scurrilous attack on a court or judge, or by an attempt to impute bias to a judge.

15.57 The leading case is *R v Gray*,[185] in which Darling J, in an obscenity trial, directed the press to refrain from publishing an account of the trial, lest they too be prosecuted for obscenity. Following the trial, Gray published a newspaper article attacking Darling J in a vitriolic fashion, insulting him personally and decrying his warning to the media and his capacity to act as a judge of the court. The article was held to be a grave contempt. Other cases have since stressed that criticism consisting of 'respectful, even though outspoken, comments of ordinary men' must not be considered to be contempt.[186] No offence is committed in such cases provided there is no imputation of improper motives to the judge.[187]

15.58 However, a publication which imputes bias to a judge, even if expressed moderately may scandalise the court. The last successful prosecution of a contempt of this type was in the *Colsey* case[188] where an article implied that a judge might have been biased when construing a statute because he had earlier been involved in initiating the legislation as Solicitor General. Prosecutions for scandalising the court only take place in the most serious cases and are very rare.[189] Critics have suggested that the offence should be abolished, since the notion of undermining public confidence in the administration of justice is so vague.[190] They argue that it is not the comment but the

---

[184] *R v Gray* [1900] 2 QB 36, 40 *per* Lord Russell; see generally, *Arlidge, Eady and Smith on Contempt* (2nd edn, Sweet & Maxwell, 1999) paras 5-208– 5-269.

[185] n 184 above.

[186] *R v Metropolitan Police Commissioner, ex p Blackburn (No 2)* [1968] QB 150; see also *Ambard v A-G for Trinidad and Tobago* [1936] AC 322.

[187] *Ambard v A-G for Trinidad and Tobago* (n 186 above) 335.

[188] *The Times*, 9 May 1931; see also *R v Editor of New Statesman, ex p DPP* (1928) 44 TLR 301; Arlidge, Eady and Smith point out that judges have brought a number of successful libel actions against newspapers in recent years in relation to allegations of incompetence or bias (n 184 above) para 5-209, n 98.

[189] One was, however, instituted in 1999.

[190] See N Lowe and B Sufrin, *Borrie and Lowe: The Law of Contempt* (3rd, edn, Butterworths, 1996) 243; Law Commission, *Offences Relating to Interference with the Course of Justice* (Law Com No 96) 67-8.

conduct which attracts comment which undermines public confidence in the justice system; and that suppressing expression is likely to cause resentment and suspicion.[191] However, it is generally recognised that there is a residual need for the protection afforded by this offence and the Law Commission has recommended a statutory offence of knowingly publishing false allegations that a court is corrupt.[192]

(b) Breach of undertakings or orders that restrict court reporting

There are a number of types of orders a court might make to restrict the media from reporting upon court proceedings. The three most important are:

15.59

- the power to 'postpone' the reporting of proceedings;
- the power to prevent the publication of the names of parties; and
- restrictions on the publication of information relating to children.[193]

Courts are also permitted to restrict reporting of: indecent matters,[194] the identity of the victims of rape and certain other sexual offences[195] and committal proceedings before magistrates' courts.[196]

A person aggrieved by orders under section 4(2) or section 11 and other orders restricting or preventing reports or restricting public access in relation to a trial in the Crown Court can appeal to the Court of Appeal.[197] This right of appeal is subject to a requirement of permission being granted.[198] There is no further appeal to the House of Lords. Where orders are made by magistrates' courts they can be challenged in applications for judicial review.

15.60

Orders for postponement of trial reporting.   Under section 4(2) of the 1981 Act, a court may order the postponement of the publication of material until the conclusion of a trial or series of trials[199] in order to avoid a risk of prejudice to the

15.61

---

[191] Cf the American position where this form of contempt is almost extinct following the case of *Bridges v California* (1941), 314 US 252 in which it was held that a display of disrespect for the judiciary should not be averted by enforced silence.

[192] *Offences Relating to Interference with the Court of Justice* (n 190 above) 213.

[193] For a full discussion of these and other powers see *Arlidge, Eady and Smith* (n 184 above) Chaps 6–8.

[194] Judicial Proceedings (Regulation of Reports) Act 1926.

[195] Sexual Offences (Amendment) Act 1976.

[196] Magistrates' Court Act 1980, s 8.

[197] Criminal Justice Act 1981, s 159; after the decision in *R v Central Criminal Court, ex p Crook*, *The Times*, 8 Nov 1984 and following the application of the journalist to the European Court of Human Rights; see also G Robertson and A Nicol, *Media Law* (3rd edn, Penguin Books, 1992) 347.

[198] Which is determined without a hearing, this provision was held to be *intra vires* in *R v Guardian Newspapers Ltd* [1994] Crim LR 912, see generally, *Arlidge, Eady and Smith on Contempt* (2nd edn, Sweet & Maxwell, 1999) para 7–231ff.

[199] N Lowe and B Sufrin, *Borrie and Lowe: The Law of Contempt* (3rd edn, Butterworths, 1996) 284 ff; *Arlidge, Eady and Smith on Contempt* (n 198 above) paras 7-82–7-231; Robertson and Nicol (n 197 above) 341–350.

administration of justice in those proceedings. The section provides that in any legal proceedings held in public:

> the court may, where it appears to be necessary for avoiding a substantial risk of prejudice to the administration of the justice in those proceedings, or in any other proceedings pending or imminent, order that the publication or any report of the proceedings, or any part of the proceedings, be postponed for such period as the court thinks necessary for that purpose.

The risk to the administration of justice must be 'substantial', and the courts have determined that 'blanket bans' on reporting are likely to be inappropriate.[200]

15.62 In assessing the necessity of such an order, the court must consider the alternatives and should not lightly interfere with the freedom of the press.[201] The test is a three stage one:[202]

- is there a substantial risk of prejudice[203] to the administration of justice?
- is an order necessary?
- should the court exercise its discretion in favour of making an order?

The operation of these tests is illustrated by the case of *Ex parte Central Television plc.*[204] A jury was required to stay overnight in a hotel and the judge, in order to insulate the jurors from the media, ordered that reporting of the trial be postponed until the next day. The Court of Appeal held that there was little evidence that reports would have been anything but fair and accurate and that the risk to the administration of justice was therefore minimal. Even if there had been a substantial risk, the order would not have been automatic, as alternative methods of preventing exposure of the jurors to the media may have been available.[205]

15.63 Orders made under section 4(2) must be formulated in precise terms and committed to writing.[206] It has been suggested that copies of all section 4 orders should be faxed by the court to the Press Association.[207] Unless the order is varied or set aside on appeal, a breach will render the press liable to be committed for contempt.[208]

---

[200] *R v Horsham Justices, ex p Farquarhson* [1982] QB 762; [1982] 2 All ER 269.

[201] *Ex p Central Television plc* [1991] 1 WLR 4; see generally, *Arlidge, Eady and Smith on Contempt* (n 198 above) paras 7-132–7-193.

[202] *MGN Pension Trustees Ltd v Bank of America National Trust and Savings Association* [1995] 2 All ER 355.

[203] Note that, in contrast to the position under the Contempt of Court Act 1981, s 2(2) (see para 15.50 above) there is no requirement that the prejudice be 'serious'.

[204] [1991] 1 WLR 4.

[205] See also *A-G v Guardian Newspapers (No 3)* [1992] 1 WLR 874; *Ex parte The Telegraph plc* [1993] 2 All ER 971; *R v Beck, ex p Daily Telegraph plc* [1993] 2 All ER 177.

[206] *Practice Direction (Contempt: Reporting Restrictions)* [1982] 1 WLR 1475.

[207] *A-G v Guardian Newspapers Ltd (No.3)* (n 205 above).

[208] Ibid 884H–885A.

An employment tribunal also has a power to make a restricted reporting order at **15.64** any stage until its decision is promulgated in any cases involving allegations of sexual misconduct[209] or in a disability discrimination case where evidence of a personal nature is likely to be heard.[210] In *R v London (North) Industrial Tribunal, ex p Associated Newspapers Ltd*[211] it was emphasised that because of the principle of the freedom of the press to report court hearings fully and contemporaneously, the power to make an order should be interpreted narrowly.

Orders to prevent publication of the names of parties. A number of statutory **15.65** provisions allow certain persons involved in the proceedings to remain anonymous.[212] Under section 11 of the Contempt of Court Act 1981, the court has limited powers to restrict the publication of material in relation to hearings which are held in private[213] and to prohibit the reporting of material, including names of participants, mentioned in open court. The section provides that:

> In any case where a court (having power to do so) allows a name or other matter to be withheld from the public in proceedings before the court, the court may give such directions prohibiting the publication of that name or matter in connection with the proceedings as appear to the court to be necessary for the purpose for which it was so withheld.

Section 11 does not confer any additional powers on the court, but simply regulates the exercise of existing powers[214] such as the well-established common law power to withhold the identity of witnesses in blackmail cases since their disclosure would prejudice the administration of justice by discouraging witnesses from coming forward in the future.[215] These policy considerations apply whether or not the accused is subsequently acquitted. Once section 11 orders are made they appear to be binding on everyone who is aware of them.[216] 'Publication' in this section is not understood in the broad sense in which it is used in the law of libel but in its ordinary sense of 'made available to the public'.[217]

An order under section 11 is a draconian measure and should only be used when **15.66** failure to grant anonymity would render the attainment of justice really doubtful

---

[209] Employment Tribunal Act 1996, s 11.

[210] Ibid s 12.

[211] [1998] ICR 1212; see also *Leicester University v A* [1999] IRLR 352.

[212] In addition to the Contempt of Court Act 1981, s 11, see: Sexual Offences (Amendment) Act 1976, s 4, in relation to complainants in rape cases and the Children and Young Persons Act 1933, s 39(1), for children.

[213] *Scott v Scott* [1913] AC 417.

[214] See N Lowe and B Sufrin, *Borrie and Lowe: The Law of Contempt* (3rd edn, Butterworths, 1996) 299; G Robertson and A Nicol, *Media Law* (3rd edn, Penguin Books, 1992) 338–41.

[215] See *R v Socialist Worker Printers and Publishers Ltd, ex p A-G* [1975] QB 637.

[216] *A-G v Leveller Magazine Ltd* [1979] AC 440.

[217] *Borrie and Lowe* (n 214 above) 85.

or, in effect, impracticable.[218] Such orders should not be made to protect the 'comfort and feelings' of parties[219] or to protect businesses from potential loss.[220] In *R v Legal Aid Board, ex p Kaim Todner (a firm)*[221] the Court of Appeal emphasised that, in principle, proceedings should be conducted in public, and that section 11 orders which prevent publication of names or require conduct of proceedings in private require objective justification.

15.67   The general rule is now that hearings are to be in public.[222] Thus, the decision to hold in private an inquiry following the convictions of Dr Shipman for 15 murders was held to be irrational.[222a] However, this general rule does not require the court to make special arrangements for accommodating members of the public.[223] A hearing, or any part of it, may be in private if:

- publicity would defeat the object of the hearing;
- it involves matters relating to national security;
- it involves confidential information and publicity would damage that confidentiality;
- a private hearing is necessary to protect the interest of any child or patient;
- it is a hearing without notice and it would be unjust to any respondent for there to be a public hearing;
- it involves uncontentious matters arising out of the administration of trusts or estates; or
- the court considers it necessary in the interests of justice.[224]

The court may order that the identity of a party or witness must not be disclosed if it considers non-disclosure necessary in order to protect the interests of that party or witness.[225] The fact that proceedings are held in private does not mean that they are secret. Other than in exceptional cases, disclosure of judgments or orders made in private and comments on what happened during proceedings in private is not improper. The court should make arrangements, so far as this is practical, for members of the public to attend hearings in private if this is requested.[226]

---

[218] *R v Westminster City Council, ex p Castelli* [1995] 7 Admin LR 840: no order to conceal the identity of HIV positive applicant; but see *R v Somerset Health Authority, ex p S* [1996] COD 244 where an order for anonymity was made on behalf of a transsexual; and see *R v Criminal Injuries Compensation Board ex p A* [1992] COD 379 (anonymity of applicant seeking compensation for sexual abuse).

[219] *R v Evesham Justices, ex p McDonagh* [1988] 1 QB 553: order banning publication of address of former MP revoked.

[220] *R v Dover JJ, ex p Dover District Council* (1991) 156 JP 433: order banning reporting of name of restaurateur being prosecuted for public health offences.

[221] [1998] 3 WLR 925.

[222] CPR, r 39.2(1).

[222a] *R v Secretary of State for Health ex p Wagstaffe* [2000] 1 All ER (D) 1021.

[223] CPR, r 39.2(2).

[224] CPR, r 39.2(3).

[225] CPR, r 39.2(4).

[226] See *Hodgson v Imperial Tobacco Ltd* [1998] 1 WLR 1056.

Restriction of publication of information concerning children.[226a]   The court   **15.68**
has a general power to restrict publication of information concerning children.
Although a child does not have any special right of privacy or confidentiality,[227]
the court will restrain publication to protect the effective administration of justice. The court must balance the protection of the child against the right of freedom of expression. In this balancing exercise the welfare of the child is not
paramount.[228] It has been recognised that the court will attach great importance
to safeguarding the freedom of the press and will take account of Article 10 of the
Convention. The need to protect the child will be weighed against the right of the
press to comment on matters of genuine public interest.[229] Where an injunction
is sought to restrain the freedom of the press the case should be transferred to the
High Court and the Official Solicitor invited to represent the child.[230]

Restrictions on publications which identify children may be effected by way of an   **15.69**
order under section 39 of the Children and Young Persons Act 1933. That section
provides:

> (1) In relation to any proceedings in any court . . . the court may direct that . . .
>
> > (a) no newspaper report of the proceedings shall reveal the name, address, or
> > school, or include any particulars calculated to lead to the identification
> > of any child or young person concerned in the proceedings, either as
> > being the person [by or against] or in respect of whom the proceedings
> > are taken, or being a witness therein;
> >
> > (b) no picture shall be published in any newspaper as being or including a
> > picture of any child or young person so concerned in the proceedings as
> > aforesaid;
> >
> > except in so far (if at all) as may be permitted by the direction of the court.

Such orders, although discretionary, are routinely made in family cases[231] and education cases; they normally should be if a child or young person is before the court.[232]
If the child is a defendant in a criminal case and is convicted then the conviction may
lead to the order being discharged, although this is not automatic.[233]

Section 39 does not confer an express power to order that publication of the name   **15.70**
of the defendant is to be restricted.[234] Nevertheless, the provision is wide enough

---

[226a] Some important changes are envisaged under the Youth and Criminal Evidence Act 1999, but
at the time of writing these are not yet in force.

[227] *R v Independent Television* [1994] Fam 192, 207A.

[228] See *Re M and N (Wards) (Publication of Information)* [1990] 1 FLR 149; and see *Re Z (A Minor)
(Identification: Restrictions on Publication)* [1997] Fam 1.

[229] See the 'guidelines' set out in *Re W (A Minor) (Wardship: Restrictions on Publication)* [1992] 1
WLR 100, 103.

[230] *Re H–S (Minors) (Protection of Identity)* [1994] 1 WLR 1141.

[231] See *Re X County Council v A* (the Mary Bell case) [1985] 1 All ER 53.

[232] *R v Leicester Crown Court, ex p S (A Minor)* [1992] 2 All ER 659, 662.

[233] See *R v Inner London Crown Court, ex p B* [1996] COD 17; *R v Central Criminal Court, ex p S
and P* [1999] Crim LR 159.

[234] *R v Crown Court at Southwark, ex p Godwin* [1991] 3 All ER 818.

to enable the court to prevent the publication of everything concerning the proceedings, including the fact that the order has been made. The Court of Appeal has, however, recognised difficulties with orders of this type and has approved the practice of the release of a summary of the court decision by the Official Solicitor.[235]

15.71 **Restrictions on reporting material made available on disclosure.** Documents which are the subject of disclosure between parties to proceedings cannot be used for any purpose other than the conduct of the litigation and cannot be supplied to the media. This is because disclosure constitutes a serious invasion of privacy and confidentiality.[236] The obligation is imposed by law[237] and applies in criminal proceedings as well as civil.[238]

15.72 The issue has arisen as to whether, once a disclosed document has been read in court, the parties are entitled to supply copies of it to journalists. In *Home Office v Harman*[239] the House of Lords held that they were not. In that case, 800 pages of documents relating to Home Office prison policy had been read in open court and copies were subsequently supplied by the plaintiffs' solicitor to a journalist. It was held that this constituted a contempt of court. The European Commission on Human Rights held that there had been a violation of Article 10.[240] A friendly settlement was reached and as a result the Rules of the Supreme Court were changed.[241] The rule provides that the implied undertaking of confidentiality ceases to apply after a document has been 'read to or by the court or referred to in open court'. This includes documents pre-read by the court, referred to in a skeleton argument or referred to in open court by counsel or the court but not read.[242] However, this rule has been given a restrictive interpretation, allowing the party to make the contents of the document known, but to use it for no other purpose.[243]

(e) Protection of journalistic sources

15.73 The common law provided limited protection for journalistic sources. In libel

---

[235] *Re G (Minors) (Celebrities: Publicity)*, *The Times*, 28 Oct 1998; and see also *Re R (A Minor)(Wardship: Restrictions on Publication)* [1994] Fam 254 (if order relates to criminal proceedings it should be made by the judge hearing those proceedings, not in wardship proceedings).
[236] *Home Office v Harman* [1983] 1 AC 280, 308.
[237] *Prudential Assurance v Fountain Page Ltd* [1991] 1 WLR 756, 764.
[238] *Taylor v Director of the Serious Fraud Office* [1998] 1 WLR 1040.
[239] Ibid; see generally, I Eagles, 'Disclosure of Material Obtained on Discovery' (1984) 47 MLR 284; N Lowe and B Sufrin *Borrie and Lowe: The Law of Contempt* (3rd edn, Butterworths, 1996) 594–6; G Robertson and A Nicol, *Media Law* (3rd edn, Penguin Books, 1992) 356–358.
[240] *Harman v United Kingdom* (1985) 7 EHRR 146, EComm HR.
[241] RSC Ord 24, r 14A was introduced (and is now CPR, r 31.22).
[242] *Derby v Weldon (No 2) The Times*, 19 Oct 1988; *Smithkline Beecham Biologicals SA v Connaught Laboratories Inc* [1999] 4 All ER 498; and see also *GIO Personal Investment Services v Liverpool and London Steamship Protection and Indemnity Association* [1999] 1 WLR 984.
[243] *Singh v Christie*, *The Times*, 11 Nov 1993; see also the comments of Lord Hoffmann in *Taylor v Director of the Serious Fraud Office* [1998] 1 WLR 1040, 1051.

cases, disclosure of sources was governed by the so-called 'newspaper rule' which meant that newspapers could not be forced to disclose sources of information before trial.[244] In other cases, however, the 'newspaper rule' did not apply.[245] The perceived need to protect journalistic sources more generally led to the enactment of section 10 of the Contempt of Court Act.[246] That section provides:

> No court may require a person to disclose, nor is any person guilty of contempt of court for refusing to disclose, the source of information contained in a publication for which he is responsible,[247] unless it be established to the satisfaction of the court that disclosure is necessary in the interests of justice or national security or for the prevention of disorder or crime.

Section 10 recognises that the protection of sources is a matter of 'high public importance'[248] and effectively creates a presumption in favour of journalists who wish to protect their sources. The presumption is, however, subject to four wide exceptions where disclosure of the source is a matter of necessity: **15.74**

- in the interests of justice;
- in the interests of national security;
- for the prevention of disorder; or
- for the prevention of crime.

The word 'necessary' has a meaning somewhere between 'indispensable' and 'useful' or expedient, the nearest paraphrase being 'really needed'.[249]

In relation to 'national security' and 'the prevention of disorder or crime', the courts have said that: **15.75**

> These two public interests are of such overriding importance that once it is shown that disclosure will serve one of those interests, the necessity of disclosure follows almost automatically.[250]

In *Secretary of State for Defence v Guardian Newspapers Ltd*[251] the House of Lords decided that the *Guardian* should disclose a photocopy of a memorandum, dealing with the arrival in the United Kingdom of cruise missiles, which had been

---

[244] P Milmo and W Rogers (eds), *Gatley on Libel and Slander* (9th edn, Sweet & Maxwell, 1998) para 30.112.

[245] *British Steel Corporation v Granada Television Ltd* [1981] AC 1096.

[246] *Arlidge, Eady and Smith on Contempt* (2nd edn, Sweet & Maxwell, 1999) Chap 9.

[247] The section applies to information received for the purposes of publication, even though it is never in fact published: see *X Ltd v Morgan-Grampian (Publishers) Ltd* [1991] 1 AC 1, 40F, in which the point was conceded.

[248] Ibid 41E.

[249] *In re An Inquiry under the Company Securities (Insider Dealing) Act 1985* [1988] AC 660, 704.

[250] *X Ltd v Morgan-Grampian (Publishers) Ltd* (n 247 above) 43B, although not if the crime was of a 'trivial nature'.

[251] [1985] AC 339.

supplied by an anonymous source, despite the absence of clear evidence of the sensitivity and urgency of the subject matter.[252] A similar result was reached in *In re An Inquiry under the Company Securities (Insider Dealing) Act 1985*[253] in which it was held to be sufficient to show that disclosure could assist in the prosecution of a crime already committed.[254] Such an application was, however, refused where a health authority sought disclosure of the identity of doctors who were practising despite having contracted AIDS: the prevention of crime was not the task of the plaintiff health authority and criminal investigation was unlikely.[255]

15.76 The question as to whether disclosure is 'necessary in the interests of justice' has given rise to considerable difficulty. The courts have construed 'interests of justice' as being wider than 'the administration of justice'. It covers the interest of the public

> in the maintenance of the system of law, within the framework of which every citizen has the ability and the freedom to exercise his legal right to remedy a wrong done to him or to prevent it being done . . .[256]

In the *Morgan-Grampian* case Lord Bridge set out a number of factors which were relevant when balancing the interests of justice against the policy of protection from disclosure underlying section 10, stating that:

> if it appears that the information was obtained illegally, this will diminish the importance of protecting the source unless, of course, this factor is counter-balanced by a clear public interest in publication of the information.[257]

15.77 In the case itself it was found 'necessary in the interests of justice' that the court should order the disclosure of the source of financial confidential information concerning the claimant's business even though the dissemination of the confidential information had been restrained by injunction. The journalist applied to the European Court of Human Rights. In *Goodwin v United Kingdom*[258] the Court held that, insofar as the disclosure order served to reinforce the injunction, the additional restriction on freedom of expression was not justified under Article 10(2). Furthermore, the Court took the view that the interest of the plaintiff in eliminating the residual threat of damage through dissemination of confidential information and in unmasking a disloyal employee was not sufficient to outweigh the public interest in protecting the journalist's source.

---

[252] *Borrie and Lowe* (n 239 above) 54; G Robertson and A Nicol (n 239 above) 202.
[253] [1988] AC 660.
[254] Rejecting the view of Hoffmann J that it was necessary to show that, in the absence of disclosure, it was likely that further crimes would be committed.
[255] *X v Y* [1988] 2 All ER 648; and see *Handmade Films v Express Newspapers* [1986] FSR 463: no order for disclosure of source of photographs taken on a film set as no serious damage threatened.
[256] *X Ltd v Morgan-Grampian (Publishers) Ltd* (n 247 above) 54C.
[257] n 247 above, 44.
[258] (1996) 22 EHRR 123 (by an 11:7 majority).

When the issue again arose before the English courts in *Camelot Group plc v* **15.78**
Centaur Communications Ltd[259] the Court of Appeal said that 'the tests which the
ECHR and the House of Lords applied were substantially the same'. There was no
public interest in protecting the source of the draft accounts of the plaintiff and
the Court upheld an order for disclosure. This decision can be contrasted with
that in *Saunders v Punch Ltd*[260] where Lindsay J refused to order the disclosure of
sources of information concerning a DTI inquiry,[261] despite the fact that some of
the disclosed information appears to have been protected by legal professional
privilege. He said that an injunction already granted to restrain the use of the information meant that the interests of justice were not so pressing as to require that
the ban on 'statutory privilege against disclosure' be overridden.[262] This approach
was approved by the Court of Appeal in *John v Express Newspapers*[262a] which held
that before overriding the public interest in protecting confidential sources, the
minimum requirement was that other ways of obtaining the information had to
have been explored.

(5) Obscenity and indecency

(a) Introduction

English law restricts freedom of expression by regulating content and prohibiting **15.79**
the publication of obscene, blasphemous or racially offensive matter.[263] The extent to which the display or publication of such material ought to be criminalised
and the content of film, theatre and telecommunications broadcasts ought to be
suppressed or regulated, remains highly contentious.

(b) The Obscene Publications Acts

Introduction. The moral and legal debate concerning obscenity focuses on **15.80**
whether obscenity falls within the realm of protected expression at all;[264] and if so,
whether there are justifiable bases for its restriction.[265] In practice, Parliament and
the courts have had difficulty devising a test of obscenity which adequately

---

[259] [1999] QB 124; see also *O'Mara Books Ltd v Express Newspapers plc*, 3 Mar 1998, Neuberger J:
following *Camelot*, disclosure ordered.
[260] [1998] 1 WLR 986; see also *Chief Constable of Leicestershire v Garavelli* [1997] EMLR 543: disclosure not necessary.
[261] The DTI inquiry concerned Mr Ernest Saunders who was ultimately convicted for his role in
the Guinness take over.
[262] At 250b–d.
[262a] *The Times*, 26 Apr 2000.
[263] For a fuller discussion, see G Robertson and A Nicol, *Media Law* (3rd edn, Penguin Books,
1992) Chap 3.
[264] See discussion in E Barendt, *Freedom of Speech* (Clarendon Press, 1985) 247ff.
[265] See J Bakan, [1984] Ottawa L Re, 1; E Barendt, *Freedom of Speech* (n 264 above) 254–279 discusses the three main grounds: specific harm to individuals, impact on the moral tone of society
(community standards) and the offensiveness principle.

distinguishes between expression which is defensible and expression which is not.[266]

15.81   The Obscene Publications Acts of 1959 and 1964[267] supersede but do not abolish the common law. They were a response to a number of prosecutions of serious literature during the 1950s followed by deliberations of a Parliamentary Committee and the recommendations of the 'Society of Authors' chaired by Sir Alan Herbert.[268] The Acts prohibit anyone from publishing an obscene article, whether for gain or not, unless it can be shown that the publication is justified as being for the common good[269] or that it can be shown that the publisher was ignorant of the nature of the article.[270] The legislation also provides powers of search and seizure, and for forfeiture of obscene articles upon conviction.

15.82   **Definition of obscenity.**   The statutory definition of obscenity provides that an article is 'obscene' if its effect tends to:

> deprave and corrupt persons who are likely, having regard to all relevant circumstances, to read, see or hear the matter contained or embodied in it.[271]

This is the common law *Hicklin*[272] test, modified (to redefine the class of persons liable to be depraved) so as to include those to whom the material is likely to be distributed, circulated or offered for sale.[273] The result is that, for example, material intended for adults will not be 'obscene' merely because it would tend to

---

[266] See eg proposals in *Pornography: The Longford Report* (1972); *The Pollution of the Mind; New Proposals to Control Public Indecency and Obscenity*, The Society of Conservative Lawyers (1972); *The Obscenity Laws: Report of Arts Council Working Party* (1969); also proposals put forward by the Defence of Literature and the Arts Society (1978) 12 NLJ 423.

[267] See also: Children and Young Persons (Harmful Publications) Act 1955; Indecent Displays (Control) Act 1981; Criminal Justice Act 1988, s 160 in relation to offence of possession of indecent photograph of child; Theatres Act 1968; Post Office Act 1953, s 11; Customs Consolidation Act 1876, s 42 in relation to controls on importation of indecent or obscene articles; Judicial Proceedings (Regulation of Reports) Act 1926, s 1(1)(a) in relation to indecent details of legal proceedings.

[268] See C H Rolph, *Books in the Dock* (Andre Deutsch, 1969) 93; G Robertson, *Obscenity* (Weidenfeld and Nicholson, 1979) Chap 2; Robertson and Nicol (n 263 above) 108–110; also *R v Martin Secker and Warburg Ltd* [1954] 1 WLR 1178, *per* Stable, J.

[269] s 4 of the 1959 Act provides that there should be no conviction or forfeiture if it is proved that the article in question is justified as being for the common good on the ground that it is in the interests of science, literature, art or learning.

[270] s 2(5) of the 1959 Act provides that 'a person shall not be convicted of an offence against this section if he proves that he had not examined the article in respect of which he is charged and had no reasonable cause to suspect that it was such that *his publication* of it would make him liable to be convicted of an offence against this section'. The 1964 Act, s 1(3), amends the 1959 reference to 'his publication' of the article to read 'his having of it'.

[271] Obscene Publications Act 1959, s 1(1).

[272] *R v Hicklin* (1868) LR 3 QB 360, 371. The old test was 'whether the tendency of the matter charged as obscenity is to deprave and corrupt those whose minds are open to such immoral influences and into whose hands such a publication might fall'.

[273] As suggested by *R v Martin Secker and Warburg Ltd* [1954] 1 WLR 1138.

corrupt a young person, to whom it would not normally be made available. In addition, there is authority for the suggestion that 'persons' means a 'significant proportion' of the likely readers,[274] and that 'likely readers' will only be excluded from consideration if they are negligible in number.[275] The provision protects not only the innocent, but also those whose morals are already in a state of corruption because it is fallacious to assume that they cannot be further depraved.[276]

The phrase 'deprave and corrupt' refers to the mental and moral corruption orig- **15.83**
inally propounded by Lord Cockburn CJ in *R v Hicklin*.[277] Depravity is not confined to sexual matters;[278] and sexual explicitness does not necessarily amount to obscenity.[279] Even the fact that an article is 'filthy' or 'lewd' may not be sufficient: it is a defence to assert that the article is so disgusting that, far from corrupting the individual, it would cause him to revolt from the activity it describes.[280] The decision in *R v Calder and Boyars Ltd*[281] suggests that the number of readers susceptible, the strength of the tendency to corrupt and deprave, and the nature of the corruption or depravity are all elements which should be considered.[282] The purpose or intention of the publisher is, however, irrelevant, for the test for obscenity depends on the article itself.[283]

Obscene Publications Act 1964. Two loopholes in the 1959 Act's definition of **15.84**
'publication'[284] were filled by the 1964 Act. The first involved the display of a priced article in a shop which was found not to be an 'offer for sale' so as to constitute publication.[285] The second problem arose because it was said that in a sale to a particular individual, it was necessary to show publication of the article to a

---

[274] *R v Calder and Boyars Ltd* [1969] 1 QB 151.
[275] *DPP v Whyte* [1972] AC 849.
[276] Ibid.
[277] (1868) LR 3 QB 360.
[278] *John Calder (Publications) Ltd v Powell* [1965] 1 QB 509.
[279] *R v Stanley* [1965] 2 QB 327; *Darbo v DPP* [1992] Crim LR 56.
[280] *R v Anderson* [1972] 1 QB 304.
[281] [1969] 1 QB 151.
[282] See also *Hoare v United Kingdom* [1997] EHRLR 678 in which the applicant had engaged in publication and distribution of pornographic videotapes by post: a brochure describing the contents of the videos was provided to those who responded to an advertisement in a Sunday paper, and the videos distributed thereafter, upon request. The applicant was convicted, and given a 30-month prison sentence. His argument that the videos could not deprave or corrupt since only those who shared his interests would have purchased them from the brochure was rejected by the Commission on Human Rights.
[283] *R v Shaw* [1962] AC 220: affirmed on other grounds, [1962] AC 237; followed in *Knuller (Publishing, Printing and Promotions) Ltd v DPP* [1973] AC 435.
[284] The 1959 Act, s 1(3), provides that a person publishes an article who distributes, circulates, sells, lets on hire, gives, lends, offers for sale or for hire an obscene article; and in the case of an article containing matter to be looked at, shows, plays or projects it.
[285] *Mella v Monahan* [1961] Crim LR 175; see also *R v Taylor (Alan)* [1995] Cr App R 131, where the Court of Appeal held that the sale by photographic developing-processing outlets of prints to the owners of developed film constituted a 'publication'.

person who was liable to be corrupted by it.[286] A person is now deemed to have an article for publication for gain if, with a 'view to publication', he has it in his ownership, possession or control.[287]

15.85 **The offences.** By section 2 of the Obscene Publications Act 1959 it is an offence to publish an obscene article or to have an obscene article for publication for gain. The maximum penalty is three-years' imprisonment on trial on indictment. An 'article' includes anything 'containing or embodying matter to be read or looked at or both, any sound record and any film or other record of a picture or pictures'.[288] This includes photographic negatives[289] video cassettes[290] and images on computer disc in digitised form.[291] 'Publication' is given a wide definition[292] and includes giving or lending. It is committed by a photographic developer who develops film sent by customers depicting obscene acts, makes prints and sends them to the customers.[293]

15.86 **Seizure and forfeiture.** By section 3 of the Obscene Publications Act 1959 a justice of the peace can issue a warrant for the search and seizure of obscene articles kept for publication for gain. The articles must be brought before the justice who may issue a summons to the occupier to show cause why the articles should not be forfeited.[294] This provision also applies to articles kept for publication abroad.[295] This procedure is often used by the police to avoid having to prove obscenity offences at a jury trial.[296]

15.87 **Defence of public good.** Section 4 of the Obscene Publications Act 1959 provides that there should be no conviction or forfeiture:

> if it is proved that publication of the article in question is justified as being for the common good on the ground that it is in the interests of science, literature, art or learning or of other objects of general concern.

The defence will only be considered once it is established that an article is obscene,[297] and may be assisted by expert evidence concerning the literary or other

---

[286] See *R v Clayton and Halsey* [1963] 1 QB 163 (where the particular persons to whom the articles were sold were police officers experienced in dealing with obscene articles and who were said to be uncorrupted by it).

[287] Obscene Publications Act 1964, s 1(2).

[288] Obscene Publications Act 1959, s 1(2).

[289] Obsence Publications Act 1964, s 2(1).

[290] *A-G's Reference (No 5 of 1980)* [1981] 1 WLR 88.

[291] *R v Fellows* [1997] 2 All ER 548.

[292] Obscene Publications Act 1959, s 1(3).

[293] *R v Taylor (Alan)* [1995] 1 Cr App R 131.

[294] See *Olympia Press v Hollis* [1973] 1 WLR 1520, see also R Stone, 'Obscene Publications: The Problems Persist' [1986] Crim PR 139.

[295] *Gold Star Publications Ltd v DPP* [1981] 1 WLR 732.

[296] See the criticism by Robertson and Nicol (n 263 above) 134–135.

[297] *R v Calder and Boyars Ltd* [1969] 1 QB 151; *DPP v Jordan* [1977] AC 699.

merits[298] of the material in question.[299] 'Learning' means the 'product of scholarship'[300] and, as a result, a publication used for the purposes of teaching cannot be defended under section 4.

(c) Other obscenity and indecency offences

The Obscene Publications Act 1959 was intended to protect defendants against the prosecution of obscene libel. Thus, section 2(4) provides that an article shall not be proceeded against at common law 'where it is of the essence of the offence that the matter is obscene'. However, this does not prevent prosecutions being brought at common law on the basis that the essence of the offence is 'indecency'.[301] The result is that the defence of 'public good' is not available. Moreover, the common law offences of conspiracy to corrupt public morals[302] and of outraging public decency[303] are unaffected by the legislation. **15.88**

It is an offence publicly to display 'indecent matter'.[304] It appears that material can be 'indecent' for these purposes without being obscene.[305] A public place does not include a place to which the public only have access on payment or a shop to which the public can only gain access by passing a warning sign.[306] **15.89**

Under the Protection of Children Act 1978 it is an offence to take or permit to be taken any indecent photograph of a child (that is, a person under 16),[307] to distribute or show such photographs,[308] to possess them with a view to distribution,[309] or to publish an advertisement likely to be understood as conveying that the advertiser distributes or shows such indecent photographs.[310] 'Indecent photographs' include films, film negatives and video recordings. The only defence to the offence of taking a photograph is that it is not 'indecent'. The motive for **15.90**

---

[298] In *John Calder Publications v Powell* [1965] 1 QB 509 it was held that a court is entitled to reject even favourable evidence and hold that the publication is not justified as being for the public good.

[299] s 4(2).

[300] *A-G's Reference (No 3 of 1977)* [1978] 1 WLR 1123.

[301] See Robertson and Nicol (n 263 above) 158–160.

[302] This would not entail the publication of the obscenity, but an agreement to do an act of a kind that may corrupt. See *Shaw v DPP* [1962] AC 220, regarding publication of a magazine offering the services of prostitutes; *Knuller (Publishing, Printing and Promotions) Ltd v DPP* [1973] AC 435.

[303] See *R v Gibson* [1991] 1 All ER 439; the criminal offence of outraging public decency, which prohibits the public display of offensive material, is aimed at protecting individuals from the shock or offence of exposure to certain material, rather than protecting public morals; see also cases on conspiracy to corrupt public morals: *Shaw v DPP* and *Knuller (Publishing, Printing and Promotions) Ltd v DPP* (n 302 above).

[304] Indecent Displays (Control) Act 1981, s 1.

[305] Cf *R v Stanley* [1965] 2 QB 327.

[306] Indecent Displays (Control) Act 1981, s 1(3).

[307] s 1(1)(a).

[308] s 1(1)(b).

[309] s 1(1)(c).

[310] s 1(1)(d).

taking the photograph is irrelevant.[311] This means that, for example, taking a photograph for medical purposes would involve the commission of the offence. It is also an offence to possess an indecent picture of a child.[312] It is a defence to show a legitimate reason for possessing the photograph.

15.91 The import into the United Kingdom of 'indecent or obscene prints, paintings, photographs, books, cards, lithographic or other engravings or any other indecent or obscene articles' is prohibited.[313] The test of 'indecency' is much less strict than that under the Obscene Publications Act. However, it was held that insofar as this prohibition related to indecent articles imported from the EC it was in breach of Article 36[314] of the Treaty of European Union[315] and the Customs no longer seize material solely on the ground that it is 'indecent'. When considering a claim for forfeiture by the Customs, the court can order forfeiture if the material is 'obscene' within the definition in section 1 of the Obscene Publications Act 1959. The court does not have to go on to consider whether a section 4 'public good' defence might be available.[316]

(6) Media regulation and censorship

(a) Introduction[317]

15.92 The regulation of broadcasting, theatre, film and video has evolved in Britain over a long period of time and reflects an ambiguous attitude towards the media, which has been seen as both providing important public benefits and as a source of potential harm. It raises issues concerning the independence of radio and television from government, political impartiality and the standards to be applied when regulating the content of broadcasts.

(b) Broadcasting regulation[318]

15.93 **Introduction.** In the 1950s, there was a movement from regulation by means of

---

[311] *R v Graham-Kerr* [1988] 1 WLR 1098.

[312] Criminal Justice Act 1988, s 160.

[313] Customs Consolidation Act 1876, s 42; see generally, G Robertson and A Nicol, *Media Law* (3rd edn, Penguin Books, 1992), 153–155.

[314] Formerly, Art 30 of the Treaty of Rome.

[315] *Conegate Ltd v HM Customs and Excise* [1987] QB 254.

[316] *R v Bow Street Metropolitan Stipendiary Magistrates, ex p Noncyp Ltd* [1990] 1 QB 123.

[317] For a fuller treatment, see for example T Gibbons, *Regulating the Media* (2nd edn, Sweet & Maxwell, 1998); R Craufurd Smith, *Broadcasting Law and Fundamental Rights* (Clarendon Press, 1997).

[318] See eg A Briggs, *The History of Broadcasting in the UK, Vol I: The Birth of Broadcasting* (Oxford University Press 1961); *Vol II: The Golden Age of Wireless* (Oxford University Press 1965); *Vol IV: Sound and Vision* (1979); B Sendall, *Independent Television in Britain; Origin and Foundations 1946–62* (Macmillan, 1982); R Negrine (ed), *Cable Television and the Future of Broadcasting* (Croom Helm, 1985); T Hollins, *Beyond Broadcasting to the Cable Age* (BFI, 1984).

the criminal law to direct statutory regulation. This change coincided with the introduction of commercial television. In contrast to the absence of direct government regulation of newspapers, there was a perceived need for careful monitoring of television by a public body.

The Independent Broadcasting Authority ('IBA') was established in 1954 to ensure that nothing in independent television programming would offend against good taste, decency or public feeling or would be likely to encourage or incite to crime or to lead to disorder; that news was presented with accuracy and impartiality; and that impartiality of presentation was preserved with respect to matters of political or industrial controversy or relating to current public policy.[319] The Board of Governors of the British Broadcasting Corporation ('BBC') in 1964 voluntarily undertook[320] to comply in general terms with the statutory duties imposed on independent television, so that in effect all broadcasting, both public and independent, was subjected to the same standards.

15.94

Public broadcasting.   Public broadcasting is currently governed by the Royal Charter of the BBC comprising in part a Licence Agreement[321] with the Home Secretary. The 1964 undertaking as to standards has been reaffirmed and is now annexed to the BBC Licence:[322] it is the responsibility of the Governors of the BBC under these instruments to produce a code of content and scheduling requirements for the guidance of programme-makers including standards to be observed for the preservation of good taste, decency, the protection of children and political impartiality. Although the undertaking is not legally enforceable against the Corporation, BBC programming is also monitored by the Broadcasting Standards Commission ('BSC') established by the Broadcasting Act 1996.[323] Manifestly inappropriate material may be subject to injunction under the code of standards elaborated by that body.

15.95

Independent broadcasting.   Independent broadcasting is now governed by the Broadcasting Acts of 1990 and 1996. In an attempt to 'deregulate' independent television, these Acts replaced the IBA with the Independent Television Commission ('ITC') and the Independent Radio Authority, endowing them with licensing and regulatory powers. By section 6(1), the 1990 Act requires that the

15.96

---

[319] See Broadcasting Act 1981, s 4.

[320] Letter from Lord Normanbrook, Chairman of the BBC to the Postmaster-General 19 Jun 1964: 'The Board accept that so far as possible the programmes for which they are responsible should not offend against good taste or decency, or be likely to encourage crime or disorder, or be offensive to public feeling. In judging what is suitable for inclusion in programmes, they will pay special regard to the need to ensure that broadcasts designed to stimulate thought do not so far depart from their intention as to give general offence.'

[321] See Cmnd 8313 and 8233.

[322] The contents of the letter are noted in the prescribing memorandum under the BBC Licence and Agreement, cl 13(4).

[323] See para 15.99 below.

ITC publish a Code to require that programmes containing politically sensitive material are balanced[324] in order to maintain impartiality.[325] Furthermore, although the Act does not impose a censorship role,[326] it establishes programme guidelines for good taste, decency and portrayal of violence.[327] A similar function is performed by the Independent Radio Authority in relation to monitoring independent radio stations.

15.97 **Satellite television.** The ITC Code only applies to broadcasters who hold an ITC licence. The Broadcasting Act 1990 requires that 'domestic' satellite services and 'non-domestic' satellite services hold an ITC licence. As defined, the two categories together do not represent comprehensive coverage of conceivable satellite services. A domestic service provides direct satellite broadcasting on one of five frequencies allocated to the United Kingdom at the World Administrative Radio Conference of 1977. Non-domestic service refers to satellite re-transmission of programmes either from within the United Kingdom, or into the United Kingdom from outside the territory if the service is nevertheless being dictated by a UK supplier. Any satellite transmission that does not qualify as either a 'domestic' or a 'non-domestic' service is not regulated by the Act.

15.98 Section 89 of the Broadcasting Act 1996, amending section 45 of the 1990 Act, permits immediate suspension of non-domestic satellite transmissions that do not meet the taste and decency standards of section 6(1)(a) of the Act. This UK legislation has been held to be contrary to the EC Directive on Transfrontier Television,[328] which requires that a service licensed from within any EC member state must be given freedom of reception within other member states. No clear exception is created for obscene material, which may create a difficulty for prosecution of satellite material beamed from other EC states.[329] No such difficulty will arise in relation to obscene publications transmitted from non-EC states.

---

[324] 'Balancing' must occur within a programme or series of programmes produced by a particular broadcasting company: it is not sufficient that the company assert that programming by another company will balance the bias exhibited by its production.

[325] The ITC published its Programme Code in 1991.

[326] This is in contrast to its predecessor, the Independent Broadcasting Authority, which previewed and approved scheduled programming; for cases unsuccessfully challenging these powers see: *A-G, ex rel McWhirter v Independent Broadcasting Authority* [1973] QB 629; *R v Independent Broadcasting Authority, ex p Whitehouse, The Times,* 4 Apr 1985.

[327] See *Broadcasting in the 90s: Competition, Choice and Quality* (1988) 517 (White Paper).

[328] 89/552/EEC; in Case 222/94 *Commission v United Kingdom* [1996] ECR-I 4025, it was found that the extraterritorial reach of the Broadcasting Act 1990, s 43 to broadcasters who fell under the regulatory jurisdiction of other member states was a violation of the Directive, Arts 2(1)(2) and 3(2).

[329] There have been a number of proscriptive orders issued under the Broadcasting Act 1990, s 177, against EC satellite channels that transmit hard core pornography: so far these have not been challenged in the European Court of Justice.

Broadcasting Standards Commission.   Part V of the Broadcasting Act 1996 es-   **15.99**
tablishes a Broadcasting Standards Commission ('BSC').[330] The BSC is an amalgam of the Broadcasting Complaints Commission[331] and the Broadcasting
Standards Council.[332] The functions of the BSC are applicable to all television and
radio services provided by the BBC and other television and radio companies in
the United Kingdom. The BSC has a duty to:

> draw up, and from time to time review, a code giving guidance as to the principles
> to be observed and the practices to be followed in connection with the avoidance
> of—
>
> (a) unjust or unfair treatment in programmes . . .
> (b) unwarranted infringement of privacy in or in connection with the obtain-
> ing of material contained in such programmes.[333]

In addition, it is required to draw up a code giving guidance as to the practices
to be followed in connection with the portrayal of violence and sexual conduct.[334]

Government powers.   The Broadcasting Act confers important powers on the   **15.100**
Government over radio and television. Powers of censorship over the BBC are
contained in sections 13(4) and 19 of the Licence Agreement: section 19 enables
the Home Secretary, in an 'emergency' and when he thinks it 'expedient', to send
in the troops to take possession of the BBC in the name of and on behalf of Her
Majesty.[335] More significant is the power under section 13(4), by which he may
ban transmission of any BBC item or programme at any time, subject to the minimal safeguard that the BBC 'may' tell the public that it has received a section
13(4) order from the Government.[336]

A parallel power in relation to independent television entitles the Government   **15.101**
under section 10(3) of the 1990 Act to order the ITC to refrain from transmitting

---

[330] s 106.
[331] Established by the Broadcasting Act 1980, s 17 and continued by the Broadcasting Act 1981,
s 53 and the Broadcasting Act 1990, s 142.
[332] See the Broadcasting Act 1990, s 151.
[333] s 107.
[334] s 108. For an example of the BSC's exercise of its powers, see the discussion of its handling of
the satellite broadcast channel 'Red Hot Dutch' in S Bailey, D Harris and B Jones *Civil Liberties:
Cases and Materials* (4th edn, Butterworths, 1995) 345; also F Coleman and S McMurtrie, 'Too Hot
to Handle' [1993] NLJ 10; and see also *R v Secretary of State for the Natural Heritage ex p Continental
Television* [1993] 2 CMLR 333.
[335] This provision was established during the General Strike when the Government under
Winston Churchill wanted to control the BBC; although it has never been used for that purpose, it
was contemplated by Sir Anthony Eden as a basis for broadcasting propaganda during the Suez crisis and was used as such to beam propaganda to Argentina during the Falklands war.
[336] Home Secretary Reginald Maudling tried to use this power to stop BBC broadcasts of a debate
about Government action in Ulster, but the safeguard was invoked by Lord Hill, Director-General
of the BBC, who threatened to make public the Government's attempts to keep the matter quiet.

any 'matter or classes of matter' on commercial television. Although the veto has been little used, it was recently applied in an attempt to deprive terrorists of publicity by imposing a ban on the broadcast of words as spoken by representatives of specified organisations.[337] A challenge was unsuccessful when the House of Lords, in *R v Secretary of State for the Home Department, ex p Brind*[338] held that Ministers and public bodies were not obliged to exercise their powers in accordance with Convention rights. The ban was lifted in September 1994, following the IRA declaration of ceasefire.

15.102 **DA Notice system.**[339] The Defence Press and Broadcasting Advisory Committee ('DPBAC') is a joint committee of the Ministry of Defence, publishers and broadcasters. It offers informal advice to the press on the content of proposed publications and broadcasts, in the interests of and for the protection of national security. The DPBAC acts as a cooperative consultative and negotiating body between the media and the Ministry: it has no judicial function and participation by the press in the DA Notice system is entirely voluntary.

15.103 The function of the DPBAC, as broadly defined by the Ministry of Defence, is to review proposed publications to identify information that the Government considers it necessary to keep secret. There are eight specific categories of information with which the Committee is concerned:

- defence plans, operational capability, state of readiness and training;
- defence equipment;
- nuclear weapons and equipment;
- radio and radar transmissions;
- cyphers and communications;
- British security and intelligence services;
- war precautions and civil defence; and
- photography etc of defence establishments and installations.

There are six 'standing' DA Notices covering highly classified information about future military operations, defence equipment, nuclear weapons installations, codes and ciphers, details of sites for the use of Government in times of crisis nad information about security and intelligence services.[340]

15.104 A publisher or broadcaster may itself approach the Committee to ask its advice on a proposed publication. The Committee may on, the other hand, initiate

---

[337] The organisations included, in addition to those identified in the Northern Ireland (Emergency Provisions) Act 1978, Sinn Fein, Republican Sinn Fein, and the Ulster Defence Association.

[338] *R v Secretary of State for the Home Department, ex p Brind* [1991] 1 AC 696.

[339] See D Fairley, 'D Notices, Official Secrets and the Law' (1990) 10 OJLS 430–40. 'D Notices' were renamed 'DA Notices' (Defence Advisory Notices) in 1993.

[340] *The Defence Advisory Notices, A Review of the D Notice System* (Ministry of Defence Open Government Document No 93/06).

contact.[341] If the DPBAC concludes that the contents of a publication threaten national security in one of its areas of responsibility, it will suggest that changes are made. If the advice is not accepted, it will issue a DA Notice.

The DA Notice serves solely as a warning device. The fact that a DA Notice has no legal force has both positive and negative implications: the media can be assured that it will not be prosecuted merely for defying the advice of the Committee; on the other hand, the DPBAC has no power to provide security clearance and provides a publisher with no defence or justification should the Government seek to restrain the publication under the Official Secrets Act[342] or on grounds of breach of confidence.[343] **15.105**

(c) Theatre, film and video censorship

The Theatres Act 1968 removed the official censorship of theatrical productions so that theatre performances are now only subject to the criminal law. Film censorship, on the other hand, continues to be governed by the Cinemas Act 1985 which establishes a licensing requirement for premises used for film exhibitions. The Act also imposes a duty on the licensing authority[344] to define regulations and conditions for the admission of children to such exhibitions. Furthermore, the Act authorises the licensing body to make regulations for the 'safety', 'health', and 'welfare' of children attending film exhibitions. **15.106**

In 1912, the British Board of Film Censors was established by the film industry to provide guidance to local authorities which had been given licensing powers under the Cinematograph Act 1909.[345] The decisions and classification criteria of the non-statutory body were well accepted and the objective of the BBFC largely achieved. Although there has been controversy over specific films, most councils have generally been happy to rely upon the judgment of the BBFC. The Board, renamed the British Board of Film Classification, is also the authority designated by **15.107**

---

[341] If a publisher does not normally participate in the DA Notice system, the DPBAC will send it a copy of the relevant DA Notice and a guide to the system called the *General Introduction to the D Notice System*: for a copy of this document, see S Bailey, D Harris and B Jones, *Civil Liberties: Cases and Materials* (4th edn, Butterworths, 1995) 470–471.

[342] There is, however, substantial overlap between the contents of a DA Notice and the relevant Government legislation in the area. DA Notice 6 in relation to British Security and Intelligence Services, for example, requests that the media refrain from publishing references to an extensive list of specific matters that comes close to comprehensive coverage of the matters that could be caught by the Official Secrets Act.

[343] For example, when the BBC approached the DPBAC in regard to a radio series exploring aspects of national security in the wake of the *Spycatcher* litigation, it was told that advice was not necessary: nevertheless, the Government sought and obtained injunctions restraining the broadcasts on grounds of breach of confidence. Although the Government eventually acknowledged that the programmes were not a threat and the injunctions were lifted, the BBC delayed their broadcast and in certain instances, declined to deliver altogether.

[344] The licensing authorities are now London boroughs and district councils across the country: see Cinema Act 1985 ss 3(10), 21.

[345] See G Robertson and A Nicol, *Media Law* (3rd edn, Penguin Books, 1992) 566ff.

the Home Secretary to deal with the arrangements for certifying videos under section 4(1) of the Video Recordings Act 1984 as:

the authority responsible for making arrangements

(a) for determining, for the purposes of [the] Act whether or not video works are suitable for classification certificates to be issued in respect of them, having special regard to the likelihood of video works in respect of which such certificates have been issued being viewed in the home,

(b) in the case of works which are determined in accordance with the arrangements to be so suitable

  (i) for making such other determinations as are required for the issue of classification certificates, and

  (ii) for issuing such certificates . . .

15.108 The Video Recordings Act 1984 gives rise to a number of problems. First, it requires classification of almost all video recordings,[346] whether or not they have already been broadcast on television. The BBFC will censor videos containing a wide range of material including cruelty to animals, drug use, violence, sexual violence and blasphemy.[347] Decisions regarding classification may be appealed to the Video Appeals Committee,[347a] which is selected by the BBFC. The decision of the Video Appeals Committee to certify the film, called 'Visions of Ecstasy', on the ground of blasphemy resulted in an unsuccessful application to the European Court of Human Rights in *Wingrove v United Kingdom*.[348]

15.109 The BBFC now classifies films and videos in accordance with its published guidelines.[349] It often makes distribution under a particular classification conditional upon cuts being made to the film.

15.110 The power of local authorities to license cinemas is contained in the Cinemas Act 1985. It is an offence to use unlicensed premises for film exhibition.[350] Conditions, which usually require compliance with BBFC classifications, may be attached to licences.[351] Local authorities can, however, prohibit the showing of films which the BBFC have certified for viewing.[352] Local authorities also have licensing powers under which they regulate sex cinemas.[353]

---

[346] For exemptions, see s 2.

[347] See Robertson and Nicol (n 354 above) 584–590.

[347a] See, eg, *R v Video Appeals Committee of the British Board of Film Classification ex p British Board of Film Classification*, 16 May 2000 (unreported).

[348] (1996) 24 EHRR 1.

[349] U (universal); Uc (universal and suitable for young children); PG (parental guidance required); 12 (passed only for persons 12 years and over); 15 (passed only for persons 15 years and over); 18 (passed only for persons 18 years and over); R18 (restricted 18: passed only for distribution through specially licensed cinemas or sex shops to which no one under 18 is admitted)

[350] s 10; licences are not required for exhibitions which are not for private gain.

[351] s 1(3).

[352] Notorious examples include 'Ulysses' and 'The Life of Brian' which were banned in many local authority areas; see generally, Robertson and Nicol (n 345 above) 569–572.

[353] Local Government (Miscellaneous Provisions) Act 1982, Sch 3.

(7) Freedom of expression and the criminal law

(a) Introduction

The criminal law has traditionally placed significant restrictions on freedom of ex- **15.111**
pression. At common law, there were four related offences: obscene libel, blasphemous libel, seditious libel and defamatory libel. Only the first of these has been
codified by statute. This is dealt with in section 5 above.[353a] There are also a number of other statutory offences which affect expression. Finally, there are statutory
restrictions on police powers to seize 'journalistic material' for the purposes of investigation of criminal offences.

(b) Blasphemous libel

It is an offence to publish material which is likely to shock and outrage the feelings **15.112**
of believers[354] in the established religion.[355] The only mental element required is
an intention to publish the offending words.[356] This offence is considered in detail in Chapter 14.[357]

Prosecutions for blasphemous libel are very rare;[358] and the Law Commission has **15.113**
recommended its abolition.[359] Nevertheless, it currently remains a potential restriction on freedom of expression; and may take on greater importance if the
Human Rights Act results in the offence becoming extended to other religions.[360]

(c) Seditious libel

It is a common law offence to publish words with a seditious intention. The words **15.114**
may be written or spoken. In *R v Chief Metropolitan Stipendiary Magistrate, ex p
Choudhury*[361] the offence was confined to

> an intention to incite to violence or create public disturbance or disorder against
> His Majesty or the institutions of government. Proof of an intention to promote
> feelings of ill-will and hostility between different classes of subjects does not alone
> establish a seditious intention. Not only must there be proof of an incitement to vi-
> olence in this connection but it must be violence or resistance or defiance for the
> purpose of disturbing constituted authority.[362]

Seditious libel involves demonstration of a more restrictive 'mental element' than
other common law libel offences. It seems, however, that the Divisional Court has

---

[353a] See para 15.88 above.
[354] See *Whitehouse v Gay News* [1979] AC 617.
[355] *R v Gathercole* (1838) 2 Lew CC 237, 254; 168 ER 1140, 1145.
[356] See *Whitehouse v Gay News* (n 354 above).
[357] See para 14.14ff above.
[358] The *Gay News* case is the first to have been brought in this area in over 60 years.
[359] See Law Commission, *Offences against Religion and Public Worship* (Law Com No 145, 1985).
[360] See para 14.77 above.
[361] [1991] 1 QB 429.
[362] Ibid 453.

extended the offence by the reference to the 'disturbance of constituted authority'[363] but the precise scope of the offence is uncertain.

15.115   Prosecutions for seditious libel are also very rare, with only one prosecution in the past 80 years. This was the 1947 case of *R v Caunt*[364] which concerned an article attacking British Jews. The editor was acquitted. On the analysis of the offence put forward in *Ex parte Choudhury*,[364a] it would appear that the judge was wrong to hold that the offence could extend to the stirring up of racial hatred or class violence.

(d) Defamatory or criminal libel[365]

15.116   The common law offence of 'defamatory' libel is the most common of the common law libel offences and is often known as 'criminal libel'. The publication must be in permanent form and the words must tend to vilify a person and to bring them into hatred, contempt and ridicule.[366] Furthermore, the words must constitute a 'serious' and not a trivial libel.[367] It is no longer necessary, however, that the libel relate to a public figure or that it should have a tendency to provoke the person defamed to commit a breach of the peace.[368] The mental element of the offence is not clear. It may be that all that is required is an intention to publish the words[369] or perhaps to prove an intention to defame.[370]

15.117   Although the principles of law applicable to civil and criminal libels are for the most part similar, there are several important exceptions. First, while a civil action requires publication of the statement to a third person, it appears that publication to the defamed person alone will sustain a prosecution in criminal libel.[371] Secondly, no civil action lies against a dead person, but if the libel was intended or tends to damage living persons or to cause a breach of the peace, it may be criminally prosecuted. Thirdly, no civil action for libel can be aimed at a group or class of people; but such defamation will be subject to the criminal law if it tends to excite public hatred against the class.[372] Finally, the truth of a defamatory statement

---

[363] See D Feldman, *Civil Liberties and Human Rights in England and Wales* (Clarendon Press, 1993) 679.

[364] Noted in (1947) 64 LQR 203.

[364a] See n 361 above.

[365] See Law Commission, *Report on Criminal Libel* (Law Com No 149, Cmnd 9618, 1985).

[366] This is the traditional definition of libel and continues to apply in the criminal law: see *Goldsmith v Pressdram* [1977] QB 83, 87.

[367] See *Gleaves v Deakin* [1980] AC 477, 487, 495; see generally, P Milmo and W Rogers (eds), *Gatley on Libel and Slander* (9th edn, Sweet & Maxwell, 1998) para 22.2.

[368] *R v Wicks* [1936] 1 All ER 384, 386; *Gleaves v Deakin* (n 367 above) 498g.

[369] *R v Wicks* (n 368 above).

[370] See J Smith and B Hogan, *Criminal Law* (7th edn, Butterworths, 1999) 729 and *Gatley on Libel and Slander* (n 367 above) para 22.3.

[371] Although *Gatley on Libel and Slander* (n 367 above) suggests that this is no longer the case, see para 22.5.

[372] See *R v Williams* (1822) 5 B & Ald 595.

has always been an absolute defence to an action under the civil law; while in the criminal law this was not so at common law. There is, however, a statutory defence of truth to an action in criminal libel, if publication is for the public benefit.[373]

Section 8 of the Law of Libel Amendment Act 1888 requires that leave must be obtained before bringing a prosecution for criminal libel against a proprietor, publisher, editor or any other person responsible for publishing a newspaper. Section 8 does not, however, apply to prosecutions of individual journalists.[374] A judge should not give leave unless there is a clear *prima facie* case and the public interest requires the institution of criminal proceedings.[375]

15.118

(e) Other criminal offences

Racial hatred. Incitement to racial hatred was first criminalised under the Race Relations Act of 1965. Part III of the Public Order Act 1986 contains a number of offences which restrict freedom of expression. The 1986 Act defines racial hatred as:

15.119

> hatred against a group of persons in Great Britain defined by reference to colour, race, nationality (including citizenship) or ethnic or national origins.[376]

It therefore does not include hatred based on grounds of religion.[377]

The Public Order Act 1986 creates three main offences relating to the incitement of racial hatred. Each requires that the accused acts either with the intention of stirring up racial hatred, or in circumstances in which there is a likelihood that racial hatred will be stirred up.[378] First, it is an offence to use threatening or abusive or insulting words or behaviour[379] or to display abusive or insulting written material. The same prohibition applies to the publication or distribution of written material,[380] the presentation or direction of public performances of plays,[381] the distribution or presentation of visual images or sounds[382] and the provision or production of a programme or programme service containing such material.[383] Finally, it is an offence to be in possession of written material or recordings of images or sounds which is threatening, abusive or insulting with a view to its being displayed or published.[384]

15.120

---

[373] Libel Act 1843, s 6.

[374] See *Desmond v Thorne* [1983] 1 WLR 163; and see *Gatley on Libel and Slander* (n 367 above) para 22.10.

[375] See *Goldsmith v Pressdram* [1977] QB 83, 89; and *Desmond v Thorne* (n 374 above).

[376] s 17.

[377] Cf the discussion of the phrase 'racial grounds' under the Race Relations Act 1976, at para 17.56 below.

[378] s 18.

[379] Ibid.

[380] s 19.

[381] s 20.

[382] s 21.

[383] s 22.

[384] s 23.

15.121 The Public Order Act 1986 also criminalises the use of threatening, abusive or insulting words or behaviour which is likely to cause, in general terms, public disorder. In some circumstances these provisions may be applicable to racially motivated actions. Section 4 provides that it is an offence to use threatening, abusive or insulting words or behaviour or to distribute or display such writing, signs or other visible representation, with intent to cause a person to believe that immediate unlawful violence will be used against him or to provoke him to use violence. Section 5 prohibits disorderly behaviour which is intended to harass. A criminal offence will be committed under that section if words or behaviour that are threatening, abusive or insulting are used or any such material displayed 'within the hearing of a person likely to be caused harassment, alarm or distress'.[385]

15.122 The racial hatred provisions of the Public Order Act 1986 have been criticised as not providing a solution to the problem of racially motivated demonstrations or marches. Although section 18 is likely to be applied in relation to processions and assemblies, it may be ineffective in protecting racial groups against intimidatory marches, which are not intended to stir up racial hatred; furthermore, public or private meetings held in a 'dwelling' are not covered.[386] Behaviour which is not an incitement to racial hatred under sections 18 through 23 may breach sections 4 and 5 if it is threatening to a particular racial group.

(f) Police powers to seize journalistic material

15.123 Material which is acquired or created for the purposes of journalism is specially protected against search and seizure by the police. By section 8 of the Police and Criminal Evidence Act 1984, a Justice of the Peace can authorise entry and search only where the material sought does not consist of or include 'journalistic material'.[387] A constable who wishes to obtain access to excluded material or special procedure material for the purposes of a criminal investigation may make an application to the circuit judge under section 9 of the Police and Criminal Evidence Act 1984 for a production order or a search warrant under and in accordance with Schedule 1. No order can be made for the production of journalistic material held in confidence[388] unless such an order could have been made under the previous law.[389]

---

[385] Animal rights demonstrators using signs designed to shock have been charged with these offences.

[386] s 18(2); hence there is no protection against attacks on racial groups meeting in the context of a pub or restaurant.

[387] Defined by Police and Criminal Evidence Act 1984, s 13.

[388] As defined by ibid s 11(3).

[389] This covers a limited range of circumstances, for example, if the material was stolen.

A circuit judge can only make a production order for other journalistic material if **15.124**
he is satisfied that a number of 'access conditions' are fulfilled.[390] There must be
reasonable grounds for believing that:

- a serious arrestable offence has been committed;
- the material is likely to be of substantial value to the investigation and is likely
  to be relevant evidence; and
- other methods of obtaining the material have failed or appear to be bound to fail.

More importantly, it must be in the public interest to make an order, having regard to
the benefit likely to accrue to the investigation if the material is obtained and to the
circumstances under which the person in possession of the material holds it.[391]

The effect of these provisions in relation to journalistic material was considered in **15.125**
Chief Constable of Avon and Somerset Constabulary v Bristol United Press.[392] The
judge ordered the production of photographs of public disorders taken for 'journalistic purposes.' Although the mere assertion that the material would be of substantial value was insufficient, the court was entitled to draw inferences; but the
respondent could produce evidence to the court, without the police seeing it, to
show that the material was not of substantial value. It was held that, to fulfil paragraph 2(a) of the access conditions in Schedule 1, it was not necessary for the material sought to relate to some particular criminal offence. The judge was prepared
to draw the inference, in the absence of contrary evidence, that photographers
would take pictures of assaults and acts of violence and that their material would,
therefore, be likely to provide evidence of 'serious arrestable offences'. The judge
was of the view that the public interest in the 'impartiality and independence of
the press' would not be undermined by making the order. Even if it was undermined in some people's eyes 'that could not outweigh the great public interest in
the conviction of those guilty of serious crime'. An application for judicial review
of this decision was refused.[393]

The court in the *Bristol United Press* case did not directly consider the impact of **15.126**
'freedom of expression'. However, in *Re an application under Police and Criminal
Evidence Act*[394] it was held that the 'public interest' condition was not satisfied.
The judge held that interference with the public interest in press freedom had to
be 'convincingly established'. The assertion that the material was needed for the
detection and prosecution of crime was not, of itself, sufficient for this purpose
and the police had to avoid treating these applications as routine.

---

[390] Police and Criminal Evidence Act 1984, Sch 1, para 1.
[391] Ibid Sch 1, para 2(c).
[392] *The Independent,* 4 Nov 1986 (Stuart-Smith J, sitting as a circuit judge).
[393] *R v Bristol Crown Court, ex p Bristol Press and Picture Agency Ltd* (1986) 85 Cr App R 190.
[394] 2 Jul 1999, Central Criminal Court, HHJ Pownall; see also *R v Central Criminal Court ex p
Bright, The Times,* 26 Jul 2000 (not reported on this point).

(8) Expression and government secrecy

(a) Introduction

15.127 Restrictions upon freedom of expression are often justified because they protect the national security interests of the state. The laws safeguarding secrecy include the law of confidence[395] and the Official Secrets Acts of 1911 to 1989. The Official Secrets Acts cover everything from serious national security offences to unauthorised releases of public information.

(b) Official secrets and the criminal law

15.128 The Official Secrets Act 1911 was passed through Parliament in one day in an atmosphere of panic and was subjected to intensive criticism over many years.[396] The catch-all provision of section 2 has now been repealed, but the 'espionage' provision of section 1 remains in force.

15.129 Section 1 of the Official Secrets Act 1911 provides that an offence is committed where

> any person for any purpose prejudicial to the safety or interests of the State . . . communicates to any other person any secret official code word, or pass word, or any sketch plan, model, article, note, or other document or information which is calculated to be or might be or is intended to be directly useful to an enemy.[397]

'Enemy' in this section includes 'potential enemy'.[398] In *Chandler v DPP*[399] the House of Lords held that 'the interests of the state' meant such interests according to the policies of the state as they in fact were, not as it might be argued they ought to be.

15.130 Section 2 of the Official Secrets Act 1911 created a very wide offence of 'disclosure of any official information, without authority'. The disclosure of the information did not have to be harmful.[400] This section was repealed by the Official Secrets Act 1989 and replaced by a number of more specific restrictions on various types of disclosure of information. These include:

- disclosure of information relating to security or intelligence by members and former members of the security and intelligence services;[401]

---

[395] See para 12.27ff above.

[396] See eg *Report of the Franks Committee on Section 2 of the Official Secrets Act 1911* (1972) Cmnd 5104; and see P Birkinshaw, *Reforming the Secret State* (Hull University Press, 1990).

[397] s 1(1).

[398] *R v Parrott* (1913) 8 Cr App R 186.

[399] [1964] AC 763.

[400] See *R v Crisp and Homewood* (1919) 83 JP 121: army clothing contracts.

[401] s 1(1), there is no requirement under this subsection that the information is 'damaging'. The House of Lords held in *A-G v Blake*, *The Times*, 3 Aug 2000, that where an intelligence officer published an autobiography which breached s 1, the Crown was entitled to confiscate his profits by obtaining an order for an account based upon his breach of contract.

- damaging disclosure[402] of security or intelligence information by other Crown servants or Government contractors;[403]
- damaging disclosure[404] of information relating to defence by Crown servants or Government contractors;[405]
- damaging disclosure[406] of information relating to international relations or confidential information obtained from another state by Crown servants or Government contractors;[407]
- disclosure of information obtained as a result of warrants issued under the Interception of Communications Act 1985 or the Security Service Act 1989.[408]

It is also an offence to disclose information which has been disclosed by Crown servants or Government contractors without lawful authority or on terms requiring it to be held in confidence.[409] The Act makes no provision of a defence of 'public interest' or 'prior publication' in relation to any type of disclosure.

(c) Official secrets and breach of confidence

In recent years the Government has increasingly relied on civil remedies against the media to prevent publication of allegedly secret material, particularly breach of confidence.[410] In the 'Crossman Diaries' case[411] the Attorney-General sought an injunction to restrain publication of the diaries, on the ground that disclosure of Cabinet discussions was contrary to the public interest. The defendants' argument that the private law doctrine of 'breach of confidence' did not apply to Cabinet discussions was rejected; Lord Widgery CJ denied that the courts should be powerless to restrain the publication of public secrets.[412] He held, however, that, in order to obtain an injunction, the Attorney-General had to show: **15.131**

(a) that such publication would be a breach of confidence;
(b) that the public interest requires that publication be restrained; and
(c) that there are no other facets of the public interest contradictory to and more compelling than that relied upon. Moreover, the court, when asked to restrain a publication, must examine the extent to which relief is necessary to ensure that restrictions are not imposed beyond the strict requirement of public need.[413]

---

[402] As defined by s 1(4).
[403] s 1(3).
[404] As defined by s 2(2).
[405] s 2(1).
[406] As defined by s 3(2).
[407] s 3(1).
[408] s 4(1), (3); there is no requirement under this subsection that the information is 'damaging'.
[409] s 5.
[410] See generally, para 12.27ff above.
[411] *A-G v Jonathan Cape Ltd* [1976] 1 QB 752.
[412] Ibid 769G–H.
[413] Ibid 770G–771A.

As much of the material was 10-years-old and three general elections had since been held, there was, on the facts no sufficient public interest in restraining publication and an injunction was refused.[414]

15.132 This principle was invoked most significantly in the *Spycatcher* litigation.[415] The House of Lords in *A-G v Guardian Newspapers Ltd (No 2)*[416] held that members and former members of the security service owed a lifelong duty of confidence to the Crown. Lord Goff, however, made clear that, in the case of Government secrets:

> it is incumbent on the Crown, in order to restrain disclosure of Government secrets, not only to show that the information is confidential, but also to show that it is not in the public interest that it should be published.[417]

(9) Freedom of information

15.133 The Government has always sought to exercise strict control over information concerning the operation of the administration.[418] In recent years, partly under the influence of 'freedom of information' legislation abroad,[419] there has been increasing pressure for greater disclosure of governmental information.[420] In 1994, the Government issued the *Code of Practice on Access to Government Information* (which applies to Government departments and public bodies under the jurisdiction of the Parliamentary Ombudsman).[421] A Freedom of Information Bill was published in 1999.[422]

15.134 There are limited rights to freedom of information from local government.[423] Part VA of the Local Government Act 1972[424] enables any member of the public to inspect and take copies of local authority minutes, reports and background papers. The minutes of decisions by the full council, committee or sub-committee are available for inspection by members of the public.[425] Members of the public are

---

[414] See also *Commonwealth of Australia v John Fairfax and Sons Ltd* (1980) 147 CLR 39.

[415] See para 15.19ff above.

[416] [1990] 1 AC 109

[417] *Per* Lord Goff, *A-G v Guardian Newspapers Ltd (No 2)* (n 416 above); see also *Lord Advocate v The Scotsman Publications Ltd* [1990] 1 AC 812.

[418] For a history see P Birkinshaw, *Freedom of Information: The Law, the Practice and the Ideal* (2nd edn, Butterworths, 1996) Chap 3 'Government and Information: An Historical Development'.

[419] Ibid Chap 2 'Freedom of Information: Overseas Experience'.

[420] See, ibid Chap 8 and also G Robertson and A Nichol, *Media Law* (3rd edn, Penguin, 1992) 412ff.

[421] Ibid 201–213.

[422] For criticism of its contents see P Birkinshaw and N Parry, 'Every Trick in the Book: the Freedom of Information Bill 1999' [1999] EHRLR 373.

[423] See Birkinshaw (n 418 above) 138ff.

[424] Introduced by the Local Government (Access to Information) Act 1985.

[425] Local Government Act 1972, s 100C.

also entitled to inspect the reports considered by officers[426] and background papers.[427] Furthermore, the *Good Administrative Guide* issued by the Local Government Ombudsman contains principles of good administration including information on policies, procedures and complaints.

However, the Local Governmment Act is subject to two significant limitations. **15.135** First, certain types of information are exempt from access to information[428] such as:

- information concerning a particular employee or office holder or former employee or office holder or applicant;
- information concerning a particular occupant or former occupant or applicant for council accommodation;
- information concerning a particular applicant, recipient or former recipient of financial assistance;
- the amount of expenditure incurred by the authority under a particular contract to buy property, goods or services;
- information about consultations or negotiations or contemplated consultations or negotiations concerning labour relations;
- instructions to and advice from counsel regarding any proceedings or determining any matter affecting the authority.

Secondly, Part VA of the Local Government Act does not apply to council working parties. Whether a particular body is a committee or a working party depends primarily on the subjective intention of the local authority; its manifest intention is decisive unless something unlawful lies behind it.[429]

There are also statutory rights to certain information from educational institu- **15.136** tions. The following must be made available on request:

- the agenda, draft minutes, signed minutes and reports, documents and papers considered at meetings of the governing bodies of schools (subject to certain exceptions);[430]
- a school's statement of its policy concerning secular curiculum;[431]
- information about school admissions procedures and public examination results in England[432] and Wales.[433]

---

[426] Ibid ss 100C, 100E.
[427] Ibid ss 100D, 100E.
[428] Local Government Act 1972, s 100I, Sch 12A.
[429] *R v Warwickshire CC, ex p Bailey* [1991] COD 284.
[430] Education (School Government) Regulations 1989, SI 1989/1503 as modified by Education (School Government) (Transition to New Framework) Regulations 1998, SI 1998/2763.
[431] Education (School Curriculum and Related Information) Regulations 1989, SI 1989/954).
[432] Education (School Information) (England) Regulations 1998, SI 1998/2526.
[433] Education (School Information) (Wales) Regulations 1998, SI 1998/1832.

C. The Law Under the European Convention

(1) Introduction

15.137   Article 10 of the Convention provides:

> (1) Everyone has the right to freedom of expression. This right shall include free-
> dom to hold opinions and to receive and impart information and ideas without inter-
> ference by public authority and regardless of frontiers. This Article shall not prevent
> States from requiring the licensing of broadcasting, television or cinema enterprises.
>
> (2) The exercise of these freedoms, since it carries with it duties and responsibil-
> ities, may be subject to such formalities, conditions, restrictions or penalties as are
> prescribed by law and are necessary in a democratic society, in the interests of na-
> tional security, territorial integrity or public safety, for the prevention of disorder or
> crime, for the protection of health or morals, for the protection of the reputation or
> rights of others, for preventing the disclosure of information received in confidence,
> or for maintaining the authority and impartiality of the judiciary.

15.138   The Convention was the first human rights instrument to make express provision for
limitations on the freedom of expression.[434] Article 10 expressly acknowledges that
freedom of expression has the potential to damage the interests of others or the public interest. The tension between the right of expression and the need to protect other
rights has been at the heart of the Convention jurisprudence under Article 10.

15.139   The right to freedom of expression has been consistently recognised as being an
'essential foundation of a democratic society' and a 'basic condition for its
progress and for the development of every man'.[435] In the recent case of *Zana v
Turkey*[436] the Court summarised and reaffirmed the fundamental principles in the
following terms:

> The Court reiterates the fundamental principles which emerge from its judgments
> relating to Article 10:
>
> (1) Freedom of expression constitutes one of the essential foundations of a de-
> mocratic society and one of the basic conditions for its progress and for each
> individual's self fulfilment. Subject to Article 10(2), it is applicable not only
> to 'information' or 'ideas' that are favourably received or regarded as inof-
> fensive or as a matter of indifference, but also to those that offend, shock or
> disturb the State or any sector of the population. Such are the demands of
> that pluralism, tolerance and broadmindedness without which there is no
> 'democratic society'. As set forth in Article 10, this freedom is subject to
> exceptions which must, however, be construed strictly, and the need for any
> restrictions must be established convincingly.[437]

---

[434] Contrast Art 19 of the Universal Declaration, see App H in Vol 2.
[435] Similar formulations are used in cases from *Handyside v United Kingdom* (1976) 1 EHRR 737
para 49 to *Zana v Turkey* (1997) 27 EHRR 667 para 51.
[436] (1997) 27 EHRR 667 para 51.
[437] *Handyside v United Kingdom* (1976) 1 EHRR 737 para 49; *Lingens v Austria* (1986) 8 EHRR
103 para 31; *Jersild v Denmark* (1994) 19 EHRR 1 para 37.

(2) The adjective 'necessary' within the meaning of Article 10 implies the existence of a 'pressing social need'. The Contracting States have a certain margin of appreciation in assessing whether such a need exists, but it goes hand in hand with European supervision, embracing both the legislation and the decisions relating to it, even those given by an independent court. The Court is therefore empowered to give the final ruling on whether a 'restriction' is reconcilable with freedom of expression as protected by Article 10.[438]

(3) In exercising its supervisory jurisdiction, the Court must look at the whole, including the content of the remarks held against the applicant and context in which he made them. In particular, it must determine whether the interference in issue is 'proportionate to the legitimate aim pursued' and whether the reasons adduced by the national authorities are 'relevant and sufficient'.[439] In so doing the Court has to satisfy itself that the national authorities applied standards which are in conformity with the principles embodied in Article 10 and, moreover, that they based themselves on an acceptable assessment of the relevant facts.[440]

(2) Scope of the right

(a) Introduction

'Expression' has been interpreted broadly to include communications of any kind or subject matter: spoken or written words, television programmes[441] and broadcasting,[442] film,[443] video,[444] pictures,[445] dress,[446] images[447] and probably electronic information systems where they are used to express ideas or to convey information. Furthermore, the concept of 'expression' covers conduct such as acts of protest (even where they involve physically interfering with the activity protested against)[448] and the physical expression of feelings.[449] However, it does not extend to linguistic freedom[450] or the right to vote or stand for election.[451]

15.140

---

[438] *Lingens v Austria* (n 437 above) para 39.

[439] Ibid para 40; and *Barfod v Denmark* (1989) 13 EHRR 493 para 28.

[440] *Jersild v Denmark* (n 437 above) para 31.

[441] See eg *Hodgson v United Kingdom* (1987) 51 DR 136, EComm HR.

[442] See eg *Autronic AG v Switzerland* (1990) 12 EHRR 485 where the Court acknowledged that the public have a right to receive broadcasts.

[443] See eg *Otto-Preminger-Institute v Austria* (1994) 19 EHRR 34.

[444] See eg *Wingrove v United Kingdom* (1996) 24 EHRR 1.

[445] *Müller v Switzerland* (1988) 13 EHRR 212.

[446] *Stevens v United Kingdom* (1986) 46 DR 245, EComm HR.

[447] *Chorherr v Austria* (1993) 17 EHRR 358.

[448] *Steel v United Kingdom* (1998) 5 BHRC 339 para 92; *Chorherr v Austria* (n 447 above); and see para 15.146 below.

[449] *X v United Kingdom* (1978) 3 EHRR 63, EComm HR (homosexual activity).

[450] See the Belgian linguistics cases: *23 Inhabitants of Alsemberg and Beersel v Belgium* (1963) 6 YB 332; *X v Belgium*, (1963) 6 YB 444, in which it was held that the applicant had no freedom of choice as to the language of instruction for his children.

[451] *Liberal Party, Mrs R and Mr P v United Kingdom* (1982) 4 EHRR 106.

15.141   Statements directed against the Convention's underlying values, such as the justification of a pro-Nazi policy, do not enjoy the protection of Article 10.[452] With
this exception, there is probably no form of expression that is excluded from the
protection of Article 10 on the basis of its *content*[453] (although the Court has oc-
casionally suggested that 'valueless' expression might not be protected).[454] This
means, for example, that 'expression' is applicable to ideas that 'offend, shock or
disturb'.[455] Thus, in *Jersild v Denmark*[456] the Court held that convicting a journalist for aiding and abetting racist insults in a television programme was disproportionate to the need to protect those whom he had insulted. Similarly, in
Lehideux v France[457] the Court held that convictions for portraying Marshall
Petain positively in a false light were disproportionate interferences with freedom
of expression. However, the Commission has applied a low standard of review
when considering whether Article 10 has been violated in cases arising from racist
literature[458] or support for terrorist activities.[459]

15.142   The distinction in Article 10 between information and ideas makes it clear that
'expression' is not restricted to statements of fact.[460] It encompasses opinions, criticism and speculation, whether or not they are objectively 'true'. In *Thorgeirson v
Iceland*[461] the Court considered that an obligation on the applicant to prove the
truth of his opinions was an interference with freedom of expression.

15.143   Furthermore, the fact that views are expressed in polemical language does not take
them outside the scope of Article 10. Thus, in *De Haes and Gijsels v Belgium*,[462]
journalists who personally insulted certain members of the judiciary for their
handling of child abuse and incest proceedings when writing critical articles
nevertheless were entitled to rely on Article 10.

---

[452] See *Lehideux and Isornia v France* (1998) 5 BHRC 540, 558 para 53.

[453] D Harris, M O'Boyle, and C Warbrick, *Law of the European Convention on Human Rights*
(Butterworths, 1995) 336–374; P van Dijk and G van Hoof, *Theory and Practice of the European
Convention on Human Rights* (3rd edn, Kluwer, 1998) 559.

[454] *Otto-Preminger-Institute v Austria* (1994) 19 EHRR 34 para 49 addressed 'abusive or inflammatory words'; *Groppera Radio AG v Switzerland* (1990) 12 EHRR 321, *per* Judge Matscher and
Judge Valticos, found that light music was mere entertainment and not 'information and ideas'.

[455] See *Lehideux and Isornia v France* (n 452 above) 558 para 55.

[456] (1994) 19 EHRR 1.

[457] (1998) 5 BHRC 540.

[458] See eg *Glimmerveen and Hagenbeek v Netherlands* (1979) 18 DR 187, EComm HR (racist
leaflets); *X v Germany* (1982) 29 DR 194, EComm HR (Nazi leaflets); *T v Belgium* (1983) 34 DR
158 (Nazi leaflet); *Kuhnen v Germany* (1988) 56 DR 205, EComm HR (Nazi leaflet); *H, W, P and
K v Austria* (1989) 62 DR 216, EComm HR (Nazi activities).

[459] See eg *Purcell v Ireland* (1991) 70 DR 262, EComm HR (political support for terrorists); *Brind
v United Kingdom* (1994) 18 EHRR CD 76, EComm HR (restrictions on broadcasting interviews
with supporters of terrorism); *Gerry Adams v United Kingdom* [1997] EHRLR 293 (exclusion order
preventing Gerry Adams speaking at House of Commons).

[460] *Lingens v Austria* (1986) 8 EHRR 103.

[461] (1992) 14 EHRR 843.

[462] (1997) 25 EHRR 1; *Jersild v Denmark* (1994) 19 EHRR 1.

Article 10 extends to expression by employees but is subject to restriction under **15.144** Article 10(2).[463] However, there are some types of employment which, by their nature, involve restrictions on freedom of expression.[464] Furthermore, it is sometimes said that an employee can contract out of his right to freedom of expression, but this is open to question.[465]

(b) The relationship with Article 10 and other Convention rights

Article 10 is often invoked in conjunction with complaints about breaches of **15.145** other Convention rights. In *K v Austria*[466] the Commission decided that passing a sentence of imprisonment on the applicant for refusing to testify against himself was a breach of Article 10 and did not require further consideration as a breach of Article 6.[467] Freedom of expression (and, in particular, the right to hold an opinion) is also closely connected to freedom of thought under Article 9.[468] However, it seems that Article 10 has wider scope than Article 9. Whereas Article 9 only applies if the opinion reflects the conviction of the person who puts it forward,[469] Article 10 contemplates the protection of *any* expression of opinion.

Complaints about freedom of expression frequently involve violations of freedom **15.146** of assembly under Article 11.[470] In *Ezelin v France*[471] the Court said that a disciplinary penalty against a lawyer for participating in a demonstration should be examined as a potential breach of freedom of association under Article 11. However, in *Steel v United Kingdom*[472] the Court accepted that arrests for breach of the peace when exercising a right of protest (even where the protests were not peaceful) could amount to an interference with Article 10(1).[473] In *Vogt v Germany*[474] a teacher was dismissed because of her political activities as a Communist and alleged that both Article 10 and 11 had been breached. The Court based its decision on Article 11 by examining the arguments put forward under Article 10.

---

[463] See generally, *Vogt v Germany* (1995) 21 EHRR 205.

[464] See eg *Morissens v Belgium* (1988) 56 DR 127, EComm HR (no breach by disciplining a teacher for criticising her superiors in a TV broadcast); see also *Ahmed v United Kingdom* (1998) 5 BHRC 111; *Rekvényi v Hungary* (1996) 6 BHRC 554 (police officers); *Wille v Liechtenstein* (2000) 8 BHRC 69 (members of the judiciary).

[465] *Vereiniging Rechtswinkels Utrecht v Netherlands* (1986) 46 DR 200, EComm HR; *Rommelfanger v Germany* (1989) 62 DR 151, EComm HR; and see generally, para 6.149ff above.

[466] (1993) Series A No 255–B.

[467] That is, of the privilege against self incrimination: see para 11.211ff above.

[468] See para 14.39 above.

[469] *Arrowsmith v United Kingdom* (1980) 19 DR 5, EComm HR.

[470] See generally, para 16.57ff below.

[471] (1991) 14 EHRR 362.

[472] (1998) 5 BHRC 339.

[473] Ibid para 92.

[474] (1995) 21 EHRR 205.

15.147 On the other hand, where restrictions on expression are an unintended consequence of a state's decision, the Court has been reluctant to consider the complaint under Article 10. For example, where interference with freedom of
expression was incidental to the expulsion of an alien, no violation was found.[475]

15.148 The Court has taken a similar (and more controversial) approach[476] where public
service employees protest about restrictions on their freedom of expression. In
Glasenapp v Germany[477] the applicant was dismissed from his post for expressing
views contrary to the German Constitution. He alleged that his Article 10 rights
had been breached. The Court took the view that the claimant, who held only a
temporary position, was seeking access to public employment (rather than freedom of expression); and that access to public employment was not a right protected by the Convention.[477a] By contrast, in *Vogt v Germany*[478] the Court decided
that the dismissal of a teacher because of her membership of the Communist Party
violated Article 10. The Court distinguished *Glasenapp v Germany*[479] and *Kosiek
v Germany*[480] on the basis that in the earlier cases, the authorities had refused to
grant temporary employees access to the civil service because they lacked one of
the necessary qualifications.[481] Public officials serving in the judiciary are expected
to show restraint in exercising freedom of expression in cases where the authority
and impartiality of the judiciary are likely to be called into question.[481a] However,
an interference with the freedom of expression of a judge calls for close
scrutiny.[481b] A statement by the Head of State that a judge would not be reap-
pointed to public office as a result of views expressed in a lecture violated his freedom of expression.[481c]

---

[475] *Agee v United Kingdom* (1976) 7 DR 164, EComm HR; but not if the purpose of the expulsion
is the restriction of freedom of expression, *Piermont v France* (1995) 20 EHRR 301.

[476] Contrast with the Commission who decided in *Glasenapp* and *Kosiek* that legislation which required an obligation of loyalty and allegiance to the Constitution as a condition of employment directly interfered with freedom of expression under Art 10(1). Van Dijk and Van Hoof (n 453 above)
564 argue that the Court should have followed the opinion of the Commission. Lester suggests that
the dissenting Court judgment of Judge Spielam in *Glasenapp v Germany* (1986) 9 EHRR 25 is to
be preferred; Judge Spielam holds that the restriction is disproportionate to the aim pursued: see A
Lester, 'Freedom of Expression' in R St John Macdonald, F Matscher and H Petzold (eds), *The
European System for the Protection of Human Rights* (Kluwer, 1993).

[477] n 476 above; see also *Kosiek v Germany* (1986) 9 EHRR 328; but see *Vogt v Germany* (1995)
21 EHRR 205.

[477a] See also *Wille v Liechtenstein* (2000) 8 BHRC 69 para 41.

[478] (1995) 21 EHRR 205.

[479] n 476 above.

[480] n 477 above.

[481] Ibid para 44.

[481a] *Wille v Liechtenstein* (n 477a above) para 64.

[481b] Ibid.

[481c] Ibid paras 67–70.

(c) The right to hold opinions and to impart information

Article 10 expressly includes the right to 'impart information and ideas'. The free- **15.149**
doms to 'receive' and 'impart' information and ideas are not mere corollaries of
one another: they are two independent rights.[482] Thus, a speaker has a right to express opinions and a willing hearer has the right to receive the communication.
The state must not stand between the speaker and his audience and thus defeat the
purpose for which the protection of expression is realised.[483] In *Groppera Radio
AG v Switzerland*[484] the Court declined to give a precise definition of 'information
and ideas'. Nonetheless, a right to impart ideas means, for example, that organis-
ing an exhibition of paintings was an exercise of freedom of expression on the part
of the organisers.[485]

However, the right to receive information under Article 10 does *not* entail a cor- **15.150**
responding right of access to information (or an obligation on the Government to
provide it), even when it is necessary for the purposes of forming an opinion or effectively exercising other freedoms. In *Leander v Sweden*[486] the applicant sought
confidential Government information so he could bring a claim arising out of an
unsuccessful job application. In dismissing the Article 10 claim, it was said:[487]

> The Court observes that the right of freedom to receive information basically pro-
> hibits a Government from restricting a person from receiving information that
> others wish or may be willing to impart to them. Article 10 does not, in the cir-
> cumstances such as those of the present case, confer on an individual a right of
> access to a register containing information about his personal position, nor does
> it embody an obligation on the Government to impart such information to the
> individual.

In *Open Door Counselling v Ireland*[487a] the court found that an injunction restraining the imparting of information to pregnant women by abortion clinics
was a breach of both the clinic's right to impart information and the women's right
to receive it. However, in the cases where the Court has accepted that there is a
right of access to information, it has done so by reference to Article 8. Thus, in
Gaskin v United Kingdom,[488] the Court decided the case under Article 8 and expressly denied that Article 10 embodied an obligation on the state to impart the
information in question to the individual.

---

[482] *Sunday Times v United Kingdom (No 1)* (1979) 2 EHRR 245 paras 65-66.
[483] *Groppera Radio AG v Switzerland* (1990) 12 EHRR 321 para 53; *Casado Coca v Spain* (1994)
18 EHRR 1 para 59.
[484] n 483 above para 55.
[485] *Müller v Switzerland* (1988) 13 EHRR 212.
[486] (1987) 9 EHRR 433.
[487] Ibid para 74.
[487a] (1992) 15 EHRR 244.
[488] (1989) 12 EHRR 36 paras 37, 52; see also *McGinley and Egan v United Kingdom* (1998) 27
EHRR 1; and see generally, para 12.90 above.

15.151   It should, however, be noted that the Consultative (Parliamentary) Assembly of the Council of Europe has resolved that the right to freedom of expression involves a:

> corresponding duty for the public authorities to make available information on matters of public interest within reasonable limits and a duty for mass communication media to give complete and general information on public affairs.[489]

Although this resolution does not have binding effect, it indicates a trend in legal opinion within Contracting States.[490]

15.152   Similarly, Article 10 does not provide a general right to broadcast time or to advertise on television.[491] However, it may in exceptional circumstances create a right to 'access to broadcast time' such as where one political party is excluded from broadcasting when others are not.[492] But the inability of an independent candidate to make a party political broadcast did not breach Article 10.[493] Nor does Article 10 create a right to be granted a commercial radio licence.[494] However, where the state provides assistance to particular information providers, this must be done in an even-handed way.[495]

15.153   Where the information is otherwise available the state must not obstruct access to it.[496] In *Autronic v Switzerland*[497] the Court held that the refusal of the Swiss authorities to allow a company to receive, without Soviet consent, a satellite broadcast of a Soviet television programme for showing at an exhibition in Zurich, amounted to a violation of its right to receive information 'without interference by public authority and regardless of frontiers'.

(d) Freedom of the press and mass media

15.154   The Court has attached great importance to freedom of the press and of the mass media.[498] There is an obligation on the press to impart information and ideas on political issues and on other areas of public interest;[499] and the public have a right

---

[489]   Res 428 (1970), 21st Ordinary Session (Third Part), 22-30 Jan 1970, *Texts Adopted*.

[490]   See P van Dijk and G van Hoof, *Theory and Practice of the European Convention on Human Rights* (3rd edn, Kluwer, 1998) 565–566.

[491]   *X and Association Z v United Kingdom* (1971) 38 CD 86, EComm HR.

[492]   *Haider v Austria* (1995) 85 DR 66, EComm HR.

[493]   *Huggett v United Kingdom* [1996] ERHLR 84.

[494]   *X v United Kingdom* (1972) 40 CD 29, EComm HR.

[495]   *Vereinigung Demokratischer Soldaten Osterreichs and Gubi v Austria* (1994) 20 EHRR 55.

[496]   *Z v Austria* (1988) 56 DR 13, EComm HR.

[497]   *Autronic AG v Switzerland* (1990) 12 EHRR 485.

[498]   See *Bladet Tromsø and Stensaas v Norway* (1999) 6 BHRC 599, 624 para 59 and *Bergens Tidende v Norway* Judgment of 2 May 2000 para 48; for a general discussion from the point of view of English defamation law, see P Milmo and W Rogers (eds), *Gatley on Libel and Slander* (9th edn, Sweet & Maxwell, 1998) para 23.20.

[499]   *Lingens v Austria* (1986) 8 EHRR 103 para 26; *Oberschlick v Austria (No 1)* (1991) 19 EHRR 389 para 58; *Castells v Spain* (1992) 14 EHRR 445 para 43; *Thorgeirson v Iceland* (1992) 14 EHRR 843 para 63; *Jersild v Denmark* (1994) 19 EHRR 1 para 31.

to receive them.[500] Journalistic freedom means that the media can have recourse to exaggeration or even provocation.[501] Otherwise the press is not able 'to play its vital role of public watchdog'.[502] The Court has emphasised that:

> Where . . . measures taken by the national authorities are capable of discouraging the press from disseminating information on matters of legitimate public concern, careful scrutiny of the proportionality of the measures on the part of the Court is called for.[502a]

Article 10 provides a safeguard to journalists in relation to reporting on issues of general interest, provided that they are acting in good faith in order to provide accurate and reliable information in accordance with the ethics of journalism.[502b]

The Court has held that prior restraint on publication in the media is not *as such* incompatible with Article 10. However, it requires very close scrutiny: even if the restraints are temporary, they may deprive the information of interest because news is a perishable commodity.[503]   **15.155**

The Court has consistently upheld the press where they have criticised politicians in strong or hostile terms.[504] The importance of press freedom also influenced the Court's approach in *Bladet Tromsø and Stensaas v Norway*[505] where it concluded that the vital interest in ensuring an informed public debate over a matter of local and national interest outweighed the interests of those who issued defamation proceedings in protecting their reputation. The Court has also stressed that it should provide very strong protection for journalistic sources which has been described as 'one of the basic conditions for press freedom'.[506] Similarly, in *Bergens Tidende v Norway*[506a] the public interest in dealing with allegations of unacceptable healthcare meant that an award of substantial damages against a newspaper on the basis of the 'natural and ordinary meaning' of the   **15.156**

---

[500] *Sunday Times v United Kingdom* (1979) 2 EHRR 245 para 65; *Fressoz and Roire v France* (1999) 5 BHRC 654 para 51.

[501] *Prager and Oberschlick v Austria* (1995) 21 EHRR 1 para 38.

[502] *The Observer and The Guardian v United Kingdom* (1991) 14 EHRR 153 para 59; *Goodwin v United Kingdom* (1996) 22 EHRR 123 para 39.

[502a] *Bergens Tidende* (n 498 above) para 52.

[502b] Ibid para 53.

[503] *The Observer and The Guardian v United Kingdom* (n 502 above) para 60; *Sunday Times v United Kingdom (No 2)* (1991) 14 EHRR 229 para 51.

[504] See cases such as *Lingens v Austria* (n 499 above); *Oberschlick v Austria* (n 499 above), and *Castells v Spain* (n 499 above).

[505] (1999) 6 BHRC 599; and see also *Dalban v Romania* (2000) 8 BHRC 91 (breach consisted of conviction for defamation as a result of an article concerning criminal activity by a director of a public enterprise and a senator).

[506] *Goodwin v United Kingdom* (n 502 above) para 39: disclosure order and fine for refusing to disclose source a violation of Art 10; see para 15.73ff above for the English cases; see also *K v Austria* (1993) Series A No 255–B.

[506a] Judgment of 2 May 2000, see also para 15.204 below.

words used[506b] was disproportionate. In contrast, the Court in *Worm v Austria*[507] decided that restrictions on pre-trial criticism of a politician were justified 'for maintaining the authority and impartiality of the judiciary'.[508]

15.157 Unfortunately, the Court has not taken a consistent approach in press freedom cases.[509] Protection has sometimes been based on the identity of the person defamed with, for example, discussion of politicians receiving the highest degree of protection.[510] In other cases, the Court has focused on the 'public interest content' of the publication itself.[511] The failure of the Court to reconcile these approaches means that the degree of protection afforded to the press remains uncertain.

(e) The licensing power

15.158 Article 10(1) states that it does not prevent states from requiring the licensing of broadcasting, television or cinema enterprises. The Court in *Groppera Radio AG v Switzerland*[512] said:

> . . . the purpose of the third sentence of Article 10(1) of the Convention is to make it clear that states are permitted to control by a licensing system the way in which broadcasting is organised in their territories, particularly in its technical aspects. It does not, however, provide that licensing measures shall not otherwise be subject to the requirements of Article 10(2), for that would lead to a result contrary to the object and purpose of Article 10 taken as a whole.

This view curtails the licensing power substantially, confining it to restrictions that can be construed as part of the licensing function as such.

15.159 The scope of the 'licensing power' is not clear. It entitles a state to establish technical and financial criteria for issuing licences to operate radio, television or cinematic facilities; and permits the taking of enforcement action against unlicensed operators (as in the *Groppera Radio AG* case)[513] provided the proceedings do not include interference with reception of programmes.[514]

15.160 The question of whether a state monopoly on broadcasting breaches Article 10

[506b] There was an 'inferred' meaning that the claimant had been reckless which the newspaper could not justify although the 'underlying facts' were true. For the English approach to meaning see para 15.25 above.

[507] (1997) 25 EHRR 454.

[508] See para 15.212ff below.

[509] See eg S Tierney, 'Press Freedom and Public Interest: The Developing Jurisprudence of the European Court of Human Rights' [1998] EHRLR 419.

[510] See eg *Castells v Spain* (1992) 14 EHRR 445.

[511] See eg *Thorgeirson v Iceland* (1992) 14 EHRR 843.

[512] (1990) 12 EHRR 321 para 61.

[513] (1990) 12 EHRR 321.

[514] *Radio X, S, W and A v Switzerland* (1984) 37 DR 236, EComm HR; *Groppera Radio AG v Switzerland* (n 513 above) para 61.

has to be considered under Article 10(2) rather than 10(1).[515] At one time the maintenance of public monopolies on broadcasting was considered by the Commission to be compatible with the Convention.[516] However, the Commission subsequently changed its view.[517] It is now clear that a public broadcasting monopoly is a breach of Article 10 as it involves a restriction which cannot be justified as being 'necessary in a democratic society'.[518]

The 'licensing power' in Article 10(1) has not been used to review the licensing process although there is scope to do so under the discrimination provisions of Article 14.[519] Nor has the 'licensing power' been invoked to regulate the content of broadcasts. Complaints about the contents of broadcast material have to be justified as interferences with freedom of expression under Article 10(2).[520] **15.161**

(3) Types of expression

(a) Introduction

The Court has distinguished three kinds of expression:[521] **15.162**

- political expression;
- artistic expression; and
- commercial expression.

The Court consistently attaches great importance to political expression; and applies rather less rigorous principles to artistic and commercial expression.

(b) Political expression

Political expression is central to a democratic system which requires that even ideas that 'offend, shock and disturb' be published.[522] Freedom of political debate and the press gives the public one of the best means of discovering and forming an opinion about the ideas and attitudes of political leaders and is a core concept of a democratic society.[523] While the electoral process is not itself protected by Article 10, expression during the course of an election is given specific protection.[524] **15.163**

---

[515] *Informationsverein Lentia v Austria* (1993) 17 EHRR 93.

[516] See *X v Sweden* (1968) 26 CD 71, EComm HR; *Sacchi v Italy* (1976) 5 DR 435, EComm HR.

[517] See *Nydahl v Sweden* (1993) 16 EHRR CD 15.

[518] See *Informationsverein Lentia v Austria* (n 515 above) and more recently *Radio ABC v Austria* (1997) 25 EHRR 185.

[519] *Verein Alternatives Lokalradio Bern v Switzerland* (1986) 49 DR 126, EComm HR where the Commission discussed this possibility.

[520] See eg *Purcell v Ireland* (1991) 70 DR 262, EComm HR; *Brind and McLaughlin v United Kingdom* (1994) 77-A DR 42, EComm HR.

[521] See generally, D Harris, M O'Boyle and C Warbrick, *Law of the European Convention on Human Rights* (Butterworths, 1995) 397–406.

[522] *Handyside v United Kingdom* (1976) 1 EHRR 737 para 49.

[523] *Lingens v Austria* (1986) 8 EHRR 103 para 42.

[524] See *Bowman v United Kingdom* (1998) 26 EHRR 1 para 42 (restrictions on election expenses a violation of Art 10).

15.164 As a result, there is little scope for restricting political speech or debate on matters of public interest.[525] Interference with the expression of politicians and, in particular, the views of the opposition, must be given the 'closest scrutiny'.[526] Politicians must be tolerant of sharp criticism of themselves, in the same democratic interest.[527] In particular, the Court has distinguished between facts and value judgments when considering the validity of criticisms made against politicians. Value judgments are not susceptible to proof and, consequently, a requirement that a publisher must prove the truth of an opinion is impossible and is therefore unjustifiable under Article 10(2).[528]

15.165 The concept of political expression is broadly interpreted. In *Thorgeirson v Iceland*[529] the Court considered a complaint about defamation of the police; and said that its jurisprudence did not warrant a distinction between political discussion and discussion of other matters of public concern. A journalist's allegations of bias against a court where two of its lay judges were employed by local government was party to proceedings before it was treated as political expression.[530] Press statements made by a veterinary surgeon about the inadequacies of an emergency veterinary service[531] have also been treated as political expression.

15.166 In a number of cases proceedings for criminal libel in relation to statements about politicians have been found to be in breach of Article 10. Vigorous criticism of a political figure is justified, so that convicting a journalist for criminal libel for failing to prove the truth of an opinion breaches Article 10. In *Lingens v Austria* the conviction of a journalist for making allegations concerning Chancellor Kreisky's views on Nazism was held to have breached Article 10.[532] Similarly, in *Castells v Spain*[533] a member of the Basque nationalist party alleged that the police were responsible for murdering Basque activists and had been protected from prosecution. He was convicted of serious insults to the Government. The Court found that the national courts had denied him the opportunity to prove the truth of his allegations, and that it was not necessary to punish him for the publication of factual assertions which were or might be true. One concurring judge regarded Castell's claims as 'matters of opinion' which were not susceptible to being proved, while another said that as his comments were of 'general interest' the truth of them

---

[525] *Wingrove v United Kingdom* (1996) 24 EHRR 1 para 58.

[526] *Castells v Spain* (1992) 14 EHRR 445 para 42.

[527] *Lingens v Austria* (1986) 8 EHRR 103; *Oberschlick v Austria (No 1)* (1991) 19 EHRR 389; *Schwabe v Austria* (1992) Series A No 242–B.

[528] *Lingens v Austria* (n 527 above) para 46.

[529] *Thorgeirson v Iceland* (1992) 14 EHRR 843 para 62.

[530] *Barfod v Denmark* (1989) 13 EHRR 493.

[531] *Barthold v Germany* (1985) 7 EHRR 383.

[532] (1986) 8 EHRR 407.

[533] (1992) 14 EHHR 445.

was irrelevant. The same approach was taken in *Oberschlick v Austria (No 1)*,[534] *Thorgeirson v Iceland*[535] and *Schwabe v Austria*[536] where criminal convictions were also held to have violated Article 10. The Court has, however, criticised journalists for not carrying out adequate research and suggested that, in the case of serious allegations, the journalist may be obliged to give the person concerned a right to comment.[537]

Furthermore, the Court has recognised that criticism of other public figures may attract some additional protection under Article 10: **15.167**

> the limits of acceptable criticism are wider with regard to businessmen actively involved in the affairs of large public companies than with regard to private individuals.[538]

When statements are published as part of a 'general interest' debate concerning matters such as public health they may also be accorded greater protection.[539]

On the present state of the Convention case law it cannot be said that Article 10 **15.168** requires the courts to allow for a 'public figure' defence in defamation actions.[540] Although Article 10 does require the courts to give special scrutiny to restrictions on political expression, the right to reputation of politicians is still acknowledged and protected. The precise balance between the two remains to be worked out.

(c) Artistic expression

Artistic expression (such as painting, exhibiting and giving an artist the opportunity to show his works in public) is an indisputable exercise of freedom of expression under Article 10.[541] However, where artistic expression offends or shocks, the Court has taken a cautious position. In *Müller v Switzerland*[542] paintings depicting activities involving homosexuality and bestiality were on public display without warnings. The Court held that the duties and responsibilities of the artist imposed on him special considerations of restraint rather than opportunities of freedom. **15.169**

---

[534] (1991) 19 EHRR 389 para 63 (conviction for publishing complaint that politician's views on immigration reflected philosophy and aims of Nazis).

[535] (1992) 14 EHRR 843 para 65 (defamation of the police).

[536] (1992) Series A No 242–B (conviction of politician for publishing spent conviction of another politician).

[537] *Prager and Oberschlick v Austria* (1995) 21 EHRR 1, para 37.

[538] *Fayed v United Kingdom* (1994) 18 EHRR 393 para 75.

[539] See *Hertel v Switzerland* (1998) 5 BHRC 260.

[540] For the 'public figure' defence, see para 15.247ff below; and cf the discussion of the Convention case law in *Reynolds v Times Newspapers Ltd* [1998] 3 WLR 862 (CA) and [1999] 3 WLR 1010 (HL).

[541] See *Müller v Switzerland* (1988) 13 EHRR 212 para 27.

[542] Ibid.

15.170   The *Müller* case was applied in *Otto-Preminger-Institute v Austria*.[543] A film was seized and forfeited because its showing created 'justified indignation' among a local population on religious grounds. However, the Court's decision has been much criticised. The reasoning adopted was very broad; the outrage of people who knew the nature of the film but had not seen it justified state interference with expression; and the reaction of persons in a small geographic area was a sufficient justification for a national ban on the film. The decision of the Court was by a majority (6:3), the majority having had to rely on their own assessment of the lack of merit of the film, an approach which was inconsistent with basic principles of freedom of expression. It is difficult to avoid David Pannick's conclusion that:

> To prohibit a film from being seen in private because the ideas which it contains may offend the religious beliefs of others is impossible to reconcile with a developed concept of free speech.[544]

This case should therefore be viewed as limited to its own particular facts and should not be treated as being of general application.

(d) Commercial expression

15.171   Commercial speech has been protected on grounds that Article 10 did not apply 'solely to certain types of information or ideas or forms of expression'.[545] In *Markt Intern and Beermann v Germany*[546] the applicant published a trade magazine which contained an article describing the experience of a chemist who was dissatisfied with a mail order firm and sought a refund; the article also described the response of the firm to its own inquiries. Although the statements in the article were true, an injunction was granted, restraining '*Markt Intern*' from repeating the allegations on the basis that it had acted contrary to honest practices in breach of the Unfair Competition Act. The Court regarded the article as information of a commercial nature which was protected under Article 10, although on the facts the interference was justified. Similarly, in *Casado Coca v Spain*[547] the Court rejected an argument that professional advertising was not protected by Article 10.

15.172   However, as the Court emphasised in *Jacubowski v Germany*,[548] not all expression of commercial value is protected: Article 10 only covers commercial expressions which are directed to furthering the economic interests of individuals and enterprises through advertising (or some other means of providing information to consumers).

---

[543] (1994) 19 EHRR 34; note though that Judge Spielmann's dissent in *Müller* has been favoured in later cases of the Commission.

[544] See D Pannick, 'Religious Feelings and the European Court', [1995] PL 7.

[545] (1989) 12 EHRR 161 paras 25–26.

[546] Ibid.

[547] (1994) 18 EHRR 1 paras 35–36.

[548] (1994) 19 EHRR 64.

In *Barthold v Germany*[549] the Court distinguished commercial advertising from public discussion of a matter of general interest when considering the conviction of a veterinary surgeon who made comments to the press about the lack of public provision in his field. His conviction in proceedings brought by fellow vets for 'instigating or tolerating publicity on his own behalf' was unjustified; the newspaper article in question was not viewed by the Court as commercial expression but as involving political expression. **15.173**

Commercial expression is treated as being of less importance than either political or artistic expression. Statements made for the purpose of competition fall outside the basic nucleus protected by freedom of expression and receive a lower standard of protection than other ideas or information.[550] Thus, in the *Markt Intern* case[551] the Court upheld an injunction against a trade magazine which prohibited it from publishing. The Court took the view that, as commercial speech, the magazine was subject to different standards. Even if statements in the publication were true, they could, nevertheless, be prohibited because of a duty to respect the privacy of others or the confidentiality of certain commercial information. However, the decisive factor in the Court's reasoning was the wide margin of appreciation it gave to the national courts.[552] By contrast, in *Hertel v Switzerland*[553] where the submission of a research paper to a scientific journal resulted in a criminal conviction, the Court took a much more restrictive approach to the margin of appreciation. It held that the conviction was a disproportionate interference with freedom of expression. **15.174**

The close regulation of advertising in some European countries has resulted in decisions holding that the national authorities have a wide margin of appreciation when interfering with an advertiser's expression. In *Colman v United Kingdom*,[554] the Commission decided that restrictions on advertising by doctors was justified. This approach was followed in *Casado Coca v Spain*[555] where it was held that, in the absence of a common European standard, the regulation of advertising by barristers did not fall outside the wide margin of appreciation which states had on the matter. **15.175**

Cases such as *Markt Intern and Beermann v Germany*[556] and *Jacubowski v Germany*[557] therefore represent a retreat from the fundamental principle estab- **15.176**

---

[549] (1985) 7 EHRR 383 para 50.

[550] *Markt Intern and Beermann v Germany* (1989) 12 EHRR 161 para 32.

[551] Ibid, the Court was split 9–9 and the case was decided on the casting vote of the President.

[552] Ibid paras 33–38.

[553] (1999) 28 EHRR 534; see para 15.207 below.

[554] (1993) 18 EHRR 119; the case was the subject of a friendly settlement.

[555] (1994) 18 EHRR 1.

[556] (1989) 12 EHRR 161.

[557] (1994) 19 EHRR 64.

lished by *Handyside v United Kingdom*[558] and *Sunday Times v United Kingdom (No 1)*[559] that an interference with expression is necessary only if the state presents convincing evidence of a pressing social need for it.[560] As Judge Pettiti observed in his dissenting judgment in *Markt Intern*:

> only in the rarest cases can censorship or prohibition of publication be accepted . . . This is particularly true in relation to commercial advertising or questions of economic or commercial policy. The protection of the interests of users and consumers in the face of dominant positions depends on the freedom to publish even the harshest criticisms of products.[561]

(4) Justifying limits on expression

(a) Introduction

15.177 Where there has been an interference with freedom of expression, it will be justified under Article 10(2) if:

- the interference is prescribed by law;
- the interference furthers a 'legitimate aim' (as there set out); and
- the interference is necessary in a democratic society.

The 'legitimate aims' which can, potentially justify restrictions on the freedom of expression are:

- the interests of national security;
- the interests of territorial integrity or public safety;
- for the prevention of disorder or crime;
- for the protection of health or morals;
- for the protection of the reputation or the rights of others;
- for preventing the disclosure of information received in confidence; or
- for maintaining the authority and impartiality of the judiciary.

15.178 When the Court (or Commission) assesses the question of justification under Article 10(2), it is essential to be clear whether its decision is based on the ground that the interference is a disproportionate restriction which is not 'necessary in a democratic society'; or whether it has decided that the interference is within a state's margin of appreciation. These doctrines are discussed in detail in Chapter 6. The principle of proportionality is a standard of judicial review.[562] On the other

---

[558] (1976) 1 EHRR 737.
[559] (1979) 2 EHRR 245.
[560] D Harris, M O'Boyle and C Warbrick, *Law of the European Convention on Human Rights* (Butterworths, 1995) 404.
[561] Judge Pettiti (n 556 above) 178.
[562] See generally, para 6.43ff above.

hand, the doctrine of the 'margin of appreciation' involves an interpretative obligation on an international human rights court to respect domestic cultural traditions and values.[563]

The potential justifications for interfering with freedom of expression under Article 10(2) must be narrowly interpreted: the 'necessity' for any restrictions must be 'convincingly established'.[564] The necessity of a restriction depends on the character of the expression, the duties and responsibilities of those exercising freedom of expression, the means of the communication, the audience to which it is directed, the significance of the interference and the purpose for which the restraint is imposed. **15.179**

The doctrine of margin of appreciation will therefore have no direct application to the Human Rights Act.[565] Nevertheless, it has played an important and controversial role in the Article 10 jurisprudence. The Court has used a number of different approaches when applying the margin of appreciation to freedom of expression cases;[566]; and it is strongly arguable that excessive use of the concept has seriously eroded the protection given by Article 10.[567] **15.180**

(b) Interferences

Prior restraint is not in principle incompatible with Article 10. However, such interference must be subject to strict scrutiny; it prevents transmission of ideas and information to those who wish to assess them for themselves and even temporary interference may be disastrous since information is a perishable commodity.[568] The burden of establishing the necessity of pre-publication measures, such as licensing schemes or court ordered injunctions, is therefore a heavy one.[569] **15.181**

The right to freedom of expression under Article 10 does not cease once information has been placed in the public domain. Post-publication sanctions such as civil and criminal actions, forfeiture of property,[570] the denial of a licence[571] or **15.182**

---

[563] See para 6.31ff above.

[564] See generally, the principles restated in *Zana v Turkey* (1997) 27 EHRR 667 para 51, see para 15.139 above.

[565] See para 6.37ff above.

[566] N Lavender, 'The Problem of the Margin of Appreciation' [1997] EHRLR 380.

[567] See for example A Lester 'Freedom of Expression' in R St J Macdonald, F Matscher and H Petzold (eds), *The European System for the Protection of Human Rights* (1993, Kluwer); and see P Mahoney, 'Universality Versus Subsidiarity in the Strasbourg Case Law on Free Speech: Explaining Some Recent Judgments' [1997] EHRLR 364 and Lord Lester, 'Universality Versus Subsidiarity: A Reply' [1998] EHRLR 73.

[568] *The Observer and The Guardian Newspapers v United Kingdom* (1991) 14 EHRR 153 para 60; but see *Wingrove v United Kingdom* (1997) 24 EHRR 1.

[569] *The Observer and The Guardian Newspapers v United Kingdom* (n 568 above) para 60; and see *De Becker v Belgium* (1962) 1 EHRR 43 regarding licensing of outlets or journalists.

[570] See eg *Müller v Switzerland* (1988) 13 EHRR 212.

[571] See eg *Autronic AG v Switzerland* (1990) 12 EHRR 485; *Radio ABC v Austria* (1997) 25 EHRR 185.

disciplinary penalties[572] will also be carefully scrutinised. The impact of the interference will depend on the kind and degree of consequences for the applicant. Criminal penalties are the most difficult interferences to justify; but high levels of damages in defamation proceedings may pose comparable dangers.[573] The seizure of original works of art also poses difficult problems;[574] and the Commission in *Otto-Preminger-Institute v Austria* expressed the view that very stringent reasons were needed to justify the seizure of a film, thus excluding any chance to discuss its message.[575] Post publication sanctions may also have a 'chilling effect' by acting as a deterrent to future publication of other information and materials.[576]

15.183 In some circumstances Article 10 creates positive obligations[577] on the state to take action to protect the freedom of expression of private individuals. In *Özgür Gündem v Turkey*[578] the Court held that genuine effective exercise of freedom of expression:

> does not depend merely on the State's duty not to interfere, but may require positive measures of protection, even in the sphere of relations between individuals.

In determining whether or not a positive obligation exists, regard must be had to the fair balance that has to be struck between the general interest of the community and the interests of the indiviudal. The obligation must not be interpreted in such a way as to impose an impossible or disproportionate burden on the state.[578a] In the *Özgür Gündem* case the state was found to be in breach of this positive obligation.

(c) Duties and responsibilities

15.184 Article 10(2) states that the exercise of the freedoms in Article 10(1) carries with it 'duties and responsibilities'. The phrase implies that, in determining the necessity of restrictions, these duties and responsibilities must not be overlooked.[579] This consideration might legitimise discriminatory distinctions between people in different positions; and could also serve to justify restrictions upon 'irresponsible' expression. It is, however, unclear how the notion of 'duties and responsibilities' is to be applied. In some cases it has justified a broad interpretation of a

---

[572] See eg *Casado Coco v Spain* (1994) 18 EHRR 1.

[573] See *Tolstoy Miloslavsky v United Kingdom* (1995) 20 EHRR 442 where the level of damages in English libel law was challenged when the award was £1.5 million; and *Markt Intern and Beermann v Germany* (1989) 12 EHRR 161 where the publisher faced a 500,000 DM fine for failure to comply with an injunction.

[574] *Müller v Switzerland* (1988) 13 EHRR 212 para 43.

[575] (1994) 19 EHRR 34 Com Rep para 77.

[576] *Barthold v Germany* (1985) 7 EHRR 383 para 58; *Lingens v Austria* (1986) 8 EHRR 103 para 44; *Jersild v Denmark* (1994) 19 EHRR 1 para 44.

[577] For the distinction between negative and positive obligations, see para 6.95ff above.

[578] Judgment of 16 Mar 2000 para 43.

[578a] Ibid.

[579] *Handyside v United Kingdom* (1976) 1 EHRR 737 para 49.

limitation, while in other cases it has had the opposite effect.[580] In *Handyside*,[581] which concerned an obscene publication intended for children, the Court emphasised the responsibilities of publishers and upheld a restriction. In *Lingens*,[582] on the other hand, the right of a journalist to criticise a politician was upheld when the press was found to have a duty and responsibility in a democratic society to 'impart information and ideas on political issues'; and in *Castells v Spain*[583] a politician enjoyed the advantage of protection of his special position.

In particular, the phrase has been used to justify interfering with freedom of expression on grounds of status. Thus, the duties and responsibilities of soldiers,[584] civil servants[585] or teachers[586] were said to justify interferences with Article 10. However, the phrase has not played a prominent role in recent cases[587] and it appears to have only minor significance as a further source of justification for interference with freedom of expression.   **15.185**

(d) 'Prescribed by law'

An interference with freedom of expression will be prescribed by law where: **15.186**

- the interference in question has some basis in domestic law;
- the law is adequately accessible; and
- the law is formulated so that it is sufficiently foreseeable.

The principle applies to a number of qualified Convention rights and is examined in detail in Chapter 6.[588] There have, however, been a number of important cases which have considered its impact on Article 10.

Restrictions on the freedom of expression must be authorised by national law.   **15.187**
Identification of the law or rule[589] in question has not been a source of difficulty.

---

[580] See A Robertson and J Merrills, *Human Rights in Europe: A Study of the European Convention on Human Rights* (Manchester University Press, 1993) 151.

[581] *Handyside v Uunited Kingdom* (n 579 above) para 49.

[582] *Lingens v Austria* (1986) 8 EHRR 103; but a more restrictive view of 'duties and responsibilities' was taken in *Prager and Oberschlick v Austria* (1995) 21 EHRR 1 where it was found that a journalist had failed to prove that he had applied the necessary diligence in his research.

[583] (1992) 14 EHHR 445.

[584] *Engel v Netherlands (No 2)* (1976) 1 EHRR 706 para 100; but see *Vereinigung Demokratischer Solidaten Osterreichs and Gubi v Austria* (1994) 20 EHRR 55 para 27 where the Court expressed the view that freedom of expression under Art 10(1) applies to servicemen just as much as to others.

[585] *B v United Kingdom* (1985) 45 DR 41, EComm HR.

[586] *X v United Kingdom* (1979) 16 DR 101, EComm HR; *Morissens v Belgium* (1988) 56 DR 127, EComm HR.

[587] Cf *Otto-Preminger-Institute v Austria* (1994) 19 EHRR 34 para 49 where the Court suggested that those who criticised the religious views of others had an obligation to avoid so far as possible remarks which were gratuitously offensive.

[588] See para 6.123ff above.

[589] It is accepted that rules made by professional or other bodies constitute 'laws' where rule-making power has been delegated to those authorities; see *Barthold v Germany* (1985) 7 EHRR 383; *Casado Coca v Spain* (1994) 18 EHRR 1.

Whether or not the law is adequately accessible is equally straightforward. However, whether a law regulating freedom of expression is sufficiently foreseeable has been challenged in a variety of applications: in the commercial area,[590] in contempt of court proceedings,[591] in licensing cases[592] and in relation to obscenity law,[593] defamation awards by juries[594] and the disclosure of journalistic sources.[595]

15.188 The law must be formulated with sufficient precision to enable the citizen to regulate his conduct. He must be able—if need be with appropriate advice—to foresee, to a degree that is reasonable in the circumstances, the consequences which a given action may entail.[596] Absolute precision is not achievable, however, and flexibility is necessary where the circumstances are constantly changing.[597]

15.189 The Court has considered on several occasions whether the common law is sufficiently foreseeable. In *Sunday Times v United Kingdom*[598] the Court accepted that a reformulation of the principles of contempt of court by the House of Lords[599] was still sufficiently foreseeable. In *Tolstoy Miloslavsky v United Kingdom*[600] it held that libel awards by juries were not too uncertain to be sufficiently foreseeable. The Court decided in *Steel v United Kingdom*[601] that breach of the peace was formulated with sufficient precision to be sufficiently foreseeable. In *Goodwin v United Kingdom*[602–603] the Court held that section 10 of the Contempt of Court

---

[590] *Markt Intern and Beermann v Germany* (1989) 12 EHRR 161; *Barthold v Germany* (n 589 above).

[591] *Sunday Times v United Kingdom* (1979) 2 EHRR 245.

[592] *Groppera Radio AG v Switzerland* (1990) 12 EHRR 321; *Autronic AG v Switzerland* (1990) 12 EHRR 485.

[593] *Müller v Switzerland* (1988) 13 EHRR 212.

[594] *Tolstoy Miloslavsky v United Kingdom* (1995) 20 EHRR 442.

[595] *Goodwin v United Kingdom* (1996) 22 EHRR 123.

[596] *Sunday Times v United Kingdom* (1979) 2 EHRR 245 para 48, 49; see also *Grigoriades v Greece* (1997) 27 EHRR 464 para 37.

[597] In *Markt Intern and Beermann v Germany* (1989) 12 EHRR 161, a law requiring 'honest practices' was sufficiently foreseeable in the sphere of competition where changes in the market and in communication precluded absolute precision; see also *Müller v Switzerland* (1988) 13 EHRR 212 in which the Court referred to 'the need to avoid excessive rigidity and to keep pace with changing circumstances'; the language comes from *Sunday Times v United Kingdom* (n 596 above) in which the Court held that a development in the common law of contempt of court was an application of a general principle which might have been anticipated by the applicants and was thus 'reasonable in the circumstances'.

[598] (1979) 2 EHRR 245.

[599] Whereas in *A-G v Times Newspapers Ltd* [1973] QB 710 the Divisional Court applied the principle that a deliberate attempt to influence the settlement of pending proceedings by bringing public pressure to bear on a party amounted to a contempt of court, the House of Lords seemed to prefer the view that it is a contempt to publish material which prejudges pending litigation: see [1974] AC 273.

[600] (1995) 20 EHRR 442.

[601] (1998) 5 BHRC 339 paras 25–28, 55.

[602–603] (1997) 22 EHRR 123.

Act 1981 was sufficiently precise to be foreseeable. On the other hand, in *Hashman and Harrup v United Kingdom*[604] the Court took the view that ordering a bind over on the basis that the applicant's conduct was *contra bonos mores* (that is, 'conduct which is wrong rather than right in the judgment of the majority of contemporary fellow citizens')[605] did not provide sufficient guidance about what sort of conduct would breach the order.

The Court has taken a broad view of the accessibility requirement in commercial **15.190** expression cases. In *Barthold v Germany*[606] the Court acknowledged a wide discretion to control unfair competition and said that absolute precision is especially difficult in regulating competition. In *Markt Intern and Beermann v Germany*[607] the requirement of honest practices in German competition law was acceptable because absolute precision could not be achieved in a competitive environment which was constantly changing because of developments in the market and in the communications field. The state was entitled to rely on the norms of public international law to prove that its domestic law was sufficiently accessible in *Groppera Radio AG v Switzerland*[608] and in *Autronic AG v Switzerland*.[609]

(e) 'Necessary in a democratic society'

The general principles which the Court applies when deciding whether an inter- **15.191** ference is proportionate[610] and necessary in a democratic society[611] are discussed in Chapter 6. A number of early cases such as *Handyside*,[612] *Sunday Times*,[613] *Barthold*[614] and *Lingens*[615] sought to give expression a preferred status over other protected interests. They also placed the burden on public authorities to show that there is a 'pressing social need' to interfere with the freedom and that the grounds for doing so are not only 'relevant and sufficient', but 'convincingly established'.[616] Although these principles were recently reaffirmed in *Zana v Turkey*,[617] in practice the Court considers a variety of factors including the value of the type of expression,[618] its medium and other circumstances of the communication, its

---

[604] (2000) 8 BHRC 104 paras 36–41.
[605] *Hughes v Holley* (1986) 86 Cr App R 130.
[606] (1985) 7 EHRR 383 para 47.
[607] (1989) 12 EHHR 161 para 30.
[608] (1990) 12 EHRR 321.
[609] (1990) 12 EHRR 485.
[610] See para 6.42ff above.
[611] See para 6.146ff above.
[612] *Handyside v United Kingdom* (1976) 1 EHRR 737.
[613] *Sunday Times v United Kingdom (No 1)* (1979) 2 EHRR 245.
[614] *Barthold v Germany* (1985) 7 EHRR 383.
[615] *Lingens v Austria* (1986) 8 EHRR 103.
[616] *The Observer and The Guardian Newspapers v United Kingdom* (1991) 14 EHRR 153.
[617] (1997) 27 EHRR 667 para 51; see para 15.139 above.
[618] See para 15.162ff above.

audience or target, the objective of the interference and its impact on the applicant.

15.192 Restrictions on freedom of expression may be difficult to justify where directed to a willing adult audience.[619] However, a different approach is taken where children are the target audience. Thus, interference was justified in *Handyside v United Kingdom*[620] on the grounds that the offensive subject matter was marketed specifically to appeal to children. The degree of access given to consumers, particularly unwilling consumers and those in need of protection, may also be decisive. A factor in the *Müller*[621] decision was that the exhibition, at which a shocking painting was observed by a young girl, was open to the public, without warning as to the subject matter of the art. In *Otto-Preminger-Institute v Austria*[622] the Commission held that access to an offensive film was limited because of a public warning about its contents and by the specialised nature of the cinema owned by the applicant. Nevertheless, the Court found that the state interference was justified because, even though no innocent viewer was likely to attend, the warnings themselves and the knowledge that the film was going to be shown, incited community outrage.

15.193 The tolerant and broadminded approach emphasised in *Handyside v United Kingdom*[623] (and recently re-iterated in *Zana v Turkey*)[624] has not prevailed in cases brought by political protesters. In *Arrowsmith v United Kingdom*[625] the Commission held that the conviction and imprisonment which resulted from distributing leaflets advising soldiers not to serve in Northern Ireland was necessary to protect national security. In *Chorherr v Austria*[626] the Court upheld the right of the state to interfere with protesters by suggesting that the commotion they created had brought the interference on themselves. The Commission has also adopted a restrictive approach when considering complaints about interferences with racist expression or support for terrorists.[627]

(f) Objective of the interference

15.194 The necessity of the public interference in a democratic society also requires that an interference furthers one of the aims set out in Article 10(2). In practice, very few disputes arise about whether an interference falls within their broad scope.

---

[619] See eg *Jersild v Denmark* (1994) 19 EHRR 1 where the expression was part of a serious news programme intended for an informed audience; note however, *Otto-Preminger-Institute v Austria* (1994) 19 EHRR 34 where willing viewers were precluded by community standards from seeing a film.
[620] (1976) 1 EHRR 737.
[621] (1988) 13 EHRR 212.
[622] n 619 above.
[623] n 620 above, see para 15.163 above.
[624] (1997) 27 EHRR 667 para 51; see para 15.139 above.
[625] (1980) 19 DR 5, EComm HR.
[626] (1993) 17 EHRR 358 para 33.
[627] See para 15.141 above.

National security, territorial integrity or public safety.   The national security   **15.195**
restriction featured prominently in the 'Spycatcher' cases which considered the le-
gitimacy of injunctions granted to restrain newspapers from publishing information about the British security services which was derived from the manuscript of
a proposed book, *Spycatcher*, written by the former secret intelligence officer, Peter
Wright.[628]

The main issue facing the Court in *The Observer and The Guardian v United*   **15.196**
Kingdom[629] and *Sunday Times v United Kingdom (No 2)*[630] was the compatibility of
injunctions issued, modified and extended and finally discharged by the House of
Lords, with Article 10. Although the book had been published in the United States,
the interlocutory injunctions were continued[631] until the main proceedings were
complete. The House of Lords[632] had refused to restrain the newspapers on grounds
that the American publication had destroyed any justification for granting the permanent injunctions. The Commission found that the injunctions had violated
Article 10. However, the Court decided that the interlocutory injunctions were not
a breach, holding that only their continuation by the House of Lords infringed freedom of expression. Initially, the Government had identified several aims to support
the ban. National security was indirectly in issue; it was said that Mr Wright's information was protected as it had been received in confidence; and the injunction was
necessary to preserve the Attorney-General's claim to confidentiality, thus maintaining the authority of the judiciary.[633] The Court found that, prior to the
American publication, revelation of the material could be damaging to the Security
Service; and that the objectives of protection of national security and of preserving
the Attorney-General's claim were legitimate ones, justifying interference in a democratic society. Once the book had been published,[634] however, this substantially
eradicated any justification for continuing the interim injunction to preserve the
case of the Attorney-General until trial.[635] Before the Court of Human Rights, the
Government argued that protection of national security required the maintenance
of the morale and reputation of the Security Service and that others should be dis-
couraged from breaches of confidentiality such as the publishing of memoirs.[636]

---

[628] For the history of the English litigation, see para 15.19ff above.

[629] (1991) 14 EHRR 153.

[630] (1991) 14 EHRR 229.

[631] *A-G v Guardian Newspapers Ltd* [1987] 1 WLR 1248.

[632] Ibid.

[633] Protecting the rights of litigants is recognised as an aspect of maintenance of the authority of
the judiciary under Art 10(2): *Sunday Times v United Kingdom* (1979) 2 EHRR 245; see para 15.213
below.

[634] Publication took place in the United States just prior to the continuation of the interlocutory
injunctions by the House of Lords.

[635] See the earlier decision of the Court in *Weber v Switzerland* (1990) 12 EHRR 508, where it
held that the defence of prior publication might limit the scope of the restrictions on Article 10.

[636] *The Observer and The Guardian Newspapers v United Kingdom* (n 629 above) para 69.

The Court did not directly assess these issues, but decided that the continuation of the injunction had a negative impact on the third party newspapers which was disproportionate to any need to protect the confidence interest.[637] Judge Walsh, dissenting, pointed out[638] that the authorities had not established any threat to national security and ought not to invoke this exception on the basis of opinion alone.

15.197   The Commission has also held that restrictions on broadcasting news material about organisations which support terrorism does not contravene Article 10.[639] On the other hand, there was an unjustified interference with the freedom of expression of soldiers[640] where they were disciplined for distributing a satirical journal within military barracks in breach of military regulations.[641] A number of cases have examined whether restrictions on national security grounds to prevent insults to the armed forces,[642] or statements of support for a terrorist separatist organisation[643] could be justified on national security grounds. In *Grigoriades v Greece*[644] a conviction violated Article 10 because the insults to the armed forces were contained in a letter to a commanding officer without wider publication, did not attack the recipient or any other individual and had little impact on military discipline.

15.198   In *Zana v Turkey*[645] a prosecution for the applicant's outspoken support for the PKK was justified on national security and public safety grounds as part of the fight against terrorism. However, in *Incal v Turkey*[646] a conviction for 'inciting the people to hatred' violated Article 10 where a leaflet was distributed containing virulent remarks about Government policy but no incitement to violence, hostility or hatred. The Court distinguished the *Zana* case on grounds that the applicant could not be regarded as being in any way responsible for problems caused by terrorism in the province of Izmir. The Court has recently considered a number of Turkish cases where convictions on terrorist or public safety grounds were said to be disproportionate restrictions on freedom of expression. Most of the

---

[637] For an analysis of the *Spycatcher* litigation at Strasbourg see I Leigh, 'Spycatcher in Strasbourg' [1992] PL 200.

[638] *The Observer and the Guardian Newspapers v United Kingdom* (n 629 above) 205 para 4.

[639] *Purcell v Ireland* (1991) 70 DR 262, EComm HR; *Brind and McLaughlin v United Kingdom* (1994) 77–A DR 42, EComm HR.

[640] The Court emphasised in *Hadjianastassiou v Greece* (1992) 16 EHRR 219 that freedom of expression under Art 10(1) extended to soldiers just as much as to civilians.

[641] *Vereinigung Demokratischer Soldaten Österreichs and Bethold Gubi v Austria* (1994) 20 EHRR 55; *Vereniging Weekblad 'Bluf' v Netherlands* (1995) 20 EHRR 189.

[642] *Grigoriades v Greece* (1997) 27 EHRR 464.

[643] *Zana v Turkey* (1997) 27 EHRR 667.

[644] (1997) 27 EHRR 464.

[645] (1997) 27 EHRR 667.

[646] RJD 1998–IV 1547.

applications were held to breach Article 10[647] although two convictions were justified.[648]

The justification for interfering with expression to maintain 'territorial integrity' **15.199**
has been considered less frequently. In *Piermont v France*[649] the applicant had
been excluded from French Polynesia after making a speech supporting anti-
nuclear and independence demands of local political parties. Although the interference with her freedom of expression was to prevent disorder and maintain territorial integrity, the interference was disproportionate as the demonstration was
non-violent and there was a strong interest in protecting political speech.

Prevention of disorder or crime.   The prevention of disorder or crime includes **15.200**
(but is not limited to) public disorder. The need to protect public order in the face
of terrorist threats is a significant justification for restricting freedom of expression[650] or international telecommunications.[651] Prevention of disorder within the
armed forces has also been found to be a legitimate aim.[652]

Restrictions on political expression, however, are likely to be difficult to justify. **15.201**
Although freedom of political debate is not absolute, the Government must react
proportionately and without excess to criticisms made of it.[653] Thus, in *Steel v
United Kingdom*[654] arresting protesters for breach of the peace was a legitimate restriction on the right of expression because the arrests were intended to prevent

---

[647] *Karatas v Turkey* Application 23168/94, 8 Jul 1999 (convictions under Prevention of
Terrorism Act for poems concerning Kurdish discontent); *Arslan v Turkey* Application 23462/94,
8 Jul 1999 (conviction of author for book maintaining that Kurds were victims of oppression);
Polat v Turkey Application 23500/94, 8 Jul 1999 (conviction for historical epic concerning Kurdish
rebel movement); *Ceylan v Turkey* Application 23556/94, 8 Jul 1999 (conviction of union leader
for Marxist explanation for Kurdish movement); *Okçuoglu v Turkey* Application 24246/94, 8 Jul
1999 (conviction for interview expressing views about Kurdish situation); *Gerger v Turkey*
Application 24919/94, 8 Jul 1999 (conviction for polemic given at funeral of political activists)
Erdogdu and Ince v Turkey Application 25067/94, 8 Jul 1999 (conviction for interview of sociolo-
gist in monthly review expressing views about Kurds); *Surek v Turkey (No 2)* Application
24762/94, 8 Jul 1999 (conviction for news report identifying officials which were alleged to be terrorist targets); *Surek v Turkey (No 4)* Application 24762/94, 8 Jul 1999 (conviction for news com-
mentary about Kurdistan).
[648] *Surek v Turkey (No 1)* Application 26682/95, 8 Jul 1999 (conviction for polemic about
Kurdistan); *Surek v Turkey (No 4)* (conviction for polemic about Kurdistan).
[649] (1995) 20 EHRR 301.
[650] *Chorherr v Austria* (1993) 17 EHRR 358.
[651] *Groppera Radio AG v Switzerland* (1990) 12 EHRR 321 and *Autronic AG v Switzerland* (1990)
12 EHRR 485.
[652] *Engel v Netherlands (No 1)* (1976) 1 EHRR 647; *Vereinigung Demokratischer Soldaten Österreichs and Gubi v Austria* (1994) 20 EHRR 55.
[653] *Incal v Turkey* (1998) 4 BHRC 476, 491–492 paras 52–59: prosecution for publication of a
leaflet urging Kurdish population to band together was a violation; see also *Janowski v Poland* (1999)
5 BHRC 672 in which the Court held that conviction of the applicant, for using offensive words to
criticise civil servants acting in an official capacity, was justified.
[654] (1998) 28 EHRR 603.

disorder and to protect the rights of others. However, the restrictions were disproportionate since the police could not justify the arrests on the basis that they had reasonable grounds to apprehend a breach of the peace.[655]

15.202   **Protection of health or morals.**   Because the Court regards 'morals' as having no objective content, and there is no European consensus to assist in a definition,[656] the Court has given national courts a wide margin of appreciation, both in deciding the content of 'morals' and in what measures are necessary to protect morals.[657] While 'morals' may attract strong local feelings,[658] it is not self evident that local considerations should govern the determination of national standards for protecting morals. On the other hand, in the *Open Door* case[659] the Court found Government interference unjustifiable. While it is primarily for the state to determine the content of 'morals', the very broad and perpetual injunction to restrain anyone (regardless of age, health reasons or necessity) from seeking advice about abortion was not necessary in a democratic society.

15.203   **Protection of the reputation or the rights of others.**   The protection of the reputation or rights of others provides the entitlement for an individual to pursue defamation proceedings. The Court has frequently stressed that the limits of acceptable criticism are wider for a politician than a private citizen. A politician lays himself open to close scrutiny of his every word and deed by both journalists and the general public and must display a greater degree of tolerance.[660] The bounds of permissible criticism of the Government is even wider.[661]

15.204   Even where there is substantial damage to reputation, a successful claim in defamation may violate Article 10. In *Bladet Tromsø and Stensaas v Norway*[662] the Court, in a long and detailed analysis of the facts, held that the vital interest in ensuring an informed public debate over seal hunting was a matter of local and national interest which was sufficient to outweigh the interests of those who issued defamation proceedings to protect their reputation. Similarly, in *Nilsen and Johnsen v Norway*[663] the Court again carefully examined the factual issues and concluded that defamation proceedings breached freedom of expression. The

---

[655] Ibid para 110.

[656] *Handyside v United Kingdom* (1976) 1 EHRR 737.

[657] See eg ibid (the sale of the Little Red Schoolbook); and *Müller v Switzerland* (1988) 13 EHHR 212.

[658] In *Handyside v United Kingdom* (n 656 above) and *Müller v Switzerland* (n 657 above) the Court accepted that a 'pressing social need' was necessary to punish expression for the protection of the morals of relatively small areas of the population.

[659] *Open Door and Dublin Well Woman v Ireland* (1992) 15 EHRR 244.

[660] See eg *Lingens v Austria* (1986) 8 EHRR 103 para 42; and see, generally, para 15.166 above.

[661] *Castells v Spain* (1992) 14 EHRR 445 para 46.

[662] (1999) 6 BHRC 599 paras 62–73.

[663] Judgment, 25 Nov 1999.

Court also took the view in *Tolstoy Miloslavsky v United Kingdom*[664] that the unpredictable nature of jury awards in libel cases was a disproportionate restriction on freedom of expression. In *Bergens Tidende v Norway*[664a] the applicant newspaper had published an article containing critical accounts given by the patients of a cosmetic surgeon, Dr R. Although the accounts were factually accurate, the Supreme Court had held that the 'natural and ordinary' meaning of the words used was that Dr R performed his activities in a reckless way—which was false. As a result, Dr R had been awarded substantial damages.[664b] The Court held that this was a violation of Article 10. It said:

> the Court cannot find that the undoubted interest of Dr R in protecting his professional reputation was sufficient to outweigh the important public interest in the freedom of the press to impart information on matters of legitimate public concern.[664c]

15.205 Where the religious beliefs of others are offended, interferences with freedom of expression may be justified. In *Otto-Preminger-Institute v Austria*[665] it justified the nation-wide seizure and forfeiture of a film which offended the rights of a local population on religious grounds. The Court found that, as with 'morals', the lack of a uniform conception of religion in European society gave a wide margin of appreciation to the state to determine the necessity of the ban for the protection of the rights of the local people. However, the case differs from the 'morals' cases because the Court accepted the application of 'local' standards to a national level, finding that the nation-wide ban did not exceed the state's margin of appreciation. Similarly, in *Wingrove v United Kingdom*[666] the refusal of the British Board of Film Classification to grant a licence for the distribution of the film 'Visions of Christ' was justified to protect the rights of Christians.

15.206 The protection of the rights of others also permits an interference to ensure 'effective political democracy'. Such interferences are not limited to circumstances in which the stability of the constitutional or political order is threatened.[667] Thus, in *Ahmed v United Kingdom*[668] regulations restricting the political activity of local authority employees were a proportionate restriction on freedom of expression. In the special circumstances of the former Eastern bloc countries, restriction on the freedom of police officers to engage in political debate was proportionate.[669]

---

[664] (1995) 20 EHRR 442.
[664a] Judgment of 2 May 2000.
[664b] 930,000 krone, or approximately £75,000.
[664c] *Bergens Tidende* (n 664a above) para 60.
[665] (1994) 19 EHRR 34.
[666] (1996) 24 EHRR 1.
[667] *Ahmed v United Kingdom* (1998) 5 BHRC 111, para 52.
[668] Ibid paras 52-54; for the unsuccessful challenge to these regulations in the English courts, see *R v Secretary of State for the Environment, ex p NALGO* [1993] Admin LR 785.
[669] *Rekvényi v Hungary* (1999) 6 BHRC 554 paras 44–49.

15.207　Interference with commercial expression may also be justified because of its impact on the rights of others. In *Hertel v Switzerland*[670] the applicant was convicted[671] for submitting to a scientific journal a research paper on the possible detrimental effects of the use of microwave ovens. Although the legislation, which was 'intended to guarantee, in the interests of all parties concerned, fair, undistorted competition', had the legitimate aim of the protection of the rights of others, the conviction could not be justified as being necessary in a democratic society. The Court emphasised that the wide margin of appreciation given to states in relation to commercial and competition areas must be reduced when the statement of an individual is not made as a matter of purely 'commercial' interest, but is part of a more general debate.

15.208　Protection of the rights of others was also claimed to justify interfering with freedom of expression in *Lehideux and Isorni v France*.[672] The applicant was convicted of the 'public defence of war crimes or the crimes of collaboration' after publishing an advertisement seeking to present in a positive light information concerning Marshall Petain to secure a retrial of his case. The interference pursued several legitimate aims including the protection of rights of others and the prevention of disorder or crime but was a disproportionate restriction.[673] On the other hand, in *Janowski v Poland*[674] a conviction for using insulting words to criticise the actions of municipal guards in a public setting was justifiable as protecting the reputation and rights of the civil servants. Similarly, in *Peree v Netherlands*[674a] the Commission held that the convictions of the applicant for 'insult and slander' for comparing an anti-discrimination organisation to the Nazi SA were justifiable.

15.209　In *Fressoz and Roire v France*[675] one of the legitimate aims for the conviction of applicants for publishing a press article was the protection of the reputation of M Calvert, the chairman of the French car manufacturer, Peugot. Although the article was intended to contribute to a wider debate, it disclosed details of M Calvert's personal income and tax assessments. The applicants were found guilty of 'the handling of photocopies of tax returns obtained through a breach of professional confidence by an unidentified tax official' and sentenced to substantial fines and damages. The convictions were held to be a disproportionate interference with freedom of expression.

---

[670] (1999) 28 EHRR 534.

[671] The Federal Unfair Competition Act included in its definition of 'unfair acts' the denigration 'of others or the goods, work, services, prices or business of others by making inaccurate, misleading or unnecessarily wounding statements'.

[672] (1998) 5 BHRC 540.

[673] Ibid paras 51–58.

[674] (1999) 5 BHRC 672.

[674a] (1998) 28 EHRR CD 158.

[675] (1999) 5 BHRC 654.

Preventing the disclosure of information received in confidence. Justification   **15.210**
on grounds of prevention of disclosure of information received in confidence
overlaps with other legitimate aims. For example, the protection of confidential
governmental information may be required 'in the interests of national security'
whilst disclosure of private information may be restricted for 'protection of the
rights of others'. However, this aim may be relevant in cases concerning confidential Government information which does not affect national security.[676]

The Court has considered justification on this basis on a number of occasions. In   **15.211**
Goodwin v United Kingdom[677] an order for the disclosure of a journalistic source
on the ground that it would enable an employer to identify a disloyal employee
was not justified by an 'overriding requirement in the public interest'. In *Fressoz v
France*[678] the objective of protecting fiscal confidentiality was legitimate but the
conviction of journalists for handling documents obtained in breach of professional confidence was disproportionate.

Maintaining the authority and impartiality of the judiciary. The need to   **15.212**
maintain the authority and impartiality of the judiciary is a ground of justification
for interference and overlaps with the right of an individual to a fair trial 'where
publicity would prejudice the interests of justice' under Article 6(1).[679] Article
10(2) is broader in scope and pre-trial comments are potentially legitimate under
this head. However, in this context the Court has recognised that account must be
taken of the central position occupied by Article 6.[680]

In the *Sunday Times* case[681] an injunction had been granted restraining the publica-   **15.213**
tion of a newspaper article about the merits of pending Thalidomide litigation, on
grounds that it would prejudice the trial. The Court decided that there was no 'pressing social need' for the injunction, that there was substantial public interest in the
case, that the article used moderate language and that the injunction was broadly
framed. The Court took the view that the 'authority and impartiality of the judiciary' were 'objectively determinable' interests; and that the margin of appreciation
afforded to the state to take measures to protect them was therefore a narrow one.[682]

The impact of criticising the judiciary has also been considered. In *Barfod v*   **15.214**
Denmark[683] the applicant was convicted of defaming two lay judges. This conviction was justified despite his arguments that the comments were aimed at the tribunal rather than the individual judges, and that they were part of a wider political

---

[676] See *X v Germany* (1970) 13 YB, 888, EComm HR.
[677] (1996) 22 EHRR 123, see generally, para 15.77ff above.
[678] (1999) 5 BHRC 654.
[679] Art 6(1); see para 11.231ff above.
[680] *Sunday Times v United Kingdom* (1979) 2 EHRR 245 para 55.
[681] Ibid.
[682] But see *Weber v Switzerland* (1990) 12 EHRR 508.
[683] (1989) 13 EHRR 493.

tax debate. In *Schöpfer v Switzerland*[684] the disciplinary punishment of the applicant lawyer was also justifiable where a lawyer publicly criticised the administration of justice in his jurisdiction in criminal proceedings which were then pending before the courts. In *De Haes and Gijsels v Belgium*[685] journalists argued that the articles, which personally insulted certain members of the judiciary for their handling of child abuse and incest proceedings, were to be seen against the background of the public debate on incest in the region. They argued that the research upon which they were based constituted objective evidence; and that it was only to protect their sources that it had not been presented in court. The Court held that, although the comments were severely critical, they were not disproportionate to the indignation caused by the subject matter of the articles.

15.215   The restriction of pre-trial comment in criminal cases was addressed in *Worm v Austria*[686] where the Court upheld the conviction of a journalist who had written an article which was critical of a former Minister in advance of his trial on charges of tax evasion. The Court held that states were not entitled to restrict all forms of public discussion on matters pending before the courts. It said:

> There is general recognition of the fact that courts cannot operate in a vacuum . . . Provided that it does not overstep the bounds imposed in the interests of the proper administration of justice, reporting, including comment on court proceedings contributes to their publicity and is thus perfectly consonant with the requirements under article 6(1) of the convention that hearings be public.[687]

The Court drew attention to the role of the media in imparting information, particularly where a public figure is involved. However:

> public figures are entitled to the enjoyment of the guarantees of a fair trial set out in art 6 . . . the limits of permissible comment may not extend to statements which are likely to prejudice, whether intentionally or not, the chances of a person receiving a fair trial or to undermine the confidence of the public in the role of the courts in the administration of criminal justice.[688]

The conviction was upheld despite the absence of a requirement in domestic law of actual influence on court proceedings. The Commission took a similar view of a pre-hearing restriction in *Channel Four v United Kingdom*[689] where it held that the broadcasting of contemporaneous reconstructions of the criminal appeal would have an impact both on the right to fair trial and on the reputation of the court.

---

[684]   [1998] EHRLR 646.
[685]   (1997) 25 EHRR 1.
[686]   (1997) 25 EHRR 454.
[687]   Ibid para 50.
[688]   Ibid.
[689]   (1989) 61 DR 285, EComm HR; see also *Hodgson v United Kingdom* (1987) 51 DR 136, EComm HR; *Atkinson Crook and The Independent v United Kingdom* (1990) 67 DR 244, EComm HR (jury trial).

D. The Impact of the Human Rights Act

(1) Introduction

The Human Rights Act will require the courts to give new weight to the freedom **15.216**
of expression which, in the past, has often been subordinated to other interests.
There was considerable debate when the Bill was enacted concerning the effect of
incorporating Article 10, and its relationship to other Convention rights. The existence of a right to freedom of expression which is subject to narrowly defined
limits which must be justified as proportionate[690] will have a significant impact on
the English law in a large number of different areas. Nevertheless, during the passage of the Bill the media expressed concerns about the effect of the right of privacy on freedom of expression. As a result, the Government introduced section 12
of the Act which was 'specifically designed to safeguard press freedom'.[691]

The Human Rights Act is likely to have important repercussions on private law **15.217**
remedies which restrict expression. In particular, it will give impetus to further developments in the law of defamation. In addition, Article 10 is likely to have an
impact in the fields of commercial law, criminal law, education, employment and
discrimination, family law, local government, media law, and prison law.

(2) United Kingdom cases prior to the Human Rights Act

(a) Introduction

A large number of United Kingdom applications based on Article 10 have come **15.218**
before the Commission and the Court. Many of these were unsuccessful, but the
Court has on eight occasions found the United Kingdom to be in violation of
Article 10.[692] Most of the Article 10 applications out of the United Kingdom fall
into one of four general categories: obscenity and blasphemy, contempt of court,
defamation and national security.

However, before considering the cases brought in Strasbourg, it is necessary to **15.219**
consider the impact that Article 10 has had on the development of domestic law.
Although, in general, Convention rights only affect domestic law indirectly[693] the
stance the courts have taken to Article 10 has been rather different.

---

[690] See generally, para 6.40ff above.
[691] See *Hansard*, HC col 538 ff (2 Jul 1998).
[692] *Sunday Times v United Kingdom* (1979) 2 EHRR 245; *Sunday Times v United Kingdom (No 2)*
(1991) 14 EHRR 229; *The Observer and The Guardian v United Kingdom* (1991) 14 EHRR 153;
Tolstoy Miloslavsky v United Kingdom (1995) 20 EHRR 442; *Goodwin v United Kingdom* (1996) 22
EHRR 123; *Bowman v United Kingdom* (1998) 26 EHRR 1; *Steel v United Kingdom* (1998) 28
EHRR 603 (the Art 10 violation incidental to an Art 5 violation); *Hashman and Harrup v United
Kingdom* (2000) 8 BHRC 104.
[693] See para 2.09ff above.

(b) The impact of Article 10 on the common law

15.220 Before the Human Rights Act came into force, Article 10 of the Convention had already had a substantial impact on the development of the common law. In the well known passage in *Derbyshire County Council v Times Newspapers Ltd*,[694] Lord Keith said:

> Lord Goff of Chieveley in *A-G v Guardian Newspapers Ltd (No 2)*[695] expressed the opinion that in the field of freedom of speech there was no difference in principle between English law on the subject and article 10 of the Convention. I agree and can only add that I find it satisfactory to be able to conclude that the common law of England is consistent with the obligations assumed by the Crown under the Treaty in this particular field.

15.221 The courts have taken Article 10 into account in refusing local authorities and political parties the right to sue in defamation,[696] in determining the extent of the defence of 'qualified privilege'[697] and in deciding how libel damages should be assessed.[698] Article 10 has had an important influence on the law of contempt[699] and, in particular, on decisions concerning disclosure of journalistic sources under section 10 of the Contempt of Court Act 1981.[700] It has also been considered when the court decides whether to exercise discretion to restrain freedom of expression[701] and as a relevant factor to be taken into account where a public body implements measures which restrain expression.[702] The Human Rights Act can only reinforce the importance of freedom of expression as a fundamental legal value in English law.

(c) Obscenity and blasphemy

15.222 None of the United Kingdom applications under Article 10 in relation to obscenity and blasphemy have been successful. Where there has been doubt as to the 'necessity' of the measures used, the Government has consistently been given the benefit of a 'margin of appreciation'. This is because:

> a wider margin of appreciation is generally available to the contracting states when regulating freedom of expression in relation to matters liable to offend intimate personal convictions within the sphere of morals or, especially, religion.[703]

---

[694] [1993] AC 534, 553F.

[695] [1990] 1 AC 109, 283–284.

[696] Ibid; see para 15.29 above.

[697] *Reynolds v Times Newspapers Ltd* [1998] 3 WLR 862, [1999] 3 WLR 1010, see para 15.29 above.

[698] *Rantzen v Mirror Group Newspapers (1986) Ltd* [1994] QB 670, see para 15.38 above.

[699] See para 15.48ff above.

[700] See para 15.73ff above.

[701] See *A-G v Guardian Newspapers Ltd (No 1)* [1987] 1 WLR 1248, 1296-7; *R v Advertising Standards Authority Ltd, ex p Vernons Organisation Ltd* [1992] 1 WLR 1289; *Middlebrook Mushrooms Ltd v Transport and General Workers' Union* [1993] IRLR 232, 235.

[702] *R v Secretary of State for the Environment, ex p NALGO* [1993] Admin LR 785, 795;

[703] See *Wingrove v United Kingdom* (1996) 24 EHRR 1 para 58.

The fact that the margin of appreciation given to national authorities has been determinative in these cases means that the Strasbourg jurisprudence will provide less than reliable guidance to the UK judiciary when such matters arise in the national courts, where 'margin of appreciation' is not relevant.[704]

The leading case of *Handyside v United Kingdom*[705] concerned the Little Red **15.223** Schoolbook, a publication which was written for schoolchildren and included a chapter on explicitly sexual topics. The applicant was convicted of an offence under the Obscene Publications Act. The issue for the Court was whether the undoubted interference with freedom of expression of the applicant was 'necessary in a democratic society for the protection of morals'. The Court referred to the 'national margin of appreciation' and said that:

> The Contracting States have each fashioned their approach in the light of the situation obtaining in their respective territories; they have had regard, *inter alia*, to the different views prevailing there about the demands of the protection of morals in a democratic society.[706]

On this basis, the Court found that the conviction of the applicant on grounds of obscenity was not a violation of Article 10.[707] In *Hoare v United Kingdom*[708] the applicant complained of a breach of Article 10 as a result of his conviction for publishing obscene articles[709] under section 2 of the Obscene Publications Act 1959 and his sentence of 30-months' imprisonment. The Commission took the view that the restriction on the applicant's freedom of expression was for a legitimate aim, namely the protection of morals and was not disproportionate.

The case of *Gay News and Lemon v United Kingdom*[710] concerned the convic- **15.224** tions of the applicant for blasphemous libel. The Commission found that this offence restricted freedom of expression for a legitimate purpose, namely 'the protection of the rights of citizens not to be offended in their religious feelings by publications'.[711] The Commission also took the view that the offence of blasphemous libel satisfied the test of 'proportionality' inherent in Article 10(2). As a result, the Commission found that the complaint was manifestly ill-founded.

---

[704] See para 6.31ff above.
[705] (1976) 1 EHRR 737.
[706] Ibid para 57.
[707] For a discussion of the case, see R Lawson and H Schermers (eds), *Leading Cases of the European Court of Human Rights* (Ars Aequi Libri, 1997) 37–42; and see A Lester, 'Freedom of Expression' and R St J Macdonald, 'The Margin of Appreciation' in R St J Macdonald, F Matscher and H Petzold (eds), *The European System for the Protection of Human Rights* (Nijhoff, 1993).
[708] [1997] EHRLR 678.
[709] The articles were hardcore pornographic video tapes distributed by post.
[710] (1982) 5 EHRR 123.
[711] Ibid para 11.

15.225   Blasphemy was again at issue in *Wingrove v United Kingdom*.[712] A video entitled
'Visions of Ecstasy' depicted St Teresa of Avila in erotic scenes. The British Board
of Film Classification had refused the video a distribution certificate. The admitted interference with freedom of expression was held by the Court to be 'prescribed by law', despite the fact that the offence of blasphemy lacked precise legal
definition: it took the view that the applicant, with appropriate legal advice, could
reasonably have foreseen that the film might fall within the scope of the offence of
blasphemy.[713] The interference was also found to have the legitimate aim of protecting the rights of others: more specifically, 'to provide protection against seriously offensive attacks on matters regarded as sacred by Christians'.[714] In holding
that the restrictions were 'necessary', the Court took into account the fact that:

> there is as yet not sufficient common ground in the legal and social orders of the
> Member States of the Council of Europe to conclude that a system whereby a State
> can impose restrictions on the propagation of material on the basis that it is blas-
> phemous is, in itself, unnecessary in a democratic society and thus incompatible
> with the Convention.[715]

The Court took into account the wide margin of appreciation for states in relation
to matters which are liable to offend intimate personal convictions.[716]

(d) Contempt of court

15.226   One of the best known decisions of the Court is that of *Sunday Times v United
Kingdom*[717] which arose out of the Thalidomide litigation. The Attorney-General
obtained an injunction restraining publication of an article commenting on the
drug 'Thalidomide' as a contempt of court.[718] The Court accepted that the rules
relating to contempt of court were 'prescribed by law' and had the legitimate aim,
under Article 10(2), of 'maintaining the authority ... of the judiciary'.[719]
However, the Court went on to consider whether the interference by injunction
was 'necessary in a democratic society' and concluded that:

> the interference complained of did not correspond to a social need sufficiently
> pressing to outweigh the public interest in freedom of expression within the mean-
> ing of the Convention.[720]

---

[712] (1996) 24 EHRR 1.
[713] Ibid para 43.
[714] Ibid para 48.
[715] Ibid para 57.
[716] For a general discussion, see S Ghandi and J James, 'The English Law of Blasphemy and the
European Convention on Human Rights', [1998] EHRLR 430.
[717] (1979) 2 EHRR 245.
[718] The injunction had been granted at first instance, discharged by the Court of Appeal and re-
stored by the House of Lords: see *A-G v Times Newspapers Ltd* [1974] AC 273.
[719] *Sunday Times v United Kingdom* (n 717 above) para 57.
[720] Ibid para 67.

The restraint was therefore a violation of Article 10. This decision resulted in the Contempt of Court Act 1981. In *Channel Four v United Kingdom*,[721] on the other hand, a restraint was acceptable where the Commission found that the broadcasting of contemporaneous reconstructions of a criminal appeal would have an impact on both the right to fair trial and the reputation of the court.

The effect of section 10 of the Contempt of Court Act 1981 was considered by the Court in *Goodwin v United Kingdom*.[722] Section 10 introduced a presumption against the disclosure of journalists' sources, subject only to a 'legitimate aim' and a 'necessity' test, requirements which mirror Article 10(2) of the Convention. The House of Lords had ordered disclosure of the identity of the source of confidential financial documents stolen from the plaintiff company.[723] In contrast, the Court decided that the order breached Article 10; it was not 'necessary in a democratic society' because there was no reasonable relationship of proportionality between the order and the legitimate aim of the protection of the rights of the company. **15.227**

(e) Defamation

The English law of defamation has generated a steady stream of applications under the Convention. The case of *Tolstoy Miloslavsky v United Kingdom*[724] was brought following the notorious libel proceedings in which the jury had awarded Lord Aldington a record £1,500,000 damages because he was alleged to have been involved in war crimes. Article 10 had been infringed as the size of the award could not be justified as being 'necessary in a democratic society'. The Court of Appeal now gives guidance to juries when they consider making awards of damages.[725] **15.228**

The applicants in *Steel and Morris v United Kingdom*[726] complained that restrictions on their expression were unjustified because the state failed to provide legal aid funding for defamation proceedings, simplified legal procedures and restrictions which would limit damage awards. The Commission declared the complaint inadmissible, commenting that the freedom of expression under Article 10 is not absolute; and does not authorise the publication of defamatory material: **15.229**

---

[721] *Channel Four v United Kingdom* (1989) 61 DR 285, EComm HR; see also *Hodgson v United Kingdom* (1987) 51 DR 136, EComm HR; *Atkinson Crook and The Independent v United Kingdom* (1990) 67 DR 244, EComm HR.

[722] (1996) 22 EHRR 123.

[723] *X Ltd v Morgan-Grampian (Publishers) Ltd* [1991] 1 AC 1; see para 15.76 above.

[724] (1995) Series A No 316–B ; see also *Times Newspapers v United Kingdom* (1990) 65 DR 307, EComm HR: similar argument could not be raised by *The Times* because it was not a victim.

[725] See para 15.39 above.

[726] (1993) 18 EHRR CD 172.

They have published their views, upon which there was no prior restraint, and, if those views are subsequently found to be libellous, any ensuing sanctions would in principle be justified for the protection of the reputation and rights, within the meaning of Article 10.[727]

In *Times Newspapers v United Kingdom*[728] the Commission rejected the applicant's contention that an apology published in a newspaper gave rise to the defence of qualified privilege.

(f) National security

15.230 The well-known *Spycatcher* litigation[729] led two newspapers to bring applications under Article 10.[730] The *Observer* and *Guardian* newspapers complained about interlocutory injunctions, granted by Millett J and continued by the House of Lords, which banned publication of excerpts from the book, *Spycatcher*,[731] on grounds of national security. By the time of the House of Lords decision, the book had been published in the United States and was obtainable in the United Kingdom. In the related cases of *The Observer and The Guardian v United Kingdom* and *Sunday Times v United Kingdom*[732] the Court held that the continuation of the injunctions after confidentiality had been lost contravened Article 10. It was accepted, on the other hand, that, until publication in the United States, confidentiality was justified; and it was, therefore, proportionate to find that publication in breach of the injunctions was a contempt.[733]

15.231 The applicants in *Brind and McLaughlin v United Kingdom*[734] challenged the Government 'broadcasting ban' on terrorists.[735] The Commission found that the interference was for the legitimate aim of protecting the interests of national security, and, bearing in mind the margin of appreciation in relation to measures against terrorism, took the view that the ban was not disproportionate.[736]

(g) Other applications

15.232 The limits of the concept of 'expression' have been tested in a number of United Kingdom applications. Expression has been held to include television

---

[727] Ibid para 2; cf the discussion of the Art 10 position by the Court of Appeal in *McDonalds v Steel* unreported, 31 Mar 1999.

[728] [1997] EHRLR 430; arising out of the case of *Watts v Times Newspapers Ltd* [1997] QB 650.

[729] For a general discussion, see para 15.19ff above.

[730] For the history of the litigation see *Sunday Times v United Kingdom (No 2)* (1992) 14 EHRR 153, 156–73.

[731] *A-G v Guardian Newspapers Ltd (No 1)* [1987] 1 WLR 1428.

[732] (1991) 14 EHRR 153, 229.

[733] See *Times Newspapers and Neill v United Kingdom* (1992) 15 EHRR CD 49.

[734] (1994) 18 EHRR CD 76.

[735] See para 15.135 above.

[736] See also *Brind and McLaughlin v United Kingdom* (1994) 18 EHRR CD 76.

programmes[737] but not the physical expression of feelings[738] or the right to vote or stand for election.[739] In *Arrowsmith v United Kingdom*[740] there was a challenge to the applicant's conviction for distributing leaflets inciting soldiers to disaffection. Article 10 was not breached, as the prosecution served the legitimate purpose of protecting disorder in the army.

In *Bowman v United Kingdom*[741] the Court had to consider restrictions on free-dom of expression in the context of elections. The applicant anti-abortion cam-paigner in that case had been prosecuted under section 75 of the Representation of the People Act 1983 for her third party expenditure in excess of £5, 'with a view to promoting or procuring the election of a candidate' during an election period. The applicant had distributed a leaflet setting out the candidates' respective views on abortion. She was acquitted on technical grounds. The Court held that the provisions of section 75 were a restriction on freedom of expression. They were not 'necessary in a democratic society' as they were disproportionate to the legiti-mate aim of securing equality between candidates. As a result, there had been a violation of Article 10. **15.233**

In *B v United Kingdom*[742] a civil servant was reprimanded by his employers for his participation in a television programme about safety at a nuclear weapons estab-lishment. The reprimand was found to be a justified interference with his freedom of expression. This approach was confirmed in *Ahmed v United Kingdom*,[743] in which local government employees unsuccessfully challenged restrictions placed on their political activities by the Local Government (Political Restrictions) Regulations 1990. Although it was accepted that there had been an interference with the expression of the applicant, one of the 'rights of others' which can justify interference with expression is the right to 'effective political democracy'. Interferences on this ground are not limited to circumstances in which there is a threat to the stability of the constitutional or political order.[744] The Court took the view that the Government had identified a 'pressing social need' to maintain the political neutrality of local government officers and that the interference was not disproportionate.[745] **15.234**

---

[737] See eg *Hodgson v United Kingdom* (1987) 51 DR 136, EComm HR.
[738] *X v United Kingdom* (1978) 3 EHRR 63, EComm HR (public displays of affection by homo-sexuals).
[739] *Liberal Party, Mrs R and Mr P v United Kingdom* (1982) 4 EHRR 106, EComm HR.
[740] (1980) 19 DR 5, EComm HR.
[741] (1998) 26 EHRR 1.
[742] (1985) 45 DR 41, EComm HR.
[743] (1998) 5 BHRC 111.
[744] Ibid para 52.
[745] Ibid paras 61–65; the Court also took into account the fact that whenever the right to freedom of expression of public servants was in issue, it had to have regard to the 'duties and responsibilities' referred to in Article 10(2): see para 15.184 above.

15.235   The case of *Colman v United Kingdom*[746] arose out of the advertising restrictions of the General Medical Council. The Commission found that there was an interference with the freedom of expression of the applicant, but that it had been carried out in pursuit of legitimate aims, namely the protection of the health of patients and the rights of other doctors. The restrictions were held to be necessary.[747]

15.236   In *Steel v United Kingdom*[748] the five applicants had been arrested and detained to prevent a breach of the peace while participating in various protests.[749] It was found that the arrest and detention of the first and second applicants conformed to English law, but that that of the third, fourth and fifth applicants had been unlawful.[750] The Court considered that the protests of the applicants constituted expressions of opinion and that the measures taken against them were accordingly violations of Article 10,[751] albeit in pursuit of the legitimate aims of prevention of disorder and protection of the rights of others. In relation to the first and second applicants, taking into account the seriousness of their conduct, the apprehensions were 'necessary in a democratic society'. Interference with the other applicants was, however, unlawful and disproportionate, in violation of Article 10.[752] In *Hashman and Harrup v United Kingdom*[753] the Court again considered the impact of a bind over on protesters. The Court held that a bind over made to prevent behaviour *contra bonos mores*[754] was not sufficiently precise to be forseeable in accordance with the law under Article 10(2).

15.236A   The case of *A and Byrne and Twenty-Twenty Television v United Kingdom*[754a] concerned a challenge to an injunction which prevented the transmission of a television programme concerning the illegitimate child of a politician. The Commission held that this was a justifiable interference with freedom of expression: the interference was proportionate to the aim of protecting the welfare of the child. It was justifiable to favour the child's welfare over any public interest in the programme.

---

[746] (1993) 18 EHRR 119.
[747] The restrictions were later relaxed and a friendly settlement reached.
[748] (1998) 28 EHRR 603.
[749] For the facts, see ibid paras 6–38.
[750] These applicants were, therefore, successful in Art 5 claims, ibid para 64.
[751] Ibid paras 92– 93.
[752] Ibid para 110.
[753] (2000) 8 BHRC 104.
[754] Conduct which is wrong rather than right in the judgment of the majority of contemporary citizens: see *Hughes v Holley* (1986) 86 Cr App R 130.
[754a] (1997) 25 EHRR CD 159; for the English case see *Re Z (A Minor) (Identification and Restrictions on Publication)* [1997] Fam 1.

(3) General impact issues

(a) Section 12 of the Human Rights Act

Section 12 of the Human Rights Act is headed 'Freedom of Expression'. It was in-   **15.237**
troduced at the Committee stage by the Government to meet concerns raised
about press freedom and the conflict with the right to privacy.[755] The Home
Secretary, Jack Straw MP,[756] explained the purpose of section 12 during the
Committee stage:

> So far as we are able in a manner consistent with the Convention and its jurispru-
> dence, we are saying to the court that wherever there is a clash between article 8 and
> article 10 rights, they must pay particular attention to the article 10 rights.

In fact, it appears that section 12 has rather broader implications.

Section 12 provides as follows: **15.238**

> (1) This section applies if a court is considering whether to grant any relief
> which, if granted, might affect the exercise of the Convention right to freedom of
> expression.
> (2) If the person against whom the application for relief is made ('the respon-
> dent') is neither present nor represented, no such relief is to be granted unless the
> court is satisfied—
> (a) that the applicant has taken all practicable steps to notify the respondent; or
> (b) that there are compelling reasons why the respondent should not be noti-
> fied.
> (3) No such relief is to be granted so as to restrain publication before trial unless
> the court is satisfied that the applicant is likely to establish that publication should
> not be allowed.
> (4) The court must have particular regard to the importance of the Convention
> right to freedom of expression and, where the proceedings relate to material which
> the respondent claims, or which appears to the court, to be journalistic, literary or
> artistic material (or to conduct connected with such material), to—
> (a) the extent to which—
> (i) the material has, or is about to, become available to the public; or
> (ii) it is, or would be, in the public interest for the material to be published;
> (b) any relevant privacy code.
> (5) In this section—
> 'court' includes tribunal;
> 'relief' includes any remedy or order (other than in criminal proceed-
> ings).

---

[755] See HC Deb, 2 Jul 1998, Col 538 ff: The Home Secretary. For *Hansard* extracts on s 12, see J
Wadham and H Mountfield, *Blackstone's Guide to the Human Rights Act 1998* (Blackstone, 1999)
227–230.
[756] *Hansard* HC 2 Jul 1998, col 543.

It is submitted that these provisions should be construed 'generously'[757] and in accordance with the principle of 'practical effectiveness'.[758] Each sub-section merits specific consideration.

15.239 **Section 12(1)** establishes the scope of application of the section. First, it is clear that what is being protected is not any English law right, but 'the Convention right to freedom of expression'. This means that the section encompasses the same wide range of 'forms of expression' as that covered by Article 10 of the Convention.[759]

15.240 Secondly, section 12 will apply with respect to 'any relief' which, if granted, 'might affect' the exercise of the Convention right. Therefore, although the section was contemplated to 'safeguard press freedom',[760] it clearly extends beyond court orders which might affect publication of material by the media. Injunctions granted, for example, in actions for breach of confidence, contract or copyright 'might affect' the exercise of the right to freedom of expression. An injunction in a matter of private and public nuisance might similarly be affected if its purpose was to restrain demonstrations.[761] Furthermore, the distinction between 'speech' and 'conduct' is not a clear one[762] and section 12 may have a wider impact than is initially apparent.

15.241 Furthermore, the words 'any relief' are not restricted to 'injunctive' relief. Relief which 'might affect' the exercise of the freedom must include awards of damages in civil actions.[763] As a result of section 12(5), tribunals[764] as well as courts must apply its principles. However, it is clear from section 12(5) that the criminal courts are outside the scope of the section. This means that the provision will not need to be considered when, for example, the court is making reporting restrictions during criminal trials.[765]

15.242 **Section 12(2)** restricts the circumstances in which an injunction may be granted in the absence of the defendant. It resembles the statutory restrictions on granting interim injunctions in industrial relations disputes;[766] and would appear to apply whenever it is genuinely claimed that relief might affect the right to expression

---

[757] See generally, para 3.23 above.

[758] See para 6.28ff above.

[759] See para 15.140 above.

[760] See n 755 above.

[761] Thus, Barendt suggests that no injunction would have been granted in *Hubbard v Pitt* [1976] 1 QB 142 if US freedom of expression analysis had been applied: (see E Barendt, *Freedom of Speech* (Clarendon Press, 1985) 43).

[762] See Barendt (n 761 above) 41–48; see para 15.140 above.

[763] See *Tolstoy Miloslavsky v United Kingdom* (1995) 20 EHRR 442.

[764] Defined in s 21(1) of the Human Rights Act as 'any tribunal in which legal proceedings may be brought'; the meaning of the phrase is discussed at para 5.43 above.

[765] See para 15.59 above.

[766] Trade Union and Labour Relations (Consolidation) Act 1992, s 222(1).

regardless of whether the claim might succeed.[767] Section 12 gives no indication that it does not also apply to final orders. If the defendant is not present at the trial, the court can only grant a final injunction or award of damages if the claimant shows that he has taken 'all practicable steps to notify the respondent'. This is a stronger test than that presently applied but is likely to be of limited practical importance.

The effect of **section 12(3)** is to raise the threshold test for the restraint of expression: to require the claimant to establish a stronger *prima facie* case.[768] As a result, the standard *American Cyanamid* test[769] for interim injunctions will no longer be applicable in any application to restrain 'expression'. Instead, the claimant will only be entitled to an injunction if he can show that he is 'likely' to succeed at trial.[770] This test does not appear to be as stringent as the rule in *Bonnard v Perryman*,[771] but its scope is much broader. The stricter test must be applied to claims for injunctions to restrain breaches of confidence, copyright or contract. | **15.243**

Section 12(4) provides that the court 'must have particular regard to' the importance of the right to freedom of expression when granting relief. Where the proceedings relate to material which the respondent claims, or which appears to the court, to be journalistic, literary or artistic material (or to conduct connected with such material), the court must also have regard to the extent of the current or pending availability of the material to the public; or interest of the public in having it published; and to any relevant privacy code. The reference to 'conduct connected with such material' appears to be intended to cover journalistic enquiries which suggest the presence of a story without the support of existing material.[772] It appears that this sub-section is intended to 'tip the balance' in favour of expression in applications for injunctions to restrain breaches of privacy. Although the rights of the claimant under Article 8 will have to be weighed in the balance, the section makes clear that the Court must pay particular regard to the Article 10 rights of the respondent. | **15.244**

The approach the Court will take when resolving conflicts between the freedom of expression and the right to privacy under section 12 is not entirely clear.[773] Although the Strasbourg authorities have stressed the important role of the | **15.245**

---

[767] See *Gouriet v Union of Post Office Workers* [1978] AC 435 in relation to s 221(1).

[768] See *Hansard* HC 2 Jul 1998, col 562.

[769] *American Cyanamid Company v Ethicon Ltd* [1975] AC 396.

[770] s 12(3); this is also the position in New Zealand: see *A-G for England and Wales v Television New Zealand* 2 Dec 1998, CA. The guidance suggested by the House of Lords in *NWL Ltd v Nelson* [1979] ICR 867 in relation to injunctions in industrial relations disputes may provide assistance when applications are made under s 12(3).

[771] [1891] 2 Ch 269, see para 15.14 above.

[772] See *Hansard* HC 2 Jul 1998, col 540 (Jack Straw MP).

[773] See generally, R Singh, 'Privacy and the Media after the Human Rights Act' [1998] EHRLR 712.

media,[774] little guidance has been given about balancing the freedom of the press against the right to respect for private life.[775] The recent case law[776] suggests that the strong public interest in informed public debate about matters of legitimate public concern will outweigh the interest of individuals in reputation, and similar reasoning may well be applied to cases involving 'privacy rights'. The balance between privacy and freedom of expression has also recently been considered by the Supreme Court of Canada[777] which decided that this depends on the nature of the information which is subject to privacy and the factual context of publication.

15.246   It has been suggested that the English courts should adopt the approach taken in Canada and Germany and take into account the following factors[778] when considering privacy:

- the nature of the information at stake;
- the public (or private) status of the claimant; and
- the nature of the place where the invasion of privacy occurred.

When weighing the right to privacy against freedom of expression, the court should examine the extent to which the information contributes to public debate, whether the motivation for publication is commercial or is informed by a desire to inform the public about a serious issue and whether there were alternatives available to the publisher which could have reduced the impact on privacy. The approach that must be taken is not different in principle from the type of public figure defence in defamation considered by the House of Lords in *Reynolds v Times Newspapers Ltd*.[779] Whether freedom of expression should prevail over the right to privacy must ultimately depend on whether the circumstances show that the restriction in question is a disproportionate interference with freedom of expression.

(b) Defamation

15.247   Article 10 has already had a significant impact in this area of law.[780] It is likely that the Human Rights Act will have further repercussions. A number of possibilities have been suggested, the most important being the potential in English law for

---

[774] See para 15.154 above.

[775] For a general discussion of the balance between press freedom and other public interests see S Tierney, 'Press Freedom and Public Interest: the Developing Jurisprudence of the European Court of Human Rights' [1998] EHRLR 419.

[776] *Bladet Tromsø v Norway* (1999) 6 BHRC 599; *Nilsen and Johnsen v Norway* Judgment of 25 Nov 1999; *Bergens Tidende v Norway* Judgment of 2 May 2000, see para 15.204 above.

[777] *Aubrey v Les Editions Vice-Versa* [1998] 1 SCR 591; see para 12.223 above.

[778] J Craig and N Nolte, 'Privacy and Free Speech in Germany and Canada: Lessons for an English Privacy Tort' [1998] EHRLR 162.

[779] [1999] 3 WLR 1010.

[780] See para 15.220ff above; for a recent discussion of Art 10 and the law of defamation, see *McDonalds v Steel* unreported, 31 Mar 1999 (CA).

recognition of a full-blown 'public figure' defence.[781] Such a defence derives from US case law and, in particular, the decision of the Supreme Court in *New York Times v Sullivan*.[782] In that case the Supreme Court held that a public official could not recover damages for defamation relating to his official conduct unless he proved 'actual malice'.[783] The defence has been extended to defamation against 'public persons'[784] and also to private persons who are defamed in relation to matters of 'public interest'.[785]

The question as to the availability of a 'public figure' defence in libel actions has been considered in several common law jurisdictions. In some, the protection of publishers has taken the form of a defence of privilege or qualified privilege against suit where the impugned statements are matters of political or public interest. The present position can be summarised as follows: **15.248**

Australia: The High Court has held that qualified privilege applies to publications concerning 'government and political matters that affect the people of Australia', provided that the publisher acts reasonably as well as honestly.[786]

Canada: The 'public figure' defence has been rejected by the Supreme Court.[787]

India: The 'public figure' defence has been recognised by the Supreme Court.[788]

New Zealand: The Court of Appeal has held that the defence of 'qualified privilege' applies to generally published statements made about politicians in relation to matters affecting their capacity to meet their public responsibilities.[789]

---

[781] Cf P Milmo and W Rogers (eds), *Gatley on Libel and Slander* (9th edn, Sweet & Maxwell, 1998) para 23.20.

[782] (1964) 376 US 254.

[783] For general discussions, see I Loveland, 'Privacy and Political Speech: An Agenda for the "Constitutionalisation" of the Law of Libel', in P Birks (ed), *Privacy and Loyalty* (Clarendon Press, 1997) 51–92; and L Leigh, 'Of Free Speech and Individual Reputation' in I Loveland (ed), *Importing the First Amendment* (Hart Publishing, 1998), 51. The case grew out of the struggle against segregation in the American south and the plaintiff, who was not mentioned by name, had recovered damages of $500,000 despite the fact that only 35 copies of the newspaper were circulated in the town in which he was a police commissioner. In the light of this extraordinary factual background, it is not surprising that the Court appeared to be anxious to reach a result favourable to the defendant newspaper. The reasoning behind the decision has attracted considerable judicial and academic criticism: see R A Epstein, 'Was New York Times v Sullivan Wrong?' (1986) 53 U Chi L Rev 782, 787; *Dun and Bradstreet Inc v Greenmoss Builders Inc* (1985) 472 US 749, 767; see generally, *Hill v Church of Scientology* [1995] 2 SCR 1130.

[784] *Gertz v Welch* (1974) 418 US 323.

[785] *Milkovich v Lorain Journal Co* (1986) 497 US 1.

[786] *Lange v Australian Broadcasting Corp* (1997) 145 ALR 96; see para 15.353 below.

[787] See *Hill v Church of Scientology* [1995] 2 SCR 1130; see para 15.297 below.

[788] *Rajagopal v State of Tamil Nadu* 1994 6 SCC 632; see para 15.364 below.

[789] *Lange v Atkinson and Australian Consoldiated Press NZ Ltd* [1998] 3 NZLR 424, see para 15.333 below.

There is no requirement that the defendant must have acted reasonably: the defence can only be rebutted by proving 'malice'.

South Africa: It has been held that a defamatory statement in the media will not be unlawful provided that the defendant can show that he acted reasonably.[790] In deciding reasonableness, all the circumstances are taken into account but greater latitude is allowed in respect of political discussion.

However, in *Reynolds v Times Newspapers Ltd*[791] the House of Lords refused to recognise a new category of qualified privilege for 'political information' but accepted that qualified privilege could apply to a publication to the world at large if the media could establish that there was a 'right to know'.[792] Although it was recognised that that, where politicians are involved, it was likely to be relatively easy for the media to establish a defence of qualified privilege,[793] the burden of establishing the privilege remains on the media in each case.

15.249   It is not clear whether this approach will be sufficient to satisfy Article 10 tests. The Convention case law does not make express provision for a 'public figure' or 'political discussion' defence in favour of publishers of potentially defamatory material. Politicians are entitled to have their reputations protected when acting in their public capacity. Nevertheless:

> the requirements of that protection have to be weighed against the interests of open discussion of political issues, since exceptions to freedom of expression must be interpreted narrowly.[794]

The Convention now recognises a species of 'qualified privilege' (described as a 'safeguard to journalists') when 'matters of legitimate public concern' are being discussed by the press.[794a] The *Reynolds* approach does not provide full recognition of this right. Furthermore, it leaves the law of defamation in a state of uncertainty in relation to media discussion of matters of public interest. In the absence of a developed body of case law, a responsible media organisation publishing material relating to matters of 'public interest' will be unable to determine whether a defence is available. It seems that the full background to the publication will have to be investigated in each case in order to satisfy the court that there is a 'right to know'. It is arguable that this uncertainty, *of itself*, constitutes an unacceptable restriction on freedom of expression.

---

790   *National Media v Bogoshi* 1998 (4) SA 1196, 1212.
791   [1999] 3 WLR 1010, see para 15.36ff above.
792   Ibid.
793   Ibid *per* Lord Hope.
794   *Oberschlick v Austria (No 2)* (1997) 25 EHRR 357 para 29.
794a   See, in particular, *Bergens Tidende v Norway* Judgment of 2 May 2000, especially paras 53 and 60.

It is submitted that the Human Rights Act, whether through positive rights   **15.250**
horizontality[795] or aiding the development of the common law,[796] will bring about
further developments on qualified privilege where it relates to public interest or
political discussion. The case law from other jurisdictions shows that there are a
number of ways in which the balance can be achieved between 'freedom of expression' and 'right to reputation'. Although a defence of qualified privilege applicable to all 'public interest discussion' seems to go too far towards the 'freedom
of expression interest', the present position in English law is unduly favourable to
the 'reputation interest'. At present the law of defamation either provides the defendant with a complete defence (for example, qualified privilege) or renders him
liable in substantial damages (whether or not actual damage can be proved). There
are a number of ways in which a better balance could be struck between freedom
of expression and the right to reputation. One possible approach would be to re-
verse the burden of proof as to truth in cases brought by elected public officials or
those seeking elected public office. Another approach would be to provide a person who is defamed with a limited right to an apology or a declaration of falsity,
while at the same time providing the media defendant with a 'public figure' defence to an action in damages.[797]

Where defamation actions are brought by public bodies, Article 10 will be of   **15.251**
direct application. In such cases, it is likely that the courts will recognise a 'public
interest defence'. The potential for such actions is, however, greatly reduced because of the restrictions on public bodies bringing proceedings.[798]

Article 10 is likely to affect the law of defamation in other respects. For example,   **15.252**
it is possible that the right to impart information under Article 10 will, in some
circumstances, entitle the court to make an interim order requiring a defendant to
publish a correction of a defamatory statement.[799]

(c) Freedom of information

Article 10 requires that everyone has the right to 'receive and impart information'.   **15.253**
The Court in *Leander v Sweden*[800] took a cautious approach in defining the scope
of the obligation although the Consultative (Parliamentary) Assembly of the
Council of Europe took a broader view.[801] However, in New Zealand it was held
that the right to impart information provided the court with jurisidiction to order

---

[795]   See, generally, para 5.87 above.
[796]   See para 5.88ff above.
[797]   See eg the proposal of the New South Wales Law Reform Commission, *Report No 75,
Defamation* (Oct 1995) para 6.2ff on a proposed 'declaration of falsity' procedure in which affirmative defences to actions for damages cannot be raised (save for absolute privilege).
[798]   *Derbyshire County Council v Times Newspapers Ltd* [1993] AC 534; and see para 15.29 above.
[799]   See eg *TV 3 Network v Eveready New Zealand Ltd* [1993] 3 NZLR 435: see para 15.331 below.
[800]   (1987) 9 EHRR 433; see para 15.331 below.
[801]   See para 15.151 above.

a mandatory interlocutory injunction to require a correction of a defamatory tele-vision programme[802] and the Supreme Court of Canada has developed a consti-tutional right to use public property for freedom of expression.[803] It is therefore uncertain whether Article 10 will affect any rights to freedom of information by, for example, creating a right to know[804] and widening the exemptions against dis-closure in the Freedom of Information Bill or in the Local Government Act 1972.[805]

(4) The potential impact

(a) Commercial law

15.254 Although Article 10 is unlikely to have an immediate substantial impact on com-mercial law outside the media field, it may have some impact on regulation of ad-vertising. This will depend on the extent to which the courts will defer to the discretion of those responsible for the regulation of commercial expression.[806] For example, in Canada[807] the Supreme Court has ruled that prohibitions on adver-tising tobacco[808] breached the right to freedom of expression whereas restrictions on advertising directed at children[809] did not. Article 10 may also affect the re-strictions on advertising in the professions. Controls on lawyers[810] and doctors[811] have been held to comply with Article 10; however, in Canada the strict regime for advertising dental services breached freedom of expression.[812]

(b) Criminal law

15.255 The various criminal offences which restrict freedom of expression may well be af-fected by the Human Rights Act. Applications to quash summons or indictments for common law offences such as criminal libel may be made under the Act, or an application could be made for a stay of the proceedings.[813] The following offences

---

[802] *TV3 Network v Eveready New Zealand Ltd* [1993] 3 NZLR 435; see para 15.331 below.

[803] See para 15.314 below.

[804] Cf *Reynolds v Times Newspapers* [1999] 3 WLR 1010, 1020A–C *per* Lord Nicholls, indicating that the 'right to know' test is preferable to the traditional 'duty and interest' test for qualified privi-lege.

[805] See para 15.134ff above.

[806] The Convention case law gives a wide margin of appreciation to commercial expression: see para 15.171ff above. Although the margin of appreciation is not directly applicable to the Human Rights Act (see para 6.82ff above), the courts may nevertheless take a broad approach when consid-ering commercial speech: see C McCrudden 'The Impact of Freedom of Speech' in B Markesinis (ed), *The Impact of the Human Rights Bill on English Law* (Oxford University Press, 1998).

[807] See para 15.310ff below.

[808] *R J R-MacDonald v A-G of Canada* [1995] 3 SCR 199.

[809] *Irwin Toy v Quebec* [1989] 1 SCR 927.

[810] *Casado Coca v Spain* (1994) 18 EHRR 1.

[811] *Colman v United Kingdom* (1993) 18 EHRR 119.

[812] *Rocket v Royal College of Dental Surgeons* [1990] 1 SCR 232.

[813] See generally, para 21.110ff below.

will be considered: criminal, blasphemous and seditious libel, obscenity and Official Secrets Act offences.

Criminal libel. The offence of criminal (or defamatory) libel has often been crit- **15.256**
icised as unduly restrictive of freedom of expression. The problem is not with the
offence itself,[814] but with the anomalies and obscurity of elements of the offence
at common law. The fact that truth is not a defence and that the burden of proving public interest rests with the defendant means that the offence potentially
places undue restriction on expression. The elements of the offence are unclear:
the 'seriousness' element is vague and the requisite mental element is obscure.[815]
As Lord Diplock said in *Gleaves v Deakin*:[816]

> The examination of the legal characteristics of the criminal offence of defamatory
> libel as it survives today . . . has left me with the conviction that this particular of-
> fence has retained anomalies which involved serious departures from accepted prin-
> ciples upon which the modern criminal law of England is based and are difficult to
> reconcile with international obligations which this country has undertaken by be-
> coming party to the European Convention.

He drew attention, in particular, to the fact that there is no onus on the prosecution to demonstrate that it is 'necessary in a democratic society to suppress or penalise' the defamatory material in order to protect the public interest. Instead, the
defendant must prove that the publication was for the public benefit. Lord
Diplock castigated the 'sorry state of the law of criminal libel'. These criticisms remain valid. It is therefore open to any person prosecuted for the offence to seek a
remedy under the Human Rights Act.[817]

Blasphemous and seditious libel. It is not clear whether blasphemous libel sat- **15.257**
isfies Convention standards on restrictions of expression. Blasphemy legislation is
still in force in a number of European countries, although prosecutions appear to
be rare.[818] The Commission and the Court have accepted that the restriction of
expression entailed by the offence has the legitimate purpose of protecting the
rights of others 'not to be offended in their religious feelings' and can be considered 'necessary in a democratic society'.[819] These decisions have, however, all been
based on the 'wide margin of appreciation in relation to morals and religion'.[820]

---

[814] Cf *Thorgeirson v Iceland* (1992) 14 EHRR 843 para 59.
[815] Cf Law Commission, *Report on Criminal Libel* (Law Com No 149, Cmnd 9618, 1985).
[816] [1980] AC 477, 482.
[817] See para 21.110ff below.
[818] See *Wingrove v United Kingdom* (1996) 24 EHRR 1 para 57.
[819] *Gay News and Lemon v United Kingdom* (1982) 5 EHRR 123, 130; and *Wingrove* (n 818 above).
[820] *Wingrove* (n 818 above) para 58.

Under the Human Rights Act, the English courts will be able to give direct application to their own assessment of what is 'necessary in a democratic society'.[821] The obscure and discriminatory nature[822] of this offence might be incompatible with Article 10.

15.258   The scope of 'seditious libel' is uncertain and it is possible that the offence could be committed by a person who promotes a campaign of peaceful civil disobedience. This might contravene Article 10, as limitation of such campaigns by use of the criminal law may not be 'necessary in a democratic society'.[823]

15.259   **Obscenity and indecency.**   The criminal law relating to obscenity and indecency places substantial restrictions on freedom of expression. The Convention case law recognises a wide 'margin of appreciation' in obscenity cases[824] so that the Convention cases are an uncertain guide to the approach to be taken by the English courts. Article 10(2) recognises 'the protection of morals' as a legitimate aim for an interference with expression. The interference for this purpose must, however, be 'necessary' and 'proportionate'.[825] It is arguable that the law governing obscenity and indecency is incompatible with Article 10 in a number of respects:

- there is a lack of clarity as to the definition of obscenity;[826]
- in relation to the common law offences[827] there is no defence of 'public good' and no requirement that the publications 'deprave and corrupt';[828]
- the use of the 'forfeiture' provisions in section 3 of the Obscene Publications Act 1959[829] arguably provides a disproportionate restraint on freedom of expression.

15.260   **Official secrets.**   Section 1 of the Official Secrets Act 1911 is likely to be regarded as an acceptable restriction on freedom of speech to the extent that it is concerned with espionage. However, an offence could be committed by, for example, a journalist publishing information about incompetence in the armed forces. It is submitted that this would be a breach of Article 10 since the restrictions on freedom of expression in section 1 may go beyond 'what is necessary in a democratic society'.

---

[821]   See para 6.146ff above.
[822]   The fact that the offence does not extend to non Christians may breach Art 9; see para 14.77 above.
[823]   See *Steel v United Kingdom* (1998) 28 EHRR 603 discussed at para 15.201 above; and see generally, D Feldman, *Civil Liberties and Human Rights in England and Wales* (Clarendon Press, 1993) 680.
[824]   See *Handyside v United Kingdom* (1976) 1 EHRR 737.
[825]   See para 15.191 above.
[826]   Cf F Klug, K Starmer and S Weir, *The Three Pillars of Liberty* (Routledge, 1996) 174.
[827]   See para 15.88 above.
[828]   See Klug, Starmer and Weir (n 826 above) 174–175.
[829]   See para 15.80 above.

The Official Secrets Act 1989 is also difficult to reconcile with Article 10.[830] In particular, where restrictions on freedom of expression are permissible without the need to prove damage, it is arguable that such restrictions are unnecessary. Under section 1 the defendant could be liable for disclosing information which is already in the public domain.

15.261

The 1989 Act does not include a 'public interest defence'. This contrasts with proceedings for breach of confidence in which such a defence is available.[831] As Feldman points out, this means that:

15.262

> under all provisions of the 1989 Act criminal liability may be imposed in circumstances when no injunction could have been obtained to restrain publication.[832]

The result of these considerations is that:

> It seems likely . . . that . . . the restraints on freedom of expression resulting from the [Official Secrets Act 1989 go] . . . further than is necessary in a democratic society.[833]

Public order. English law has increasingly accepted a right to protest when considering public order offences such as obstructing the highway[834] or trespassory assembly.[835] However, Article 10 will give explicit recognition to the right to protest. Where, for example, an individual is bound over, he must be able to foresee with sufficient precision what sort of conduct will breach the order;[836] and Article 10 will require the prosecution to justify any interference with freedom of expression as being a proportionate restriction. The decision in *Steel v United Kingdom*[837] suggests that interferences with peaceful protests will breach Article 10.[838] However, in many cases it will be argued that peaceful protest engages the right to assemble under Article 11[839] rather than freedom of expression issues under Article 10.

15.263

Racist speech. The criminal law substantially restricts expression which exhibits an intent to stir up racial hatred.[840] In general, such interference will be for a legitimate aim and will be necessary.[841] Where the offences apply to media reporting of racist speech, it is possible that there could be a breach of Article 10.[842]

15.264

---

[830] See generally, Feldman, (n 823 above) 668–73.
[831] See para 12.34ff above.
[832] Feldman, (n 823 above) 669.
[833] R Stone, *Textbook on Civil Liberties* (2nd edn, Blackstone, 1997) 184.
[834] See eg *Hirst v Chief Constable of West Yorkshire* (1986) 85 Cr App R 143.
[835] *DPP v Jones* [1999] 2 AC 240.
[836] *Hashman and Harrup v United Kingdom* (2000) 8 BHRC 104; see para 15.189 above.
[837] (1998) 5 BHRC 339, see para 15.146 above.
[838] See also *Levy v Victoria* (1997) 146 ALR 248; see para 15.354 above.
[839] See para 16.57ff below.
[840] See Public Order Act 1996, Pt III.
[841] The Commission has applied a low standard of review when examining whether restrictions on racist expression breach Art 10: see para 15.141 above.
[842] See eg *Jersild v Denmark* (1994) 19 EHRR 1.

15.265   **Other offences restricting expression.**   By section 5 of the Public Order Act 1986 it is an offence, *inter alia*, to use words or to 'display any writing, sign or other visible representation' which is 'threatening or abusive or insulting' within the hearing or sight of a person 'likely to cause harassment, alarm or distress thereby'. This offence is often used to arrest demonstrators displaying placards which police officers believe to be offensive.[843] The operation of the restrictions on expression contained in this section may be a breach of Article 10.[844]

15.266   By section 1 of the Public Order Act 1936 it is an offence for a person to wear a uniform:

> signifying his association with any political organisation or with the promotion of any political object.

It is possible that the wearing of a uniform might be treated as a form of 'expression';[845] as such, it is difficult to see how this offence, given its broad scope, could be justified under Article 10.[846]

(c) Education

15.267   There are a number of restrictions on freedom of expression in the field of education.[847] Local Education Authorities, governing bodies and head teachers of state schools must, for example, forbid pupils under the age of 12 to pursue partisan political activities.[848] This is a clear breach of Article 10.[849] Furthermore, those responsible for state schools are obliged to forbid the promotion of partisan political views in the teaching of any subject.[850] There is no statutory definition of 'promotion' in this context and the statute may be held to place undue restrictions on the Article 10 rights of both pupils and teachers.

(d) Employment and discrimination

15.268   It is clear that Article 10 rights extend to the workplace[851] and will affect standard

---

[843] See F Klug, K Starmer and S Weir, *The Three Pillars of Liberty* (Routledge, 1996) 178 for other examples.

[844] Cf the American cases on symbolic speech such as *Cohen v California* (1971) 403 US 15 (jacket with insignia 'Fuck the draft' protected speech under the First Amendment).

[845] Cf Barendt's suggestion that the wearing of a uniform would be 'speech' in the United States (E Barendt, *Freedom of Speech* (Clarendon Press, 1985) 44.

[846] Cf the American cases which treat symbolic speech as protected under the First Amendment such as *Cohen v California* (1971) 403 US 15.

[847] See generally, D Feldman, *Civil Liberties and Human Rights in England and Wales* (Oxford University Press, 1993) 568–571.

[848] Education Act 1996, s 406(1)(a).

[849] It is also a breach of the right of freedom of expression in the UN Convention on the Rights of the Child, 1989 (Art 13).

[850] Education Act 1996, s 406(1)(b). Regarding the 'promotion' of homosexuality, see para 15.276 below.

[851] *Vogt v Germany* (1995) 21 EHRR 205, see para 15.144 above.

public authorities[851a] in their capacity as employers. An employee also owes duties of loyalty and confidentiality to his employers, however, and restrictions designed to enforce these duties may be justified under Article 10(2). There are a number of potential areas of impact on the rights of employees, including restrictions on political activity, workplace dress codes and the rights of whistleblowers.

The Convention case law indicates that the actions of an employer in dismiss-   **15.269**
ing[852] or disciplining[853] employees who are exercising freedom of expression are within the scope of Article 10. However, a refusal to appoint probationary employees to the civil service is not.[854] The justification for this distinction is not persuasive[855] and contrasts sharply with the American approach which has rejected the idea that public employment can be made conditional on surrendering constitutional rights.[856] It is submitted that where a standard public authority interferes with freedom of expression in appointing staff, this will be unlawful under the Human Rights Act.

However, the current restrictions on the political activities of local government   **15.270**
employees will be lawful under Article 10, provided these serve the proper public interest of preserving the impartiality of officials.[857]

It has been argued that the right to freedom of expression includes a right to   **15.271**
choose styles of dress.[858] It appears, however, that the protection will be limited to a 'right to express ideas or opinions' by dressing in a particular way.[859] On this basis, 'dress or grooming codes' imposed by public authority employers will constitute violations of Article 10 only if the employee can show that his appearance is intended to express some idea or opinion.[860] Such a violation may be justified by the employer if it can be shown that a 'legitimate interest' was served by the

---

[851a] The meaning of 'standard public authorities' is discussed at para 5.14ff above; they are to be distinguished from 'functional public authorities' which are discussed at para 5.16ff. The question of whether employees of functional public authorities have Convention rights is complex; see para 5.32ff.

[852] *Vogt v Germany* (1995) 21 EHRR 205.

[853] See eg *Morrissens v Belgium* (1988) 56 DR 127, EComm HR.

[854] See *Glasenapp v Germany* (1986) 9 EHRR 25; *Kosiek v Germany* (1986) 9 EHRR 328.

[855] See para 15.148 above.

[856] See eg *Perry v Sinermann* (1972) 408 US 593, 597 and *Rutan v Republican Party of Illinois* (1990) 497 US 62; and see, generally, G Morris, 'The European Convention on Human Rights and Employment: To Which Acts Does it Apply?' [1999] EHRLR 498.

[857] See *Ahmed v United Kingdom* (1998) 5 BHRC 111, and para 15.234 above; and the unsuccessful domestic challenge in *R v Secretary of State for the Environment, ex p NALGO* [1993] Admin LR 785; and see generally, G Morris, 'Political Activities of Public Servants and Freedom of Expression' in I Loveland (ed) *Importing the First Amendment* (Hart Publishing, 1998) 99.

[858] See G Clayton and G Pitt, 'Dress Codes and Freedom of Expression' [1997] EHRLR 54.

[859] See *Stevens v United Kingdom* (1986) 46 DR 245 para 2, EComm HR.

[860] For example, wearing of black armbands as an anti-war protest: see *Tinker v Des Moines School District* (1969) 393 US 503; cf *Boychuk v Symons Holdings* [1977] IRLR 395: dismissal for wearing a 'Gay Liberation' badge at work, held to be fair.

restriction and that it was 'necessary'. Dress or grooming which does not relate to the expression of ideas is unlikely to attract Article 10 protection.[861] The issue of dress codes also raises questions about an employee's right to personal autonomy; these are addressed in Chapter 12.[862]

15.272   It has also been argued that the failure of English law in the past to protect 'whistle blowers' from disciplinary action could violate Article 10.[863] However, it is unlikely that Article 10 will have an impact on this area in the light of the Public Interest Disclosure Act 1998.[864] Although the Court[865] has not directly considered the issue, it is clear that the restriction on the ability of employees to publish information about their employers is justifiable under Article 10(2). In any case, the limitations contained in a contract of employment on maintaining confidentiality may waive any right of an employee to rely on Article 10.[866]

15.273   It is likely that peaceful picketing will be protected as expression under Article 10 as it is in Canada[867] and the United States.[868] If peaceful picketing is within the scope of Article 10, the court would have to apply section 12 of the Human Rights Act[869] when an application is made seeking an injunction; and would proceed on the basis that a peaceful picket was *prima facie* lawful unless a restriction on the right was justified as proportionate.[870] On the other hand, it is arguable that it is

---

[861]   Cf *New Rider v Board of Education* (1974) 414 US 1097: suspension of school students for having long hair not reviewed.

[862]   See para 12.185 above.

[863]   See J Bowers and J Lewis, 'Whistleblowing: Freedom of Expression in the Workplace' [1996] EHRLR 637; L Vickers, 'Whistleblowing in the Public Sector and the ECHR' [1997] PL 594; Sir Gavin Lightman and J Bowers, 'Incorporation of the ECHR and its Impact on Employment Law' [1998] EHRLR 560.

[864]   The Act prevents an employee within its scope from being subject to a detriment (Employment Rights Act 1996, s 47B); nor can he be dismissed (s 103A) even if he has not worked for one year (s 108(3)(ff)) or is above the upper age limit (s 109(2)(ff)). However, an employee must show that the nature of the information revealed makes it a 'protected disclosure' under s 43A. If the disclosure is a 'qualifying disclosure' under s 43B, the question of whether the disclosure is *actually* covered by the Act depends on the circumstances in which the information is revealed which are strictly and narrowly defined in ss 43C–H.

[865]   But see the Commission decision in *B v United Kingdom* (1985) 45 DR 41, EComm HR where the reprimand of a civil servant for participating in a television programme about safety at a nuclear weapons establishment was a justified interference with his freedom of expression.

[866]   See *Vereiniging Rechtswinkels Utrecht v Netherlands* (1986) 46 DR 200, EComm HR; and see generally, para 6.148ff above.

[867]   See *Retail, Wholesale and Department Store Union v Dolphin Delivery* [1986] 2 SCR 573; *BCGEU v BC* [1988] 2 SCR 214; *Union Food and Commercial Workers v K Mart Canada*, [1999] 2 SCR 1083; see para 15.318 below.

[868]   *Thornhill v Alabama* (1940) 310 US 88; however, it is not protected as free speech where the picketing is for a legal purpose; see, for example, *Teamsters Local 695 v Vogt* 354 US 284 (1957).

[869]   See para 15.237ff above.

[870]   Cf *DPP v Jones* [1999] AC 240 at 254, 255 where Lord Irvine held that the common law recognised that the public had the right to use the highway for any reasonable purpose provided the activity was not a public or private nuisance and did not unreasonably interfere with the rights of others to pass and repass.

more appropriate for picketing to be considered in relation to freedom of assembly.[871]

(e) Family law

It seems unlikely that the jurisdiction of the court to restrict the publication of information relating to children will be in breach of Article 10.[872] The general policy of conducting in private those trials which relate to children is also likely to be held to be consistent with the Convention.[873]

15.274

(f) Local government law

Any regulation of the use of local authority property which circumscribes the type of meetings which may be held or material which may be distributed thereon could potentially breach Article 10. A right of access to public property has been derived from the right to freedom of expression in Canada[874] and in the United States.[875] The implications of Article 10 on the freedom of information provisions of the Local Government Act 1972 are discussed above.[876]

15.275

Section 28 of the Local Government Act 1988 makes it unlawful for local authorities to 'promote homosexuality'.[877] This constitutes a restriction on freedom of expression. It is difficult to see how it can be justified under Article 10. The Government proposes to repeal it shortly.[878]

15.276

(g) Media law

Introduction. The impact of the Human Rights Act on the law relating to the media is likely to be substantial. The impact on the law of defamation has already been considered.[879] In addition, the Act will affect contempt, the regulation of broadcasting and the certification of films and videos.

15.277

Contempt. It is arguable that the Contempt of Court Act 1981, which was intended to bring the law into line with the Convention, fails to do so. While the new strict liability rule supersedes the 'prejudgment' test applied by the House of Lords in the *Sunday Times* case,[880] its scope does not encompass unintentionally

15.278

---

[871] For the position in English Law, see para 16.31 below.
[872] Cf *Re H–S (Minors) (Protection of Identity)* [1994] 1 WLR 1141; and *Arlidge, Eady and Smith on Contempt* (2nd edn, Sweet & Maxwell, 1999), para 6–37.
[873] *Re P-B (A Minor) (Child Cases: Hearings in Open Court)* [1997] 1 All ER 58; *Official Solicitor v News Group Newspapers* [1994] 2 FLR 174 and see *Arlidge Eady and Smith* (n 872 above) para 7-42–7-43, 8–91.
[874] *Committee for the Commonwealth of Canada v Canada* [1991] 1 SCR 139; *Ramsden v Peterborough* [1993] 2 SCR 1084; see para 15.291 below.
[875] Cf *Martin v City of Struthers* (1943) 319 US 141: restrictions on leafleting.
[876] See para 15.253 above.
[877] Cf F Klug, K Starmer and S Weir, *The Three Pillars of Liberty* (Routledge, 1996) 178.
[878] See *Hansard* HL 5 Jun 1998, col 654 (Lady Blackstone).
[879] See para 15.247ff above.
[880] *A-G v Times Newspapers Ltd* [1974] AC 273; see para 15.46 above.

prejudicial conduct apart from publications[881] and all forms of contempt which deliberately impede or prejudice the administration of justice.[882] In these instances, the restrictive common law approach might still be applied, a possibility contemplated by the Act itself,[883] at least in relation to intentional contempts. It should not be assumed, therefore, that the facts of the *Sunday Times* case, should they arise again, could not be successfully prosecuted a second time: this time as an intentional contempt.[884]

15.279   It is arguable, furthermore, that the 'exception' for the 'discussion of public affairs' contained in section 5[885] does not accord with the proper approach under Article 10. The exception does not require the courts to engage in any 'balancing exercise' and does not recognise the importance of the protection of freedom of expression. The application of the exception would not have assisted in the *Sunday Times* Thalidomide case,[886] and the approach adopted by the courts in relation to the affairs of Robert Maxwell[887] suggests that the exception will be of limited value in protecting freedom of expression.

15.280   Section 10 of the Contempt of Court Act has led to a finding by the Court of a violation of Article 10 of the Convention.[888] The section is expressed in the language of Article 10: disclosure will not be ordered unless it is necessary in the interests of justice or national security or for the prevention of disorder or crime. The English courts have, however, been prepared to give a broad construction to the listed 'exceptions'. The interpretation given to 'prevention of crime' extends its ambit beyond specific crimes to include prevention of future crime,[889] and the 'interests of justice' have been held to cover the freedom of private individuals to exercise their legal rights.[890] The difference of approach between the English courts and the European Court of Human Rights is illustrated by the decisions in the *Goodwin* case: while the House of Lords ordered the disclosure of the journalist's sources,[891] the Court of Human Rights held this to be a violation of Article 10.[892] The Human Rights Act may require the English courts to reconsider their approach.

15.281   The maintenance of the authority of the judiciary is a 'legitimate aim' under Article 10(2). It has been suggested that the common law offence of 'scandalising

---

[881] This exempts private conduct including questions such as payments to witnesses and other forms of pressure on individuals which might be unintentionally prejudicial.

[882] s 6(c).

[883] s 6(c).

[884] See Lord Diplock's comments to this effect in *A-G v English* [1983] 1 AC 116, 143.

[885] See para 15.52 above.

[886] See n 880 above; cf *A-G v English* (n 884 above) 144.

[887] See *Arlidge, Eady and Smith on Contempt* (2nd edn, Sweet & Maxwell, 1999) para 4–296.

[888] *Goodwin v United Kingdom* (1996) 22 EHRR 123.

[889] *In re An Inquiry under the Company Securities (Insider Dealing) Act 1985* [1988] AC 660.

[890] See *X Ltd v Morgan-Grampian (Publishers) Ltd* [1991] 1 AC 1, 54C.

[891] Ibid.

[892] *Goodwin v United Kingdom* (1996) 22 EHRR 123.

the court'[893] is not compatible with Convention rights.[894] However, the Convention case law shows a recognition of the need to protect the judiciary from unfounded attacks[895] and the offence has been accepted as being consistent with freedom of expression in a number of Commonwealth jurisdictions.[896] It seems unlikely that it will be affected by the Human Rights Act.

Reporting restrictions.   The Human Rights Act will require that greater empha-   **15.282**
sis is placed on freedom of expression[896a] as opposed to the right to a fair trial. The case law on the Canadian Charter may be particularly pertinent;[897] and, in partic-
ular, the decision of the Supreme Court in *Dagenais v Canadian Broadcasting Corporation*[898] which took a robust view about the value of adopting alternatives where the court is asked to impose a restriction on freedom of expression.

The police and the media.   The right to freedom of expression will significantly   **15.283**
alter the principles to be applied when the police seek orders which affect the media. The court must not act incompatibly with Article 10; and the starting point is that interferences with expression must be justified as proportionate where the police seek journalistic material[899] or apply for search warrants to be ex-
ecuted on the premises of the media.[900]

Regulation of broadcasting.   The Human Rights Act will mean that the approach   **15.284**
of the courts in *R v Secretary of State for the Home Department, ex p Brind*[901] will be radically transformed. That case upheld the Sinn Fein broadcasting ban on the ground that Ministers and public bodies were not then required by law to exercise their powers in accordance with the Convention. The Government veto power on broadcasts has until now been subject only to the threshold test for judicial review at common law. The effect of the Human Rights Act is to require that such Government action be measured, instead, against the European standard of proportionality.

Whether the change in perspective will affect the outcome in any particular case   **15.285**
is unclear. In the *Brind* case,[902] considered by the Commission, it held that, given the importance of measures against terrorism and the margin of appreciation to be

---

[893] See para 15.56 above.

[894] See D Feldman, *Civil Liberties and Human Rights in England and Wales* (Clarendon Press, 1993) 747; and cf *R v Kopyto* (1987) 62 OR (2d) 449 (see para 15.300 below); and contrast *Secretary of Justice v The Oriental Press Group* [1993] HKLY 49 (see para 15.360 below).

[895] See eg *De Haes and Gijesels v Belgium* (1997) 25 EHRR 1; see para 15.143 above.

[896] See *Arlidge, Eady and Smith on Contempt* (n 887 above) paras 5-259–5-269.

[896a] See, eg, *R v Secretary of State for Health ex p Wagstaffe* [2000] 1 All ER (D) 1021; and see para 15.67 above.

[897] See para 15.301ff below.

[898] [1994] 3 SCR 835; see para 15.303 below.

[899] See para 12.17 above.

[900] See cases under the Canadian Charter of Rights at para 15.309 below.

[901] [1991] 1 AC 696.

[902] (1994) 18 EHRR CD 82.

afforded states, the interference occasioned by the Sinn Fein ban was not disproportionate to the aims pursued.

(h) Prison law

15.286 The freedom of expression of prisoners is, of course, restricted by the fact of their
imprisonment. These restrictions must now be justified under Article 10. Any restriction which cannot be so justified will be unlawful and the courts will have
power to strike down Prison Rules and other secondary legislation which contain
them.

15.287 The Prison Rules allow Governors to impose conditions upon prison visitation.
Under paragraph 37 of Standing Order 5A, for example,[903] a journalist or author
permitted to visit a prison must give a written undertaking to, *inter alia*, ensure
that material is not used for professional purposes, in the absence of permission of
the Governor.[904] In *R v Secretary of State for the Home Department, ex p Simms*[905]
the prison authorities had refused to allow interviews with journalists to take place
unless they signed written undertakings not to publish such material. The House
of Lords[906] held that although oral interviews with prisoners required careful control, a blanket ban was unlawful. The provisions of the prison standing orders did
not affect the prisoners' fundamental right to freedom to communicate with journalists with the object of obtaining a review of their convictions. This right could
only be defeated by demonstrating a 'pressing social need'[907] which the Home
Secretary had failed to do. The House of Lords refused to follow US cases to the
opposite effect.[908]

Appendix 1: The Canadian Charter of Rights

(1) Introduction

15.288 The Canadian Charter of Rights and Freedoms, section 2(b) states:

> (2) Everyone has the following fundamental freedoms: . . .
>
> > (b) the freedom of thought, belief, opinion and expression, including freedom of the
> > press and other media of communication.

---

[903] Made by the Home Secretary pursuant to rule 33 of the Prison Rules 1964, under the authority of the Prison Act 1952, s 47(1).
[904] For a general discussion, see S Livingstone and T Owen, *Prison Law* (Oxford University Press,
1999) para 7.34.
[905] [1999] 2 WLR 730.
[906] Reversing the Court of Appeal, [1999] QB 349.
[907] *Per* Lord Steyn, at 411.
[908] See eg *Pell v Procunier* (1974) 417 US 817, partly based on judicial deference to the views of
prison authorities which 'does not accord with the approach under English law', for a general discussion of the US case law on news media interviews, see J Palmer and S Palmer, *The Constitutional
Rights of Prisoners* (6th edn, Anderson Publishing, 1999) 43–46.

The Supreme Court in *Irwin Toy v Quebec*[909] expressed the view that freedom of expression is to be valued because: **15.289**

> (1) seeking and attaining the truth is an inherently good activity; (2) participation in social and political decision-making is to be fostered and encouraged; (3) the diversity in forms of individual self-fulfilment and human flourishing ought to be cultivated.

In *Libman v A-G of Quebec*[910] the Supreme Court said that:

> It is difficult to imagine a guaranteed right which is more important to a democratic society than freedom of expression. Indeed, a democracy cannot exist without that freedom to express new ideas and to put forward opinions about the functioning of public institutions. The concept of free and uninhibited speech permeates all truly democratic societies. The vital importance of the concept cannot be over-emphasised. No doubt that is the reason why the framers of the constitution set forth s 2(b) in absolute terms which distinguishes it, for example, from s 8 of the Charter which guarantees the qualified right to be secure from unreasonable search. It seems that the rights enshrined in s 2(b) should only be restricted in the *clearest* of circumstances.

Nevertheless, restrictions on the right of expression may be justified under section 1 of the Charter as being such reasonable limits prescribed by law as can be demonstrably justified in a free and democratic society.

The Supreme Court of Canada has defined 'expression' as activity which attempts to convey   **15.290**
meaning.[911] It therefore includes all forms of art,[912] commercial expression[913] and could even extend to parking a car as part of a protest against parking regulations.[914] Freedom of expression is content neutral so that a statement cannot be deprived of constitutional protection no matter how offensive it is.[915] Thus, it includes communicating for the purpose of prostitution,[916] promoting hatred against the Jews (or other racial group),[917] threats of violence[918] and a conviction for the offence of publishing false news by denying the Holocaust.[919]

(2) Justifiable limitations

(a) The limitation clause

The limitation provision in section 1 of the Charter applies equally to the freedom of expression as to other Charter rights. 'Prescribed by law'[920] requires that a law must not be   **15.291**

---

[909] [1989] 1 SCR 927 , 976 *per* Dickson CJ, Larmer and Wilson J; *R v Keegstra* [1990] 3 SCR 697, 762, 763 *per* Dickson CJ.

[910] [1997] 3 SCR 569, 581; see also *UFCW Local 1518 v K Mart Canada Ltd* [1999] 2 SCR 1083 para 21.

[911] *Irwin Toy v Quebec* [1989] 1 SCR 927, 968; *Re ss 193 and 195.1 of the Criminal Code (Prostitution Reference)* [1990] 1 SCR 1123, 1180; *Rocket v College of Dental Surgeons* [1990] 2 SCR 232, 244; *R v Keegstra* [1990] 3 SCR 697, 729, 826.

[912] *Re ss 193 and 195.1 of the Criminal Code (Prostitution Reference)* (n 911 above) 1182.

[913] See para 15.171ff above.

[914] *Irwin Toy v Quebec* (n 911 above) 969.

[915] *R v Keegstra* (n 911 above) 828.

[916] *Re ss 193 and 195.1 of the Criminal Code (Prostitution Reference)* (n 911 above).

[917] *R v Keegstra* (n 911 above) 828.

[918] Ibid 733 *per* Dickson CJ for the majority.

[919] *R v Zundel* [1992] 2 SCR 731.

[920] See generally, para 6.146ff above.

excessively vague,[921] and the two-stage *Oakes*[922] test dictates that: first that the legislative objective of the limitation must be justifiable on the grounds of pressing and substantial concerns, and, secondly, that the specific means adopted to implement the objective are proportionate. The principle of proportionality[923] ensures that the means be rationally connected with the legislative objective, that the means result in as little impairment of the right or freedom as possible, and that the effects of the measure be proportional to the objective. It is more difficult to justify a complete ban on a form of expression than a partial ban.[924]

15.292 An application of the proportionality test to expression is exemplified in *Butler*,[925] where the criminal prohibition of pornographic material breached section 2(b) of the Charter by restricting pornography on the basis of its content.[926] The prohibition was, nevertheless, justified because it was no wider than was necessary to accomplish the goal of preventing harm to society: it did not prohibit sexually explicit material that was neither violent nor degrading; neither did it attack private possession or viewing of the obscene materials or prohibit material that was required by the internal necessities of serious artistic work.

(b) The value of expression

15.293 The Canadian courts do not treat all types of expression as being of equal worth.[927] Political speech is considered indispensable,[928] while artistic and commercial speech are less so. Under the Charter the value of the expression becomes relevant only at the stage of the section 1 assessment of the necessity of limitations on it and has nothing to do, in the first instance, with its protection under section 2(b). The approach taken does not, for example, apply special tests to restrictions on commercial expression; instead, the court considers a conflict between expression and the other values said to justify a restriction on expression by examining its social and factual context while taking account of the special features of the expression in question.[929]

(c) Types of restrictions on expression

15.294 The expansive definition of expression and the very general terms in which interferences can be justified under section 1[930] mean that the freedom of expression cases have been argued in a wide variety of contexts.

---

[921] In *Ontario Film and Video Appreciation Society v Ontario Board of Censors* (1984) 45 OR (2d) 80n a film censorship law was held invalid for failure to supply standards of censorship; *R v Butler* [1992] 1 SCR 452, 491: the Criminal Code prohibition of obscenity was construed not merely as moral disapprobation but as 'the avoidance of harm to society', which gave it sufficient precision to be considered an intelligible standard.

[922] *R v Oakes* [1986] 1 SCR 103.

[923] See generally, para 6.42ff above.

[924] See *Ramsden v Peterborough* [1993] 2 SCR 1085, 1105, 1106; *Ford v Quebec* [1988] 2 SCR 712, 772, 773.

[925] Ibid.

[926] *R v Butler* [1992] 1 SCR 452.

[927] *R v Keegstra* [1990] 3 SCR 697, 760.

[928] *Re Alberta Statutes* (1938) SCR 100, 133 *per* Duff J; *Samur v City of Quebec* [1953] 2 SCR 299.

[929] *Rocket v Royal College of Dental Surgeons* [1990] 2 SCR 232, 246, 247 *per* McLachlin J.

[930] See para 15.291 above.

Prior restraint.   The Courts have struck down a variety of prior restraints under section   **15.295**
2. These include: legislation authorising film censorship where there were no statutory
standards laid down;[930a] an injunction to prohibit peaceful picketing,[930b] restrictions on
the importation of books of an immoral or indecent character.[930c] Before ordering a ban
on publication the judge must be convinced that there are no reasonable alternatives less
restrictive of freedom of expression, that the ban is as limited as possible in time and scope
and that the value of the right protected by the ban outweighs the harm caused to freedom
of expression.[930d]

Defamation.   The most controversial issue that has arisen is whether the Charter pro-   **15.296**
vides constitutional protection to public officials by entitling them to a defence of qualified privilege along the lines of *New York Times v Sullivan*.[931] In that case the American
Supreme Court held that a defendant had a complete defence where statements made concerned the plaintiff's official conduct unless the defendant was guilty of express malice. At
common law the mere existence of a public interest in the subject matter of a publication
was insufficient to provide a defence of qualified privilege.[932] There was therefore considerable debate about whether the Charter might affect this principle.[933]

The question was addressed by the Supreme Court in *Hill v Church of Scientology of*   **15.297**
Toronto.[934] The action was brought by a Crown Attorney in relation to allegations of criminal contempt made by the defendant. The defendant argued that the common law of
defamation was contrary to section 2(b) of the Charter. However, the Supreme Court held
that the Charter did not have any direct application to non-governmental action.[935]
Nevertheless, it went on to consider how the common law should be interpreted in accordance with Charter values[936] and concluded that the common law of defamation did so.
The Court acknowledged the criticism which the 'actual malice' rule in *New York Times v
Sullivan* had attracted[937] and said *per* Cory J that:

> The *New York Times v Sullivan* decision has been criticised by judges and academic writers in
> the United States and elsewhere. It has not been followed in the United Kingdom or
> Australia. I can see no reason for adopting it in Canada in an action between private litigants.
> The law of defamation is essentially aimed at the prohibition of the publication of injurious

---

[930a] *Ontario Film and Video Appreciation Society v Ontario Board of Censors* (1983) 147 DLR (4th)
766.
[930b] *Halifax Antiques v Hildebrand* (1985) 22 DLR (4th) 289.
[930c] *Luscher v Canada* (1985) 17 DLR (4th) 503.
[930d] *Dagenais v CBC* [1994] 3 SCR 835.
[931] *New York Times v Sullivan* (1964) 376 US 254.
[932] *Banks v Globe and Mail* (1961) 28 DLR (2d) 343, SCC.
[933] See M Doody, 'Freedom of the Press, the Canadian Charter of Rights and Freedoms, and a
New Category of Qualified Privilege' (1983) 61 Canadian Bar Rev 126; also D Madott, 'Libel Law,
Fiction, and the Charter' (1983) 21:4 Osgoode Hall LJ, 741 786 where she suggests that the time is
ripe for an expanded defence of qualified privilege.
[934] [1995] 2 SCR 1130.
[935] For a discussion about the application of the Canadian Charter to private litigation, see para
5.64ff above.
[936] For a discussion of indirect horizontality under the Canadian Charter, see para 5.66 above.
[937] Citing academic criticism such as: R A Epstein, 'Was New York Times v Sullivan Wrong?'
(1986) 53 U Chi L Rev 782, R P Bezanson, 'Libel Law and the Realities of Litigation: Setting the
Record Straight' (1985) 71 Iowa L Rev 226; P N Leval, 'The No-Money, No-Fault Libel Suit:
Keeping Sullivan in its Proper Place' (1988) 101 Harv L Rev 1287.

false statements. It is the means by which the individual may protect his or her reputation which may well be the most distinguishing feature of his or her character, personality and, perhaps, identity. I simply cannot see that the law of defamation is unduly restrictive or inhibiting. Surely it is not requiring too much of individuals that they ascertain the truth of the allegations they publish. The law of defamation provides for the defences of fair comment and of qualified privilege in appropriate cases. Those who publish statements should assume a reasonable level of responsibility.[938]

15.298   The impact of the right to freedom of expression on criminal libel was examined in *R v Lucas*.[939] The Supreme Court took the view that the protection of reputation was a pressing and substantial objective; and that the negligible value of defamatory expression significantly reduced the burden on the prosecution to demonstrate that the offence minimally impaired expression.

15.299   **Contempt of court.**   The law of contempt of court in Canada is broadly similar to that of Britain. Contempt can be either civil[940] or criminal in nature. Criminal contempt is a common law offence[941] and may be 'direct'[942] or 'indirect';[943] it commonly takes the form of a statement prejudicial to the merits of a case. 'Scandalising' of the Court, in which slanderous or insulting remarks are directed at a judge in his official capacity, or impugning his impartiality, is a form of contempt which has been long recognised but rarely invoked.

15.300   In Canada the law of contempt of court has generally favoured the administration of justice over freedom of expression through the press.[944] Obviously, reasonable criticism of the court is not a contempt at common law.[945] However, in *R v Kopyto*[946] the Ontario Court of Appeal found that the contempt of scandalising the court did not survive the adoption of the Charter (although it may be significant that the statement in question was made by the defendant after the trial ended). On the other hand, the Supreme Court has held that an injunction prohibiting a union from picketing the courthouses on the ground that it was a contempt amounted to a restriction on the right of freedom of expression; but it was justified under section 1 in order to ensure unimpeded access to the courts.[947]

15.301   **Reporting restrictions.**   Freedom of expression includes freedom of the press to publish proceedings in court. In *Edmonton Journal v Alberta (A-G)*[948] the Supreme Court held

---

[938]   At para 139, *per* Cory J; see generally, L Leigh, 'Of Free Speech and Individual Reputation' in I Loveland (ed), *Importing the First Amendment* (Hart Publishing, 1998) 51–68.

[939]   [1998] 1 SCR 439.

[940]   The Charter will have no application to civil contempt proceedings where the order in question resolves a dispute between private parties based on the common law. See *Retail, Wholesale and Department Store Union v Dolphin Delivery* [1986] 2 SCR 573.

[941]   The offence was preserved by s 8 of the Canadian Criminal Code. The absence of a statutory definition of contempt was not a breach of fundamental justice under s 7 (see generally, para 11.386ff above) of the Charter: see *UNA v Alberta* (1992) 89 DLR (4th) 609.

[942]   A direct contempt is committed in the face of the court by words or acts in the courtroom which are intended to disrupt proceedings.

[943]   An indirect contempt is committed by words or acts outside the courtroom that are intended to obstruct the administration of justice.

[944]   For a review of the area of contempt and freedom of expression, see J Watson, 'Badmouthing the Bench: Is There a Clear and Present Danger? To What?' (1992) 56 Saskatchewan L Rev 113.

[945]   *Hebert v A-G Quebec* [1967] 2 CCC 111.

[946]   (1987) 62 OR (2d) 449.

[947]   *BCGEU v BC* [1988] 2 SCR 214.

[948]   (1983) 146 DLR (3d) 673.

that provincial legislation prohibiting press reports of matrimonial cases (with some exceptions) violated freedom of expression because the courts must be open to public scrutiny and to public criticism.[949] It went on to decide that the restriction was wider than necessary to safeguard the privacy of litigants.

A provision in the Criminal Code which prohibited disclosure of the identity of the complainant in a sexual assault was challenged in *Canadian Newspapers Company Ltd v Canada (A-G)*.[950] The Supreme Court took the view that the limitation on expression was justified to foster the victims who needed such an assurance.

15.302

In *Dagenais v Canadian Broadcasting Corporation*[951] a fictional television programme concerning sexual abuse of children at a Catholic home was restrained from being broadcast. An injunction had been granted in favour of several priests who were charged with offences in circumstances which were very similar to those depicted in the programme. The injunctions were to continue until the last of four trials took place: on the basis of a common law power to prevent a real and substantial risk of interference with the fairness of a trial. However, the Supreme Court took the view that the common law gave too much weight to a fair trial and too little to freedom of expression; the limit on expression was disproportionate since alternative measures could be taken falling short of an injunction: such as adjourning the trial, changing venues, sequestering jurors, allowing challenges for cause and providing strong judicial directions to the jury.[952] The Supreme Court therefore concluded that the restriction on expression could not be justified under section 1.

15.303

Prohibiting the press from having access to juvenile trials has also been tested under the Charter. In *Re Southam and the Queen (No 1)*[953] the Ontario Court of Appeal held that an absolute bar on access could not be justified as using the least restrictive means of protecting the interests of a child. The legislation was then changed to require juvenile trials to be held in public with the trial judge having a discretion to order a hearing in private. That provision was regarded as a justifiable restriction on expression in *Re Southam and the Queen (No 2)*.[954]

15.304

In *Canadian Broadcasting Corporation v New Brunswick (A-G)*[955] the press was excluded from part of a sentencing hearing where the offences committed by a sex offender against young girls were being detailed. Although the power to exclude the press was unconstitutional as a breach of freedom of expression, the Supreme Court took the view that the legislation pursued an important purpose by permitting an exclusion order to be made where openness was inimical to the proper administration of justice; furthermore, La Forest J went on to identify the principles to be applied when the court is requested to exericise its discretion to make reporting restrictions.

15.305

Obscenity and pornography. In *R v Butler*[956] the Supreme Court held that the prohibitions on obscenity breached freedom of expression because they restricted communication

15.306

---

[949] Ibid 1337.
[950] [1988] SCR 122.
[951] [1994] 3 SCR 835.
[952] Ibid 881.
[953] (1983) 41 OR (2nd) 113.
[954] (1986) 53 OR (2nd) 663.
[955] [1996] 3 SCR 480.
[956] [1992] 1 SCR 452.

on the basis of its content.[957] However, the restriction was justified to prevent the 'harm associated with the dissemination of pornography';[958] the justification was therefore 'sufficiently pressing and substantial to warrant some restriction on full exercise of the right to freedom of expression'.[959] Sopinka J said that pornography was not unacceptable because it offended morals; they were perceived by public opinion as being harmful to society, particularly women.[960]

15.307   The *Butler* case has attracted feminist criticism,[961] on the basis that the harm done to women by pornography was misunderstood by the Court: its offensiveness lay in the search for a causal link between pornography and violence towards women, and in the fact that the decision requires censorship of sexually explicit material. A similar debate has occurred in relation to prostitution following the *Prostitution Reference*,[962] in which the Court found that it is legitimate to criminalise public communication for the purpose of prostitution, despite the fact that prostitution itself is clearly legal. While all judges agreed that the criminal provisions did not violate the Charter, there was divergence over whether they could be justified as a limitation under section 1.[963]

15.308   **Racial hatred.**   In *R v Keegstra*[964] the Supreme Court stated that the objective of the hate propaganda provisions of the Criminal Code was to 'prevent the pain suffered by target group members and to reduce racial, ethnic and religious tension in Canada'.[965] This was a justified restriction on expression. Similarly, in *Ross v New Brunswick School District No 15*[966] a decision by a human rights tribunal which required a teacher to be removed from his post for disseminating anti semitic literature was held to be a justified restriction on freedom of expression. However, in *R v Zundel*[967] the Supreme Court struck down the conviction for 'spreading false news' of a defendant who had claimed that the Holocaust was a fraud invented by an international Jewish conspiracy. The offence was an unjustified restriction on freedom of expression as the restriction was not confined to any particular type of statement or statements which caused any particular type of injury.

---

[957]   Ibid 489.

[958]   See J Cameron, 'Abstract Principle v Contextual Conceptions of Harm: A Comment on *R v Butler*' (1992) 37 McGill LJ 1135.

[959]   *R v Butler* (n 956 above) 449; see V Ramraj, 'Keegstra, Butler and Positive Liberty: A Glimmer of Hope for the Faithful' 51:2 University of Toronto Faculty of Law Rev, 304, 305.

[960]   Ibid 479.

[961]   See eg 'Pornography, Harm and Censorship: A Feminist (Re)Vision of the Right to Freedom of Expression' 52:1 University of Toronto Faculty of Law Rev, 132; R Moon, 'R v Butler: The Limits of the Supreme Court's Feminist Re-Interpretation of Section 163' (1993) 25:2 Ottawa L Rev 361.

[962]   *Re ss 193 and 195.1 of the Criminal Code* [1990] 1 SCR 1123.

[963]   For a discussion of the reasoning of the judges, their construction of the legislative objectives, and imposition of legal moralism generally see D Dyzenhaus, 'Regulating Free Speech' (1991) 23:2 Ottawa L Rev, 289; also *Ontario Film and Video Appreciation Society v Ontario Board of Censors* (1984) 45 OR (2d) 80n.

[964]   [1990] 3 SCR 697; see also *R v Keegstra (No 2)* [1995] 2 SCR 381 and *R v Keegstra (No 3)* [1996] 1 SCR 458.

[965]   *R v Keegstra* (n 964 above).

[966]   [1992] 2 SCR 731.

[967]   [1992] 2 SCR 731; For a discussion of the distinction between *Keegstra* and *Zundel* see P W Hogg, *Constitutional Law of Canada* (4th edn, Carswell, 1997) para 40.9.

Police powers.   The Supreme Court has considered the use of search warrants to obtain   **15.309**
film taken by television crews of a crime in progress in *Canadian Broadcasting Corporation
v Lessard*[968] and *Canadian Broadcasting Corporation v New Brunswick (A-G)*.[969] It was argued that the search warrants breached freedom of expression because of their 'chilling' effect on newsgathering. The Court said that the constitutional protection of freedom of
expression provides a backdrop against which the reasonableness of a search had to be eval-
uated: the justice should give careful consideration not only to whether a warrant should
issue but also to the conditions which might properly be imposed upon any search of
media premises. A warrant would impede the media from fulfilling its news gathering
functions and should only be issued where there is a compelling state interest. This could
only be demonstrated by showing that there was no reasonable alternative source for the
information or if the offence was a grave one and there was an urgent need to obtain the
information. On the facts, the warrants were upheld, although the majority stressed that
the film had already been shown.

Commercial expression.   The need to regulate commercial expression such as the ad-   **15.310**
vertisement is well recognised under the Charter. The American jurisprudence on commercial expression was analysed by the Supreme Court in *Ford v Quebec (A-G)*[970] where it
held that provincial legislation requiring commercial signs to be in French only was unconstitutional.

There have been a number of cases which have considered restrictions on advertising. In   **15.311**
Irwin Toy v Quebec[971] the issue concerned provincial legislation aimed at advertising for
children. The legislation did not ban advertising absolutely; but required, for example,
that advertisement of toys and breakfast cereals did not use cartoons. The Supreme Court
accepted that a ban directed at children was a sufficiently important purpose to limit expression; and upheld the legislation.

The acceptability of restricting advertisements by professionals arose in *Rocket v Royal*   **15.312**
College of Dental Surgeons.[972] The Supreme Court concluded that the regulations on den-
tists were unjustified because they had an impact far broader than was needed to ensure
high standards of professional conduct; and prevented advertising information which
would be genuinely useful if it was made available to the public.

The important case of *RJR-McDonald v A-G of Canada*[973] considered the constitutional-   **15.313**
ity of federal legislation banning the advertisement of tobacco and other tobacco products. The Supreme Court struck down the legislation because the restrictions imposed
were not carefully tailored to ensure expression was impaired no more than was reasonably
necessary.

Access to public property.   Because the Charter does not apply to private individuals,[974]   **15.314**
it cannot create a right to use private property for the purposes of expression.[975] However,

---

[968] [1991] 3 SCR 421.
[969] [1991] 3 SCR 459.
[970] [1988] 2 SCR 712.
[971] [1989] 1 SCR 927.
[972] [1990] 1 SCR 232.
[973] [1995] 3 SCR 199.
[974] See generally, para 5.64ff above.
[975] *Committee for the Commonwealth of Canada v Canada* [1991] 1 SCR 139, 228 *per* McLachlin J.

in *Committee for the Commonwealth of Canada v Canada*[976] the Supreme Court decided that there is a constitutional right to use public property for freedom of expression although the reasoning of different members of the Court varied significantly. Nevertheless, it held that a manager of a Montreal airport had acted unconstitutionally by prohibiting political leaflets from being distributed at the airport.

15.315   The issue was again considered in *Ramsden v Peterborough.*[977] In that case a musician advertised performances of his band by placing posters on public property in contravention of a bye-law which forbade posters on public property. The Supreme Court did not attempt to reconcile the different approaches taken in *Committee for the Commonwealth of Canada v Canada*;[978] instead, it said that, applying any of the views expressed in the earlier decision, postering on public property was protected by the Charter. The Court also concluded that the limit on expression was not justified under section 1 because it was broader than necessary to accomplish its objective of reducing litter and blight.

15.316   **Picketing.**   The Supreme Court has accepted that picketing is entitled to constitutional protection as 'expression' under the Charter. In the *Dolphin Delivery* case[979] a union challenged the constitutionality of an injunction on secondary picketing where the union had induced a breach of contract. The Court decided that the Charter did not apply to the common law in private litigation.[980] However, McIntyre J said *obiter* that picketing came within the scope of 'expression' under the Charter;[981] but went on to decide that secondary picketing could be justified under section 1 in order to prevent industrial conflict spreading beyond the parties in dispute.

15.317   After seeing a picket line outside the Vancouver court house, the Chief Justice of British Columbia of his own motion and without notifying the union issued an injunction restraining the picket. The Supreme Court in *BCGEU v BC*[982] held that the injunction on the picket restricted freedom of expression; but that limitation on expression was justified so as to ensure unimpeded access to the court.

15.318   Peaceful leafleting of customers by pickets at secondary sites was restrained by an order of the Industrial Relations Council which the union then claimed was a restriction on freedom of expression. The Supreme Court in *Union of Food and Commercial Workers v K Mart Canada*[983] held that:

> workers, particularly those who are vulnerable, must be able to speak freely on matters that relate to their working conditions. For employees, freedom of expression becomes not only an important but an essential component of labour relations. It is through free expression that vulnerable workers are able to enlist the support of the public in their quest for better conditions of work. Thus their expression can often function as a means of achieving their goals.[983a]

---

[976] [1991] 1 SCR 139.
[977] [1993] 2 SCR 1084.
[978] Ibid.
[979] *Retail, Wholesale and Department Store Union v Dolphin Delivery* [1986] 2 SCR 573.
[980] See generally, para 5.66ff above.
[981] *Dolphin Delivery* (n 979 above) 105.
[982] [1988] 2 SCR 214.
[983] [1999] 2 SCR 1083.
[983a] Ibid para 25.

The Court decided that leafleting did not have the same coercive effect as a picket and that, in the circumstances, leafleting was lawful.

Political restrictions on public employees. The restrictions preventing federal civil ser-   **15.319**
vants from engaging in work for a Parliamentary candidate or for a federal political party
were challenged in *Osborne v Canada*.[984] The Supreme Court ruled that the restrictions
limited freedom of expression and could not be justified under section 1. The objective of
maintaining a neutral public service could justify imposing limits; but the legislation did
not adopt the least restrictive means of achieving that objective since the range of activities
prohibited and employees covered was wider than needed to accomplish the objective.

Restrictions on the political process. In *Libman v A-G of Quebec*[985] the Supreme Court   **15.320**
considered a challenge to the constitutional validity of spending limits which had been
placed on political groups in the campaign periods for referenda. The restrictions on expression were justified to prevent political debate being dominated by the most affluent.
However, the limits did not meet the minimum impairment test required under the proportionality principle; the ceiling was so restrictive that it amounted to a total ban on
spending by groups who did not meet the criteria in the legislation which authorised campaign spending.

The prohibition on disseminating information about opinion polls during the last three   **15.321**
days of a federal election was examined in *Thomson Newspapers v Canada*.[986] The Supreme
Court held that a total ban was wider than necessary to guard against the influence of inaccurate polls late in an election campaign; and that the benefits of the ban were outweighed by its detrimental effects.

Appendix 2: The New Zealand Bill of Rights Act

(1) Introduction

Section 14 of the New Zealand Bill of Rights Act 1990 provides: **15.322**

> **14. Freedom of expression**—Everyone has the right to freedom of expression, including the
> freedom to seek, receive, and impart information and opinions of any kind in any form.

The White Paper which explained the proposed bill described this provision as being of
'central importance' but did not give any detailed analysis and suggested that most laws
which were found to infringe freedom of expression would 'no doubt' be held to establish
reasonable limitations on the freedom.[986a]

Section 14 has had an impact in several areas: defamation, contempt of court, reporting   **15.323**
restrictions, obscenity, racial hatred and police powers. However, section 14 does not impose any positive duties on the state to ensure freedom of expression.[987]

---

[984] [1991] 2 SCR 69.
[985] [1997] 3 SCR 569.
[986] [1998] 1 SCR 877.
[986a] *A Bill of Rights for New Zealand: A White Paper* (Government Printer, 1985) 79–80; see generally G Huscroft, 'Defamation, Racial Disharmony and Freedom of Expression' in G Huscroft and
P Rishworth (eds) *Rights and Freedoms* (Brooker's, 1995).
[987] *Mendelsson v A-G* [1999] 1 NZLR 268.

15.324   The New Zealand courts have drawn heavily on the case law of the Canadian Charter of Rights and Freedoms.[988] In *Solicitor-General v Radio NZ Ltd*[989] the Canadian approach to the scope of the right was adopted, the court stressing that the Bill of Rights protects all expression that conveys or attempts to convey meaning except threats of violence.[990]

15.325   Freedom of expression under section 14 includes the right to impart information, a feature that it shares with Article 10(1) of the European Convention.[991] This right provides jurisdiction in an exceptional case for the court to grant a mandatory injunction before trial compelling a defendant to broadcast a correction where he has clearly established that he has been defamed.[992]

15.326   There is a public interest in freedom of expression which exists over and above the rights of the individual. In *Police v O'Connor*[993] it was said:

> While the right in section 25(a) (right to fair and public hearing) is couched in terms of an individual right as is Article 14 of the ICCPR, the right to freedom of expression as expressed in section 14 of the NZ Bill of Rights is not. The latter is to be perceived as a public right. While, therefore, the position adopted by the particular defendant will no doubt be significant, it is not a right which he or she can automatically waive. The public interest in freedom of expression is to be recognised apart from the interests of the individual.

(2) Justifiable limitations

(a) Introduction

15.327   The freedoms set out in the New Zealand Bill of Rights Act are subject to such reasonable limits prescribed by law as may be justified in a free and democratic society.[994]

15.328   The basic principles to be applied when deciding whether a limitation on a right is justified under section 5 were described in *Ministry of Transport v Noort*.[995] First, the New Zealand courts have applied the Canadian authorities both on the meaning of 'prescribed by law'[996] and the general approach to justifying limitations on rights.[997] Secondly, the

---

[988] For a comparison of the general features of the New Zealand Bill and the Canadian Charter, see *Solicitor-General v Radio NZ Ltd* [1994] 1 NZLR 48, 60, 61.

[989] [1994] 1 NZLR 48, 59.

[990] *Solicitor-General v Radio NZ Ltd* (n 988 above) 59 relying on *Irwin Toy Ltd v Quebec* [1989] 1 SCR 927, 970: 'a murderer or rapist cannot invoke freedom of expression in justification of the form of expression he has chosen'; also McIntyre J in *Retail, Wholesale and Department Store Union v Dolphin Delivery* [1986] 2 SCR 573, 588 who said 'that freedom of course, would not extend to protect threats of violence or acts of violence'. However, in *R v Keegstra* [1990] 3 SCR 697, 733 the Supreme Court reversed its views and now accepts that threats of violence are within the scope of expression under the Charter.

[991] Also with the Universal Declaration of Human Rights, Art 19, and the ICCPR 1966, Art 19(2). Cf the Canadian Charter, s 2(b), and the US First Amendment, which do not specify the right to impart information.

[992] *TV3 Network Ltd v Eveready New Zealand Ltd* [1993] 3 NZLR 435.

[993] [1992] 1 NZLR 87.

[994] ss 4, 5 and 6 of the New Zealand Bill of Rights Act.

[995] [1992] 3 NZLR 260, 282-283.

[996] See generally, para 6.146ff above.

[997] The general approach of the Canadian courts, 'modified to New Zealand conditions', was adopted by the Court of Appeal in *Solicitor-General v Radio New Zealand* [1994] 1 NZLR 48 (reviewing *R v Oakes* [1986] 1 SCR 103 and *Irwin Toy Ltd v Quebec* [1989] 1 SCR 927); see also *Ministry of Transport v Noort* (n 995 above).

burden of proof rests with those seeking to rely on section 5 to demonstrate the reasonableness of the limit and that it can be justified in a free and democratic society. Thirdly, the Court of Appeal defined the process of the inquiry under section 5: it should use the Canadian approach in *R v Oakes*[998] as a starting point;[999] and consider all economic, administrative and social implications, taking into account the following factors:

- the significance of values underlying the Bill of Rights;
- the importance of the public interest in the intrusion;
- the limits sought to be placed on the protected freedom; and
- the effectiveness of the restriction in protecting the interests put forward to justify those limits.

The means used must have a rational relationship with the objective and there must be as little interference as possible with the right or freedom affected:

> Ultimately, whether the limitation in issue can or cannot be demonstrably justified in a free and democratic society is a matter of judgment which the Court is obliged to make on behalf of the society which it serves.[999a]

(b) Restrictions on expression

Prior restraint. The New Zealand courts have recognised that the principle of freedom of expression means that any applicant seeking an injunction to prevent a legitimate publication faces an uphill task.[999b] Nevertheless, such an injunction was granted to restrain the broadcast of a television programme about student suicides on the highly speculative ground that it was possible the programme might trigger a young person to commit suicide.[999c]   **15.329**

Defamation. In the field of defamation the Bill of Rights Act has been invoked largely in support of decisions favouring expression. However, its impact has been explained in terms of providing assistance in areas of uncertainty where the law is developing[1000] and to reinforce long established principles.[1001]   **15.330**

Thus, in *Quinn v Television New Zealand Ltd*[1002] it was observed that section 14 did not extend the boundaries of the right of expression, affirming the historic common law right of a person to protect his reputation. In particular, it drew attention to section 28 of the Bill of Rights Act which requires that an existing right or freedom should not be abrogated or restricted by reason only that it was not included in the Bill of Rights. On the other hand, in *TV3 Network v Eveready New Zealand Ltd*[1003] a manufacturer which alleged that a television broadcast libelled its produce applied for a mandatory interlocutory injunction to require the television company to broadcast a correction. It held that section 14 did   **15.331**

---

[998] [1986] 1 SCR 103.
[999] See generally, para 15.291 above.
[999a] *Moonen v Film and Literature Board of Review* (1999) 5 HRNZ 224 para 18.
[999b] *Board of Trustees of Tuakau College v TVNZ* (1996) 3 HRNZ 87, 96.
[999c] Ibid.
[1000] *TV3 Network Ltd v Eveready New Zealand Ltd* [1993] 3 NZLR 435.
[1001] *Auckland Area Health Board v A-G* [1992] 3 NZLR 406 (the jurisdiction to grant interlocutory injunctions to restrain publication of defamatory statements); see also *Quinn v Television New Zealand Ltd* [1995] 3 NZLR 216 which affirmed of historic right to reputation.
[1002] [1995] 3 NZLR 216.
[1003] n 1000 above; see also *TV3 Network Services v Fahey* [1999] 2 NZLR 129 (no injunction to restrain publication of defamatory material where the defendant announced an intention to justify).

not preclude the court in an exceptional case from providing mandatory injunctive relief; in fact, the statutory definition of expression created a right to impart information and supported the claim for an injunction.

15.332   The question of parliamentary privilege was the subject of the Privy Council decision in *Prebble v Television New Zealand.*[1004] The case arose out of an investigative television programme of a former Government by one of its MPs. When the defendant pleaded particulars of speeches and other statements made by the plaintiff in 'proceedings of Parliament' by way of defence, the plaintiff was successful in having them struck out on grounds of parliamentary privilege. The Court of Appeal ordered a stay of proceedings unless and until parliamentary privilege was waived by both the House and the MP, a solution which precludes both action in defamation by persons maligned by statements in the House and suit by an MP to protect his reputation. The Privy Council held that where the exclusion of privileged material makes it impossible fairly to determine the issue between the parties, a stay of proceedings may be required; but allowed the appeal on the facts because the allegations related to statements which were made outside of the House. However, there has been criticism of the broad approach taken in view of the right to freedom of expression under the Bill of Rights Act.[1005]

15.333   In *Lange v Atkinson and Australian Consolidated Press NZ Ltd*[1006] the Court of Appeal considered section 14 in the context of a claim to qualified privilege in respect of 'political expression' based on *New York Times v Sullivan.*[1007] It took the view that a newspaper report on a matter of public interest could, of itself, give rise to a 'common interest' between the newspaper and the general public in the publication of the report. In particular, it was stressed that:

> a proper interest does exist in respect of statements made about the actions and qualities of those currently or formerly elected to Parliament and those with immediate aspirations to such office, so far as those actions and qualities directly affect or affected their capacity . . . to meet their public responsibilities.[1008]

The Court of Appeal refused to follow the Australian approach[1009] and held that whether or not the defendant had acted reasonably was irrelevant.[1010] However, the plaintiff's appeal was allowed by the Privy Council[1011] which remitted the case back to the New Zealand Court of Appeal to reconsider in the light of the decision of the House of Lords in *Reynolds v Times Newspapers.*[1012]

15.334   **Contempt.**   Freedom of expression may be restricted by competing fundamental freedoms such as the right of an accused to a fair hearing[1013] and by the law of contempt of

---

[1004] [1995] 1 AC 321, 332.

[1005] See eg R Best, 'Freedom of Speech in Parliament: Constitutional Safeguard or Sword of Oppression?' (1994) 24 VUWLR 91, 97; and see also the comment of Cooke P in his judgment [1993] 3 NZLR 513, 522; and his subsequent analysis of the case in 'A Sketch From the Blue Train. Non-discrimination and Freedom of Expression: The New Zealand Contribution' (1994) NZLJ 10, 13.

[1006] [1998] 3 NZLR 424 approving [1997] 2 NZLR 22; see also the discussion of this case in *Reynolds v Times Newspapers Ltd* [1998] 3 WLR 862.

[1007] (1964) 376 US 254.

[1008] *Lange v Atkinson* (n 1006 above) 613g–h.

[1009] See para 15.232ff above.

[1010] *Lange v Atkinson and Australian Consolidated Press NZ Ltd* (n 1006 above) 615a-f; 619e-620c.

[1011] [2000] 2 LRC 802.

[1012] [1999] 3 WLR 1010.

[1013] New Zealand Bill of Rights Act 1990, s 25.

court. The conflict between expression in the media and the due administration of justice has traditionally been resolved in favour of the right to a fair trial. The protection of the justice system is considered a substantial and pressing concern;[1014] and the sanction of contempt in achieving this objective has been regarded as being reasonable and demonstrably justified.[1015]

Prior restraints have been imposed on publication in several cases to ensure a fair trial.[1016] **15.335**
The approach in the past has been to impose restraints very readily. More recently, the courts have shifted markedly towards favouring freedom of the media in both law and practice.[1017] *R v Chignell and Walker*[1018] involved an attempt by the Crown to invoke the inherent jurisdiction of the court to restrain a threatened contempt by preventing further public comment concerning an unnamed witness pending a retrial of the accused homicide suspect. The court declined, citing section 14 of the Bill of Rights Act in support of freedom of expression. It held that a mere risk of activity which could undermine a fair trial was insufficient to outweigh the competing considerations of freedom of expression and information; there must be a real likelihood of prejudice to the accused.[1019]

The court in *Police v O'Connor*[1020] went further and said that the English cases:[1021] **15.336**

> fairly read, suggest a balancing exercise in which the interests of justice will prevail over freedom of expression only where the publication of the material will seriously prejudice the conduct of the litigation. Any lingering notion that, where a conflict is found to exist, freedom of expression is to be at once subordinated to the interests of justice is now laid to rest with the enactment of section 14.

However, in *Gisborne Herald v Solicitor-General*[1022] the Court of Appeal held that, in cases in which it was not possible to assure both freedom of expression and fair trial rights:

> it is appropriate in our free and democratic society to temporarily curtail freedom of media expression so as to guarantee a fair trial.[1023]

[1014] *Solicitor-General v Radio NZ Ltd* [1991] 1 NZLR 48: the protection of the due administration of justice, the impartiality and the freedom of deliberation of a jury, the finality of its verdict and preservation of the juror's anonymity are all substantial and pressing concerns of a free and democratic society.

[1015] Ibid 64.

[1016] See *Duff v Communicado Ltd* [1996] 2 NZLR 89; *Greenpeace New Zealand v Minister of Fisheries* [1995] 2 NZLR 463; *R v H* [1996] 2 NZLR 487.

[1017] R E Harrison, 'Mass Media and the Criminal Process: Public Service or Public Circus?' (1992) NZLJ 271; for the media response to Harrison see K Hill, 'Freedom of the Media and the Criminal Law' (1992) NZLJ 278; see the pre-Bill of Rights cases cited in support of the changing style of media coverage: *R v Harawira* [1989] 2 NZLR 714; *The Queen v Tamihere* CA 428/90, 21 May 1992; *Solicitor-General v BCNZ* [1987] 2 NZLR 100; *TV New Zealand Ltd v Solicitor-General* [1989] 1 NZLR 1.

[1018] (1990) 6 CRNZ 476.

[1019] The Court viewed the requested action, which was equivalent to an injunction against the world prohibiting publication of information about the witness, as an unwarranted overreaction to the need for responsibility and restraint to ensure that there was a fair and proper retrial.

[1020] [1992] 1 NZLR, 87, 98-99.

[1021] *A-G v Times Newspapers Ltd* [1974] AC 273; *A-G v British Broadcasting Corporation* [1981] AC 303.

[1022] [1995] 3 NZLR 563.

[1023] At 575, *per* Richardson J.

In *Duff v Communicado* [1024] it was stressed that the relationship between section 14 and contempt is best approached by balancing freedom of expression against the benefits of protecting the administration of justice by examining the facts of each case to see if the particular interference was so serious as to override freedom of expression. The Court went on to hold that remarks made on radio to put pressure on another litigant in proceedings amounted to a contempt.

15.337 **Reporting restrictions.** It is a responsibility of the state to ensure that the administration of justice is carried out in public, so as to safeguard against judicial arbitrariness or idiosyncrasy and to maintain public confidence in the system. [1025] This entails not only the admission of the public to judicial proceedings, but also the publication of fair and accurate press reports so that the public can scrutinise the workings of the courts. The right of the public should not be readily restricted, [1026] reflecting the fact that section 14 provides for the news media to publish information and a public right to receive that information; and in the right of an accused, under section 25, to be given a hearing that is public as well as fair. In *R v H* [1027] a prosecution of an adult for gross indecencies against a child was withdrawn. He subsequently sought an order permanently suppressing his identity. The interference on expression was justified; there was no relevant public interest or need to know that the accused had been charged.

15.338 By contrast, the issue in *Television New Zealand v R* [1028] arose out of a trial where the defendant who had murdered his parents, brother and two sisters wished to adduce certain evidence. An order was made prohibiting publication of the witness and the evidence which was confirmed by the Court of Appeal; however, a television company then applied to rescind the order. The Court of Appeal emphasised that in the absence of compelling evidence to the contrary, criminal justice is public justice; and held that the right to information to the public outweighed the family right to privacy.

15.339 The decision in *National Newspaper Association v Family Court* [1029] considered reporting restrictions in relation to a child suffering from cancer whose parents objected to chemotherapy treatment. The child was taken into hiding and there was widespread public and media interest when the Family Court approved a news release so he could be found. An order was then made suppressing any information relating to the child or the case. The High Court said that great significance should be attached to freedom of the press but that it must bend to the extent necessary to protect the child; and it was necessary to distinguish between mere curiosity and matters of public interest. As a result, any suppression order had to be tailored to intrude only to the extent necessary to ensure that the child's welfare was protected.

15.340 **Obscenity and pornography.** The Bill of Rights Act 1990 appears to have had minimal impact on the regulation of obscenity and pornography. The New Zealand Indecent Publications Act has a statutory definition of indecent [1030] and establishes a tribunal [1031] to

---

[1024] (1995) 2 HRNZ 370.
[1025] See *Police v O'Connor* [1992] 1 NZLR 87, 95.
[1026] Ibid.
[1027] [1994] 2 NZLR 143.
[1028] [1996] 3 NZLR 393.
[1029] [1999] 2 NZLR 344.
[1030] Under s 2.
[1031] The Indecent Publications Tribunal: see s 11(1) of the Act.

classify or determine the character of any book or magazine, to consider the dominant effect of the magazine as a whole and the persons, classes of persons or age groups to or amongst whom the magazine might be made available. The limitations on expression required under the Act were demonstrably justified in a free and democratic society.[1032] In the important case of *Moonen v Film and Literature Board of Review*[1032a] the Court of Appeal considered the relationship between section 14 and the 'censorship provisions' of The Films, Video and Publications Classification Act 1993. It was held that these provisions must be given a meaning that impinges as little as possible on freedom of expression.[1032b]

Racial hatred.   In *Zdrahal v Wellington City Council*[1033] the appellant painted swastikas   **15.341**
on the exterior wall and a window of his house, attracting complaints from two neighbours. The Planning Tribunal under the Resource Management Act issued an abatement order, on grounds that the symbols were offensive and objectionable. The Act in question authorised the prohibition of 'anything . . . that in the opinion of the enforcement officer, was likely to be noxious, dangerous, offensive, or objectionable to such an extent that it has or is likely to have an adverse effect on the environment'. The court accepted that the Tribunal was entitled to find that the ordinary person, members of the public, would find the swastikas offensive. The order had been made for a legitimate legislative objective and the means used were proportionate.[1034]

Police powers.   The restrictions on expression resulting from the imposition of a bind   **15.342**
over were considered in *Bracanov v Moss*.[1035] In that case an anti royalist was ordered to enter into a bond to keep the peace because of a royal visit. The court held that any limitations on freedom of expression were justified to ensure a citizen respects the rights and freedoms of others in the community.

Appendix 3: Human Rights Cases From Other Jurisdictions

(1) Introduction

The right to freedom of expression is firmly established as a constitutional right in many   **15.343**
European countries.[1035a] However, the principles of freedom of expression have been most extensively developed in the United States. American authorities have already had a significant impact on the evolution of the common law on defamation[1036] and, although

---

[1032] *Society for Promotion of Community Standards Inc v Waverley International (1988) Ltd* [1993] 2 NZLR 709.
[1032a] (1999) 5 HRNZ 224.
[1032b] Overruling *Re News Media Ltd v Film and Literature Review Board* (1997) 4 HRNZ 410.
[1033] [1995] 1 NZLR 700.
[1034] Applying s 5 as analysed in *MOT v Noort* [1992] 3 NZLR 260.
[1035] [1996] 1 NZLR 445.
[1035a] See eg S Micahelowski and L Woods, *German Constitutional Law* (Dartmouth, 199) Chap 12.
[1036] See eg *Derbyshire County Council v Times Newspapers Ltd* [1993] AC 534; *Reynolds v Times Newspapers Ltd* [1999] 3 WLR 1010.

the point is not uncontroversial,[1037] it seems likely that American constitutional principles will provide important guidance on the development of freedom of expression under the Human Rights Act.[1038]

15.344   In particular, the American courts have accorded a high priority to political speech. Freedom of expression is said to create a market place of ideas. As Holmes J said in his famous dissenting judgment in *Abrams v United States*:[1039]

> when men have realised that time has upset many fighting faiths, they may come to believe even more than they believe the very foundations of their own conduct that the ultimate good desired is better reached by a free trade in ideas—that the best of truth is the power of the thought to get itself accepted in the competition of the market, and that truth is the only ground upon which their wishes can be safely carried out.

As a result, free speech promotes the search for truth. It also secures the right of the citizen to participate in the democratic process:

> Those who won our independence believed that the final end of the State was to make men develop their faculties, and that in its government the deliberate forces should prevail over the arbitrary . . . They believed the freedom to think as you will and to speak as you think are means indefensible to the discovery and spread of political truth; that without free speech and assembly, discussion would be futile; that with them, discussion affords ordinarily adequate protection against the dissemination of noxious doctrine; that the greatest menace to freedom is the inert people; that public discussion is a political duty; and that this should be the fundamental principle of American government.[1040]

Thus, Meiklejohn argued that the purpose of freedom of expression is to ensure that self government guaranteed under the American constitution is achieved by self education.[1041]

15.345   Nevertheless, it must be borne in mind that there are important differences in philosophy and the political culture between England and the United States which limit the value of directly transposing expression principles.[1042] Furthermore, the drafting of the First Amendment is very unlike Article 10 since it prohibits interference with freedom of speech in absolute terms.[1043] A literal interpretation of the First Amendment would per-

---

[1037] Sir Stephen Sedley takes a more sceptical view about the value of borrowing ideas from the First Amendment, arguing that freedom of expression is at the head of the queue for judicial protection because the media has the funds to underwrite litigation and that it places no sanctions on the mass media to act responsibly: see Sir Stephen Sedley, 'The First Amendment: A Case for Import Controls?' in I Loveland (ed), *Importing the First Amendment* (Hart Publishing, 1998).

[1038] See eg E Barendt, 'The Importance of United States Free Speech Jurisprudence' and I Loveland, 'The criminalisation of Racial Violence' in I Loveland (ed), *A Special Relationship* (Clarendon Press, 1995); R Singh, *The Future of Human Rights in the United Kingdom* (Hart Publishing, 1997) Chap 4; I Loveland (ed), *Importing the First Amendment* (Hart Publishing, 1998).

[1039] (1919) 250 US 616, 630.

[1040] Brandeis J in *Whitney v California* (1927) 274 US 357, 375.

[1041] See A Meiklejohn, *Free Speech and its Relation to Self Government* (Harper & Sons, 1948); 'The First Amendment is an Absolute' [1961] Sup Ct Rev 245; and see, eg W J Brennan, 'The Supreme Court and the Meiklejohn Interpretation of the First Amendment' (1965) 79 Harv L Rev 1; and Sir John Laws, 'Meiklejohn, the First Amendment and Free Speech in English Law' in I Loveland (ed), *Importing the First Amendment* (Hart Publishing, 1998).

[1042] C McCrudden, 'The Impact on Freedom of Expression' in B Markesinis, *The Impact of the Human Rights Bill in English Law* (Oxford University Press, 1998).

[1043] The case law has developed important implied limitations to free speech; some of the basic principles are summarised at para 15.346 below.

mit no interference with freedom of speech. The absolutist approach to the First Amendment is most closely associated with Black J. Thus, in his dissenting judgment in the obscenity case of *Ginzburg v United States*[1044] he said:

> I believe that the Federal Government is without power under the Constitution to put any burden on speech or expression of any kind (as distingusihed from conduct).

He later explained the position, writing extra-judicially in the following terms:

> Some people regard the prohibitions of the Constitution, even its most unequivocal commands as mere admonitions . . . and that all constitutional problems are questions of reasonableness, proximity and review. I cannot accept this approach to the Bill of Rights. It is my belief that there *are* 'absolutes' in our Bill of Rights and that they were put there on purpose by men who knew what the words meant and meant their prohibitions to be 'absolutes' . . . I am discussing here whether liberties *admittedly* covered by the Bill of Rights can nevertheless be abridged on the ground that a superior public interest justifies the abridgement. I think the Bill of Rights makes its safeguards superior.[1045]

However, under the First Amendment even political speech is curtailed where there is a **15.346** clear and present danger of harm.[1045a] Its regulation is subject to strict scrutiny which must be 'narrowly tailored' to serve a 'compelling governmental interest';[1045b] this means, for example, that First Amendment protection covers lewd epithets[1046] and extends to symbolic speech such as flag burning[1047] or to demonstrators in Nazi uniforms marching through a Jewish community.[1048] In practice, the case law of the American Supreme Court has developed a complex system for justifying limitations on freedom of expression:

- by imposing content based restrictions where certain types of speech are singled out as not being sufficiently worthy to attract First Amendment protection[1049] (such as speech which is not essential to the exposition of any idea, libel,[1050] obscenity[1051] and insulting or 'fighting' words)[1052]

[1044] (1966) 383 US 463.

[1045] H L Black, *A Constitutional Faith* (Knopf, 1968); see also, H L Black, 'Bill of Rights' (1960) 35 New York University L Rev 865.

[1045a] The test was formulated by Holmes J in *Schenck v United States* (1919) 249 US 47 52; see *Brandenburg v Ohio* (1969) 395 US 444.

[1045b] The starting point for the strict scrutiny doctrine is the famous passage from the judgment of Stone J in *United States v Carolene Products* (1938) 304 US 144 footnote 4 which he said that: 'there may be narrower scope for the operation of the presumption of constitutionality when legislation appears on its face to be within a *specific prohibition of the Constitution*, such as those of the first ten amendments'.

[1046] See eg *Cohen v California* (1973) 403 US 15 where the Supreme Court held that wearing a badge on a jacket saying 'Fuck the draft' in the corridor of a Los Angelos courtroom could not amount to a criminal offence because it was protected as free speech.

[1047] See eg *Texas v Johnson* (1989) 491 US 397; *United States v Eichman* (1990) 496 US 310.

[1048] *Smith v Collins* (1978) 436 US 953.

[1049] The principles set out in *Chaplinsky v Hampshire* (1942) 315 US 568 268, 269 should now, however, be treated with caution.

[1050] The scope of First Amendment protection depends on whether the plaintiff is a political figure (see *New York Times v Sullivan* (1964) 376 US 254 or a private citizen (see *Gertz v Robert Welch* (1974) 418 US 323).

[1051] Which is confined to hard core pornography: see *Roth v United States* (1957) 354 US 476 and *Miller v California* (1973) 413 US 15.

[1052] The doctrine was radically changed in the controversial decision in *RAV v City of St Paul, Minnesota* (1992) 505 US 377 where a city ordinance against hate crime laws breached the First Amendment because it selectively silenced free speech on the basis of its content; it now seems that only inflammatory words intended to bring about imminent violence are unprotected.

- by regulating conduct which only incidentally affects speech;[1053] or
- by permitting restrictions on the time, place or manner of expression provided they are 'content neutral'.[1054]

15.347   Nevertheless, there are numerous expression issues which the American case law illuminates including: the distinction between speech and conduct[1055] (and in particular, the protection of symbolic speech such as flag burning);[1056] the degree of protection given to extreme political views[1057] or to commercial speech;[1058] and whether restrictions on expression require greater justification because they apply in a public place.[1059]

(2) Antigua and Barbuda

15.348   Section 12(1) of the Constitution of Antigua and Barbuda provides that:

> Except with his own consent, no person shall be hindered in the enjoyment of his freedom of expression.

Restrictions on this freedom must be reasonably required for various stated objectives and must also be 'reasonably required in a democratic society'.

15.349   In *Hector v Attorney-General of Antigua and Barbuda*[1060] the applicant newspaper editor had been charged with printing a false statement which was 'likely to cause fear or alarm in or to the public, or to disturb the public peace, or to undermine public confidence in the conduct of public affairs'. The Privy Council accepted his argument that his rights

---

[1053] The distinction between conduct and speech originates in *Thornhill v Alabama* (1940) 310 US 88 where a state law prohibiting all union picketing was constitutionally protected free speech; the principle means that conduct such as a demonstration is characterised as 'speech plus' and is entitled to a lesser degree of First Amendment protection than 'pure speech': see *Cox v Louisiana* (1965) 379 US 559 *per* Goldberg J at 563. However, the speech/conduct dichotomy is very difficult to maintain: see eg L Tribe, *American Constitutional Law* (2nd edn, Foundation Press, 1988) 12–7.

[1054] See eg *Lloyd Corp v Tanner* (1972) 407 US 551 (rejecting First Amendment protection to distributing antiwar leaflets in a shopping centre).

[1055] See eg *United States v O'Brien* (1968) 391 US 367 (burning a draft card); and see, generally, Tribe (n 1053 above) 12–6, 12–7; E Barendt, *Freedom of Speech* (Clarendon Press, 1985) 41–48.

[1056] See eg *Texas v Johnson* (1989) 491 US 397; *United States v Eichman* (1990) 496 US 310.

[1057] Unless they are directed at inciting (or producing) imminent lawless action and are likely to incite (or produce) such action; see *Brandenburg v Ohio* (1969) 395 US 444; and see generally, Tribe (n 1053 above) 12–9.

[1058] See the seminal case of *Virginia State Board of Pharmacy v Virginia Citizens Consumer Council* (1976) 425 US 748 which struck down legislation preventing a pharmacist advertising the price of prescription drugs in order to protect the interest of the consumer in the flow of information about prices); and includes the right of professionals to advertise fees on a limited factual basis (see eg *Bates v Arizona Bar Association* (1977) 435 US 350; *Shapero v Kentucky Bar Association* (1989) 486 US 466); a prohibition against bans on advertising (see eg *Central Hudson Gas v New York Public Service Commission* (1980) 447 US 557); the right to use the mail to send unsolicited contraceptives (*Bolger v Youngs Drug Products* (1983) 463 US 60); the right to solicit door-to-door within reasonable hours (see eg *Linmark Associates v Willingboro* (1977) 431 US 85; and see generally, Tribe (n 1053 above) 12–16.

[1059] See eg *Hague v CIO* (1939) 307 US 496 (leafleting, parades and other speech related uses of street and parks cannot be banned or subjected to a discretionary licence); *Police Department of City of Chicago v Mosley* (1992) 408 US 92 (city cannot enforce ordinance prohibiting picketing within 150 feet of schools); see generally, Tribe (n 1053 above) 12–24.

[1060] [1990] 2 AC 312.

under section 12 of the Constitution had been contravened by this prosecution. Lord Bridge said:

> In a free democratic society it is almost too obvious to need stating that those who hold office in government and who are responsible for public administration must always be open to criticism. Any attempt to stifle or fetter such criticism amounts to political censorship of the most insidious and objectional kind. At the same time it is no less obvious that the very purpose of the criticism levelled at those who have the conduct of public affairs by their political opponents is to undermine public confidence in their stewardship and to persuade the electorate that the opponents would make a better job of it than those presently holding office. In the light of these considerations their Lordships cannot help viewing a statutory provision which criminalises statements likely to undermine public confidence in the conduct of public affairs with the utmost suspicion.[1061]

The case of *de Freitas v Permanent Secretary of Ministry of Agriculture, Fisheries, Lands and Housing*[1062] concerned a provision of the Civil Service Act restricting the freedom of expression of civil servants. All civil servants were forbidden to communicate 'any information or expressions of opinion on matters of national or international political controversy'. The Privy Council held that a blanket restraint which imposed the same restrictions on all categories of civil servants was not reasonably required for the proper performance of their functions. In addition, the restriction was not reasonably justifiable in a democratic society.

15.350

(3) Australia

The Constitution Act 1900 does not contain a Bill of Rights but, over recent years, the High Court has implied a number of rights into it.[1063] In two judgments delivered on 30 September 1992, the High Court found that the system of representative government gave rise to an implied constitutional guarantee of freedom of communication in relation to the political and electoral processes.[1064] The right of the electorate to choose members of the legislature carried with it:

15.351

> the right to convey and receive information, opinions and arguments concerning such elections and the candidates who are involved in them.[1065]

Breaches of this 'implied freedom' rendered statutes invalid. Thus, in *Nationwide News*[1066] the High Court held that a statute making it an offence to use words calculated to bring a member of the Industrial Relations Commission into disrepute was invalid.[1067]

[1061] At 318 B–D.

[1062] [1998] 3 WLR 675.

[1063] See generally, G Williams, *Human Rights Under the Australian Constitution* (Oxford University Press, 1999) Chap 7.

[1064] *Nationwide News Pty Ltd v Wills* (1992) 177 CLR 1 and *Australian Capital Television Pty Ltd v The Commonwealth of Australia* (1992) 177 CLR 106 (relying heavily on Canadian authority, see generally Williams (n 1063 above) 171–173).

[1065] *Australian Capital Television v Commonwealth of Australia* (n 1064 above) 232.

[1066] n 1064 above.

[1067] Mason CJ, Dawson and McHugh JJ held that it was invalid because, applying a proportionality test, it was not within the implied incidental power to legislate on industrial relations matters. Brennan, Deane, Toohey and Gaudron JJ held that it was invalid because it breached the implied freedom of political communication.

In *Australian Capital Television Pty Ltd v The Commonwealth of Australia*[1068] the High Court held that a statute prohibiting political advertising during federal elections (coupled with 'free time' for established parties) was invalid because it infringed the implied freedom.

15.352 This approach led the High Court in *Theophanus v Herald and Weekly Times Ltd*[1069] to conclude that the law of defamation raised constitutional issues and unduly limited freedom of communication in political matters. They took the view that the defendant who published material relevant to 'political discussion' should have a defence of qualified privilege if he could show that he had acted reasonably. The same principles were applied by the High Court in *Stephens v West Australian Newspapers Ltd*.[1070]

15.353 The decisions in *Theophanus* and *Stephens* were unsuccessfully challenged by the plaintiff in *Lange v Australian Broadcasting Corp*[1071] In that case, the High Court held that:

> each member of the Australian community has an interest in disseminating and receiving information, opinions and arguments concerning government and political matters that affect the people of Australia. The duty to disseminate such information is simply the correlative of the interest in receiving it.[1072]

As a result, a defence of qualified privilege was available to anyone disseminating such information. However, because the damage from publication to the whole world was potentially very great, the privilege could only be relied on if the defendant was reasonable as well as honest.[1073] In relation to the 'reasonableness requirement', this must depend upon all the circumstances of the case:

> But, as a general rule, a defendant's conduct in publishing material giving rise to a defamatory imputation will not be reasonable unless the defendant had reasonable grounds for believing that the imputation was true, took proper steps, so far as they were reasonably open, to verify the accuracy of the material and did not believe the imputation to be untrue. Furthermore, the defendant's conduct will not be reasonable unless the defendant has sought a response from the person defamed and published the response made (if any) except in cases where the seeking or publication of a response was not practicable or it was unnecessary to give the plaintiff an opportunity to respond.[1074]

15.354 This implied constitutional freedom does not, however, cover all types of discussion which could be described as 'political'. Its purpose is to 'contribute to protecting and reinforcing the system of representative government provided for by the Australian Constitution'.[1075] The freedom has been held to be applicable in relation to criticism of the conduct of members of the Parliament,[1076] the operation of electoral law,[1077] legislation restricting criticism of a pub-

---

[1068] n 1064 above.
[1069] (1994) 182 CLR 104.
[1070] (1994) 182 CLR 211; for general discussions of these cases see, I Loveland, '*Sullivan v The New York Times* Goes Down Under' [1996] PL 126; L Leigh, 'Of Free Speech and Individual Reputation' in I Loveland (ed), *Importing the First Amendment* (Hart Publishing, 1998) 62–65.
[1071] (1997) 145 ALR 96; see also *Kruger v Commonwealth* (1997) 146 ALR 126.
[1072] *Lange v Australian Broadcasting Corp* (n 1071 above) at 115.
[1073] Ibid 116–118.
[1074] Ibid 118.
[1075] *Levy v Victoria* (1997) 146 ALR 248, 273, 291.
[1076] *Lange v Australian Broadcasting* (n 1071 above) (the New Zealand Parliament).
[1077] *Australian Capital Television Pty Ltd v The Commonwealth of Australia* (1992) 177 CLR 106; *Muldowney v South Australia (State of)* (1996) 186 CLR 352.

lic body,[1078] the administration of a Commonwealth ordinance,[1079] and to campaigns for legislative change.[1080] The freedom extends to conduct as well as to speech.[1081]

However, the freedom does not extend to advocacy of law breaking. Thus, in *Brown v* **15.355** *Classification Review Board*[1082] the Federal Court upheld a decision of the Classification Review Board refusing classification of a publication containing an 'Art of Shoplifting'.[1083] The Classification Code was enacted for the legitimate aim of preventing crime and was compatible with the maintenance of representative and responsible government, was reasonably appropriate and adapted to achieving the legitimate end.[1084]

(4) Hong Kong

(a) Introduction

Article 16 of the Hong Kong Bill of Rights Ordinance gives effect to the right to freedom **15.356** of expression contained in Article 19 of the International Covenant on Civil and Political Rights.[1085]

A number of challenges based on the freedom of expression have been unsuccessful in the **15.357** courts. In *Ming Pao Newspapers v A-G of Hong Kong*[1086] the Privy Council held that the Prevention of Bribery Ordinance, which prohibited the disclosure of details of investigations into bribery offences, was necessary to preserve the integrity of investigations into corruption. Great weight was given to the fact that the Legislative Council and the Hong Kong Court of Appeal had recognised such a need.[1087] In *Chim Sing Chung* v *Commissioner of Correctional Services*[1088] the Hong Kong Court of Appeal held that the prison authorities decision to remove racing supplements from newspapers did not violate the applicant's right to receive information under Article 16 because the restriction was 'authorised by law'.

In *Hong Kong Polytechnic University v Next Magazine Publishing Ltd*[1089] the Hong Kong **15.358** Court of Appeal rejected an attempt to argue that a university was a 'public authority' which cannot maintain an action in defamation. It was held that the university was entitled to bring an action for defamation to protect its reputation.[1090] In *Re Lee Kwok Hung*[1091] a challenge was brought to a notice issued by the Securities and Futures Commission Ordinance requiring the applicant to attend an interview with an inspector. The challenge based on breach of

---

[1078] *Nationwide News Pty v Wills* (1992) 177 CLR 1.
[1079] *Kruger v Commonwealth* (1997) 146 ALR 126.
[1080] *Levy v Victoria* (n 1075 above).
[1081] Ibid (the entry of protestors into an area in which duck hunting was taking place).
[1082] (1998) 5 BHRC 619, the issues of the limits of the implied constitutional freedom of expression are comprehensively discussed in this case.
[1083] Rendering the publication, sale or distribution of the article an offence.
[1084] Ibid, 631f-g.
[1085] See App J in Vol 2.
[1086] [1996] AC 907.
[1087] The appeal was in fact allowed on the ground that s 30 did not apply when no specific suspect was being investigated.
[1088] (1997) 1 BHRC 394.
[1089] [1996] 2 HKLR 260..
[1090] See generally, Sze Ping-fat, 'Freedom of the Press' (1996) 16 Lit 291; and 'Freedom of the Press Revisited' (1997) 17 Lit 50.
[1091] [1993] HKLR 49.

rights to freedom of expression was rejected. Article 16 was concerned with the right of freedom of opinion and expression, not with providing an immunity from the disclosure of information. In *HKSAR v Ng Kung Siu*[1092] the Court of Appeal held that a law prohibiting the desecration of the national flag was contrary to Article 19 of the ICCPR because it could not be justified as being 'necessary for the protection of public order'.[1093]

(b) Defamation

15.359 In *Cheung Ng Sheong v Eastweek Publisher Ltd*[1094] the unsuccessful defendant in a libel case challenged the award of damages made by the jury. The Court of Appeal held that excessive awards in defamation cases could constitute an impediment to freedom of expression and opinion as guaranteed in Article 16. The Court noted that, although the Bill of Rights did not apply directly to the case as both parties were private individuals, the Court could nevertheless take into account the Bill of Rights when interpreting the common law. The Court of Appeal took a similar approach to that of the English Court of Appeal in *Rantzen v Mirror Group Newspapers (1986) Ltd.*[1095]

(c) Contempt of court

15.360 In *Secretary for Justice v The Oriental Press Group*[1096] it was held that the offence of scandalising the court was compatible with freedom of expression. That case concerned a newspaper group which, after some unfavourable judicial decisions concerning copyright and obscenity, published a series of articles designed to vilify the judiciary. The articles contained abuse and racist slurs. The staff members of the newspaper group also conducted a 'paparazzi' type pursuit of a senior judge, with 24 hour surveillance of the judge, and reports and photographs being published in the paper. The articles and pursuit led to proceedings for scandalising the court. The court found the newspaper guilty of scandalising the court. The court observed that the offence of scandalising the court existed not only for the benefit of the judiciary, but also to maintain public confidence in the legal system. Permissible criticism had to be distinguished from scurrilous abuse, which might have an effect on the administration of justice. The court stated there was a strong argument that the offence of scandalising the court had been developed to preserve the rule of law. The offence was not a restriction of freedom of expression since conduct which jeopardised the rule of law could not be said to be an exercise of the right of freedom of expression at all. Even if there was a breach of freedom of expression, the breach was justified with reference to the need for public order.

(5) Human Rights Committee

15.361 Article 19 of the International Covenant on Civil and Political Rights sets out the right to freedom of expression.[1097] In *Faurisson v France*[1098] the Human Rights Committee con-

---

[1092] (1999) 6 BHRC 591.
[1093] The Court relied on the US 'flag burning' cases, *Texas v Johnson* (1989) 491 US 397 (US SC) and *United States v Eichman* (1990) 496 US 310, US SC; see generally, J Nowak and R Rotunda, *Constitutional Law* (5th edn, West Publishing, 1995) 1170–1172.
[1094] [1996] 1 LRC 168.
[1095] [1994] QB 670.
[1096] [1998] 2 HKLRD 123.
[1097] See App J in Vol 2 for the text.
[1098] (1997) 2 BHRC 1.

sidered a communication which contested the provisions of a French statute making it an offence to deny the existence of Nazi war crimes. The Committee took the view that restrictions on freedom of expression under Art 19(3) of the Covenant[1099] could relate to the interests of the 'community as a whole'. As the statements made were such as to raise or strengthen anti-semitic feelings, the restriction on the author's freedom of expression were permissible under Art 19(3)(a) and were necessary to serve the struggle against racism.[1100]

(6) India

By Article 19 the Constitution of India provides: **15.362**

(1) All citizens shall have the right—

(a) to freedom of speech and expression . . .

(2) Nothing in sub-clause (a) of clause (1) shall affect the operation of any existing law, or prevent the State from making any law, in so far as such law imposes reasonable restrictions on the exercise of the right conferred by the said sub-clause in the interests of the sovereignty and integrity of India, the security of the State, friendly relations with foreign States, public order, decency or morality, or in relation to contempt of court, defamation or incitement to an offence.[1101]

Freedom of expression is a 'preferred right which is always very zealously guarded by the **15.363** court'.[1102] In the context of Article 19(2), 'reasonableness' is applied to each individual statute impugned and no abstract standard can be laid down:

The nature of the right alleged to have been infringed, the underlying purpose of the restrictions imposed, the extent and urgency of the evil sought to be remedied thereby, the disproportion of the imposition, the prevailing conditions at the time, should all enter into the judicial verdict.[1103]

Any law which prohibits the circulation of a newspaper in a particular area[1104] or seeks to **15.364** control the size of a newspaper[1105] will be contrary to Article 19. In *Rajagopal v State of Tamil Nadu JT*[1106] the Supreme Court held that under Article 19 the state had no authority in law to impose prior restraint on publishing which defamed its officials. They went on to hold that:

government, local authority and other organs and institutions exercising governmental powers . . . cannot maintain a suit for damages for defaming them.[1107]

[1099] See App J in Vol 2.
[1100] See also *X v Germany* (1982) 29 DR 194, E Comm HR (in which the Commission declared inadmissible a complaint under Art 10 of the Convention against a prohibition on the display and sale of brochures arguing that the Holocaust was a Zionist fabrication).
[1101] See generally H M Seervai, *Constitutional Law of India* (4th edn N M Tripathi Ltd, 1991) Chap 10; and S Kulshreshtha, *Fundamental Rights and the Supreme Court* (Rawat Publications, 1995), 119–131.
[1102] *Odyssey Communication Pvt Lted v Lokvidyavan Sansthan* (1988) 3 SCC 410, 414 para 5; see also *Ramesh Thappar v State of Madras* AIR 1950 SC 124.
[1103] *Madras v V G Row* [1952] SCR 597, 607.
[1104] *Ramesh Thappar v State of Madras* AIR 1950 SC 124.
[1105] *Benett Coleman & Co v Union of India* AIR 1973 SC 106.
[1106] 1994 6 SCC 632.
[1107] Ibid 582c.

15.365   The Indian courts have relied on Article 19(2) to uphold a provision which prohibited an election candidate from advocating voting (or not voting) for any person on the ground of his religion or community.[1108] The Court held that the words 'decency' and 'morality' in Article 19(2), which permits the freedom of expression to be limited, should not be confined to sexual morality alone. The Indian Constitution was explicitly secular. Further, promoting hatred between different classes of citizens tended to create public unrest and disturb public order. Given their influence, politicians had a particular duty to be circumspect in their language.

(7) Ireland

15.366   Article 40.6.1 of the Irish Constitution provides that:

> The State guarantees liberty for the exercise, subject to public order and morality, of . . .
>
> i. The right of the citizen to express freely their convictions and opinions.
>
>> The education of public opinion being, however, a matter of such grave import to the common good, the State shall endeavour to ensure that organs of public opinion, such as the radio, the press, the cinema while preserving their rightful liberty of expression, including criticism of Government policy, shall not be used to undermine public order or morality or the authority of the State.
>>
>> The publication or utterance of blasphemous, seditious, or indecent matter is an offence, which shall be punishable in accordance with law.

The precise scope of the protections to be found in this article is controversial.[1109]

15.367   A number of 'limitations' on freedom of expression for reasons of 'public order and morality' have been recognised. It is clear that there is a restriction in the interests of 'state security'[1101] and the protection of official secrets.[1111] This extends to protection of the authority of the courts from the publication of 'scandalous' material and from material tending to obstruct the course of justice.

15.368   Freedom of expression is also restricted in the interest of an individual's right to reputation.[1112] In *Hynes-O'Sullivan v O'Driscoll*[1113] the Supreme Court rejected the argument that the constitutional guarantee of freedom of speech meant that qualified privilege should be recognised in a situation in which the defendant honestly but wrongly believed that the person to whom the communication was made had a right to receive it.[1114] The 'public figure' defence in defamation actions does not appear to have been considered in an Irish case.[1115]

[1108] *Dr Ramesh Yeshwant Prabhoo v Prabhakar Kashinath* (1996) 1 SCC 130.

[1109] See J M Kelly, *The Irish Constitution* (3rd edn, Butterworths Ireland, 1994) 923–926.

[1110] Although not to the interest of other states, see *A-G for England and Wales v Brandon Book Publishers* [1986] IR 597.

[1111] See generally, Kelly (n 1109 above) 926–933.

[1112] Protected by Art 40.3.2.

[1113] [1988] IR 436.

[1114] For criticism of this decision see Mcdonald, 'Towards a Constitutional Analysis of Non-Media Qualified Privilege' (1989) 11 DULJ (ns) 94; and generally, Kelly (n 1109 above) 942–943.

[1115] A Lexis search in Nov 1998 disclosed no references to *New York Times v Sullivan* in the Irish cases on that database.

A broadcasting ban on advertisements with a religious or political aim, or in relation to any **15.369** industrial dispute, was upheld in *Murphy v IRTC.*[1116] In relation to the challenge based on freedom of religion, the court observed that the ban did not constitute discrimination on the ground of religious belief: as it operated regardless of the particular religion involved. Moreover, to the extent that the ban was a breach of freedom of expression, it was justified. Irish people with religious beliefs tended to belong to different churches, and religious advertising from a different church could be regarded as proselytising or offensive.[1117]

Freedom of expression issues have arisen in the context of Article 40.3.1 of the Irish **15.370** Constitution, which provides that:

> The State guarantees in its laws to respect, and, as far as is practicable, by its laws to defend and vindicate the personal rights of the citizen.

That Article has been held to include the right to communicate.[1118] The courts have held that it is a justifiable restriction on that right for prisoners' letters to be read by prison staff, but the non-delivery of mail to prisoners as a result of a strike by the prison staff was a breach of that right.[1119]

(8) Namibia

By Article 21(1)(a) of the Constitution of Namibia, all persons have the right to 'freedom of **15.371** speech and expression, which shall include freedom of the press and other media'. In *Kauesa v Minister of Home Affairs*[1120] the Supreme Court struck down a police regulation that prevented police officers from publicly criticising the Government. That regulation had been used to penalise a police officer for publicly commenting unfavourably about the affirmative action policies of the police force. The court noted that the police have the same rights of freedom of speech as ordinary citizens; but accepted that that right had to be balanced against the interest of the police in maintaining discipline. However, there was no rational connection between the impugned regulation and that aim. The Court also noted that the fact that some of the appellant's comments were insulting or defamatory or rendered him criminally liable did not automatically deprive him of his right to free speech.

(9) South Africa

(a) Introduction

Section 16 of the South African Constitution provides that: **15.372**

> 16.(1) Everyone has the right to freedom of expression, which includes—
> > (a) freedom of the press and other media;
> > (b) freedom to receive and impart information and ideas;
> > (c) freedom of artistic creativity; and
> > (d) academic freedom and freedom of scientific research.

[1116] [1997] 2 ILRM 467.
[1117] See also *Colgan v IRTC* [1999] 1 ILRM (broadcasting ban applied to group lobbying for change in abortion laws).
[1118] *Attorney-General v Paperlink Ltd* [1984] ILRM 343.
[1119] *Kearney v Minister for Justice* [1986] IR 116.
[1120] [1995] 3 LRC 528.

(2) The right in subsection (1) does not extend to—

    (a) propaganda for war;

    (b) incitement of imminent violence; or

    (c) advocacy of hatred that is based on race, ethnicity, gender or religion, and that constitutes incitement to cause harm.[1121]

It has been held by the Constitutional Court that constitutional provisions as to freedom of expression do not have direct 'horizontal' effect in private law actions in defamation.[1122] However, constitutional considerations are taken into account when considering the development of the common law.

(b) Defamation

15.373 The South African courts have taken the constitutional guarantee of freedom of speech into account in reforming the common law of defamation.[1123] In *Gardener v Whitaker*[1124] it was held that the constitutional guarantee of freedom of expression meant that the plaintiff should now bear the onus of proving the falsity of a defamatory statement and the absence of defences.[1125] In *Holomisa v Argus Newspapers*[1126] the judge held that a defamatory statement regarding 'free and fair' political activity is constitutionally protected even if false, unless a plaintiff can establish that the defendant acted unreasonably. However, in *Buthelezi v South African Broadcasting Corporation*[1127] this approach was criticised on the grounds that it led to the right to freedom of expression being given precedence over the right to reputation. It was suggested that it would be preferable to develop the common law of defamation by expanding the concept of 'public interest' and placing a burden on the defendant to show that he had acted reasonably. This conflict of approach was resolved by the Supreme Court of Appeal in *National Media v Bogoshi*.[1128] It was held that:

> the publication in the press of false defamatory allegations of fact will not be regarded as unlawful if, upon a consideration of all the circumstances of the case, it is found to have been reasonable to publish the particular facts in a particular way and at a particular time.[1129]

In considering reasonableness, account had to be taken of the nature, extent and tone of the allegations.[1130] Greater latitude is allowed in cases of political discussion. The Court held that the burden of establishing that the publication was reasonable was on the defendant, in accordance with the decision in *Buthelezi*. This approach was held to be in conformity with constitutional values.

[1121] See generally, M Chaskalson, J Kentridge, J Klaaren, G Marcus, D Spitz and S Woolman (eds), *Constitutional Law of South Africa* (Juta, 1996) Chap 20.

[1122] *Du Plessis v De Klerk* 1996 (3) SA 850, in relation to the Interim Constitution see generally, para 5.71ff above .

[1123] See generally, Chaskalson (n 1121 above) 20–34.

[1124] 1994 (5) BCLR 19; the Constitutional Court refused leave to appeal on the grounds that no constitutional issue was raised, 15 May 1996.

[1125] Ibid 37D-H.

[1126] 1996 (6) BCLR 836 (W), Cameron J; see also *Hall v Welz* 1996 (4) SA 1070; *Rivett-Carnac v Wiggins* 1997 (4) BCLR 562.

[1127] (1997) (12) BCLR 1733.

[1128] 1998 (4) SA 1196.

[1129] Ibid 632e-f.

[1130] Ibid 632f.

(c) Obscenity

In *Case v Ministry of Safety and Security*[1131] the majority dealt with the law of obscenity in terms of the right to personal privacy. However, two of the judges[1132] held that the protection of section 15 extended to sexually explicit material and the criminal law on obscenity unjustifiably violated that right.   **15.374**

(d) Political restrictions on employees

The case of *South African National Defence Force Union v Minister of Defence*[1133] concerned a law which prohibited members of the armed forces from participating in public protest actions and from joining trade unions. The Court decided that prohibiting participation in acts of public protest violated the right to freedom of expression of Defence Force members. Their rights to receive and express opinions on a wide range of issues, whether in public or private gatherings, was a grave infringement on the fundamental rights of soldiers. Furthermore, such an infringement was unjustifiable, although the Court indicated that a different, narrower legislative provision might be constitutionally justified.   **15.375**

(e) Privilege

The issue of parliamentary privilege was considered in *De Lille v Speaker of the National Assembly*.[1134] The applicant had named in parliamentary debate eight senior members of the ANC as spies for the apartheid government. The applicant was formally charged with abusing her privilege of freedom of speech, and the House recommended her suspension from the House for 15 days. The applicant succeed in setting aside that recommendation. The court found that the investigation into the applicant's conduct had been flawed and in breach of natural justice. The court held that the nature and exercise of Parliamentary privilege had to be consonant with the Constitution. The court recognised that the principle of separation of powers and the proper exercise of parliamentary privilege was a matter for Parliament alone. Nevertheless, the court could interfere where Parliament improperly exercised that privilege. Furthermore, the suspension of the member was in breach of her freedom of expression.   **15.376**

(10) Sri Lanka

(a) Introduction

Article 14(1)(a) of the Constitution of Sri Lanka provides that: **15.377**

> Every citizen is entitled to the freedom of speech and expression including publication.[1135]

Article 15(7) permits such restrictions to the right as may be prescribed by law, in the interests of national security, public order and the protection of public health or morality, or for the purpose of securing due recognition and respect for the rights and freedoms of

---

[1131] 1996 (5) BCLR 609.
[1132] Mokgoro and Sachs JJ.
[1133] (1999) 6 BHRC 574.
[1134] 1998 (3) SA 430, CPD.
[1135] See generally, J Wickramaratne, *Fundamental Rights in Sri Lanka* (Navrang, 1996) Chap 7; S Sharvananda, *Fundamental Rights in Sri Lanka* (Arnold's International Printing House, 1993) Chap XII.

others, or of meeting the just requirements of general welfare in a democratic society. There must be proximate and reasonable nexus between the restriction and the object sought to be achieved by the restriction. Article 15(2) also permits such restrictions as may be prescribed by law in the interests of racial and religious harmony or in relation to parliamentary privilege, contempt of court, defamation or incitement to offence. Freedom of the recipient is included within the freedom of speech and expression. Thus, regular readers of a newspaper which had been banned by emergency regulations had standing to seek relief.[1136]

(b) Public order

15.378   A number of cases have been brought raising issues about freedom of expression. In *Joseph Perera's* case,[1137] a regulation which provided that nobody could distribute leaflets or handbills without police permission was struck down, as giving unguided and unfettered discretion to police. The police regulation of a public meeting was held to be a breach of freedom of expression in *Mohottige v Gunatilleke*.[1138] The organisers of the meeting applied for a police permit to use loudspeakers at the public meeting. The police asked for the names of the speakers, and then issued a permit subject to two conditions, that only the named speakers would be permitted to speak, and that the speakers should refrain from criticising the Government, any organisation, or any individual. The Supreme Court held that both conditions violated the freedom of speech and expression. The Court noted that demanding the names of people beforehand can have the effect of silencing people who may otherwise wish to contribute to proceedings by participating.

(c) Defamation

15.379   The case of *A-G v Siriwardana*[1139] arose out of a defamation case where a newspaper criticised the speech of an MP in Parliament, likening MPs in general to bulls and donkeys. The Supreme Court found the remarks to be defamatory, and rejected the newspaper's defence of fair comment. The Supreme Court did not decide the question of whether the defence of fair comment was available, as the newspaper had not engaged in fair criticism. Likewise, a newspaper which contained a false statement concerning a Supreme Court trial, was penalised.[1140] The Court held that the publication was deliberate and wilful, holding the Court to odium and an undue interference with the administration of justice.[1141]

(d) Media regulation

15.380   In *Siriwardena v Liyanage*[1142] the closure of a newspaper was upheld on the basis that its contents were likely to inflame sections of the community to violence and breaches of the

---

[1136] *Visvalingam v Liyanage* [1985] LRC Const 909.
[1137] *Perera v A-G* [1992] 1 Sri LR 199.
[1138] (1992) 2 Sri LR 246.
[1139] (1978-79-80) 1 Sri LR 377.
[1140] *In the matter of a rule on De Souza* [1916] 18 NLR 41.
[1141] See also *Hulugalle's Case* [1937–39] 39–40 NLR 294 (article which imputed to Supreme Court judge serious breach of duty by taking an unauthorised holiday for the purposes of going to race meetings was disrespectful; press criticism of administration of justice should be honest and in good faith, and not step beyond its bounds).
[1142] [1985] LRC Const 909.

peace, and thereby endanger the maintenance of law and order.[1143] The constitutionality of the establishment of a Sri Lankan Broadcasting Authority was considered in *Athukorale v A-G of Sri Lanka*.[1144] It decided that the existence of such an authority was not, of itself, a breach of Article 14.[1145] However, it was held that such an authority had to be independent of the Government. Since the proposed authority lacked independence and was susceptible to ministerial interference, the right of freedom of speech was placed in jeopardy.

(e) Other cases

The Sri Lankan Supreme Court held in *Karunaratne v Bandarnaike*[1146] that a member of a political party has freedom of expression, and cannot be expelled from the party for voicing unpopular views. An MP had urged the party leadership to hold internal party elections for various party committees. When that course of action failed, he made a statement to a newspaper expressing concerns at the non-holding of elections by a party committed to democracy. The petitioner was expelled by the party after a disciplinary enquiry to which he refused to submit. The Supreme Court held that the petitioner's expulsion was unlawful. While the Court accepted that freedom of speech may be limited by voluntarily joining a political association, the petitioner in this case had made every effort to obtain internal party change, before making a public statement. In the circumstances, his public statement was justified as having been made under the exercise of his freedom of speech and therefore guaranteed under the Constitution. His expulsion was therefore invalid.

15.381

(11) Zimbabwe

(a) Introduction

Section 20 of the Constitution of Zimbabwe provides, *inter alia*, that:

15.382

> (1) Except with his own consent or by way of parental discipline, no person shall be hindered in the enjoyment of his freedom of expression, that is to say, freedom to hold opinions and to receive and impart ideas and information without interference and freedom from interference with his correspondence.
>
> (2) Nothing containing in or done under the authority of any law shall be held to be in contravention of subsection (1) to the extent that the law in question makes provision:
>
> > (a) in the interests of defence, public safety, public order, the economic interests of the State, public morality or public health;
> > (b) for the purpose of:
> > > (i) protecting the reputations, rights and freedoms of other persons or the private lives of persons concerned in legal proceedings;
> > > (ii) preventing the disclosure of information received in confidence;
> > > (iii) maintaining the authority and independence of the courts or tribunals or Parliament;
> > > (iv) regulating the technical administration, technical operation or general efficiency or telephony, telegraphy, posts, wireless broadcasting or television or creating or regulating any monopoly in these fields;

[1143] See also *Visvalingam v Liayanage* FRD (2) 310.
[1144] (1997) 2 BHRC 610.
[1145] Relying, *inter alia*, on *Groppera Radio AG v Switzerland* (1990) 12 EHRR 321 and *Informationseverein Lentia v Austria* (1993) 17 EHRR 93.
[1146] [1993] 2 Sri LR 90.

(v) in the case of correspondence, preventing the unlawful dispatch therewith or other matter;

or

(c) that imposes restrictions upon public officers;

except so far as that provision, or, as the case may be, the thing done under the authority thereof is shown not to be reasonably justifiable in a democratic society.

The Supreme Court has held that freedom of expression is a 'core value' of society.[1147] The Zimbabwe courts have taken a generous approach to the meaning of freedom of expression.

(b) State funding of political parties

15.383   In *United Parties v Minister of Justice*[1148] the Supreme Court considered the provision of state funding to political parties. The practical effect of the provision was that only the ruling party, ZANU(PF), qualified for funding. The applicant political party complained that this provision infringed its rights to freedom of expression. The Court considered the systems for the public funding of political parties in a number of jurisdictions. It was held that, as political effectual communication required the expenditure of money, restrictions on state funding caused a reduction in effective political expression. As a result, the statutory provisions for party funding were struck down.

(c) Media regulation

15.384   A generous approach was also taken in *Retrofit (Private) Ltd v Posts and Telecommunications Corp*,[1149] in which the Supreme Court held that a telecommunications monopoly was in breach of freedom of expression. The application was brought by a company which had unsuccessfully applied for a licence to provide a mobile telephone network. The respondent was a public corporation which had a monopoly on the provision of telecommunications services in Zimbabwe. The Court considered the four broad purposes of freedom of expression: assisting the individual to obtain self-fulfilment, assisting in the discovery of truth, strengthening the capacity of the individual to participate in decision-making and providing a mechanism to balance stability and change.[1150] The Court stated that protection of freedom of expression involved protecting the means of expression as well as its content. It went on to hold that for the respondent to monopolise telecommunications services in Zimbabwe and then to furnish a public network of notoriously poor quality:

> manifestly interferes with the constitutional right of every person in the country to receive and impart ideas and information by means of this 'pervasive two-way communications system.[1151]

This monopoly was not 'reasonably justifiable in a democratic society'. Further, the constitutional right to free expression applied to corporations as well as individuals.

[1147]   See *Retrofit (Pvt) Ltd v Posts and Telecommunications Corp* [1996] 4 LRC 489, 499–501.

[1148]   (1997) 3 BHRC 16.

[1149]   n 1147 above.

[1150]   Ibid 500f-501f.

[1151]   Ibid 505f.

(d) Prisoners

In *Woods v Minister of Justice*[1152] the Supreme Court considered restrictions on the letters **15.385** which could be sent and received by prisoners. It was held that while the restriction addressed the legitimate objective of public order and safety, the extent of the restrictions were not reasonably justifiable in a democratic society.

(e) Other cases

The case of *Mutasa v Makombe*[1153] concerned a finding of contempt of Parliament against **15.386** a member of Parliament. The Supreme Court held that this was a justifiable interference with his freedom of expression in accordance with section 20(2)(b)(iii) of the Constitution.[1154] Furthermore, the power of Parliament to commit its members for contempt was 'reasonably justifiable in a democratic society'.

[1152] [1994] 1 LRC 359.
[1153] (1997) 2 BHRC 325.
[1154] See also *Smith v Mutasa NO* (1990) (3) SA 756.

INDEX

For reference, we reproduce here the Summary Table of Contents from *The Law of Human Rights* (OUP 2000, 0–19–826223–X) from which these chapters are extracted.

THE LAW OF HUMAN RIGHTS

CONTENTS

Foreword by Lord Bingham of Cornhill

VOLUME 1

VOLUME 2

APPENDICES

United Nations Materials

Domestic Bills of Rights